DARIO FO
PEOPLE'S COURT JESTER

DARIO FO
PEOPLE'S
COURT JESTER

TONY MITCHELL

METHUEN DRAMA

Published by Methuen 1999

1 3 5 7 9 10 8 6 4 2

First published as a paperback original
in 1984 by Methuen London Ltd
Second revised and extended edition 1986

This revised and expanded edition was first published in 1999
by Methuen Publishing Ltd
215 Vauxhall Bridge Road, London SW1V 1EJ

Peribo Pty Ltd, 58 Beaumont Road, Mount Kuring-Gai
NSW 2080, Australia, ACN 002 273 761
(for Australia and New Zealand)

Methuen Publishing Limited Reg. No. 3543167

A CIP catalogue record for this book is available from the British Library

ISBN 0 413 73320 3

Typeset in Bembo by MATS, Southend-on-Sea, Essex
Printed and bound in Great Britain by
Creative Print and Design (Wales), Ebbw Vale

CONTENTS

AUTHOR

Tony Mitchell is a senior lecturer in Writing and Cultural Studies at the University of Technology, Sydney. He was born in New Zealand, and received a PhD in Drama from Bristol University in 1976. He lived in Rome from 1978 to 1983 and was a correspondent on Italian theatre and cinema for *Plays and Players* and *Sight and Sound,* among other publications. *Dario Fo: People's Court Jester* first appeared in 1984. His translations of plays by Dario Fo have been performed in Australia, New Zealand, Papua-New Guinea and South Africa. He is the author of a number of books, including *Popular Music and Local Identity: Rock, Pop and Rap in Europe and Oceania* (University of Leicester Press, 1996).

ACKNOWLEDGMENTS

I would like to thank the following people who have provided me with valuable assistance in preparing this book: Dario Fo and Franca Rame, Piero Sciotto, Walter Valeri, Joe Farrell, Antonio Scuderi, Michael Imison, Diana Hoskers, Nicholas Hern, Mary Remnant, Joel Schechter, Steve Grant, Catherine Itzin, Mary Fulton, Marian Farrugia, Tim Fitzpatrick, Lesley Ferris, Michael Earley and Heidi Gledhill. I am particularly grateful to Ed Emery for copy-editing the manuscript and for his helpful comments and suggestions, and to Elizabeth Hornby for her scrupulous copy-editing.

Parts of Chapter 1 originally appeared in *Theatre Quarterly*, vol. ix, no. 35, Autumn 1979.

INTRODUCTION

Dario Fo's Nobel Prize for Literature in October 1997 provided
a great sense of vindication to those who had followed and
admired his work since the 1950s and 1960s. Fo has established
himself as a *giullare* (jester) in the oral tradition of the medieval
strolling players, presenting political satire against the Italian
political and religious establishment, and making militant
interventions in Italian political life. In the 1990s, Fo and his
wife Franca Rame had begun to be taken for granted in Italy.
This was despite their relentlessly controversial and savagely
comic attacks against most of Italy's religious, political and
judicial 'sacred cows' over four decades – which had occasioned
250 lawsuits against them and two brief stints by Fo in prison. It
was also despite their enormous success outside Italy. Notwith-
standing the difficulties actors, directors and translators have in
adapting his highly idiosyncratic, topical and performance-based
texts, Fo is arguably the most widely performed contemporary
playwright in world theatre. News of the Nobel came as a shock
to most Italians, who tended to regard Fo and Rame as comic
actors rather than 'serious' literary figures. Their topical satire,
based on the oral traditions of popular theatre, was regarded as
a form of theatre far removed from the high literary culture
associated with the Nobel Prize. But the prize also came as a
shock in most of the rest of the world, and in particular the
English-speaking world, where Fo was associated with a
politically committed, agitational form of theatre that had been
largely confined to the 1970s and 1980s. Fo's acceptance of the
Nobel Prize for a lifetime's work of more than 70 plays also
contrasted with his more iconoclastic reaction to being
considered for it previously in 1975. This was when he was

perhaps at his peak as a militant actor-director-playwright-designer, after writing and performing plays like *Accidental Death of an Anarchist* and *Can't Pay? Won't Pay!* which had prised open some of Italy's most glaring, embarrassing and painful political scandals. In 1975 he was clearly not ready for the pomp and circumstance of the Nobel, and had speculated on the absurdity of dressing up in a tuxedo and genuflecting to the King of Sweden like a court jester:

> I have become famous for my aversion to figures of reverence and genuflections of any kind. This Nobel business is a real comedy. I can imagine the look on the faces of certain state officials, magistrates and politicians I know. They take great pains to shut me up and clap me in handcuffs, and the Swedes go and play a trick like this . . . [Receiving the prize] would be like acting in one of my plays.[1]

Twenty-two years later, the Swedish Academy acknowledged Fo's iconoclasm and irreverence as an essential part of his work as a 'serious satirist':

> He if anyone merits the epithet of jester in the true meaning of that word. With a blend of laughter and gravity he opens our eyes to abuses and injustices in society and also the wider historical perspective in which they can be placed.[2]

For the occasion Fo, aged 71, devised and performed a topical, historical and satirical performance entitled 'Contra jogulatores obloquentes' (Against Jesters of Irreverent Speech). This, accompanied by a series of paintings, and performed in the style of his highly acclaimed *giullarate*, was his acceptance speech for the award. It was undoubtedly the most flamboyantly theatrical and comical acceptance speech ever seen at the Swedish Academy. It celebrated the international acknowledgment of Fo as a major figure in twentieth-century world theatre, while he thumbed his nose at the literary snobbery of those who thought him unworthy of the honour. As Antonio Scuderi has commented, in being awarded the Nobel Prize, Fo 'has succeeded in raising the status of the oral tradition to the level of literary prestige, and has helped in redefining the concept of "literature" in that now it must comprehend the oral tradition and performance.'[3]

By 1984, when the first edition of this book first appeared, the work of Dario Fo and Franca Rame had finally received some of the acclaim it deserved in the UK and the rest of the English-speaking world. *Can't Pay? Won't Pay!*, *Accidental Death of an Anarchist* and *Female Parts* had all run for nearly two years in the West End of London. Their acclaim was confirmed when the two Italian author-actors did performances of *Mistero buffo* and *Tutta casa, letto e chiesa* (*Female Parts*) in London in 1983 and in the USA in 1986. But behind these four plays lay 30 years of theatrical activity which was largely unknown to English-speaking audiences. In chronicling Fo and Rame's theatrical and political development from the revue sketches of the early 1950s through their commercial successes in Italy in the 1960s, and their subsequent formation of an alternative circuit of militant political theatre in 1968, I had to rely mostly on secondary sources and the authors' own retrospective accounts of their work up to 1977.

My own direct acquaintance with their plays and performances dates from that year, when most of their major plays, including *Mistero buffo*, were transmitted in a retrospective series on Italian television. At the time, I was living near Cisternino, in an isolated rural area in Apulia in the south of Italy, and spoke little Italian. I had become involved with a local Communist theatre group, Il Collettivo Teatrale di Base, in Cisternino, and we all gathered at one of their members' houses to watch *Mistero buffo*. It was a total revelation, even on television, and although I could understand little of Fo's Italian, let alone his dialect and *grammelot*, and my friends were all laughing too much to be able to explain much to me in what little English they knew, I could understand the language of his gestures. I resolved to start work on a project to ensure that the work of this prodigious actor-playwright became known in the English-speaking world, and began translating *Accidental Death of an Anarchist*. This book, the first on Fo to appear in English, and my first book, was the result of that project. A second, rather hastily updated edition of it appeared in Methuen's *Theatrefile* series in 1986. The current edition is an extensively revised, updated and expanded version which includes Fo's most recent work up to the end of 1998. It also incorporates and updates material from my *File on Dario Fo*, which appeared in Methuen's *Writer Files* series in 1989.

There is little doubt that Dario Fo is one of the world's great modern comic actors, as well as being an exceptional mime. He himself has described the chief quality of great acting as *souplesse*:

> what distinguishes great actors from average actors is their *souplesse*. This means that they have a great understanding of the *technique* of acting, and they understand so deeply, and are involved in, what they are performing, that they don't 'splash about' . . . They don't show that they are exerting themselves. They make you forget that they are acting.[4]

This definition could have been tailor-made to fit Fo himself. However, as well as pinpointing one of the main difficulties a foreign actor has to encounter in performing the massive parts which Fo writes for himself in his plays, it also raises the question that often Fo's performances are simply acclaimed (as *Mistero buffo* was in London) as 'great acting'. Such evaluations tend to overlook that the plays are essentially political vehicles of an 'epic', 'popular' theatre in which a Marxist, but satirical critique of modern society and its institutions and injustices is put forward in no mean terms.

Unlike Laurence Olivier, or Paul Scofield, or most other actors who could fit Fo's definition of *souplesse*, Fo is also an improviser. He frequently performs topical sketches about current political events in an off-the-cuff way which enables audiences to witness a process of creation at work in which a political discourse becomes a piece of theatre. At the same time, he is a political worker, negating all the distinctions and role-divisions involved in conventional theatre set-ups. He will often step onto the stage (with the house-lights still up) from the audience, where he has been chatting to people, selling books and political pamphlets, or helping stage hands and front-of-house workers, and, once on stage, directly address the audience as equals. In his work there is none of the paraphernalia of a star performance which is normally associated with 'great acting'. In his definition of the type of theatre he proposes as the 'destruction of the fourth wall', he intends not only a rejection of naturalism and the representation of a character in favour of direct address, asides and presentational commentary, but also a rejection of the hierarchical form of the conventional theatre situation.

As an actor and a playwright, Fo is essentially a political animal, who has exerted considerable influence on attempts to unify a fragmented and conflicting Italian Left through the medium of political satire. This unification of the Italian Left could be said to have come to fruition in 1995 when the Olive Branch coalition under Prime Minister Romano Prodi formed Italy's first left-wing government since the Second World War. This occurred after the ruling Christian Democrat government had been toppled by the exposure of a huge network of bribery and corruption which formed the basic fabric of Italian society, and after a brief interregnum by media magnate Silvio Berlusconi's novelty Forza Italia (Come On Italy) government. Fo and Rame presented satirical chronicles of the corruption scandals and the rise of the Berlusconi regime in their plays in the 1990s. Previously their debunking of the follies of repression in the 1970s and 1980s had become a rallying-point for audiences of several thousands at a time in football stadiums, converted cinemas, circus tents, public squares, occupied factories and deconsecrated churches. A good proportion of these audiences in the 1970s and 1980s were people who felt too alienated to set foot inside a red-plush, establishment theatre. Fo and Rame performed to workers, students, housewives and unemployed people in an environment of truly 'popular theatre' in which it was the normal theatregoer's turn to feel alienated. They shared the stage with workers reading statements about sackings, about occupied factories and other political struggles, and with the relatives of prisoners detained without trial on political charges, and then called for donations from the audience to numerous political causes. They also catered for the neglected middle-class theatregoer in the 1980s and 1990s by performing in traditional theatres, packing them out nightly. Audiences who managed to get into the relatively tiny Riverside Studios in London for Fo's and Rame's performances in 1983 were seeing them very much out of context. In Italy, frequently their style of performance had to be modified, and they had to use microphones, in order to get across to audiences of up to 5,000.

Fo's and Rame's theatrical and political activities have often created a mistaken impression of them both within and outside Italy as being ultra-left extremist propagandists. Their activities have been interpreted as calling for the total overthrow of the bourgeois state and sympathising with the philosophies of armed struggle propagated by the Red Brigades and other Italian terrorist groups. But the fact that Fo and Rame were considerably further to the left of the Italian Communist Party (PCI) does not automatically equate them with a terrorist position. Nor does the continued help they have given to political detainees held in prisons under laws which find them guilty until proven innocent. In fact, since Franca Rame left the PCI in the 1970s, Fo and Rame have not been members of any political party or group, but became comic and satirical mouthpieces for a vast, post-1968 movement on the left of the PCI. This movement was increasingly ostracised, victimised and depleted in the 1980s, while the PCI modified and revised its political stance until it became little more than a reformist social democratic party. After the collapse of the Communist regimes in Eastern Europe in 1989, the PCI 'remade' itself as the Partito Democratico della Sinistra (Democratic Party of the Left). In 1995 the PDS became the majority party in government, a progression which Fo and Rame initially did not support. Ironically, it was the Communist Refoundation (Rifondazione Communista) party, which attempted to restore the 'traditional' values of the old PCI, which caused the collapse of the Prodi government in October 1998, after it had spent the second-longest period in government in postwar Italian history. Prodi, whom Fo and Rame had had amicable meetings with both before and after he came to power, lost a vote of confidence in the Italian parliament by a single vote. Consequently Rame attacked the Rifondazione Communista leader Bertinotti and expressed support for Prodi:

> I am astonished by [Bertinotti's] behaviour. He has done enormous damage to the country: we've reached a huge impasse, the stock exchange has crashed, and the whole world is criticising us . . . Prodi is an honest person, one of the best presidents [sic] of the last 30 years. He has done a great deal in the past two years, and realised numerous points of his four-year programme. And his economic programme, which everyone has criticised, is not bad at all. And we've joined the European Union.[5]

The depletion of the extra-parliamentary Italian Left which occurred in the 1980s, and which led to a more moderate phase in Fo's and Rame's work and views, was a direct result of terrorism and the repressive laws it led to. As a result, innocent people were likely to be branded as terrorist sympathisers if they took part in any politically militant activity. Many of these repressive laws came into effect due to direct pressure on the Italian state by the PCI. In 1983, the number of people held in Italian prisons on political charges was estimated at 5,000. Franca Rame described the situation in the Italian Left at the time as

> a coma of consciousness . . . people are afraid to even start up a petition, because the State immediately criminalises you, and brands you as an 'aider and abetter' or a fellow traveller.[6]

So, far from being supporters of terrorism, Fo and Rame suffered both from being mistakenly associated with it and from the state repressions it generated. This is not, however, tantamount to depicting them as moderates. On the contrary, in their continued involvement in situations of political struggle, they showed an indomitable energy in applying theatrically the precepts of Marx, Brecht, Gramsci, Mayakovsky and Mao Ze-Dong in the teeth of state and institutional repression. They also continued to be subjected to frequent censorship of their work, even in the 1990s, and from as far back as the 1950s.

In the 1990s Fo and Rame continued to be exponents of a cultural revolution, in the sense of restoring the culture of the peasant and the working class to those from whom it had been expropriated by the middle class. One of the principal tools of this cultural revolution, and one of the most difficult for non-Italians to appreciate, is Fo's restoration of Italian regional dialects to prominence in the Italian theatre. A great part of the tradition of Italian comedy, as exemplified in modern form in the Neapolitan plays of Eduardo de Filippo, is based on the numerous and widely differing, idiosyncratic regional languages to be found throughout Italy and in Sardinia and Sicily. But these dialects began to die out as young people moved to the cities and the regularised, standard Italian of television became more and more widespread. In influencing a resurgence of dialect in modern Italian comedy by adapting the language of the Po valley in the sixteenth century in *Mistero buffo* and its sequels, Fo went a step beyond a mere re-excavation of popular culture. He combined dialect with *grammelot,* an invented onomatopoeic language devised by medieval strolling players to avoid political censorship. Consequently he created what is virtually a new theatrical language, which, combined with mime and gesture, almost transcends linguistic boundaries. This language is yoked to the voice of the underdog railing against the machinations of politicians and authority figures of church and state. While *Mistero buffo* is largely dependent on an ecclesiastical background of corruption and repression, it is by no means exclusively so, and its political implications remain universal. Many of Fo's other plays, however, often rely on a more contemporary political background which I have tried to sketch in where necessary. But the most universal aspect of Fo's work is its most lively and communicative – its farcical and iconoclastic comedy. Not the reactionary comedy of the Whitehall farce or the TV comedian, but the irreverent, popular comedy and political satire of the militant opposed to all forms of social and political repression. As Fo once replied to a member of one of his audiences in one of the many debates after performances of his plays in the 1970s:

As far as a preoccupation with ridicule, laughter, sarcasm, irony and the grotesque is concerned, I have to say – I'd be a liar if I said otherwise – it's my job. I've been teaching this lesson for years – the origins of the grotesque and Marxist and pre-Marxist culture and irony . . . Nothing gets down as deeply into the mind and intelligence as satire. The end of satire is the first alarm bell signalling the end of real democracy.[7]

At the end of the 1990s, well into his seventies, Fo is still teaching this lesson. Proof of his continued ironic and comic militancy is his 1998 monologue *Marino at Large*. This is a topical documentary satire about three former left-wing militants imprisoned on trumped-up evidence for the assassination of a police inspector who had also figured in the events surrounding *Accidental Death of an Anarchist*. And Fo's 1997 Nobel Prize was an acknowledgment that he has succeeded in his satirical fight for democracy against all forms of oppression in Italy and elsewhere in the world.

Fo's work is inseparable from its grounding in a direct engagement with Italian political life of the past half-century. It is also inseparable from the traditions of popular performance he works in, which go back to the Atella farces of the ancient Romans, Carnival Saturnalia and the medieval *giullari*. And, as Joseph Farrell has indicated, he is always straightforward in his approach; there is little to be gained from subjecting his plays to deconstructive theories, postmodern readings or psychoanalysis:

There is no value in approaching Fo with a post-modern primer of deconstructionalism, post-structuralism or reception aesthetics. There is no subtext to be uncovered, no hidden ambiguities to be revealed, no delicate psychology of character to be probed, no curiosities of flawed personality to be dissected and analysed, no alternate world of fantasy to be contemplated.[8]

This may risk overlooking what Paolo Puppa has identified as 'magical or fairy-tale motifs, surreal flights of fantasy or wildly imaginative metaphors [which] overwrite and nullify the banalization of politics, and raise the work to the dream dimension.'[9] But one might also add, there is also little value in applying the rigours of feminist theory to his and Franca Rame's plays and performances, as some critics have attempted, usually with disappointing results. Both tend to espouse a rather conventional commitment to heterosexual relationships, and Rame critiques many of the precepts expounded by Italian feminists, as well as probing Marxist orthodoxies. Another danger is in taking any of the numerous pronouncements Fo has made about his work, and the theatrical and historical tradition he works in, at face value. As he himself indicated at the beginning of his 1987 encyclopedic *Short Manual for the Actor*, his memory for names of authors and for quotations is often faulty. He often invents highly credible historical stories and arguments and mixes them with incredible actual events and details, and admits he is 'a professional liar'.[10] Although this means that some of what he says has to be taken with a pinch of salt, it does not detract from the enormous inventiveness, imagination and cogent political analysis of most of his work.

PART ONE

THE THEATRE OF DARIO FO AND FRANCA RAME

Chapter 1

MISTERO BUFFO AND THE *GIULLARATE*

Popular culture, the *giullari* and the grotesque

As well as being an actor-playwright Dario Fo also combines the roles of director, stage designer, songwriter, and political campaigner. He has performed his solo *pièce célèbre*, *Mistero buffo*, throughout Europe, Eastern Europe, Scandinavia, and in Canada and Latin America over a 30-year period, and it has become one of the most controversial and popular spectacles of postwar European theatre. When *Mistero buffo* was presented on Italian television in 1977, after Fo had performed it live more than 1,000 times to audiences in Italy of more than a million and a half, and throughout the world to an estimated 40 million, there was public outcry. This came from sources as varied as the Vatican (which described it as 'the most blasphemous show in the history of television')[1] and the Italian Communist Party, and was as vociferous as the widespread public acclaim.

What Fo did in *Mistero buffo*, virtually single-handedly, was to distil the popular, comic, irreverent elements of medieval mystery plays and religious cycles into a political and cultural onslaught against the repressions of the Catholic church and the landowning classes throughout history. He expressed this in the language of the Italian peasantry (and, by extension, every class of oppressed people), fuelled by the epic-didactic concepts of Brecht and Mayakovsky, and the political precepts of Mao Ze-Dong and Gramsci.

Recovering 'illegitimate' forms of theatre – the *giullari*

The title *Mistero buffo* (literally 'comical mystery') is borrowed from *Mystery-Bouffe,* an 'epic-satirical representation of our times' written by the Russian poet Mayakovsky in 1918. This was a hymn to socialist optimism and 'the road to revolution' which was performed under Meyerhold's direction with Mayakovsky playing the role of the Man of the Future. Mayakovsky's play deals with seven couples, representing the proletariat of different countries, who are encouraged by the Man of the Future to steal Jove's thunderbolts for electricity and expel the devils from hell and the angels from heaven (including Rousseau and Tolstoy). They finally create a promised land full of 'good things' such as machines, cars, trains, technology and food. Mayakovsky was an important influence in Fo's plays in the late 1960s and 1970s, one of which, *The Worker Knows 300 Words, the Boss Knows 1,000 – That's Why He's the Boss* (1969) has the Russian poet as one of the protagonists in a series of stories intended to convey a sense of the urgency of building a working-class culture. However, the main origins of Fo's *Mistero buffo* reside in the surviving texts and descriptions of the *giullari,* the medieval strolling players who performed in the streets and piazzas of Europe:

> *Mistero* [mystery] is the term used since the second and third centuries AD to describe a sacred spectacle or performance. Even today in the Mass we hear the priest announce 'In the first glorious mystery . . . In the second mystery . . .' and so on. So *Mistero* means a sacred performance, and *mistero buffo* means a grotesque spectacle.[2]

In extracting the grotesque elements of the mystery plays, Fo's intention is to bring to the foreground their popular origins. He also mocks the pomp and postures of the church hierarchy while popularising Christ and biblical legend, which is seen from the medieval peasant's point of view.

> The inventors of the *mistero buffo* were the people. From the first centuries after Christ the people entertained themselves – although it was not merely a form of entertainment

– by putting on and performing in spectacles of an ironic and grotesque nature. As far as the people were concerned, the theatre, and particularly the theatre of the grotesque, had always been their chief means of expression and communication, as well as putting across ideas by means of provocation and agitation. The theatre was the people's spoken, dramatised newspaper.[3]

At the basis of almost all of Fo's more than 70 plays is the theatrical tradition of the *giullare* (the Italian equivalent of the Latin *jocularis*, the French *jongleur*, the German *Gaukler*, the Spanish *juglar* and the English *juggler*). This term, which emerged in the ninth century, refers to the medieval strolling player who busked and performed to the peasants of Europe, frequently on the run from persecution from the authorities, censorship, and co-option into the courts. As Antonio Scuderi has noted, the '*giullari* were itinerant players mostly of the lower classes who worked within the oral tradition. They included a wide variety of performers: musicians, dancers, acrobats, tumblers, storytellers, and mimes.'[4] From the *giullari* arose the 'official' tradition of the *commedia dell'arte*. Fo's task in *Mistero buffo* was the retrieval and recovery of this unofficial, 'illegitimate' theatre contained in the original repertoires of the *giullari* before it was appropriated and transformed by court influences. This process was described by one of Fo's foremost Italian commentators, Lanfranco Binni:

> The 'epic theatre' of the medieval *giullari*, in which the *giullare* became the choral, didactic expression of an entire community and the feelings, hopes and rebellion of exploited people to whom he performed in a piazza, projected their desire for liberation from the religious sphere set up by the authorities. Performances expressed an insistently human passion, with a human, exploited, peasant Christ who refutes the injustices of the hypocritical religion of the rich to such an extent that this 'epic theatre' of the *giullari* was either physically suppressed (by persecuting the *giullari* and cutting off their heads) or neutered and re-translated into an aristocratic vein. Thus the *giullare* who

performed in the piazza, sharing a rapport with whoever recognised themselves and their own sufferings in his stories, became the 'court jester' who had the sole task of entertaining courtiers. As a result, his expressions of anger and hope through physical means and rapport with others were transformed into the recitation of verses of 'quality' whose chief value lay in the weaving of amorous rhymes, or even the dehumanised, objectified description of peasants 'at work'. The latter were mocked for their 'vulgarity' or transferred into an aristocratic context and given an abstract, 'pastoral' dimension, accompanied by flutes and amorous sighs for gentle nymphs.[5]

A common misconception is that the theatrical traditions of farce and comedy in Fo's theatre stem solely from the *commedia dell'arte*. But the *giullari* are essentially pre-*commedia*, the popular, unofficial mouthpieces of the peasant population, while the performers of the *commedia* are regarded by Fo as the professional 'court jesters' officially recognised by the ruling classes. Although a number of Fo's routines were culled from the repertoires of *comici dell'arte* like Ruzzante, who survived the transition from piazza to court, and Harlequin, Fo sees these performers as essentially idiosyncratic and rebellious in terms of the canons of the *commedia*, and as peasant rather than court figures. Fo himself, in the context of the contemporary Italian theatre, experienced the acclaim and stature of a 'bourgeois court jester' when he became a prominent figure in the established, mainstream Italian theatre during the mid-sixties. After the political upheavals in Europe in 1968, he and Rame renounced this position of commercial success and sought an alternative, 'fringe' theatre network, performing in factories, piazzas, and *case del popolo* (Communist Party community centres) to a predominantly non-theatre-going audience. It was in this alternative context that *Mistero buffo* was first performed.

Language as burlesque – *grammelot*
One of the most notable features of *Mistero buffo* is its language, which Fo describes as 'fifteenth-century Padano'. This

comprises a mixture of the various dialects of the Po valley, Lombardy, Veneto and Piedmont, which Fo adapted, sometimes modernised, and frequently completely invented, devising an incomprehensible foreign language which relies on the actor's physical illustration and verbal explanation. Mime, action and gesture assume primary importance in Fo's solo performances, and he has continually modified and stylised the language of the plays to such an extent that it functions like a codified system of sounds similar to 'scat song' in jazz. Particularly when performing outside the Po valley, Fo developed an onomatopoeic language which served to complement his mimic gestures and express the physicality of situations rather than conveying information about them, which Fo frequently consigned to an explanatory prologue.

Alongside this emphasis on the physical sound-structure of the Padano dialect, Fo also elaborated a totally invented language called *grammelot*. This is a phonic, abstract sound-system in which few recognisable words of any language occur, and which relies on suggestion. In his prologue to *Zanni's Grammelot*, with which he frequently opens performances of *Mistero buffo,* Fo explains the tradition of *grammelot*:

> *Grammelot* is a form of theatre that was reinvented by the actors of the *commedia dell'arte*, but it goes back to even before the 1500s. It was developed as an onomatopoeic theatrical technique to put across concepts by way of sounds which were not established words in the conventional sense. *Grammelot* was invented by the *comici dell'arte* to escape censorship, and at the time when they fled to other countries in the 1500s because of the enormous repression they suffered under the Council of Trent, which effectively denied them the possibility of performing in Italian towns and cities. The majority of them went to France, and we are told that, in order to make themselves understood, they used a form of language similar to French, although only a few words were actually French. Just as there is a foreign-language *grammelot,* so too there is an Italian one, particularly in its dialects. The most famous

Grammelot was Zanni's. Zanni is the prototype of all the characters of the *commedia dell'arte*, or at least the father of the most important ones, such as Harlequin. But he's no invented character, he was real. The character of Zanni is directly linked to a category of people, or at least a social class: the peasants of the Po valley and the mountains that extend down to the Po valley.[6]

The term *grammelot* derives from the French word *grommeler*, to mumble, and Fo first developed it when he performed *Mistero buffo* in France in 1973.[7] It has been used primarily to imitate the sounds of foreign languages, and in the course of his performances Fo even built up an American *grammelot* in a piece called *The American Technocrat*. He performed this at anti-nuclear rallies, and it is a grotesque parody of an American nuclear technician in which he mimes and utters the sounds of aeroplanes and space craft, producing perhaps one recognisable English word in ten (such as 'yeah' or 'OK' – Fo speaks fluent French but virtually no English), but with a deceptively exact inflection and accent. He also uses this American *grammelot* in his frequent topical burlesques on American politics, such as his famous impersonation of President Ford tripping while getting out of a helicopter and almost getting killed by the blades. In one of his asides in the television version of *Mistero buffo,* he relates how *The American Technocrat* caused several Americans to walk out of a Paris performance because they could not understand a word of what he was saying, but could detect he was satirising Americans.

Grammelot, then, chiefly functions as a form of burlesque mimicry in *Mistero buffo* and a number of Fo's other plays, such as the version of Stravinsky's *The Soldier's Tale* which he rewrote and directed for La Scala in 1978, where it was used to embody the different dialect the soldier spoke. Fo has extended its onomatopoeic potential to more modern contexts such as the Grandfather's simulated drug hallucinations in *Mother's Marijuana is the Best* (1976) and to a representation of the working of factory machinery and a production line in *Mistero buffo,* in a highly orchestrated gibberish of machine language. In *Knock Knock! Who's There? Police!* (1972), his sequel to *Accidental*

Death of an Anarchist, Fo recounts another branch of *grammelot* which places it in the tradition of Molière, through the mouthpiece of a Superintendent of Police whom Fo impersonates in the play:

> Scapino, Antonio Scapino, went to France in the 1500s and met Molière . . . and immediately Molière said, 'Save me, you must save me, they've censored my latest play *Tartuffe,* and cut the entire ending. You must help me!' 'But I'm a bad actor, and I'm even worse in French.' 'Yes, but you act with gestures, with your face, your hands, you're an extraordinary mime – you come out and act with gestures, and add the odd word or two here and there for effect, or just snort or mutter or talk nonsense, it makes no difference – you put your message across with your hands, with gestures, with pantomime, and they can't censor that.' 'All right then, but who do I have to play, what do I have to say, what's my character?' 'A servant – you can call yourself Scapino, you're a servant in one of the richest households in France, whose eldest son goes into politics, and you teach this youth all the tricks of the trade, the art of hypocrisy, of *tartuffaggine,* the ultimate in Jesuitry . . . OK?' . . . Now for your information this marvellous talk is called *grammelot,* it's all muttered and spat out in a continuous stream. It doesn't matter if you can't pick up the words, the gestures are what matter.[8]

In this extraordinary set-piece, Fo is using the character of the Police Superintendent to describe *grammelot* as an example of the speechifying antics of the Italian Christian Democratic Party in the 1970s. This illustrates how Fo continually makes historical leaps to refer to present political realities, a technique which is continually present in *Mistero buffo.* His use of *grammelot* and the techniques of the *giullari* is educational in serving to stress and illustrate the origins of popular culture. But it is no mere academic, intellectual exercise, since Fo continually roots his historical didacticism in contemporary political and social reality to score comic points and make gags at the expense of political authority figures. As the critic Jean Chesneaux has put it:

9

Dario Fo is indifferent to both the elitist little world of the professional scholars and to that of theatre professionals. He has moved out of that world to find the workers and the common people. For Dario Fo history is an active relationship with the past, and a distant epoch like the Middle Ages – as *Mistero buffo* shows – can be just as fertile as a more recent period when it comes to fuelling the active social struggle of the present. What matters is the political quality of this link between the present and the past, not the distance of centuries.[9]

The language used in *Mistero buffo,* in both its inventiveness and its historic complexity, is a major factor in Fo's achievement in bringing to life the origins of an essentially popular, politically aware, peasant theatre. As he performs it, it becomes entertaining and enjoyable as well as culturally and politically relevant to popular audiences. Perhaps the most apt description of the language of *Mistero buffo* was given by the critic Renzo Tian:

> . . . Padano, which is reminiscent of Ruzzante, but isn't the language of Ruzzante insofar as its concern is to provide an example of an imaginary Esperanto of the poor and dispossessed.[10]

In freeing the popular peasant theatrical culture represented by Ruzzante from the academic and bourgeois mystifications it has suffered from over the centuries, Fo restores its wit, comedy and enjoyment value by taking imaginative liberties with it. He also uses it to illustrate to his audience a key concept which he extrapolates from Gramsci: 'If you don't know where you come from, you don't know where your potentialities lie.'[11]

Addressing the audience – prologues, interludes and asides
The diverse nature of the material in *Mistero buffo,* the complexity of Fo's verbal acrobatics, his continual paring, modification and stylisation of the texts, and the 'living newspaper' aspect of the spectacle, have necessitated often

lengthy explanatory prologues to the individual pieces Fo performs. These prologues have become concretised into *discorsi* or *interventi,* direct addresses in which Fo speaks to the audience to explain the situation of a particular piece. In these he often uses satirical illustrations from topical political events, incorporating impersonations of popes and politicians as well as analyses of current events. These have in turn become an expected part of the performances, set pieces and sketches which exist alongside and complement the *canovacci* (literally 'canvasses' or plot-lines for improvisations) which comprise the source material of *Mistero buffo.* Fo traces the origins of these asides to Cherea, a contemporary of Ruzzante:

> . . . sometimes when he was performing he'd pretend there was a wasp annoying him . . . Eventually the wasp was flying all over the place, off the stage and into the audience even. Cherea would follow it and involve the audience in the comic situation. Ruzzante also used direct address with his audiences, not for any aesthetic contrast, but to enable them to participate in the events on stage with a constant awareness of their fiction.[12]

A key concept in Fo's theatrical praxis is his adoption of the concept of 'breaking down the fourth wall', and these moments in which he addresses the audience directly are similar to Brecht's alienation effects, allowing the audience to detach itself from the historical frame of reference of the pieces and make contemporary analogies. Fo's topical sketches, such as Pope John Paul II skiing, his impersonation of John Paul I as a grinning simpleton whom he compares to Pinocchio, or Paul VI riding a brakeless bicycle down the hill in Castel Gandolfo, or a skit about *carabinieri* spotting UFOs, become performance vehicles in themselves, contextualising the religious and spiritual aspects of the biblical plays by producing a modern counterpoint. As Ugo Volli stated, reviewing a performance in Milan in March 1979 in the newspaper *La Repubblica:*

The *discorsi,* analyses and polemics have their own separate place in the spectacle, introducing and motivating the individual pieces Fo performs or relates. The structure of *Mistero buffo* takes the form of a text, an explanation, and another text. The fact that the explanations are as entertaining and as well received as the pieces in the play doesn't change the situation. The opposition between language and dialects, between direct dialogue with the audience and fictional story-telling to an ideal audience, between mime and the display of vocal resources, distinguishes perfectly the two areas of the spectacle, which are integrated and complementary, both bringing laughter and applause.[13]

The form of the *discorsi* or addresses is modified in the same way as the texts themselves – according to audience response, feedback and discussion. In the 1970s, Fo frequently ended performances with what he referred to as the 'third act'. These were debates and discussions with the audience, who expressed criticisms and suggestions which often helped to shape the development of the play in terms of political content, style, language and entertainment value.

Fo regards his audiences as an essential element of the process in which he shapes his performances, and their reactions are a strong factor in his elaboration of the frequent improvisations he makes around the texts of *Mistero buffo* as well as in the prologues and *discorsi.* The rhythm of each performance of the play he sees as being the result of a spontaneous but guided (by the performer) collaboration between the comic and a participating audience who it is the comic's job to keep involved and participating by means of a technique he refers to as 'fishing for laughs':

The comic fishes for laughs by virtually throwing out a comic line, or a hook, into the audience. He indicates where the audience's reaction has to be gathered in and also virtually where the hook is cast, because otherwise the tension built up between stage and audience would die down. Winding in the hook doesn't mean snuffing out the audience reaction, but correcting its flow with a flick of the rod. The comic's ability lies in knowing that if he carries on for a while on the same tack he'll snap the audience's capacity to keep up with his theme. So he breaks into the stage action, using something extraneous (a spectator's funny way of laughing, for example, or imitating the way La Malfa* speaks). Then the comic casts out the hook again, for a bigger laugh (although he can fish for laughs by casting out the hook more than once before provoking one big laugh) . . . One could talk endlessly about techniques of laughter. In Nancy, Lecoq [the French mime] gave veritable lessons about techniques of laughter: head laughter, throat laughter, silent laughter, side-splitting laughter, rolling in the aisles . . . I think, however, the audience's real way of laughing can be divided into just two types: when it is symptomatic of involvement in the play and when it is not. The difference lies between the mechanical reaction of laughing and the relationship through which an audience collaborates in building the play. The first is about the star-satisfaction of the comic who sees the effects of his technique and is pleased with himself, and it is quite different from the comic's reaction to a sort of confrontation which prompts him immediately, on the spot, into developing what he is saying, preferably through improvisation, and the action he is building up on stage with the audience. The comic provokes the audience's laughter with his resources, but audience laughter is a response which itself recharges the comic – it's not just a technique – maybe even feeding the yeast of his stage reactions in the course of a given play, or maybe just adding to the further exercise of his craft . . . All popular theatre requires the audience to be 'inside', and take part in the rhythm of laughter.[14]

* Ugo La Malfa: economist and statesman, leader of the Italian Republican Party (PRI) and Minister of Foreign Trade and Councillor of the Exchequer until his death in 1979.

The texts in performance

Fo excavated the texts which he uses as a basis for his performance in *Mistero buffo* from a wide variety of Latin, Provençal, Italian, Middle English, and even Yugoslavian, Czech and Polish sources. The criteria behind his choice and adaptation of the texts were based on a desire to highlight their popular aspect as vehicles of the people's struggle against capitalistic and ecclesiastical oppression. This frequently involved a process of stripping down rather than augmentation, paring away the additions and superimpositions of subsequent adaptors of the original texts (who include even Dante), rescuing the material from the appropriations of 'cultural aristocrats'. In *Rosa fresca aulentissima* (A Fresh Fragrant Rose) for example, Fo is dealing with a story which is presented in school textbooks as a coy, courtly love story of a boy whose physical lust is checked by the polite blandishments of the girl who is the object of his lust. Fo restores the tale to a brutal example of sexual oppression in which the boy, a rich tax collector, is able to have his way with the girl, and owing to a special law protecting the wealthy, can even charge her with rape, rather than vice versa.

Mistero buffo has frequently been attacked from academic quarters as well as from Vatican sources. In a book entitled *Giullari e Fo* (1978), the musician and critic Michele Straniero retitles the play 'Mistero Bluff', and sets out to debunk Fo's spurious sense of history. Straniero produces a list of historical inaccuracies and anachronisms which occur in *Mistero buffo* (such as, for example, the fact that the term 'mystery' is not found in the Mass but in the Rosary), and accuses Fo of falsifying historical facts and simplifying the popular elements of his source material. Straniero maintains that Fo, in his zeal to reappropriate popular culture from the mystifying hands of bourgeois commentators, ignores or mutilates texts which are of bourgeois origin. This leads to an accusation of 'inviting young people to burn books instead of reading and criticising them and discussing the difficulties of cultural mediation, together with the importance of mastering sources like these which the bourgeoisie tends to keep to itself.'[15] Fo regards such arguments as arid and over–academic, while pointing out that many of the historical inaccuracies that Straniero picks up are deliberately ironic anachronisms: 'Only a person as deficient in irony as Straniero wouldn't notice they were put there deliberately.'[16] In reply to the 'book burning' charge, Fo points to the lengthy bibliography included in the published edition of the play, the fact that some of his material, such as the apocryphal pieces, are in fact culled from bourgeois sources, and cites the numerous university theses on medieval theatre sparked off by *Mistero buffo,* as well as the increase of sales of books on the subject.

There is no doubt that Fo's aims in *Mistero buffo* are didactic and educational, but in performance he repeatedly demonstrates the entertainment and amusement to be gained from his medieval popular sources. Performances of *Mistero buffo* in the 1970s frequently lasted up to four hours; no two performances were ever the same, and the critic Chiara Valentini estimated that if all the pieces Fo had performed in *Mistero buffo* were placed end to end, the performance would last an entire day. Fo performs alone on a bare stage, dressed in black sweater and trousers, with no lighting effects and the aid of only a microphone slung round his neck to carry his voice to the outer reaches of the vast halls, sports stadiums, converted cinemas, deconsecrated churches, public squares and open spaces where he has performed the play. He keeps up a constant patter of witty repartee, constantly ad-libbing with the audience, rather like a thinking person's Lenny Bruce. He displays a staggering physical dexterity, continually changing character, and running through an enormous variety of grotesque, vain, pathetic and comic characterisations of human folly. He uses his hooded eyes, Chaplinesque mouth, and physical largeness and gaucheness in a mimic style often reminiscent of Jacques Tati. (Fo studied with the French mime Jacques Lecoq in the 1950s, and Lecoq taught him how to use his large frame, long limbs and big feet to advantage, and his lolloping physique and vastly expressive face seem capable of evoking any number of physical idiosyncrasies.)

Fo establishes an instant rapport with his packed audiences of enthusiastic and predominantly young supporters who often spill onto the stage at the actor's invitation. Using the familiar, informal *tu* form, he ad-libs (in one performance in Vicenza during a thunderstorm he conversed with the thunder, addressing it as the voice of God), and jokes with the spectators. One particularly notable performance took place in Milan in April 1974, in a field opposite the newly occupied Palazzina Liberty, which Fo and his group La Comune had adopted as their home theatre. The audience was estimated at about 30,000 and as Fo recalls:

> At least 30 per cent were people from the local area: housewives, old age pensioners, workers, entire families, and hundreds of children, who caused inevitable confusion during the performance, running around, getting lost . . . I had to interrupt the play every ten minutes to find the mothers of kids who were up on the stage crying desperately.[17]

Typically, Fo used the situation to improvise a discussion about the necessity for more state-run crèches. A strong sense of solidarity tended to develop between actor and audience, also owing to the fact that in the 1970s audiences often had to undergo a police search before entering the theatre because of Fo's status as a politically subversive figure in Italy. *Mistero buffo* is a prime example of 'epic' theatre in the true sense of the word, at once a recreation of popular history and culture and an affirmation of the political potency of this recreation.

The TV performances

For the television transmission of *Mistero buffo,* which took place in April and May of 1977 (in four parts), and which can be regarded as something of a definitive version of the play, Fo was filmed in performance on his home base in the Palazzina Liberty. He performed to a live audience, going through his array of political caricatures, such as his satirical portrait of the then Italian Prime Minister, Giulio Andreotti. It was a definitive performance, then, in the sense that it was transmitted to an audience of some five million, and that Fo has not performed

Mistero buffo so frequently since then. But it was still subject to the spontaneous developments which always take place in Fo's live performances of the play. As Fo has said,

> *Mistero buffo* has always relied on improvisation, since the audience is involved in it and doesn't play a passive part, since it imposes its rhythms, and provokes off-the-cuff lines. This type of theatre is recreated from performance to performance, and is always different, and never repetitive.[18]

The television performance is worth describing in some detail, since the highly idiosyncratic and virtually untranslatable language of the play, and the demands it makes on the actor, make it an unrepeatable performance, an 'epic', 'total' theatre experience which establishes Fo as an actor/dramatist of unique status. *Mistero buffo* is also the linchpin of Fo's prodigious output of works, propagating most of the theatrical and political concepts which are embodied in a different dimension in his other plays.

Zanni's Grammelot

The piece with which Fo opens *Mistero buffo* is a *lazzo,* or improvised sketch from the *commedia dell'arte,* as it was performed by the Zanni, or servant figure. The name is a diminutive of Giovanni or Gianni, and the English word 'zany' derives from it. Zanni, Fo explains in his introduction to the piece, here represents the plight of the peasants of the Po valley, who were displaced by the 'origins of capitalism' in the Middle Ages, and forced to abandon their land because they could not face the competition of imported produce. Zanni as Fo represents him is a starving peasant who, in his hunger, imagines that he is eating himself – which Fo represents in minute gestural detail. He then mimes Zanni's dream, in which he prepares an enormous Pantagruelian feast, stirring an enormous bubbling pot of polenta, frying chicken, eggs, cheese and sauce, making the sounds of the boiling pot, the sizzling meat and the rising steam. He goes on to represent the pans and the cooker with gestures in mid-air, and then abruptly makes everything disappear. Zanni, awakening from his dream, hunts down and captures a fly, dismembers it and eats it with all the relish of someone devouring the feast he has dreamed up previously, his stomach distending grotesquely. The ironic Epicureanism of the sketch conveys a desperation and self-parody which combines hunger and anger. Fo's onomatopoeic utterances and mimed gestures are a prime example of what he refers to as a theatre of *gesto mimico* (mimed gesture), which

> originates from an extremely old tradition, but which has been renewed through the generations, and allows past and present to coexist simultaneously. It also amplifies the point being made on stage by continually fixing it on the level of technical experience, projected out to the audience without verbal retractions connected with lighting or atmosphere.[19]

Zanni's Grammelot is followed by another *Grammelot, The Story of Saint Benedict of Norcia,* about a wall-builder who founded an order of levitating monks. The monks become concerned about their bellies when their cook also starts levitating, which induces them to abandon the spiritual sophistication of contemplating their navels in favour of cultivating the land in order to fill their stomachs.

The Massacre of the Innocents

In *The Massacre of the Innocents* Fo represents a number of different characters, including a mad woman who has substituted a sheep for her dead baby, and who is accosted by a soldier who takes the sheep for a baby. The woman then tells her story to a statue of the Madonna, and the Madonna unsuccessfully attempts to console her. Fo alternates between the mother, the ruthless and merciless soldier, and the Madonna with impressive speed and physical differentiation, while emphasising the peasant environment of deprivation of the distraught mother, who at the end goes off rocking the sheep and singing it a lullaby. Fo avoids sentimentality both through the grotesqueness of the situation he depicts, and the 'chorality' of his performance, in which he is continually swapping characters like a quick-change artist. The unusual pathos and sense of tragedy of this piece is immediately juxtaposed with a comic, grotesque, almost Beckett-like performance, *The Morality Play of the Blind Man and the Cripple*.

The Morality Play of the Blind Man and the Cripple
This sketch is attributed to Andrea della Vigna in the fifteenth century, but exists also in French and Belgian versions. A blind man and a cripple join forces, the latter riding on the former's back, and run into Christ on his way to Calvary. They try to flee and hide from Christ, since they do not want to run the risk of being cured of their afflictions by a miracle, which would oblige them to look for work with a master and lead considerably harder lives. In their attempt to avoid Christ's glance, the blind man trips and the pair fall in a heap at the feet of Christ, who heals them and leaves them to fend for themselves.

Here a grotesque situation of peasant degradation exists alongside a revolutionary message which advocates by implication the overthrow of the *padroni* – the masters and landowners. The piece also pinpoints the charlatanry of contemporary beggars in a way which echoes Peachum's rabble of false cripples and afflicted in Brecht's *Threepenny Opera*. In the piece Fo 'doubles up' between two very distinct and separate physical types – the blind man who has lost his dog, and the cripple who has lost his cart. He presents them comically, and almost naturalistically, although he frequently speaks the words of one character while physically representing the other. This character crossover exemplifies his concern with presenting a theatre of situation rather than identifying with the characters he plays. It is characteristic that Fo does not represent Christ in the piece, but makes him a described objective presence whom his two protagonists are trying to avoid. Hence the focus of the piece is not 'supernatural', but concentrates exclusively on the misery and deprivation of the plight of the blind man and the cripple.

The Marriage at Cana
Like the previous piece, *The Marriage at Cana* presents one of Christ's miracles from the people's point of view. The supernatural overtones are played down to emphasise the joyous, Dionysian, pagan view of the gospels, presenting Christ

as a catalyst for festivity and enjoyment and even Bacchanalian excess. The piece begins with an argument over who is going to present the story. A stiff, refined archangel wants to present the correct, official and celestial version of the miracle, and an ape-like, drunken, shambling wedding guest wants to tell the story from a more earthy, boozy and materialist point of view. In this dialectic, the Drunk, a character linked to Fo's line of peasant protagonists like the Blind Man, the Cripple, and Zanni, prevails through brute force and vulgarity. He chases the archangel off the stage, after plucking some of the feathers out of his wings like a chicken. The Drunk then narrates the wedding feast from a fool's point of view, emphasising the pleasure principle, and relishing his description of the epicurean delights of the feast. He echoes Zanni's dream about his meal in expressing the full 'tragedy' of the discovery that the wine has turned into vinegar (and not run out as in the official version, which is changed to the focus of a *contadino,* or peasant farmer). He describes Christ's entrance like that of a magician, and goes into a rapturous, onomatopoeic and alliterative description of the miracle and the resulting wine on which he proceeds to get drunk. Commenting on Christ's insistence that his mother try the wine as well, he reflects that if Adam had had a good glass of wine in his hand when he and Eve were tempted by the serpent and the apple, or if the apple had been made into good cider, the Fall of Man could have been avoided, along with the necessity to work. This hedonistic and decidedly secular irreverence, which includes the Drunk's vision of heaven as a vat of wine, is free of the orthodox socialist condemnation of the excesses of alcohol as an escape from the rigours and constraints of working-class life. Fo, in the tradition of the Lombardian travelling players, embraces an almost utopian vision of communal festivity in which the joys of food and drink play an important part.

Mistero buffo was shown on Italian television at the same time as Franco Zeffirelli's comparatively pious and reverent film version of the gospels, *Jesus.* Fo and Zeffirelli consequently had a debate about their disagreements over interpreting the gospels, which was set up by the newspaper *La Repubblica.* Zeffirelli maintained that *Mistero buffo* was too 'scurrilous' to be shown to 'unprepared television audiences', and that its 'elitist' political satire would be over the heads of television audiences. But it is difficult to see how popular forms and traditions can be regarded as elitist, and Fo defended his position by attacking the lack of a popular viewpoint in Zeffirelli's film:

> Zeffirelli's most serious defect is the fact that he has stifled the festivity, joy and fantasy which exist in all Christian popular tradition and also in the gospels, where there are moments of great festivity and real community. He avoids the miracle of the wedding feast of Cana, for example, the transformation of water into wine. This is one of the greatest passages in the gospels, and it's strange that Zeffirelli censored it. In his *Jesus* there's no miracle of Cana, and it's a serious omission, because the audience doesn't get the idea that Christ is also the god of joy and spring, the social and religious continuation of Dionysus . . . His film was a ruling-class operation, because he has cut out all the popular content of the gospels.[20]

Fo's emphasis on community and festivity is part of a political vision of popular culture in which the spirit of enjoyment and even excess plays an important part. The 'popularity' of *The Marriage at Cana,* and the fact that it is frequently requested by live audiences, is ample proof of the success and comprehensibility of Fo's cultural operation. 'Popular culture,' he has stated, 'doesn't mean just taking things that are of the people *per se*. It means taking everything that the masters have taken from that culture and turned upside down, and revealing their origins and developments.'[21] *The Marriage at Cana* is an outstanding example of this operation, while Zeffirelli's film is a perpetration of the 'masters'' viewpoint of that culture.

The Birth of the Jongleur

La nascita del giullare (The Birth of the Jongleur) is a key text of *Mistero buffo,* and derives from a twelfth-century Sicilian text of Eastern origin. It reveals the peasant origins of the *giullare* and the secular, down-to-earth, popular nature of their treatment of

Christ and supernatural religious events. A serf discovers a mountain and cultivates it with crops until a landowner tries to confiscate the now fertile land. The landowner calls on a bishop to lend his support to the appropriation and give it the sanction of the Church. When the peasant still refuses to give up his land, the landowner rapes the peasant's wife in front of his children. The peasant's family deserts him, and he is about to hang himself, having lost his land as well, when a man arrives and asks him for water. The peasant obliges, offering him some food as well. The man then reveals that he is Christ, confirming the peasant's growing suspicions. Christ promises to perform a miracle which will give the peasant 'a new language' which will 'cut like a knife', deflating and mocking the class of landowners and overlords. He makes the peasant a *giullare,* and instructs him to spread the message of his oppression and that of his class throughout the country.

So the mission of the *giullare* is political rather than religious, despite his sacred origins, and his message is the subversive mockery of the ruling class. Fo performs the piece in the first person as the *giullare,* presenting Christ as an ordinary person without supernatural trappings. The *giullare* originates from poverty, degradation and anger, which gives his satire a strong cutting edge. As Fo explains:

All the forms in which the *giullare* expresses himself are intrinsically satirical, because of the very fact that he . . . originates from the people and takes their anger in order to give it back to them, mediating it with the grotesque, and with rationality, so that the people can become aware of their own condition. . . . When I relate the origin of the *giullare* in *Mistero buffo,* I'm able to tell the story in a convincing way because I believe in it. I believe in the mission which the *giullare* originally chose for himself as the jester of the people. I also believe in it because I've experienced what it means to be the jester of the bourgeoisie. When we put on plays for . . . occupied factories, our greatest joy was being able to follow our comrades' struggles from close at hand, and then to make use of them.[22]

Fo sees his role as the modern equivalent of the medieval *giullare* playing to an industrial working-class audience instead of medieval peasants. In fact in *The Birth of the Villeyn,* his companion piece to *The Birth of the Jongleur,* Fo makes a historical leap in order to relate the predicament of the medieval peasant to that of the modern working class. He does this by breaking out of the story to mime a worker on the production line programmed as to when he can go to the toilet so as not to slow down the conveyor belt. This serves to contextualise the predicament of the medieval peasant as the social and cultural predecessor of the modern working class.

The Birth of the Villeyn

This text is presented in virtually its original form, as used by the *giullare* Matazone da Caligano. It relates the creation of the peasant-serf (*villano*) 'from an ass's fart' after Adam has refused to lend his rib, so the master can have someone to do his unpleasant work for him. The master teaches the serf, under the guise of religious instruction, that his lot is to be a vulgar, repellent creature. He nevertheless has an eternal soul, through which he can transcend the misery of his fate. Then an angel appears to instruct the landowner how to treat the serf, concluding, 'How can this idiotic serf have a soul when he was born from an ass's fart?' The angel thus exposes the overlord's religious blackmail and sows the seeds for the peasant's revolt and rejection of his lot. Fo sees a strong affinity between the *villano* and the *giullare* in the fact that both are soulless and see through the overlord's religious duping. The origin of the *villeyn* is also the origin of the *giullare*:

> The *giullare* was a peasant-serf; he was oppressed – maybe he was even born from an ass like the *villeyn*, as the *giullare* Matazone describes the first villeyn born on this earth. If the *giullare* had a soul, he would feel it like lead, and wouldn't be able to fly because the soul would weigh him down. He'd say, as Bonvesin de la Riva suggests, 'You should thank God you haven't got a backside, soul, because I'd kick it till it was black and blue.' It's because he was born

without a soul that the *giullare* can refuse to accept the blackmail of 'having a good conscience', and prick and gnaw away at the overlord with his satire, and arm the oppressed against him.[23]

The Resurrection of Lazarus

The chameleon-like capacity of Fo's mimicry is taxed to the utmost in *The Resurrection of Lazarus,* where he represents an entire crowd of people straining to see Christ's miracle of raising Lazarus from the dead. First he portrays the cemetery guard receiving the first arrivals, and then, through a series of one-line utterances and physical changes, the curious, pushing and voyeuristic crowd gathering and renting chairs for a ring-side view, with brief vignettes of a sardine-seller and even a pickpocket. As Fo states in his spoken introduction to the piece:

> The text of *The Resurrection of Lazarus* is a test for a virtu-oso because the *giullare* often found himself having to play as many as 15 or 16 characters one after the other, with no way of indicating the changes except with his body – by striking a posture, without even changing his voice. It's the kind of piece which calls on the performer to improvise according to the audience's laughter, cadences, and silences. In practice, it's an improvisation which requires occasional ad-libbing.[24]

The piece is a satire on the 'mystical experience' of a miracle, and Fo's performance emphasises the fairground-spectacle aspect of the miracle. It is seen from the peasant spectators' point of view, complete with references to the smell of the decomposing body and the worms inside it. The cries of the market sellers mix with the sounds of bets being made on the outcome of the miracle, and the final cries of admiration and astonishment are mixed with the shouts of the person whose pocket has been picked, in a truly 'choral' finale. Here the allusiveness of Fo's performance is paramount, as he suggests characters and situations with a few swift gestures and changes of position, relying on the audience's imagination to fill in the details. The audience is virtually presented with a mirror image of itself in terms of assisting at a prestidigitous spectacle in which the spectator plays an active role. As Fo has explained:

> I am able to express my personal resources as a comic, because I believe in the *giullaresque* function of the comic. The ability of the medieval *giullare* to play as many as 15 characters . . . depended on the necessity of doing everything on his own. It wasn't just exhibitionistic wishful thinking. We know that the medieval *giullari* performed their plays alone from the stage directions in the texts and their allusions to doubling. Even the most able inventions of the *giullare* required audience participation. The play of allusions and the collaboration of the audience who picked them up redoubled the poetic and comic charge. So what has been referred to as a 'didactic operation' wasn't really so at all, at least not in the sense that the audience was indoctrinated. Rather their imaginations were stimulated – this was the only way they could reach an awareness of their origins, their past, and their culture.[25]

When Fo and the Associazione Nuova Scena first began working on *Mistero buffo* in 1969, the original intention was to have the plays performed by more than one actor. This idea was rejected as impracticable after experimentation, as it detracted from the necessary allusiveness of the performance of the *giullare,* and broke the rhythm and flow of the pieces. It also filled in too much unnecessary detail by introducing minor subsidiary characters, who frequently had very little to do and distracted attention from the principal comic's performance. By performing alone, Fo brings a predominantly imaginative element to Brecht's idea of didactic entertainment. *Mistero buffo* not only invites rational detachment from the audience, but also an imaginative filling-in and fleshing-out of details and situations rather in the same way as listening to a radio play. There is no space or time for the actor to detach himself from the characters he is playing, who are often only fleeting vignettes in a narrative.

Boniface VIII

Fo's allusive mimic capacity also relies heavily on the audience's imagination in *Boniface VIII*. Here, as the critic Paolo Puppa has described:

> On a completely bare stage, the audience's imagination is directed towards real objects which are conjured up with a minimum of signs; everything that is named is shown. The pope's charismatic dressing-up is shown in this way, while he recites an ancient extra-liturgical chant, assisted by priests and attendants'. . . . The aesthetic aspect . . . is elaborated in tandem with the political connotations, since the self-investiture lays bare the power which it accumulates by building up its own connotations.[26]

Boniface VIII is introduced by an account of that pope's celebrated Good Friday orgy in 1301, with an array of prostitutes, bishops and cardinals, at which candles are extinguished at three metres' distance by farts. The piece presents Pope Boniface preparing for a ceremony, singing a hymn, and praying. The prayer becomes a response to an interrogation by Christ, who finally, appearing invisibly, gives the pope a series of kicks in the backside. Fo mimes in detail Boniface's fastidious dressing-up, choosing caps, mirrors, gloves and cloaks. The piece also illustrates the capacity of fascistic authorities to oscillate between supreme arrogance and abject self-deprecation and servitude. When Boniface is confronted by Christ carrying the cross, who is not shown, but described as a country bumpkin, he becomes sycophantic and toadying. He releases a monk he has imprisoned and even kisses him for Christ's benefit, although he is unable to disguise his disgust. Fo's Boniface could almost take his place in Pasolini's film of fascist debauchery, *Salò*. As Puppa points out, Fo's Boniface 'dressing-up' is almost a direct Italian equivalent to Hitler's preparation for public appearances in Brecht's *The Resistible Rise of Arturo Ui*. Both lay bare the narcissism which lies behind the temptations of absolute power.

Fo takes a number of historical liberties in *Boniface VIII*, for which he has been severely criticised, especially by the Vatican.

But the implied political leap of the imagination in the piece, especially in his anachronistic reference to a peasant Communard movement in the same historical period, is executed with such theatrical skill that his detractors are inevitably disarmed. Zeffirelli's comments on the piece are a typical example of the censure he has received:

> Satire about the church and the papacy's bad worldly operations is as legitimate as any other form of satire, but it's a different matter when it's extended to the subject of the gospels. I don't think it's right to elaborate the contents of the gospels in a satirical way.[27]

Fo's satirical Christ is unacceptable to Zeffirelli, although he is forced to admit that 'Fo is one of the greatest Italian theatrical phenomena and his performances are always brilliant. I am also aware that the scurrility of his theatre derives from the roots of our theatre, from Plautus and the *commedia dell'arte*.'[28] This opinion led Fo to make a distinction between 'those who become militants of the proletariat, and those who become militants of the Vatican.'[29]

Texts from the Passion
The television version of *Mistero buffo* also included four 'Texts from the Passion'. The first of these, *Death and the Madman*, presents a Madman playing a Tarot-like card game, while the inn-keeper of the hotel where he is staying announces that 13 people have come for supper. Meanwhile the Madman wins a large sum of money, and the game culminates in his drawing the card of Death. At this point Death enters in the form of a beautiful virgin, grieved by her task of coming to take Christ away. The Madman proceeds to seduce her and divert her from her duty. The role of the Madman (*Il Matto*) combines the characters of the *villano* (villeyn) and the *giullare*. He could also be seen as a prototype of the protagonist of Fo's later play, *Accidental Death of an Anarchist,* who is also called *Il Matto* (the Maniac) and wreaks similar havoc in a much more modern political context. In *Mistero buffo* he is part fool, part idiot, part pagan and part charlatan, a profane character-actor who is also

capable of laudable motives (his attempts to seduce Death are a ploy to warn Christ).

Mary Comes to Know of her Son's Sentence, performed by Franca Rame, relates the attempt by friends of the Madonna to conceal Christ's crucifixion from his mother. Mary finds out what is going on only when she sees Veronica with the imprint of Christ's face after the scourging and the crowning of thorns. This piece is a prototype of a series of mother figures whom Franca Rame has performed in Fo's plays since the 1960s. Highlights of these were gathered together in a television show, *Parliamo di donne* (*Let's Talk about Women*), which was broadcast by RAI television as part of the 1977 Fo season. Rame's mother figures, who will be dealt with later in this study, have a toughness, political awareness, and sense of sisterhood which sometimes risks sentimentality in their more tragic mani-festations. But they also often become a springboard for parody of the archetypal Italian *mamma* in Fo and Rame's collaborations after *Mistero buffo.* Here Mary's total acceptance of Mary Magdalene and her determined desire to find out the truth about what is happening to Christ make her a very assertive, determined figure. The piece ends with Mary's realisation that Christ is about to be crucified, but is cut off abruptly as she rushes off in desperation to look for him, and there is no direct presentation of her maternal emotion.

In *The Madman beneath the Cross,* the Madman presents the stripping and preparation of Christ for the crucifixion as a theatrical spectacle, while the Roman soldiers bet on the number of hammer blows needed to nail him to the cross. The Madman and the Soldiers then play cards for Christ's clothes in a kind of grotesque 'Strip Jack Naked'. The Madman reveals that he has collected the 30 pieces of silver that Judas has thrown away, and he offers the money to them in exchange for Christ's body. When Christ voices his refusal of the Madman's offer, the latter concludes that Christ is mad. At this point the Madman-Samaritan becomes angry and embittered, declaring that the only really appreciable action Christ performed was driving the money-lenders from the temple.

In the fourth text from the passion, Franca Rame returns to perform *Mary's Passion at the Cross*. Here, rather like Fo's Madman, but in a more distraught fashion, the Madonna tries to bargain with the Roman soldiers to save Christ from being crucified. Graphically envisaging the crucifixion, she offers them a silver ring and gold earrings. The soldiers claim that they are just doing their job, and that to accept her bribes is to risk losing their jobs. The Archangel Gabriel then appears to attempt to explain to Mary the purpose of her son's death, but it is left ambiguous as to whether the Archangel's appearance is a 'real' supernatural manifestation or a hallucination of the grief-stricken Madonna. Mary accuses him of not understanding the condition of being a mother, since he was a mere messenger at the Annunciation. Gabriel apologetically reminds her that her grief, her sacrifice and her son's sacrifice 'will split the heavens, and enable men for the first time to enter into paradise.'[30]

At the end of the second television transmission of *Mistero buffo* Fo added a *Grammelot* of English origin, dating from the end of the sixteenth century, *The English Lawyer*, which tells the story of a man on trial for raping a girl of the nobility. Like *A Fresh Fragrant Rose*, the piece turns the tables on plaintiff and defendant. In a brilliantly histrionic display, the English lawyer proves that the girl is to blame for the rape because her physical attributes and provocative appearance induced the 'poor' young man to rape her. Here Fo reflects an argument which is still frequently used in Italian rape cases in the present day.

A Chinese *Mistero buffo*: *Tale of a Tiger*

Mistero buffo was a success on Italian television, and the high audience figures were helped along by the free 'scandal' publicity afforded by the Vatican's outrage at the play. The television version of *Mistero buffo* formed part of a 20-hour retrospective of Fo's major plays. Fo added another one-man show to his ample repertoire three years later with *La storia della tigre e altre storie* (*Tale of a Tiger and Other Stories*). This was first performed in 1980, in the same theatrical conditions as *Mistero buffo*. Interviewed in Rome during his premiere of *Tale of a Tiger* in a converted cinema rented by a feminist organisation, Casa della donna (Women's House), Fo commented on the need for the 'community spirit' of performing to live audiences in a politically charged situation:

> People are tired of solitude, which television only serves to make more acute. And cinema is no substitute for cohesion or collective movement. The theatre, on the other hand, gives people the opportunity of really meeting one another, especially the type of theatre that we and other rank-and-file groups put on, where there's a real sense of involvement and participation. And in recent years the need to get together has increased considerably.[31]

Tale of a Tiger is based on a story which Fo heard in Shanghai in 1975, as related to a Chinese audience of 20,000. It was performed by a local country storyteller in a minority dialect, which was translated into Mandarin and then into Italian for Fo. The dialect of the piece reminded him of his own adapted Padano dialect in *Mistero buffo,* and so he set about preparing a Padano version of the story. He then tried it out in public, reshaping it, and ultimately expanding it from 15 to 45 minutes, sharpening the details. He performed his 'final' version before a script of the piece even existed.

The story concerns a Chinese soldier from Mao's army who is wounded during the war of liberation against Chiang Kai-shek, with gangrene setting in. He tells his comrades to leave him in a cave, where, like Romulus and Remus, he is adopted by a tigress. He teaches the tigress how to cook meat in exchange for learning the laws of survival in the jungle. When his wound finally heals, he persuades the tigress and her cub to accompany him to his home town. The tigers help the local inhabitants to get rid of the last vestiges of Chiang Kai-shek's army by intimidating them with their roars. After the war is won, the Popular Government takes over the town's administration, and is intimidated by the tigers. The government tries to have them sent to the zoo, since they maintain that the tigers are a redundant force under the peace-time regime. The villagers are not happy with this proposed solution, and at the end they use the tigers to chase away the new administration. The piece ends with a tedious polemical speech by one of the new administrators, exhorting the people to obey him, punctuated by an almighty roar from the family of tigers. In the Chinese context of the fable, as Fo explains in his spoken introduction to the piece, the tiger represents the spirit of self-management, self-determination and endurance:

> The tiger has a very precise allegorical significance: they say that a woman, or a man, or a people, have the tiger when they are confronted by enormous difficulties, and at the point where most people are inclined to flee, scarper, run away and abandon the struggle, and even reach the point of denigrating themselves and everything generous they've done before, they insist on standing firm and resisting . . . Another clear allegorical meaning the tiger has, which is perhaps fundamental, is this: a person has the tiger when he never delegates anything to anybody, and never tries to get other people to resolve his own problems . . . The person who has 'the tiger' gets directly involved in the situation, participating in it, controlling it, verifying it, and being on the spot and responsible right up to the end.[32]

Fo's introduction spells out the contemporary political implications of the fable and indicates his involvement in working-class political struggles, as well as his role as a cultural spokesman for the extra-parliamentary Italian Left.

From a performance point of view, *Tale of a Tiger* is a *tour de force*. Fo plays both the soldier with his gangrenous leg, and the tigress, relishing her roars, snarls and growls, which he modulates through a whole range of emotions. He even represents the deer she brings back for her cubs, whose childlike playfulness he performs without ever stooping to the compromise of getting down on all fours. He even represents a bullet coming out of the soldier's gun, and winds up the piece as a pompous party bureaucrat personifying the denial of the spirit of the tigress. One of the most hilarious sequences in the play is when the tigress gives roaring lessons to the soldier's countrymen. As Renzo Tian described it:

Dario Fo does all this . . . without using words. At the most there are some fragments of words. He moves a few centimetres and becomes the teacher, then becomes the pupil, strains his vocal cords to an almost frightening extent, saws the air with his long paws, does both the real roars and the apprentice ones, and multiplies his hands, legs and utterances to let us 'see' rather than just hear the roaring class. And he succeeds. He succeeds because he has adopted everything that's been going round the theatre theory scene about gesture, mime, the *giullare,* body language, metaphor and audience involvement, and he incorporates it all into the sole ingredients of dust and sweat, without mediators, without indirect asides, and without playing his cards close to his chest.[33]

Fo's onomatopoeic language, which here even transcends *Grammelot* in its representation of the world of the tigers, manages to translate the context of the Chinese fable into an easily comprehensible contemporary Italian context. The piece can also be understood by a multinational audience, as the English critic John Francis Lane, reviewing the Rome performance of the play, testifies:

It is an invented language which he speaks as if he (and we) spoke it naturally. It isn't too difficult to understand, even if the pace at which he rambles on requires a great deal of concentration on the part of listeners of any language background . . . As happened a few weeks ago, when I watched Fo perform for an audience of British theatre people who didn't understand Italian and weren't getting much help from Fo's official translator, he revealed an ability to communicate concepts and images with characters and events and ideas. One man in three hours runs the whole gamut of theatrical experience from primitive self-expression to the latest invention of media sophistication.[34]

Much of the international success of Fo's work is due to the fact that he is an 'animal of the stage', as the Italian expression goes, capable of communicating through sound and gesture in a way which leaves language barriers behind. As Fo himself has said, referring also to Franca Rame's performances and the plays they have collaborated on together:

> We're often asked why our plays are performed so frequently abroad. Part of the answer is this: we talk about real things, which we reinterpret in an ironic and satirical vein. We talk about Italy, but in countries like Germany and France, talking about Italy means talking about their problems.[35]

The 'other stories'

The three other stories in *Tale of a Tiger* are adapted from the Apocryphal gospels, and hence are much more similar to *Mistero buffo* in content. The first of these, *The First Miracle of the Boy Jesus*, presents Christ as a Palestinian immigrant in Egypt who, out of boredom and loneliness, starts performing bizarre tricks. He projects lightning from his eyes, working up to his first miracle, which is a political act. In it he changes the son of the city governor into a terracotta pot, because he never allows the other children to play with him and ride his horses. Mary persuades Christ to change the boy back to his original form, since she and Joseph have just found a job and have no wish to be on the run again. Another of Fo's 'Gospels of the Poor', which invariably have a political twist to them, is *Abraham and Isaac*. The sacrifice is revealed to have been based on a bet between God and the devil as to the extent of Abraham's love for God. This is revealed to Isaac only after the Angel has appeared to stop Abraham carrying out the killing. The piece ends with Isaac throwing a stone which lands on his father's head, claiming that it has come from heaven and is for his own good. The piece illustrates Fo's irreverence for the official gospels, which he uses as a basis for religious satire. He also attacks the traditional notion of patriarchal power invested in the father figure.

Daedalus and Icarus explores the same theme of the power fathers exert over their children. Icarus and Daedalus are lost in the labyrinth they have themselves built for King Minas at Knossos, and the piece ends with Icarus' tragic fall as he tries to fly with the wings Daedalus has made. Fo's interpretation of the story is based on a version by the Greek satirical poet of the second century BC, Luciano di Samosata. Fo claims Samosata was one of the first ever satirists, and a big influence on Rabelais, whose influence in turn is omnipresent in *Mistero buffo*. Fo uses *Daedalus and Icarus* to stress the importance of the imagination and inventiveness, and to attack resorts to surrogates for the imagination like drugs, horoscopes and UFOs. In exhorting his audience to seek out more creative activities, Fo himself presents a formidable example.

Obscene Fables

Il fabulazzo osceno (*Obscene Fables*) is a third edition of *Mistero buffo*, based on more secular sources, which Fo first performed in March 1982. It consists of a group of three stories, all tried out and developed by Fo in public with an audience. The stories deal with popular sexuality and scatology in a way which was usually censored by medieval church and state authorities, but which was preserved through oral tradition. Fo recounts how he was unable to find any academic source material for the stories, and hence has added his own embellishments to the pieces. They convey a popular spirit of bawdry and earthy humour similar to that of Boccaccio, but with more political bite. The *fabulazzo osceno* is a Franco-Provençal story, which Fo plays in roughly the same dialects he uses in *Mistero buffo*, with a bit of Provençal dialect thrown in to tease the audience. These stories are also known as *Fabliaux,* and Fo stresses that they are obscene in the erotic and anti-scandalous sense, as opposed to mere dirty stories. As the US critic Joel Schechter explained in his article, 'Dario Fo's Obscene Fables':

Few of the tales that Fo recites can readily be found in books. He discovers them in obscure sources, invents details, and turns them into performance scenarios. In doing this he brings to the public some chapters of Italian history and folklore that went unrecorded because the scholars who preserved past culture favoured the ruling class; it was not in their interest for stories of political and sexual unrest to survive . . . Fo notes that Popes and noblemen in the Middle Ages were free to write obscene literature, and circulate it among their friends, while stories for the general public survived – if they survived at all – through the oral tradition of minstrelsy in which Fo places himself.[36]

The first piece, *Il tumulto di Bologna* (*The Bologna Riot*), is 'obscene' in the sense that it deals with excrement, which the local peasants of Bologna in 1334 used as weapons in their revolt against papal legates and the Provençal troops protecting the pope. Fo mimes with relish the local peasants throwing buckets of shit over the walls of their fortress, and the high-ranking Vatican officials being splattered by it. He continually switches from the role of a detached narrator to that of the gleeful participants in this ultimately successful peasants' revolt, and the disgruntled and finally banished Vatican troops.

The second piece, *La parpaja topola* (*The Butterfly-Mouse*) is a twelfth-century sexual fable about a wealthy but simple-minded goatherd who is tricked on his wedding night by his wife. She has been married off to him to avoid scandal arising from the fact that she has been having an affair with the local parish priest. When her new husband finally returns from a wild-goose chase on their wedding night, she, tired from her frolicking with the priest, tells him she has left her sex (the 'butterfly-mouse' of the title) at her mother's house. Following his new wife's instructions, the goatherd goes to his mother-in-law's house, and is given a cardboard box with a cloth and a mouse in it, and told not to open it until he gets back to his wife. But he is impatient, and unwraps the parcel, and the 'sex' escapes. At the end of the story the goatherd's wife takes pity on him and tells him the mouse has come home of its own accord, showing him where to find it. Fo originally intended this piece to be performed by Franca Rame, but she demurred due to

certain passages which were so crude in their erotic satire, and so ruthless in their paradoxicality, that they made me feel uneasy. I would have had to do violence to myself to manage to play it: the perennial condition of sexual inhibition of a woman faced with the blackmailing myth of modesty and shame.'[37]

The piece is a satire on Victorian-type sexual repression and euphemisms, which frequently amount to the imposition of ignorance, and Fo's performance is in itself a revolt against censorship and sexual oppression.

When he first performed it, Fo prefaced his third story in *Il fabulazzo osceno* with an improvised monologue about the P2 scandal in Italy, which he performed on its own in an extended form in Pisa in 1982. At the time, the secret lodge P2 had been exposed and shown to include some of the most prominent Italian politicians, businessmen, industrialists and even entertainers. It was a type of secret Mafia which contained more power and influence than the Italian government. In this *P2 Prologue,* Fo simply talks to his audience, acting out situations and inventing allusions and analogies as he goes along. He is particularly scathing about the role of entertainers in the lodge, and the theatrical overtones of Italian public life:

P2 is a totally Italian story, with all the drama of espionage, slaughter and crime, but also all the ridiculousness of farce. An example? One of the members of P2 was Claudio Villa, the king of popular song, who immediately admitted everything, since he's no politician and so has nothing to be ashamed of. Well, Gelli [the head of P2] took Villa into P2 for just one reason: women. The king of popular song directed a revue company and Gelli invited them all to his house in Arezzo, to have a few dancing girls . . . Don't you find it funny [buffo] that a Masonic Lodge doesn't allow women to be members, and yet Gelli used his secret lodge to get some dancing girls? Don't get me wrong, having dancing girls can be a wonderful thing, but can you imagine a country where secret sects are used to get access to women? . . . Compared to these masons, terrorists are mere amateurs. They don't just strike at the heart of the state, they've taken over its eyes, brain, heart, stomach and all the rest.[38]

Fo goes on to describe scenes which recall the orgies of *Boniface VIII*. He uses the political scandal to tease out sexual high-jinks in order to prove his point about the double standards of sexual repression and the sexual decadence of church and state authorities in whose interest sexual repression operates. Here Fo reveals the real 'living newspaper' aspect of his theatre, in which he is continually editorialising and improvising sketches based on events in the news, which he changes in every performance, providing a live running commentary and dramatisation of political news.

The piece which followed the *P2 Prologue*, *Lucio e l'asino* (*Lucio and the Donkey*), has sexual overtones similar to those between Bottom and the Queen of the Fairies in *A Midsummer Night's Dream*. A poet suffering from 'phallocratophantas-magoria' tries to perform an Ovidian transformation of himself into an eagle, imitating one of Jove's miracles, in an attempt to increase his sexual prowess. He mixes the wrong potion, however, and ends up as a donkey, who is stolen by brigands and forced to carry the beautiful daughter of a wealthy family. Fo portrays the randy, constantly sexually aroused donkey with vigour and high comedy, using onomatopoeic sounds to parody male sexual ambition in a way which echoes ancient Greek comedies like *Lysistrata*. As a donkey, the poet is constantly kicked in the testicles by all and sundry, but manages to rescue the girl and return her to her parents, who seek to gratify his insatiable sexual appetite with horses. After they discover his ability to write, they sell him to a circus, where he is rented out to an aristocratic lady for sexual purposes. This leads to his employment in the circus in a love-making act with a slave girl. He then discovers the antidote for his metamorphosis and is changed back into a man. He seeks out the lady with whom he made love as a donkey, only to be rejected by her on the grounds that he is no longer an exceptional representative of the Priapic principle, but merely a man like any other.

This fable originates in the second century BC, and was, like *Daedalus and Icarus*, written by Luciano di Samosata, a Greek satirical poet who lived in Italy, and whose writings were later an influence on Machiavelli, Rabelais and Voltaire. The 'obscene fables' reveal Fo in a more 'scabrous' vein than *Mistero buffo*, exploring a more Rabelaisian vein of satire than the religious subjects of the earlier texts. They also illustrate Fo's venture into the field of sexual politics, a process which started with his television compilation *Parliamo di donne* in 1977, and which became a dominant feature in his subsequent collaborations with Franca Rame.

Obscene Fables also emphasises Fo's direct link with the scatological 'grotesque realism' and the 'world upside down' of medieval carnival depicted by Mikhail Bakhtin in his book *Rabelais and his World*. The shit-slinging in *The Bologna Riot* is a direct illustration of Bakhtin's notion of the 'material bodily principle' in which the lofty intellectual and emotional affairs of the mind and heart are brought down to earth by excrement. It is also an illustration of the popular festive culture of folk humour in which excrement transforms fear into laughter. Similarly, the frank and comical approach to sex in *The Butterfly-Mouse* and *Lucio and the Donkey* draw on popular carnival celebrations of sexuality and the 'reproductive lower stratum' as a way of mocking the pomposity and humourlessness of church and state authority. As Bakhtin put it:

> Festive folk laughter presents an element of victory not only over supernatural awe, over the sacred, over death; it also means the defeat of power, of earthly kings, of the earthly upper classes, of all that oppresses and restricts.
>
> Medieval laughter, when it triumphed over the fear inspired by the mystery of the world and by power, boldly unveiled the truth about both. It resisted praise, flattery, hypocrisy. This laughing truth, expressed in curses and abusive words, degraded power. The medieval clown was also the herald of this truth.[39]

In his *giullarate*, Fo works directly within this tradition of the 'medieval clown', subverting religious and state authorities and expressing a reversal of their precepts of order and control. While Fo himself has resisted discussing his affinities with Bakhtin,[40] they are evident in almost all of his work. And as Antonio Scuderi has pointed out, Fo was familiar with other texts on carnival culture, such as Paolo Toschi's 1955 study, *Le origini del teatro italiano*.[41] In tracing Fo's work back to the improvised social inversion, mockery, abuse and marketplace language of the Roman Saturnalia, and through the *giullari* and the *commedia dell'arte*, Scuderi has demonstrated how

> the Saturnalian tradition suits his needs in his chosen role and function as subversive clown, forever challenging the power structure in an attempt to unmask the hoax of hypocrisy, the pretence of those who have the responsibility inherent in the privilege of power.[42]

Il fabulazzo osceno concludes with a revised and adapted version of Franca Rame's monologue about the 'suicide' of the German terrorist Ulrike Meinhof, *Io, Ulrike, grido . . . (I, Ulrike, Cry Out . . .)*. This was first performed on a stage covered in cellophane in Milan in 1977 to commemorate the first anniversary of Meinhof's death. Here it is presented as an 'obscene tragedy' and used to focus on political torture and the 'obscene' Italian *legge sui penitenti*. This was a law which offered reduced sentences to terrorists who gave information to the state about terrorist activities, and often led to the conviction of innocent people. The monologue, based on letters and documents by and about Ulrike Meinhof, is a bleak, static and intense depiction of her attempts to stay sane and rational in prison, and overcome the oppressive torture of sterile, white silence. She does this by painting her cell with the imaginary 'colours' of West German consumerist capitalism and speculating about the 'state clean-up' which will harness dissent and stamp out all forms of protest and political opposition in West Germany after the Stammheim deaths. Fo and Rame were careful to point out that they did not agree with the ideology of the Baader-Meinhof group, but used the monologue as a vehicle to condemn the sense of apathy and impotence which had blighted much of the post-1968 revolutionary Left and extra-parliamentary political groups both in Germany and Italy since the late 1970s. The piece is a rare example in the Fo canon of direct political address in a non-comic form, and illustrates a growing sense of disillusionment with the heady, optimistic and positive form of communal didactic theatre of the early days of *Mistero buffo*.

Mistero buffo and its legacies

Mistero buffo and its many offshoots, together with the countless improvised routines and sketches on topical events which Fo frequently makes up on the spot, reveal him as a 'theatrical animal', and show his unique capacity for turning a one-man show into a piece of epic and total theatre. Ron Jenkins has described, for example, the cinematic complexity and Bakhtinian scatology of Fo's impersonation of the attempted assassination of Pope John Paul II in Spain, performed as a prologue to *Mistero buffo*:

Fo uses a performance style that is a one-man theatrical equivalent of cinematic montage. . . . Fo plays all the roles himself. Images and characters appear and dissolve with a rapidity that gives the audience the impression of watching a televised documentary of the event, with the camera angles changing every few seconds. Fo portrays the gun-man waiting to shoot the pope, the Bulgarian agents with walkie-talkies directing the gunman's movements, the police asking the gunman what he is doing with bullets in his hand, and the gunman replying that they are a new kind of rosary bead . . . Shifting back into the role of narrator, Fo wonders why no one was able to stop the gunman, given that so many photographs were taken of him as he prepared for the assassination. Then Fo becomes a one-man slide show, reenacting a series of still photographs that lead up to the gunshots. Another round of theatrical jump-cuts enables Fo to act out the fall of the wounded pope, the television commentator's announcement that he has been shot in the sphincter, and an indignant Vatican spokesman who refuses to acknowledge that the pope has a sphincter, insisting that the pontiff's bowels be referred to as a divine conduit.[43]

Fo's presence as an actor, director and frequently designer, charges his plays with a dynamism both stylistic and political which is often far less apparent in the printed texts of his plays. Most of these are in fact only written down after Fo has knocked them into shape through performance, and exist as records of performances rather than constructed literary texts. *Mistero buffo* is an unrepeatable experience tailor-made for and by Fo, which fortunately surmounts language barriers (at least to a certain extent), and performances of it by other actors either in an Italian dialect or in translation seem virtually inconceivable. This has, however, occurred on a number of occasions: first in Brussels in November 1972, when Arturo Corso performed *Mistero buffo* in French and Flemish at the TRIH, and in February 1983, when Charles Cornette performed selections from *Mistero buffo* in French under the title *La Jonglerie* at the Atelier rue Ste-Anne. It has also been performed in Sweden by Bjorn Granath. The young Sicilian actor Antonio Venturino performed an adaptation of it in Sicilian dialect in March 1993 in a production directed by Claudio Russo for the Cooperativo Aquarius at the Teatro dell'Aquario in Cosenza. Venturino's version presented four of Fo's pieces: *The Massacre of the Innocents*, *The Marriage at Cana*, *The Morality Play of the Blind Man and the Cripple*, and *The Birth of the Villeyn*, the second and fourth of which originated in Sicily in the first place, facilitating a smooth adaptation. According to Antonio Garro's review in *Sipario*, Venturino's performance stood up to comparison with Fo's original, and 'managed to retain the real spirit of the *commedia dell'arte* very well, without being conditioned too much by the often uncomfortable substitutions and adaptations made to the text, which was not merely subjected to a simple translation.'[44]

The Veneto actor Marco Paolini is another performer who has continued Fo's legacy of dialect performances of monologues which make satirical comments on current events, as well as using *grammelot*. Paolini, who regards Fo and Rame as his *maestri*, has achieved considerable success in Italy. According to the director Roberto Tarasco, 'Paolini is working very precisely in the tradition of Dario Fo. He does not use Fo's texts directly but attempts to recycle his methods and theatrical qualities.'[45] Another prominent left-wing Italian comedian who has been influenced by Fo and also uses dialect and *grammelot* is Paolo Rossi, who worked with Fo as a student on his production of *The Soldier's Tale*. Rossi has since become one of the most popular stage, television and film comedians in Italy in the 1980s and 1990s, and appeared with Fo in Stefano Benni's 1988 film *Music for Old Animals*. And in her book on Fo's monologues, Marisa Pizza suggests that the comic actor Roberto Benigni, best known to English-speaking audiences in Jim Jarmusch's film *Down By Law*, could be said to 'descend indirectly'[46] from Fo. Benigni's film *Johnny Stecchino* (Johnny Toothpick) was the highest grossing film in Italy in 1994, and his 1999 Oscar-winning film *La vita è bella* (*Life is Beautiful*), about a father who convinces his son that the concentration camp they are imprisoned in is just a game, was the most successful Italian film in cinema history and also won a major prize at the 1998 Cannes Film Festival and at the 1999 British Academy Awards. (This film also starred Fo's 1950s collaborator Guistino Durano.) Pizza argues that Benigni's use of monologues, Tuscan dialect, and an onomatopoeic language similar to *grammelot*, as well as his gestural style of performance, use of scatological references, improvisation, surreal irony and political satire align him with Fo. But it is arguable that Benigni represents a much broader, cruder and more slapstick, sentimental and populist mode of comic performance than Fo, and rarely achieves the more subtle carnivalesque and grotesque aspects of Fo's performances.

There have also been productions of *Mistero buffo* in English. Some of the pieces were performed in a puppet show format by Malcolm Knight and his Maskot Puppet Theatre in Scotland and at the 1983 Edinburgh Festival. This production relied on rod and glove puppets to illustrate the gestural range of Fo's monologues in Knight's own translation. In 1984 a young, six-member English and American collective theatre group called the 1982 Theatre Company did an 'ensemble' version of *Mistero buffo*. This included performances in London at the Riverside Studios in 1983, and one performance at the Half Moon Theatre in February 1984. The group worked from a very accurate, literal translation of the pieces by Ed Emery, who also translated the Fo Riverside Theatre Workshops and has done most of Fo's other plays into English. (In 1998 Emery undertook to produce authorised, literal and performable English translations of Fo's entire collected works.) The 1982 Theatre Company adapted *The Hymn of the Flagellants*, *The Slaughter of the Innocents*, *The Marriage at Cana*, *The Morality Play of the Blind Man and the Cripple*, *The Birth of the Peasant* and *The Birth of the Jongleur* into a condensed, 90-minute production. This managed to maintain the spirit of the original from an oblique, contemporary standpoint, with little attempt made at finding an English equivalent of Fo's *grammelot*.

The group used a collective narrative style reminiscent of Paul Sills' Story Theatre and the Bread and Puppet Theatre (appropriately, as this latter group was also an influence on Fo's stagecraft). Performing without sets and costumes, they simplified Fo's texts into a modern English idiom, frequently resorting to corny jokes and slapstick devices in a limited but likeable dramatisation of the monologues. Many of Fo's necessary explanatory and introductory prologues to the pieces were maintained, while an extract from the Wakefield Mystery Cycle's *Shepherd's Play* was interpolated to illustrate similarities between Fo's sources and the English Medieval Mystery Play tradition. These similarities involve not only features of dialect, but also the religious mystification of texts by academic commentators. The group illustrated this by reading a footnote from the English texts which suggested that the shepherd's expression of misery at his plight was merely intended to reflect the greater sufferings of Christ. Ensemble 'alienation devices' were incorporated, like performing the *Morality Play of the Blind Man and the Cripple* with two actresses, and staging the conflict between the Angel and the Drunk in *The Marriage at Cana* as a battle between two actors trying to upstage each other. By drawing on English theatre traditions such as pantomime and music-hall double acts, the group's performance was rooted in a 'popular' format. A modern political parallel illustrating 'state brutality similar to that of the sixteenth century' was made by reciting Franca Rame's account of her improvised *interventi* at the gates of the Fiat factory in Turin in 1980 after the wholesale sackings there. While sacrificing most of the onomatopoeic richness and mimic range of Fo's performance of *Mistero buffo,* the 1982 Theatre Company production did demonstrate that by approaching the pieces from a respectful distance, an English equivalent to Fo's 'popular theatre', albeit impoverished, is possible.

The most successful British version of *Mistero buffo* was performed by Scottish actor Robbie Coltrane in 1990, in an adaptation by Joe Farrell from Ed Emery's translation, directed by Morag Fullerton for Borderline Theatre. This production toured Scotland and was subsequently broadcast in a television version by BBC Scotland in a series entitled 'Big Stars in Wee Productions'. Coltrane's version included *The Resurrection of Lazarus, The Morality Play of the Blind Man and the Cripple, The Marriage at Cana* and *Boniface VIII*. All had prologues which related the pieces to Scotland and contemporary political issues in the UK and adapted Fo's medieval pieces smoothly and lithely to a contemporary Scottish setting. In his introduction to *Boniface VIII*, for example, Coltrane speculated whether Pope John Paul II would kiss the airport tarmac when he visited Scotland, or perform the gesture only once at Heathrow Airport for the whole of Britain. Using a vast array of accents covering different regions of England, Scotland and Ireland as well as different classes, Coltrane found a successful English equivalent for the polyvocal *Resurrection of Lazarus*. His performance of *Boniface VIII* in a New York Italian accent reminiscent of Martin Scorsese's mobster films seemed entirely appropriate, as well as being highly amusing. Performing in a perhaps ill-advised outfit consisting of pink shirt and trousers, with minimal sets and props (including some feathers which were plucked from the Angel's wing in *The Marriage at Cana*), Coltrane's version was engaging, entertaining theatre entirely in the spirit of Fo's original, and deserved to be seen far more widely.

The most recent performance of *Mistero buffo* in English was in 1997 by the Oxford Stage Company, which toured the UK and was performed at the Greenwich Theatre in London.

CHAPTER 2

BIOGRAPHY AND OUTPUT
1951–1967

Our theatre became more and more provocative, and left
no space for 'théâtre digestif' ['after-dinner theatre'].
Reactionaries raged, disturbances broke out in the audience more than once, and fascists tried to provoke
disturbances in the auditorium ... Our theatre could be
criticised on all counts, but it has to be admitted it was a
'living' theatre, which dealt with 'facts' that people wanted
to know about. This, together with the direct language we
used, made it popular theatre.
(Franca Rame, Preface to *Le commedie di Dario Fo*, vol.2.)

English-speaking theatre audiences are likely to be familiar with
at least five of Dario Fo's plays: *Accidental Death of an Anarchist*
(*Morte accidentale di un anarchico*, 1971), *Can't Pay? Won't Pay!*
(*Non si paga!, Non si paga!*, 1974), *Female Parts* (*Tutta casa, letto e
chiesa*, 1977), *Mistero buffo*, and *Trumpets and Raspberries* (*Clacson,
trombette e pernacchi*, 1981). The first three received numerous
productions in the UK, the USA, and Australasia, and Fo and
Rame performed *Mistero buffo* and *Tutta casa, letto e chiesa* in
London at the Riverside Studios in April 1983 to considerable
acclaim, and in the USA in 1986. In addition, there have been
productions in English of *Tale of a Tiger* (*La storia della tigre*,
1982), *The Open Couple* (*Coppia aperta*, 1983), *Elizabeth* (1984),
Archangels Don't Play Pinball (*Gli arcangeli non giocano al flipper*,
1959) and *The Pope and the Witch* (*Il Papa e la strega*, 1989), as well
as some of Fo's early one-act farces, and many of the 25
monologues for women which Fo and Rame have produced.

These works nonetheless represent the tip of the iceberg of
Fo's and Rame's output. Over a 45-year period of activity Fo

has written, directed, designed and acted in more than 70 plays, as well as numerous short sketches for television, and other occasional political pieces. From the comic radio monologues of *Poer nano* (*Poor Dwarf*, 1952) to the scurrilous, sixteenth-century-style legal comedy, *The Devil in Drag* (*Il diavolo con le zinne*, 1997), Fo has produced a vast repertoire of ensemble plays, one-person shows, revue sketches, farces, clown shows, political documentaries and agit-prop musicals. He has also written numerous songs for his own plays, and for popular Italian singers such as Enzo Jannacci, Ornella Vanoni and Giorgio Gaber, as well as performing 'living newspaper' sketches for political demonstrations in piazzas, streets, sports stadiums, converted cinemas, occupied factories and deconsecrated churches.

Fo's and Rame's output forms an extraordinary mosaic of popular political and satirical theatre which can be divided into five parts, corresponding to their five decades of activity. In the 1950s they explored revue, French farce, the popular repertoire of Rame's theatrical family and Italian neo-realist cinema. In 1959 they adopted the role of 'court jesters to the bourgeoisie' with the Compagnia Fo–Rame, through which they achieved enormous popular success working within established commercial theatre while exploring political issues which frequently encountered censorship problems. In 1968 they broke with this 'bourgeois theatre' in order to propagate a popular, militant political theatre of class struggle on an alternative circuit, playing to non-theatregoers. In this period they produced topical plays of an agit-prop nature which nonetheless became internationally acclaimed and made Fo the best-known living political playwright in world theatre. In the 1980s, with the *riflusso* or decline in left-wing political activity in Italy, they moved back into a more mainstream theatre circuit to pursue a theatre of sexual politics and personal relationships. They also explored the historical antecedents of their form of popular theatre in the *commedia dell'arte*. In the 1990s they continued exploring these antecedents, while producing more topical political satire which related directly to the dramatic events of Italy's 'second republic', the 'Mani pulite' (clean hands) investigations and the 'Tangentopoli' (bribe city) corruption scandals. Throughout these five decades, they have continued to provoke controversy with their political satires and plays about sexual dilemmas.

Early influences

Dario Fo was born on 24 March, 1926, in Leggiuno Sangiano, a small town in the province of Varese on the shores of Lake Maggiore in Lombardy, in the north of Italy. His father, Felice Fo, was a socialist employee of the Italian state railways (at a time when the Italian Communist Party was yet to be formed) who worked as a station master. Fo senior was frequently transferred from one station to another along the Swiss border, but still found time to act in an amateur theatre company which performed plays by Ibsen, among other authors. Fo's mother, Pina Rota Fo, came from a peasant family, and is the author of a book of reminiscences of life in the Lake Maggiore area between the wars, *Il paese delle rane* (*Land of Frogs,* 1978). Dario was the eldest child of the family, followed by a brother, Fulvio, who became a theatre administrator, and a sister, Bianca Fo Garambois. Bianca has written two books about the Fo family's experiences: *Io, da grande mi sposo un partigiano* (*When I Grow Up I'll Marry A Partisan,* 1976) a book of childhood war time reminiscences, and *La ringhiera dei miei vent'anni* (*My First Twenty Years,* 1981), about the Fo family's life in Milan in the 1950s and her experiences in the rag trade and as a theatre costumist.

The Lake Maggiore region was a vital influence on Fo's subsequent career in the theatre because of the *fabulatori,* storytellers who performed in the towns and villages around the shores of the lake. These amateur performers, who often worked as glass-blowers or fishermen, told stories to the local people about fantastic undersea adventures and other imaginary worlds. Fo was an attentive listener to these stories, many of which he learned by heart. He also picked up a large repertoire of fishermen's tales, as his sister recalls:

He would often sit on the steps of the jetty where the fishermen mended their nets and told stories about the legends
of the lake. At night in bed he would repeat them to Fulvio
and me, reconstructing them in his own fashion, and passing
them off as true. Stories about green, mossy, enchanted
towns buried under the waters of the lake, inhabited by
giant silver fish with human heads.[1]

Fo also studied and imitated the gestures and actions of the
fabulatori. At the age of seven he built a puppet theatre with his
brother, inventing stories, making sets and creating characters
for their home-made marionettes, which he animated in the
courtyard of their house. Later he came to be considered by the
local people as an expert in the techniques of the *fabulatori*. Fo
has given his own account of how he achieved this status and
the influence of the *fabulatori* on his subsequent popular,
'illegitimate' theatrical vision:

I lived in a town of smugglers and fishermen, to whom it
wasn't enough just to have guts, you had to have a lot of
imagination. People who use their imagination to break
the law always keep part of it in reserve to entertain themselves and their friends. In that sort of environment,
everybody's a character in, as well as the author and the
protagonist of, any story he tells. I built up a collection of
these stories from the time I was seven, when I started
hanging out with these smugglers and fishermen. I didn't
just learn the content of their stories, but also their way of
telling them. It's first and foremost a particular way of
looking at and interpreting reality. The way these people
used their eyes, classifying people in a flash into characters
or a chorus, into story-builders or story-repeaters (authors
and actors), was my main weapon when I arrived in the
city (for us the city meant Milan). My fellow townspeople
who I got on best with were the *fabulatori,* who went
around the part of Lake Maggiore where I lived, telling
stories in the piazzas and the *osterie* – stories they hadn't
got from books, but had made up themselves. They were
stories which arose from an observation of everyday life,

full of a bitterness which they channelled into satire. Their 'fables' would start off from any old story, and then pick up momentum until they often reached the point of hyperbole. They always told their stories in the first person. One fellow had got angry and cast out his line too far and got it snagged on a bell-tower hidden on the bottom of the lake. Another was in a race and had forgotten to untie his moorings and came in second. Another one was trying to be cunning betting on a snail race, and when his snail came in first, he smashed it against a stone, and then got all upset and didn't have the heart to scrape it up and eat it . . .[2]

In almost all of Fo's plays, first-person storytelling plays a prominent part. In the French-language edition of *Mistero buffo* (1973), Fo referred to the stories of the *fabulatori* as a 'structural storehouse' (*blocco strutturale*), a model and constant background source of reference for the satirical stories, fables and tales which form the backbone of both his monologues and his more conventionally-staged ensemble plays.

One of the places Fo lived in as a child was a town called Portoraltravaglia, a colony of glass-blowers which was reputed to have the highest percentage of insane people in Italy. 'It was here,' Fo has recalled, 'that I began to see the figure of the madman as something familiar. This intuition I later found writ large in popular theatre, where the madman is a fundamental character.'[3] (He is also fundamental to a number of Fo's plays, from *Mistero buffo* to *Accidental Death of an Anarchist*.)

While he was accumulating these local, indigenous theatrical stimuli, Fo was also sketching and painting, and by 1940 he had made up his mind to study at the Brera Art College in Milan. During his second year at the college, Fo returned to Varese to help his father in the wartime Resistance, assisting escaped English, American and South African prisoners of war to cross the border by disguising them as Lombard peasants. Subsequently, while his father was still underground working with the partisans, Fo decided to join the anti-aircraft division of the navy, in the hope that he would be given an immediate discharge owing to the lack of munitions. Instead Fo found himself sent to a camp in Monza where Mussolini arrived to give instructions about going to Baden-Baden to retrieve dead Italian soldiers. Fo made false documents for himself and some companions and deserted, wandering at large for a time before joining a parachute squadron. This was later to lead to accusations against him of being a member of Mussolini's Republican army. (Mussolini's armed forces were referred to as 'Republican'.) In fact Fo deserted again after less than two months and tried to regain contact with the Resistance movement, without success, wandering through the countryside and sleeping rough. 'At the end it was like coming out of a nightmare,' he has recounted:

> an absurdity which seemed endless. This is another reason why I get angry when I'm accused of having been a Republican. I see it as an insult against all those years of suffering which my family, my friends and the people of my town had to go through.[4]

In 1945 Fo returned to the Accademia di Brera, but also enrolled at the Milan Polytechnic in the faculty of architecture. This decision helped shape his later work as a stage designer and playwright, and is a feature which links him with the English political playwright with whom he has most in common, John Arden. Fo was particularly interested in vernacular and popular architecture, and began a thesis on Roman architecture. He later abandoned his studies seven examinations short of a degree, disillusioned by what he saw was expected of architects in a postwar environment of building speculation and cheap, impersonal housing. After suffering a nervous breakdown, Fo was advised by a doctor to pursue what he found enjoyable, which resulted in his gravitating towards the theatre.

In this period he began painting and moving in artistic circles, reading Gramsci, Brecht and Mayakovsky, who were to become his chief sources of inspiration when he moved into the theatre. He also discovered the Neapolitan farces of Eduardo de Filippo, after whom he was later to become the second most successful popular actor-playwright in Italy. (One of Fo's favourite later stories is of how he and Eduardo were almost run over while crossing the road together in Milan. Eduardo cheerfully accused the driver of the offending car of trying to kill two birds with one stone.) Fo also recalls how he used to hide in the stalls of the Piccolo Teatro of Milan to watch the work of the director Giorgio Strehler, another major figure in the postwar Italian theatre. Strehler was at first one of Fo's main influences, but later became his chief rival in Milan. Fo was impressed by Strehler's sense of stagecraft, and also his anti-naturalistic, anti-Stanislavskian use of actors in creating a theatre based on situation. The two colleagues discussed Brecht's theatre of alienation, but Fo later regarded Strehler's famous productions of Brecht as reducing him to a glossy, bourgeois, 'théâtre digestif' format. Fo maintained this opinion despite the fact that Brecht himself was impressed with Strehler's interpretation of his work, and gave him permission to be his principal Italian director.

At this time Fo also met some of the important figures of Italian neo-realist cinema, such as Roberto Rossellini, Gillo Pontecorvo, and Carlo Lizzani, with whom he was later to work in Rome. He acquired a reputation as an improviser of stories and player of practical jokes. One of these involved announcing the arrival of Picasso in Milan, and organising a reception with flowers and reporters at Milan central station. The part of Picasso in this mock-masquerade was played by one of the Brera caretakers, who failed to turn up to the reception for Picasso. Nonetheless various happenings took place, including an impersonation by Fo of an old Milanese drunk who had known the artist in 1911, until the police intervened. Fo also made occasional visits to Paris, where he was particularly impressed by French cabaret.

Radio origins

Fo had written his first farce in 1944, and in 1948 he wrote and mounted a stage production in Luino of a play called *Ma la Tresa ci divide* (*But the Tresa Divides Us*), which he also designed as well as playing the part of an Angel. This occurred after elections which were a severe disappointment for the Italian Left. Although not a member of the Communist Party, Fo moved in predominantly left-wing and PCI circles, worked for the party, and read the periodical *Politecnico*. The play tells the story of a contested cow in a wild, surreal environment of live farm animals and racing motorbikes, and in it a white town and a red town argue for the rights to the cow's milk. The plot bears a faint resemblance to Brecht's *Caucasian Chalk Circle* but in form appeared to be more similar to Fo's student pranks, although it directed satire against the Catholic church, the Christian Democrat Party and the elections through the character of the Angel.

In 1950 Fo approached the actor Franco Parenti, noted for his performance in Strehler's Piccolo Teatro production of Goldoni's *Harlequin, Servant of Two Masters*. Parenti had also written and starred in a radio comedy entitled *Anacleto the Gas Man,* but had become disillusioned with the art-house and predominantly stylistic concerns of the Piccolo and moved into Revue. He was organising a variety show of radio actors in Intra, and Fo asked him if he could take part in this. Parenti hired him, and a collaboration between the two actors began which lasted until 1954. For the show, Fo drew on his rich stock of material from his home town, telling stories which, as Parenti recalls:

> were absolutely original, with an extraordinary humour, wit and personification. When the show was over, we'd go for walks round the lake and he'd tell me more stories. In this way we originated a project in which we would work together on a new type of revue, one which didn't copy reality, but which involved people and took a stand.[5]

This first revue, in which Fo had his first experience as an actor in front of an audience, embarked on a series of what the participants referred to as 'punitive expeditions' in Piedmont, Lombardy and Veneto. These took the form of variety shows performed outdoors with a minimum of scenery, and required a special emphasis on mime and gesture.

As a result of his theatrical exposure with Parenti, Fo was accepted by the RAI, the Italian national radio network, to do his own solo radio comedy series, *Poer nano* (*Poor Dwarf*), for 18 weeks at the end of 1951. *Poer nano* went on air on Saturday evenings after Parenti's *Anacleto the Gas Man*. In it Fo built up a series of reversals of biblical, historical, and even Shakespearian stories, turning accepted commonplaces upside-down. This series of adult fairy tales represented Fo's first experience as a fully-fledged solo author-performer. The 'poor dwarf', the narrator, presented the point of view of the underdog, as in the story of Romulus and Remus who build Rome because other children's mothers would not allow them to play with children raised by a wolf. The story of Hamlet is presented as that of a prince who kills his father in order to continue his affair with his mother, who is in fact his stepmother. Hamlet's uncle tries to get him to marry Ophelia, who is the uncle's transvestite mistress. The ghost of Hamlet's father, who only appears to Hamlet when the latter is drunk, is in fact Horatio (who is trying to steal Hamlet's stepmother's favours) dressed up in a sheet. Similarly, Othello is not a Moor but an albino who is offended because Desdemona won't give her sexual favours to his old drinking companion. Romeo is the victim of a sadistic Juliet who keeps him in her garden with savage dogs. In his preface to the 1976 book which included the most successful of the pieces, *Cain and Abel* and *Samson and Delilah*, illustrated in comic-strip form by his son Jacopo, Fo stated:

> The key point of these stories was always paradox, oppo-
> sites and contraries . . . Cain was the victim and not the
> executioner, the Almighty knew everything but was
> absent-minded and caused chaos and confusion which his
> son had to remedy – witness the story of original sin . . .
> These reversals were not done just for their own sake, but
> were an absolute refusal to accept the logic of convention,
> a rebellion against the moral contingent which always sees
> good on one side and evil on the other . . . The comedy
> and the liberating entertainment lies in the discovery that
> the contrary stands up better than the commonplace . . .

There is also the fun of desecrating and demolishing the sacred and untouchable monuments of religious tradition.[6]

This iconoclasm against established forms of Catholicism was later to inform the more grotesque satire of *Mistero buffo,* which included *Cain and Abel.* Fo also continued to perform one of the pieces in *Poer nano, Abraham and Isaac,* in his monologue *Johan Padan* in 1991. The radio format of *Poer nano* also gave Fo valuable experience in acting from a text without gestures, and in developing the tonalities of his remarkably deep, sharp and resonant voice in order to discriminate acoustically between the various characters. This experience was also later to come into its own in *Mistero buffo.*

Revue and *avanspettacolo*

In 1952, Fo performed *Poer nano* on stage at the prestigious Teatro Odeon in Milan. This offered him his first opportunity to flesh out his religious satire and championing of the underdog with gesture and action in the official Italian theatre. He also co-wrote and acted in other radio comedy series: *Chicchirichì (Cock-a-doodle-doo),* with Giustino Durano, creating the character of the civil servant Gorgogliati. In the same year, he acted in a revue entitled *Cocoricò* together with Giustino Durano. *Cocoricò* reflected the current Italian trend of 'colossal', American-influenced, 'imported revue', with superficial, but mildly satirical content. In the early 1950s the most prominent revue company in Milan was I Gobbi (The Hunchbacks), who reacted against the musical spectacularity of 'imported revue' and opted for a more intellectual, satirical cabaret form of 'chamber revue'. This could perhaps be compared with the Cambridge Footlights and *Beyond the Fringe* in the UK.

Cocoricò did contain some degree of social comment, such as, for example, in a 20-minute sketch about the situation of black people in the USA, but by and large it was a conventional revue. The following year Fo, Parenti and Durano formed their own revue company, calling themselves I Dritti (The Stand-ups, a joke at the expense of I Gobbi). I Dritti wrote, directed and performed in a revue called *Il dito nell'occhio* (*A Finger in the Eye*) which opened at the Piccolo Teatro in June and later toured all over northern and central Italy. Fo designed the sets and costumes as well as co-writing and co-directing, and the lighting was done by Strehler, while the French mime Jacques Lecoq was choreographer. The cast also included a Milanese actress, Franca Rame, who came from a popular touring theatre family, the Teatro Famiglia Rame. Fo had first met her while performing in a summer revue called *Sette giorni a Milano* (*Seven Days in Milan*), a 'girlie' show with a troupe called the Sorelle Nava (the Nava Sisters). Fo and Franca Rame were married in June 1954 and the following year had a son, Jacopo.

Il dito nell'occhio broke new ground in the Italian revue scene for its political satire and irreverent comedy, and critics called it an 'anti-revue'. Fo has claimed that it was more in the theatrical tradition of *avanspettacolo*, or curtain-raiser, rather than cabaret, although French commentators on Fo's work were later to see many resemblances between it and French cabaret. But as Fo explained to a US interviewer:

> I've never done cabaret, but rather a form of theatre tied to popular traditions; if anything, in the framework of *avanspettacolo*. (A kind of variety theatre performed between two movie showings. It was very much in vogue in Italy between 1930–1940.) All our comics, from Petrolini himself, to Ferravilla and Scarpetta, have all contributed to this type of theatre.

> When, for example, we did *Il dito nell'occhio* . . . the ambience was not that of a cabaret – the space itself, 700 seats, the stage being 12 to 13 yards wide, the complete set, the number of people acting (there were 12 of us), and finally, the concept of the piece, which, yes, was a string of sketches, but had a logical continuity of its own . . . It had little to do with the French or German tradition in cabaret. That is, it was something better than cabaret, which forces one to adopt a certain unnatural format: a cafe performance requires a very private and intimate form of speaking. With us, instead, everything was flung out: the action, the amount of physi-

cal expression inherent in our way of acting . . . [and] pantomime . . . Moreover, there was a popular element that
consisted of the storyteller's visual narration . . .[7]

A Finger in the Eye consisted of 21 sketches which ran through a
potted satirical history of the world, and used the reversal
technique of *Poer nano*. The expression 'a finger in the eye',
which was also the title of a regular column in the Italian
Communist Party newspaper *L'Unità*, roughly corresponds to
the English concept of 'nose-thumbing'. The revue overturned
the perspective of school history books, as in a sketch about the
Trojan war in which the idea for the Trojan horse originates
from an unknown soldier. (In 1954 Fo was to declare that his
favourite playwrights were Chekhov and Shaw, and here one
can see some influence of the Shaw of *Ceasar and Cleopatra*.) Fo
later commented:

> The basic idea was to dismantle the mythical mechanisms
> imposed by fascism and retained by the Christian
> Democrats. Like the myth of the hero, in which history is
> made up of prominent figures, and the myth of the family,
> and morality, and culture as the product of an intellectual
> elite, of patriotism, efficiency, virility, and history as the
> 'school of life'.[8]

Fo's sets and costumes also broke with traditional forms of
revue. The split-level set allowed two playing areas and took the
form of a parallelepiped with a curtain – a kind of stage within
a stage in which scene changes took place in full view of the
audience. All the cast wore a basic black costume over which
they put a few additional items to suggest a historical period and
the nature of their characters.

Il dito nell'occhio, apart from being the last play in which Fo
played a supporting role, was also important for the influence of
Lecoq. Lecoq's work, unlike the 'deaf-mute', 'white' mime of
Marcel Marceau, espoused 'black' mime, which incorporated
language, song and dance. He had been in Italy since 1948,
assisting on two of the first Italian productions of Brecht, and in
Il dito nell'occhio he provided what one critic called a 'perfect

geometrical mechanism'.[9] He schooled the company in rhythmic gestures, and taught Fo a considerable amount of mimic and vocal techniques to shape his spontaneous improvisations. Lecoq also trained Fo to use his physical defects to advantage rather than hiding them, and instructed him in the different forms of laughter. He also introduced him to *Grammelot* and character-transformation, ingredients which were to come into their own in *Mistero buffo*.

Il dito nell'occhio was a box-office success, running for 113 performances from June 1953 at the Piccolo Teatro before going on tour. It also led to Fo's first involvement in Italian cinema as a screenwriter and actor, when the director Domenico Paolella included a sketch from it in his film *Rosso e nero* (*Red and Black*). This was a series of short episodic sketches parodying US musicals in the style of Neapolitan *sceneggiature* (film-plays).

Musical activities and the cinema

In 1953 Fo also began his activity as a songwriter, in collaboration with Fiorenzo Carpi, who was to provide the music for all of Fo's plays up to 1967. Their first song, 'La luna è una lampadina' (The Moon is a Lightbulb) remains one of Fo's best-known individual songs – a piece of whimsy which Fo sang in a raunchy, vaguely rock 'n' roll vein. The protagonist has been betrayed by Lina, who has gone off with a wealthy barber, leaving him to lament under her window. But instead of complaining about a broken heart, he complains about his sore feet, and the fact that he will have to walk home because the last trams have left. The anti-romantic irony of this song is typical of Fo's early songs about the Milanese *mala* (underworld) written for Ornella Vanoni and Enzo Jannacci. Fo also adapted a sketch from *Il dito nell'occhio*, about a chicken thief who is imprisoned for offences against the fascist regime, for Jannacci, as well as writing and directing an entire musical show for him, *22 Songs*, in 1967. The language of Fo's early songs has been described by Lanfranco Binni as expressing

an instinctive positiveness expressed with immediacy, naturalness and irony. It is the type of language which we can
find in Jannacci's most popular songs, and it is no coincidence that Dario Fo struck a chord with him which led to
an important collaboration. It is a language which expresses
detachment from the world of the bourgeois city, with its
luxurious shop windows in the centre of town, in favour of
the squalor of the industrial outskirts where the streets are
populated by 'poor barstards' who are regarded as defeated
people, but who nonetheless have a humanity which is
lacking from the cold bourgeoisie with their purses where
their hearts should be. A language which instinctively finds
emotional truth and knows which side is right, but which
does not yet see the 'rich' and 'poor' divided into classes,
into the 'bourgeoisie' and the 'proletariat'.[10]

Fo's songwriting came into more prominence in the second
revue on which he collaborated with Parenti, Durano, Lecoq
and Carpi, *I sani da legare* (*Fit to be Tied*). This opened at the
Piccolo Teatro a year after the critical and commercial success
of its predecessor. It consisted of 24 sketches about
contemporary life in the big city – which is never mentioned by
name, but is easily recognisable as Milan – from daybreak to
nightfall. With more immediate subject matter, the revue was
more forceful in its political satire than *Il dito nell'occhio,* and ran
into censorship problems from Italy's equivalent of the British
Lord Chamberlain, the Ministero dello Spettacolo. Mario
Scelba was Minister of the Interior at the time, and
administering a repressive, violent police force made up of ex-
fascist recruits. The new American ambassador, Clare Booth
Luce, was also pressurising the Italian government to stamp out
the spread of communism. This situation occasioned a sketch in
the play about McCarthyism in Italy. Another sketch entitled
'The Compromise', about a dissident Soviet scientist who is
killed by his orthodox son, ends with a characteristic Fo touch
– a film director rushes onstage to ask how the scene has gone
down with the censor. The repressive political climate of the
time was typified by what became known as the *legge truffa*

(fraud law), a proposal to give a party which obtained 50 per cent of the vote a two-thirds majority in parliament. This was reminiscent of the strategy which Mussolini used to seize parliamentary power in 1923. In this political climate, in which police frequently appeared in the audience to check the cuts which had been enforced on *I sani da legare,* many critics seemed to be cautioned into giving the play a lukewarm reception.

Formally very similar to *Il dito nell'occhio,* the play concentrated on the underdogs of Milan – tramps, thieves, the unemployed, poker players, production-line workers, and lovers, while satirising middle-class charitable institutions, journalists and film-buffs. Stylistically, the influence of the French absurdists was apparent, and the poet Salvatore Quasimodo described the play as mixing decadent French surrealistic elements with 'a form of popular theatre'.[11] This acknowledged a feature which was to become more and more predominant in Fo's subsequent work.

Due to the financial failure of *I sani da legare,* I Dritti broke up. They had discussed doing a Milanese adaptation of Brecht's *Threepenny Opera,* a project which Fo was to realise almost 30 years later, and in the meantime Strehler premiered the play at the Piccolo in 1955. Durano returned to more conventional revues, but Parenti had difficulty getting back into radio drama in the RAI – although he and Fo collaborated on an 11-part radio comedy series called *You Don't Live on Bread Alone (Non si vive di solo pane)* in 1955. He went on to do traditional French farce, only venturing back into political theatre briefly in the 1970s with a production of Mayakovsky's *The Bath House.* Fo decided to move with his new family to Rome and try his hand as a screenwriter in the cinema.

Despite working on a high salary with prominent screenwriters like Tullio Pinelli (Fellini's scriptwriter), Age and Scarpelli, living next door to Roberto Rossellini and Ingrid Bergman in Rome, and designing film sets, Fo's three-year stint in the Italian cinema capital did not yield many substantial results. In 1956 he co-wrote and acted with Franca Rame in *Lo svitato (The Screwball),* which was directed by Carlo Lizzani and produced by Carlo Ponti, who employed Fo as a comedy sketch writer. *The Screwball* was influenced by the comedies of Jacques Tati, as well as Keaton and Chaplin, and was loosely based on the idea of a day in Milan on which *Fit to be Tied* was also based. Fo plays the part of a disoriented hotel porter cast adrift in a neo-capitalist Milan of skyscrapers and modern technology. But his essentially improvisational, gestural style of acting was at odds with the more concise and naturalistic needs of the cinema. The prominent Italian film critic Tullio Kezich described *The Screwball* as 'a satirical film which misses all its probable targets'.[12] Although it can still occasionally be seen on privately owned Italian television channels, it achieved little apart from giving Franca Rame a certain degree of prominence.

Fo also collaborated with the minor neo-realist director Antonio Pietrangeli on two films, co-writing the screenplay and acting – along with prominent neo-realist director Vittorio De Sica – in *Souvenir d'Italie* (*It Happened in Rome*, 1957) and *Nata a marzo* (*Born in March*, 1958). He also worked on unrealised screenplay projects with Pier Paolo Pasolini and Pinelli (a project entitled *Sarajevo*), and the director Guido Leoni. More importantly, he wrote, directed and acted in television commercials for Agip petrol and Recoraro, at a time when a popular TV programme called *Caroselli* (Carousels) featured commercials by a number of well-known Italian film directors. Fo later recalled:

> *Caroselli* was an incredible learning experience, because they were short sketches which went at a furious pace . . . At the time they were the *ne plus ultra* of speed, and every-thing had to happen in a few short minutes, but the story had to be told in its entirety, complete with jokes, situ-ations, cuts, editing . . . I did everything: the treatment, the screenplay, the *mise en scène*, the acting, the editing and the directing.[13]

But when Rame was offered parts in a series of farces at the Arlecchino Theatre in Milan in 1958, the Fo family returned definitively to the city which has been their base ever since. Fo later stated:

For me the lesson of the cinema meant learning from a technical point of view what audiences had already grasped: a story divided into sequences, a fast pace, sharp dialogue, and getting rid of the conventions of space and time. Working on screenplays gave me an apprenticeship as a playwright and I was able to transfer the lessons of the new technical means to the theatre.[14]

The early farces

For his return to the Piccolo Teatro in Milan in June 1958, with the newly formed Compagnia Fo–Rame, Fo put on four one-act farces under the general title of *Ladri, manichini e donne nude* (*Thieves, Dummies and Naked Women*). Fo wrote three of the plays, while the fourth was an adaptation of a farce by Feydeau with the title *Non andartene in giro tutta nuda* (*Don't Go Around Naked*), for which a fourth Fo play was later substituted. At a time of unprecedented economic stability in Italy with the beginning of what was to be called the 'economic miracle', Fo turned his attention to the relatively frivolous area of sex comedy. Nonetheless all four pieces show his concern with developing a theatre of situation, and at the time they were regarded as an indigenous response to the predominantly literary, pessimistic plays of Ionesco, Adamov and Beckett.

One of these pieces, *Non tutti i ladri vengono a nuocere* (*The Virtuous Burglar*), a '*pochade*' or boulevard farce of mistaken identities, was revived in Rome in 1980 – an indication that these early farces are by no means ephemeral. A reviewer commented on the 1980 production:

> Seeing this risqué type of theatre now, one laughs at the way we used to laugh, in rediscovering the heretical humour of a stage which was still not very permissive . . . it re-evokes the late *dolce vita* atmosphere of the Kinsey report and the scandal magazines.[15]

The play is about a burglar who is surprised in a house by the owner and his mistress. The burglar's wife rings him 'at work' to check up on him, and he manages to escape when the house-owner's wife arrives with her lover. In his insightful study of the influence of Feydeau on Fo's early farces, Joseph Farrell describes *The Virtuous Burglar* as 'the play of Fo's in this period that most invites comparison with Feydeau'. He also sees it as proof of the paradox that while iconoclastic and revolutionary in politics, Fo has remained 'an unremitting conservative in theatre. This respect for tradition in Fo takes the form of reverence for plot and situation.' Farrell analyses the play in terms of Bergson's three identifying aspects of the comic situation: repetition (in the pattern of events), inversion (of the burglar as a positive hero) and the reciprocal interference of series (the clash of the moral code of property with the moral code of adultery).[16] In portraying the burglar as 'virtuous', Fo introduces a class analysis which satirises the hypocrisy of bourgeois sexual permissiveness by overturning it through a carnivalesque reversal of social order. This play also has the distinction of being, together with a later short Fo farce, *La Marcolfa* (also revived in Rome in 1980), probably the first of Fo's plays to receive a professional English-language production. This took place at the off-Broadway theatre the Cubicolo in New York, where it ran for nine performances in August 1969, and was translated and directed by Maurice Edwards.

I cadaveri si spediscono, le donne si spogliano (*Women Undressed and Bodies to be Despatched*), a 'thriller farce', was Fo's first play to be transmitted on Italian television, in 1959, stripped of the second half of its title. It deals with a transvestite detective investigating a divorce agency – divorce did not become legal in Italy until 1974 – which is in fact a cover for a kind of human mincemeat factory. Three women have killed their husbands and despatched their bodies in parcels in the Italian post, believing that they will disappear, but the parcels are returned to them. The confusion of identities and the macabre nature of the situation make this one of Fo's more absurdist plays, but as Farrell notes, 'this is a black comedy on the disposal of murdered bodies, not a tragi-farce of universal death.'[17] Despite surface similarities to the theatre of the absurd, such as a naked man in a dustbin and two philosophising road-sweepers in *One Was*

Nude and One Wore Tails, which seem to parody Samuel Beckett, Farrell argues convincingly that Fo's use of class reversals for social satire is too materialist and rationalist to be aligned with the metaphysical tragi-comedy of Ionesco or Beckett. Some of the stage business in these short pieces, like characters losing their clothes, furniture and objects becoming animated, and immobilising injections in the backside (used to good effect in the brothel setting of *Housepainters Have No Memories*), were to recur in Fo's later work like *Clacson, trombette e pernacchi* (*Trumpets and Raspberries*, 1981).

In January 1959, Fo made his acting debut on Italian television in the part of a clumsy clerk in a play by Paolo Emilio D'Emilio, entitled *Monetine di cinque lire* (Five-Lire Coins). He was also commissioned by the Teatro Stabile of Turin, where his brother Fulvio was working as an administrator, to write and direct a play to open its new season. The theatre's artistic director, Gianfranco De Bosio, was one of a group of postwar directors who had pioneered the plays of Brecht in Italy. He had also done research into one of the major figures of the *commedia dell'arte*, Ruzzante, who was to be a major influence on Fo's work, and on *Mistero buffo* in particular. De Bosio had proposed doing a production of a Ruzzante play which Fo would act in, but Fo refused, as he was not comfortable with De Bosio's approach to Ruzzante. (He later criticised him in similar terms to his condemnation of Strehler's interpretation of Brecht, for creating a 'Ruzzante who looks like Goldoni, all nudges and winks.'[18]) Fo instead excavated some of the nineteenth-century popular farces which the Teatro Famiglia Rame had performed, rewriting and restructuring them into four one-act plays which De Bosio co-directed.

The overall title of the plays, *Comica finale* (*Comic Finale*), derives from that of the brief, improvised topical farces which travelling players performed at the end of a tragedy or 'serious' play. These belong to a tradition of popular theatre akin to that of the 'comic interlude' in Shakespeare's time. The recourse to this popular tradition was reflected in *Comica finale* by having a wagon onstage with painted backdrops, and in the opening song, 'Ma che aspettate a batterci le mani' (What are you waiting for – clap!) the audience are exhorted to put out their flags on their balconies for the arrival of the 'charlatan kings'. The tradition is that of the *guitti,* popular strolling players similar to the *giullari,* and the *lazzi,* improvised comic routines which formed interludes in the repertoire of the *comici dell'arte.*

The first of the four farces, *Quando sarai povero sarai re (When You're Poor You'll Be King)* is important insofar as it reflects a carnival tradition, that of the 'Feast of Fools'. The roles of rich and poor, nobleman and servant, are reversed, and the poor man is 'king for a day'. This tradition is a basic influence in Fo's work. *La Marcolfa* also echoes this tradition – the eponymous servant is courted by all and sundry in an aristocratic household when it is discovered she has the winning lottery ticket, but she opts for her good-for-nothing fiancé. *Un morto da vendere (A Dead Man for Sale)* is based on a newspaper article about a simpleton who beats some cheats at cards, and when they try to 'rub him out' they discover that he is a dangerous criminal. This situation could be seen as a precursor to the 'Death and the Madman' sequence in *Mistero buffo.* The final piece, *I tre bravi (Three Bold Lads),* turns on a misunderstanding between three daughters of a wealthy landowner and three applicants for menial jobs, whom the daughters take for suitors. This situation finds its antecedent in the ancient Roman comic playwright Plautus' *Miles Gloriosus,* another important influence on Fo's farces. Fo has commented on how these early farces taught him to reject literary notions of theatre and the 'theatre of words':

> These farces were an important exercise for me in writing a theatrical text. I learnt how to dismantle and reassemble the mechanisms of comedy, and to write directly for the stage without any literary intermediary. I also realised how many antiquated, useless things there were in many plays which belong to the theatre of words.[19]

In 1962, Fo's farces gained considerable national exposure. The second channel of RAI was inaugurated with one of the pieces from *Comica finale,* and other short Fo farces were broadcast weekly for a five-week period.

The 'bourgeois period'

In September 1959 the Compagnia Fo–Rame began a series of full-length plays, six in all, which were performed every season at the Teatro Odeon. This was the equivalent of a London West End theatre, although it could also boast that it was the first theatre to bring Eduardo de Filippo to Milan. It also led Fo and Rame to considerable success in the Italian theatrical establishment. The first play Fo wrote for the Odeon, *Gli arcangeli non giocano al flipper* (*Archangels Don't Play Pinball*), remains one of Fo's most accomplished farces. It is a three-act play with music, based on a short story by Augusto Frassineti, with whom Fo had written the screenplay for the film *Lo svitato*. Fo noted that the play had a cinematic structure, insofar as it shifts between more than a dozen different locations, including a train, and there is evidence also of the influence of Italian neo-realist cinema in the play's 'street kid' protagonists.

Gli arcangeli was also Fo's first play to be performed outside Italy, receiving productions in the 1960s in Yugoslavia, Poland, Holland, Sweden and Spain. It was also 'rediscovered' in the UK and the USA – where it was directed by Fo and Rame – in the mid-1980s. The play was revived a number of times in Italy, including productions in Milan in 1980 and Rome in 1983, where it was presented as a 1950s period piece. It is Fo's first play to combine political-satirical content with a Brechtian form (evident in the play's songs, but also in its reliance on paradoxical situations to make its points), in which he abandons the revue-sketch and short farce form for a consistent plot line and character development which almost makes it a 'well-made play'. It satirises both government bureaucracy – the protagonist discovers that he has been registered by mistake as a hunting dog and is sent to the municipal dog pound – and government ministers – the protagonist steals a government minister's trousers on a train, impersonates him at a reception, and receives a bribe for his troubles. As a result, it ran into censorship problems, as did most of Fo's work before 1968. This was an inevitable result of combining a topical, satirical perspective with a mainstream theatre circuit, as Fo has noted:

I took the starting point of the play from current events and the striking contradictions which illustrated the more para-doxical contradictions of the Christian Democrat state, and I took the subject into areas which would clash with audiences on the commercial circuit. Having accepted this circuit and these audiences, we had to put across political and social truths under the guise of satiric licence.[20]

The play is set in the industrial outskirts of Milan, and deals with a group of *balordi,* or 'louts', vaguely resembling English Teddy Boys, enabling Fo to mine a rich vein of Milanese street slang. The *balordi* are petty criminals who live on their wits, and resort to theatrical con-tricks reminiscent of those of Fellini's early films like *Il bidone. Gli arcangeli* is also notable for the first reference in Fo's work to the *giullari.* This takes place in an exchange between the protagonist Il Lungo (Stretch, played by Fo) and the Blonde (Franca Rame), a streetwalker who is used by the *balordi* to set up a fake marriage with Il Lungo:

STRETCH: Being a fall-guy is more or less my job.
BLONDE: You mean you work as a fall-guy?
STRETCH: Right – have you heard of the *giullari*?
BLONDE: Of course I have. (*Eruditely, like an encyclopedia.*) The *giullari* used to make royalty laugh – isn't that right?
STRETCH (*laughing*): Exactly. The same goes for me too, except for one thing. Since royalty doesn't exist any more . . . I make my coffee-bar mates laugh. I'm a poor man's Rigoletto.[21]

The *balordi* are cheerful, good-natured Milanese cousins of the doomed, down-and-out Roman *ragazzi di vita* of Pier Paolo Pasolini's gritty, naturalistic early novels and films. The play follows Il Lungo's successful attempt to extricate himself from this desperate demi-monde of pranks and petty crime, get his papers in order, and find an identity for himself. The critic Paolo Puppa has commented that the play breaks new ground in

presenting, for the first time, a *socially determined group* as opposed to a previous concentration on fixed absurdist types. They are good-natured, sulphuric louts, a kind of proletariat of the outer suburbs who have to live on their wits in order to survive. Coming from the tradition of naturalistic melodrama . . . which had been euphemistically presented in recent works by Zavattini [De Sica's screenwriter] and Fellini, they represent a type of marginalised underworld, cheerful and desperate at the same time, from which the protagonist has to free himself in order to assert himself as an individual and a social being.[22]

Fo uses the metaphor of the pinball machine – a novelty in Italy at the time, and both Fo and Rame were fanatical pinball players – to parody mechanisation and conspicuous consumption. But he rejects any deterministic, tragic notion of human actions being manipulated by a higher force (the archangels), and replaces it with a farcical situation in which the protagonist's wit and ingenuity enable him to succeed in life. The complex events of the play are revealed to have been a dream and Stretch ends up marrying the Blonde for real. The characterisation of Stretch is partly influenced by Bertoldo, the archetypal dim-witted figure from seventeenth-century Italian comedy who proves to be cleverer than he looks. The play develops a series of ingenious and elaborate sight gags – one example being the office where Stretch applies for a disability pension, and five clerks manage to elude him by pulling down their shutters in a dizzying, ballet-like conundrum which also involves a waiter with coffee and a number of other members of the public.

Another notable feature of *Archangels* is its songs. 'Stringimi forte i polsi' (Hold My Wrists Tightly Together) is an apparently trite, sentimental love ballad sung by Stretch to the 'Albanian' prostitute his mates set him up with in the mock wedding in which the couple have their wrists bound together. In Fo's detached, bemused, but resonant rendition, with music by Piccolo Teatro stalwart Fiorenzo Carpi, who was to work regularly with Fo until 1967, the bluesy setting, with 'boppy', rhythmic piano and 'whiplash' scratch guitar effects, gives the song an urbane quality which rescues it from sentimentality. The song later became the theme tune to the television programme *Canzonissima*, and a later version recorded by prominent Italian pop singer Mina became a hit, milking emotion from the rather corny lyrics:

Hold my wrists tightly together
Tightly in your hands
And even though my eyes are closed
I'll see you with my heart[23]

The celebrated Italian jazz trumpeter Enrico Rava rather surprisingly included his jazzed-up, Latinised version of the song, with vocals by Barbara Casini, on his 1997 album *Italian Ballads*, recorded in New York. This placed Fo's humble love song in the company of Nino Rota's Gelsomina theme from Fellini's *La Strada* as well as his theme from *Juliet of the Spirits*, 'Un bel di, vedremo' from Puccini's *Madama Butterfly*, the Neapolitan favourite 'Return to Sorrento' and Riz Ortolani's theme from the 1960s scandal film *More*. The opening song from *Archangels*, 'Non fare tilt' (Don't Go Into Tilt) is also worth noting, a Pop Art-like portrayal of Stretch and his gang as a group of petty criminals playing the city like a pinball machine. Late 1950s US rock 'n' roll influences are apparent, with jazzy brass and flute arrangements and a rhythmic dance beat. Another song, 'Fratelli d'ufficio' (Brothers of the office), is a satire on bureaucracy which parodies the Italian national anthem 'Fratelli d'Italia'. The songs contribute substantially to the light-hearted, optimistic, and relatively gentle satire of the play, in which the petty criminal underworld of the street kids exposes the intransigence and corruption of politicians and government bureaucracy.

As Joseph Farrell has noted, *Archangels* was the first of many Fo plays to be published in *Sipario*, the Milan-based monthly theatre magazine, in its September 1959 issue. This lengthy text, later shortened when included in the first Einaudi volume of Fo's plays, came complete with the elaborate stage directions describing the play's many and often complicated sight gags. In a brief introduction to the text, a critic, 'G.D.C.', opened what was to become a long-standing debate on Fo's status as an actor-playwright. He questioned whether Fo's 'physical and biological presence' as an actor could be excluded from the text, or whether Fo's 'literary creations' could be considered separately from his acting.[24]

The influence of Brecht, and of *The Threepenny Opera* and *Arturo Ui* in particular, is strongly apparent in Fo's second play for the Odeon. This was a black comedy described as 'a play in 3 acts and 2 interludes' which again deals with a criminal underworld. *Aveva due pistole con gli occhi bianchi e neri (He Had Two Pistols with White and Black Eyes,* 1960) is partly based on a couple of newspaper crime stories. Its farcical plot turns on a 'double' and a series of mistaken identities in a way which closely resembles Fo's later play *Trumpets and Raspberries* (1981), where he also plays a double role. Political satire is more predominant (although the play is far from being a piece of agit-prop) at a time when Fo and Rame were drawing closer to the Italian Communist Party. In 1960 there were deaths in Sicily and Reggio Emilia after clashes between workers and police, a general strike which caused the Christian Democrat government to fall, and the trade unions were gaining in strength. Grafting a topical newspaper story onto a situation taken from American *film noir*, the play deals with a priest in a mental hospital who has lost his memory and is appropriated into a gang of mobsters. In an interview published in the US *Drama Review,* Fo claimed that the play

> satirised latent fascism. It was the story of a bandit whose two-sided character was portrayed through the use of doubles, in the tradition of Greek and Roman theatre. Censorship had become just about intolerable, and we almost ended in jail for having refused to submit the text for approval by the authorities, knowing that permission could be obtained only after they mutilated the work beyond recognition.[25]

Fo was beginning to develop a repertoire of running gags and farcical situations such as mistaken identities, and the play included one gag which was later repeated at the end of *Accidental Death of an Anarchist* when the 'real' judge finally appears. In a reversal of expectations, the amnesiac priest protagonist of *He Had Two Pistols* is revealed to be the organiser of a thieves' strike, and not the crime boss he is believed to be impersonating. *He Had Two Pistols* continues in the light-hearted vein of *Archangels*, with the thieves' strike for a percentage of the income gained from their thefts by insurance companies, dog trainers, crime reporters and others being a particularly ingenious idea. The play also included a number of Brecht-styled songs, most notably one entitled 'The World Upside Down'. This derives from popular carnivalesque traditions of topsy-turvy bestiaries, and is set to a catchy Carpi melody:

> Horses fly through the sky
> Fishes swim through flowering trees
> A flower sucks butterflies
> And settles on a hornet's back
> You see a thief hearing a priest's confession
> And a little orphan giving a home to nuns
> Government ministers join a political rally
> And cops beat them up with their truncheons[26]

The hymn-like group chorus on the final line consolidates the song's satirical inversion, and emphasises the carnivalesque dynamic of class inversion which Fo uses almost continually in his work.

Fo's play for the Odeon the following year, *Chi ruba un piede è fortunato in amore* (*He Who Steals a Foot is Lucky in Love*) was a sentimental comedy with an imbalance between a highly farcical form and slight content, and was judged harshly by left-wing Italian theatre critics. A modern version of the myth of Apollo and Daphne, with a series of running gags punning on the word 'foot', it could be compared with the neoclassical plays of Shaw and Giraudoux in form. It is centred on a naive, honest taxi driver (Apollo), an 'emigrant' from the south of Italy who is cast in the same mould as Il Lungo and the Gangster-Priest. Apollo manages to extort money to buy a taxi from a group of big-time building speculators by burying the foot of a statue of Mercury in land they are developing, and impersonating an archaeologist. He then becomes involved in a series of scams and misunderstandings with Daphne, the wife of the boss of the construction company, with the marble foot providing a running sight gag throughout the play. Despite the topicality of the play at a time when the Italian economic boom was in full swing and building speculation was rife, the bourgeois comedy form of the play did not help its satire to hit its mark. It remains one of Fo's minor works, although it was revived in Rome in 1987. Paolo Puppa saw in it the emergence of a political perspective which distinguished it from Fo's earlier works:

> The attack on the corrupt bourgeois customs and the ruling class elites of the 1960s shows clearly that [Fo's] political targets are beginning to come into focus, and move away from generic [satire]. The topography of the adulterous tri-angle, the stereotypes of the *pochade* (the building contractor knows the engineer is his wife's lover and finds it perfectly normal, in terms of class solidarity) are aug-mented by cultural deprivation, illicit actions, wrangling and speculation which are exposed with an attitude mid-way between facetiousness and anger.[27]

Fo regards it as being closer in form to his revues of the early 1950s than to his other plays, but it has no songs and the antics between Apollo and Daphne resemble a boulevard bedroom farce. An English version of it was performed at the 1983 Edinburgh Festival by the Channel 5 Theatre Company, using what Joseph Farrell described in *The Scotsman* as 'the Frankie Howerd slapstick approach'. This resulted in 'a mess of asides to the audience, improvised gags, over-the-top acting, and curious accents ... There is little that is memorable, and it is not particularly funny.'[28]

The television fiasco

In 1959, as a result of Italy's first centre-left government coming into power, Fo and Rame had been invited by the more permissive and progressive second channel of RAI TV, the Italian state television network, to present some of their one-act farces on national television. RAI is controlled by the Italian government, and its first channel tended, at least until the early 1990s, to reflect the opinions of the Christian Democrat Party. With the entry of the smaller left-wing parties into the government, its policy relaxed somewhat, and a system of political 'lottizzazione' (allotment) of the two channels came into operation. Consequently the second channel became slightly more left-oriented, with programmes like *Tribuna politica*, introduced in 1962, which gave a hearing to the parties of the Italian Left.

Fo was appointed artistic director of the musical revue programme *Chi l'ha visto?* (*Who's Seen Them?*), and then, in 1962, to write and perform sketches and songs in the highly successful musical variety programme *Canzonissima*. Fo took advantage of the popularity of *Canzonissima* to produce satirical sketches and songs which attacked building speculation, working conditions in factories, prisons and the Mafia, almost immediately causing censorship problems, despite the considerable public appeal of the series. Fo's and Rame's conflict with the programme's producers culminated in their walking out of the studios on 29 November 1962, just before the eighth programme of the series was due to go on air. They had refused to accept the cuts ordered in a sketch which referred to the dangerous conditions undergone by workers on building sites. Although the sketch had initially been approved, RAI refused to transmit it because the building workers' unions were involved in a dispute about the issue at the time.

The termination of the programme made headlines in the daily newspapers, and caused questions to be asked in the Italian parliament. Fo and Rame were then sued by RAI, who subsequently destroyed all the recordings they had made for *Canzonissima,* and effectively excluded them from Italian television for 14 years. Fo has described one incident which led to the vetting and cutting of their transmissions:

There was one sketch which caused an avalanche of protest. It showed a worker who was in the habit of kissing the effigy of his boss as if it were a saint. This worker had a fat aunt who weighed a ton, and who came to visit him one day in the factory. It was a canned meat factory. The aunt tripped and fell into a machine, and came out as mincemeat because they couldn't stop the production line. The worker was given 150 cans of meat which he kept in a cupboard at home and showed to his friends every so often, telling them 'This is my aunt'. There were no reactions against this from aunts, but a lot from canned meat producers and industrialists in general.[29]

This type of grotesque humour satirising capitalist exploitation of workers and reflecting the grim reality of Italian factories, in which accidents were a common occurrence, was a foretaste of the political satire of Fo's post-1968 plays. It was evidently too close to the bone for television programme controllers in 1962. It was as if Monty Python had got together with the Red Ladder agit-prop theatre in a prime-time comedy show on BBC 1. *Canzonissima* and its 15 million spectators gave Fo his first direct experience of the potentialities of the mass medium. He used the opportunity to undermine the diversionary, trivial aspects of Italian television, which is one of the world's leaders in 'junk TV', especially in its numerous quiz shows, chat shows and musical variety programmes. Fo and Rame instead attempted to expose and condemn the social injustices and exploitation which lay behind the 'economic miracle' which TV was a part of, giving Italian viewers their first taste of a brand of humour which derived from the popular origins of theatre.

The songs in *Canzonissima* included one of Fo's most distinctive early compositions which deals with the 'industrial outskirts' of Milan, 'La brutta città che è la mia' (This Ugly City of Mine), with music by Carpi. Loosely based on Jacques Brel's 'Le plat pays' (The Flat Country), it is a melancholy lament, with a plangent flute and piano accompaniment, and with orchestral augmentation in the choruses which reprise the title. A world of pipes and pylons and 'walls disguised as houses' is described, with only one tree, where 'all the dogs queue up to pee'. The land is flat, there is no wind, instead of the Duomo of Milan, there is a marble quarry, and instead of the Navigli (the canals which run through Milan), there is a stagnant pond where the fish suffocate. Nonetheless, going into the piazza on Sundays to meet up with girls creates wind and movement, and the song ends with the image of doves flying over the holy ground of 'this ugly city of mine'.[30] It is an evocative but sad song, later recorded by the popular singer Milly, and anticipates a later tradition of Italian *canzoni d'autori* about cities such as Lucio Dalla's 'Milano' (where 'you speak to someone in German and they reply in Sicilian dialect'), Antonello Venditti's sentimental paeans 'Roma Capoccia' (Rome's the Boss) and 'Torino' and Paolo Conte's 'Genova per noi' (Genoa for Us).

Another song featured in *Canzonissima* (and later performed and recorded by Enzo Jannacci) is 'Il foruncolo' (The Pimple), a parody of the *canzonette* (trivial love songs) which prevailed in the Italian pop music industry of the early 1960s. The protagonist has discovered a pimple on his ear while he is shaving. As his girlfriend cannot bear pimples, or cysts, or blackheads, or any other form of acne, he knows this is the end of his relationship. The song fades out on a debate with himself as to whether it is a pimple or a blackhead. Fo performs the song with a mock gravitas that underscores the triteness of the teenage-romance content of what must be his silliest song. Nonetheless the song was taken to court by two priests from Novara who claimed it contained a swear word, but had to admit in court that they were mistaken.

One particularly controversial sketch in *Canzonissima*, which led to the sacking of one of the RAI 'censors' for allowing it to be broadcast, was 'The Level-Crossing Woman' (*La casellante*), performed by Franca Rame. A journalist interviews a woman working for the railways, who lives with her family in an isolated, smoke-filled shack by the railway line without electricity, gas or heating. She cheerfully recounts all the hardships of her grotesquely primitive life-style, the stresses and illnesses of her three children, and her husband's imprisonment due to a colleague's negligence at his job which caused an accident. This exposure of the shocking working and living conditions of employees of the Italian state railways caused letters of outrage and hastened the demise of *Canzonissima*. Nonetheless, according to Franca Rame, during their stint on the programme taxi drivers in the main Italian cities used to complain that it brought their trade to a standstill because everyone was home watching it.[31]

Historical drama in an epic context

Fo returned to the Teatro Odeon with a play which for him was a radical new departure – a two-act piece about Christopher Columbus entitled *Isabella, tre caravelle e un cacciballe* (*Isabella, Three Sailing Ships and a Con Man*). This play appeared in the same year as Strehler's celebrated production of Brecht's *Galileo* at the Piccolo, and there are evident resemblances to Brecht's play, although the way their protagonists clash with the political regimes in each case is quite different. Fo's play was primarily an attempt to demystify and debunk the traditional history-book image of Columbus, as it was reflected, for example, in the naming of a street after him in EUR, the fascist-designed modern business and government ministry area of Rome. Fo was undoubtedly influenced by Maxwell Anderson's and Kurt Weill's *The Nina, the Pinta and the Santa Maria,* again using songs to comment on the action, but he used the historical format as a framework in which to couch comments on contemporary Italian social and political problems. As he has commented, the play was a criticism of the 1963 'historic compromise', in which the Socialist Party (PSI) joined forces with the Christian Democrats (Democrazia Cristiana, DC) to form a centre-left government, and the Communist Party began to consider joining this alliance:

I wanted to attack those Italian intellectuals who, with the centre-left and the Socialist Party in the government, had discovered power and its advantages and leapt on it like rats on a piece of cheese. I wanted to dismantle a character who had been embalmed as a hero in school history books, whereas he is in fact an intellectual who tries to keep afloat within the mechanisms of power, play games with the King and be cunning with power figures, only to end up reduced to a wretch. I'd started to view the present with the tools of history and culture, in order to assess it better, and in this play I invited the audience to use these tools.[32]

Fo uses the mechanism of the play-within-a-play to present Columbus through a further filter of Brechtian detachment. The protagonist is an actor condemned to death under the Spanish Inquisition for performing a play by the controversial playwright Rojas, author of *The Spanish Bawd*. At the gallows he improvises a play about Columbus and Queen Isabella of Spain (played by Franca Rame, who also played Isabella's mad, soothsaying daughter Giovanna La Pazza). This play is exempt from censorship according to a law which allows a condemned prisoner to do anything he likes at the gallows. This was clearly a tongue-in-cheek reference (both the actor and Columbus were, of course, played by Fo) to Fo's own problems with censorship. The play also included a degree of erotic comedy deriving from the sailors' enforced sexual abstinence while at sea, in which Fo drew on medieval popular comic texts. It was also Fo's first play to use *grammelot*, the invented onomatopoeic language which Fo was later to use to great effect in *Mistero buffo* and his other one-man shows.

After a performance of the play at the Teatro Valle in Rome, Fo and Rame were physically attacked by a group of fascists, who tried to pelt them with rubbish, and another performance was called off due to a bomb scare. Fo received threatening letters, and was even challenged to a duel by an Italian cavalry officer. Fo agreed to the duel as long as it was fought along the lines of Thai boxing, at which he was a regional champion, and the challenge was never taken up. Franca Rame was charged with giving offence to the Italian armed forces in the following dialogue:

ISABELLA: You are allowed certain concessions, such as looting and plundering. That's covered by the war law. Then there's those four rallying words – King and Country! Family and Morality! The blood that our sons spill so generously – you'll fall right on your feet.

FERDINANDO: Not just on my feet – I'll be up to my neck in the shit.

ISABELLA: So that's why all you soldiers always walk with
   your chins up . . .[33]

The final line of this exchange, which was later used by Fo in a
slightly transposed form as the final line of *Accidental Death of an
Anarchist* to attack the Italian government's manipulation of
scandals, here had to be modified by adding, 'I mean here in
Spain, of course.' But the play also used its historical framework
to make allusions to contemporary Spain under Franco. It ends
with a defeated Columbus, after his entire fleet has sunk in the
Indies, directing a speech of 'self-criticism' (*autocritica*) at the
audience. In it he expresses his awareness of the mistakes he has
made, and the misguidedness of trying to play the
establishment's game. As he is about to suggest an alternative
course of action, he is interrupted by the executioner, and the
Columbus actor is made ready for the gallows. There is a
blackout, and then Fo appears, headless, holding a head in his
hands, in a *Grand Guignol* finale.

The final song of the play expresses clearly where Fo's
sympathies lie: 'The really cunning person is always the honest
man/Not the opportunist,/but the man who come what may/is
always on the side/of the underdogs,/of the just.'[34] In many
ways, not least its focus on the plight of the underdog actor who
is finally executed, and its use of a devious, double-dealing
intellectual as its protagonist, the play has affinities with the
historical, Brechtian works of John Arden, especially *Armstrong's
Last Good Night,* which appeared in the UK the following year.

But according to Paolo Puppa, the ideological perspective of
Isabella is ambiguous, with its criticism of the Italian centre-left
and exposure of petit-bourgeois illusions resolving into a vague
and generalised moralism in the final chorus.[35] Despite a cool
reception from the critics, *Isabella* broke box-office records in
Italy at a time when the theatre was in dire economic straits.
After having achieved considerable popularity and notoriety in
Italy, Fo became the most widely performed contemporary
Italian playwright in Europe the year after. Productions of
Isabella were mounted in Sweden in 1965 and in Paris in 1971,
and in 1992 Fo revived the play in a production in Valencia in

Spain, when it became a critique of the European and American quincentennial celebrations of Christopher Colombus' first voyage. The text of the play was published in *Sipario* in August 1963, again with an introduction stating the problems of appreciating Fo's plays in printed form 'separately from the actor and the director'.[36]

In 1963 Fo also wrote *La fine del mondo, o Dio li fa, e poi li accoppia* (*The End of the World, or God Makes Them and Then Matches Them*). This remained unperformed until February 1969, when it was produced at the Teatro Belli in Rome by the film and TV director and actor Jose Quaglio, supervised by Fo, with music by Fiorenzo Carpi. The play presents a contemporary Adam and Eve, who survive a world cataclysm by hiding in a sewer. They believe they are the sole remaining people in the world until they encounter a corrupt General of counter-espionage and an Angel. Meanwhile the world is being taken over by cats in the absence of human power figures, and here the influence of popular puppet shows on Fo's work is apparent. The play's whimsically surreal situation accommodates a series of discussions about sexual relationships, an area which comes to prominence in Fo's work after 1976, while Fo updated the piece to make comments through the General on current political events and scandals. There was also a critique of the state of the Left in Italy since the 'historic compromise', which had caused a number of splinter groups to leave the PCI. As a reviewer of the 1979 production of the play commented, its rather flimsy science-fiction metaphor is too generalised to sustain the political points the play makes, and it remains a curiosity piece, with its faint echoes of Beckett:

> Fo's metaphor does not have anything like the gloomy tragedy of Beckett, though it has all the signals or signposts: rubbish bins, for example, or tape recorders, which recall and pay homage to *Krapp's Last Tape,* which also announced the end of the world . . . Fo . . . believes above all that his plays deal with the representation of difference and contrariness, and the crisis of the commonplace. But he doesn't take into account that sometimes playing tricks

with commonplaces results in sinking into the swamp the commonplaces invite.[37]

Graveyard humour and witchcraft

Meanwhile, back at the Odeon, Fo produced *Settimo: ruba un po' meno* (*Seventh Commandment: Steal a Bit Less*) for the 1964 season. This was a return to farce in a contemporary setting, and was specially written for Franca Rame, whose performance as Isabella had been one of the high points of Fo's previous play at the Odeon. The play, like *He Who Steals a Foot*, attacks building speculation, but with considerably more impact. In one scene Enea, the female gravedigger protagonist, witnesses a clash between armed police and striking demonstrators, which, although it takes place offstage, is the first time an event of such immediate political implications had appeared on an Italian stage.

Settimo charts the political education of Enea, who is a departure from Rame's previous 'vamp' roles, and a step towards 'epic acting' in which situation takes precedence over psychology. After she is made aware of the building-speculation scandal in which the graveyard's director is immersed, Enea does a brief stint in the 'elevating, emancipating' profession of prostitution. She then disguises herself as a nun in order to get hold of compromising documents for blackmail purposes. This takes her into a mental asylum, and Fo presents us with a highly ironical, carnivalesque and satirical scene in which mental patients act out a 'game of the nations'. This portrays the jostling for political power positions between various countries, including England, which is represented by 'an inmate with a grotesque mask resembling a lion, and a large military hat with flags and pennants all over it, and three Tudor lions on the front: all of which resembles the warlike divinity of the Chinese theatre in the guise of a clown, with "typical commedia dell'arte trimmings" '.[38] The scene bears a striking resemblance in its grotesque pageantry to the World War One human chess game in Joan Littlewood's *Oh! What a Lovely War*. But Fo was probably more influenced by the Peking Opera, which had performed in Milan shortly before he wrote the play and had impressed him with the simplicity and evocativeness of its stagecraft, at a time when he was impressed by the progress of the Chinese cultural revolution.

As in *Archangels* and *Isabella*, most of the cast of *Settimo* played multiple roles, with Fo playing the part of a wily 'coffin maniac' commercial salesman who wants to rent a coffin from Enea. The stagecraft made use of multi-functional objects, such as a coffin which became a bath and then a rowing boat in a later scene, a stove which was transformed into a safe, and a hearse–cart which became a theatre cart in which the gravediggers perform songs like the *guitti* in *Comica finale*. There was also another burst of *grammelot* in a scene in which a dead man speaks. *Settimo* was considered by many to be Fo's most impressive play to date, with Enea being Fo's most fully-developed female role, although the play's political satire got up the noses of the more conservative theatre critics. The popular weekly magazine *Oggi* deplored what it regarded as the play's political preaching, but nonetheless described Fo as 'an explosive talent' and 'the most extraordinary personality in Italian theatre'.[39] Puppa maintains that it was the play which initiated a long 'braccio di ferro' (literally 'arm wrestle', or trial of strength) between Fo and the mainstream Italian theatre circuit, and that reviewers tried to reduce its political protest by concentrating on its more amusing and entertaining aspects:[40]

> The play's themes rummaged about in the dense thicket of Italian national scandals, not just in a generalised way, but with a concreteness which reflected the uproar which had broken out at the time about attempted state coups and the long succession of building speculations, and other scams involving the ruling class. The play exposed these scandals with a judicious frenzy and an obsession with telling all.[41]

Settimo's topical satire on corruption inspired Fo to reuse the title for the monologue he and Rame developed in 1992 to satirise the 'Tangentopoli' (bribe city) corruption scandals and the 'clean hands' judicial investigation. The play toured 51 Italian cities in the 1964–65 theatre season, and its cast included the noted film actress Mariangela Melato – who was later to rise to prominence in the films of Lina Wertmuller – as well as Franca's sister Pia Rame (who had also performed in *Isabella*). It also included the actor-director Arturo Corso, a long-time collaborator with Fo, who subsequently mounted a production of *VII: Tu voleras un peu moins* in Liège in 1970, with four different actresses taking the part of Enea.

By 1965 Fo's plays had been performed in Stockholm, Oslo, Vienna, Prague, Copenhagen, Warsaw, Zurich, Hamburg, Reykjavik, Budapest, Bucharest, Amsterdam and Zagreb, among other places. He was awarded a prize of 5 million lire by the government's Ministero dello Spettacolo, which he donated to support university theatres. The next play he wrote, directed and performed with the Compagnia Fo–Rame was to be his last at the Teatro Odeon. *La colpa è sempre del diavolo* (*Always Blame the Devil*) anticipates *Mistero buffo* both in its medieval setting and its satire on established forms of Catholicism as manifested in its most vicious form in medieval times by witch-burning. However, satire of religious corruption is at the basis of almost all of Fo's plays, many of which include a burlesqued representative of the Catholic church as an almost instant source of comedy. As Fo has commented:

> Unlike *Mistero buffo*, *La colpa è sempre del diavolo* is not a *giullarata,* and not a reconstruction of medieval texts, but a totally invented story in a farcical vein, which takes advantage of its medieval setting to tell a few truths about Catholicism, like showing that the authorities maintained that the gospels were too embarrassing to put into practice, as well as too dangerous, because if they were applied they would take away all their privileges.[42]

La colpa è sempre del diavolo is important in marking the beginning of Fo's research into medieval theatre, but it was a critical flop. Reviewers judged it an unintegrated combination of a demystifying historical format and contemporary social comment on subjects such as the Vietnam war, which did not quite hang together structurally or conceptually. After its run in Milan, which attracted audiences of only 600 people, Fo completely rewrote sections of the text, and the play had been strengthened considerably when it opened in Rome.

The plot concerns Amalasunta (Franca Rame), a kind of twelfth-century 'con woman' who is wrongly accused of witchcraft, and sets about becoming a witch for real. (A similar role was reprised by Rame in later plays such as *The Pope and the Witch*, 1989 and *The Devil in Drag*, 1997.) She enlists the aid of a devil–dwarf, Brancaleone (a famous name in Mafia circles), played by Fo in a guise he later elaborated and perfected in his political satire about the Italian government minister and sometime prime minister, Fanfani. This involved combining his head with the body of another actor (Corso) in a mimic technique which owes something to the influence of Lecoq. Fo played three other roles in the play, including a mannequin, and made use of an old Venetian dialect which was a forerunner of the Padano of *Mistero buffo,* as well as sophisticated stagecraft and stage machinery which evoked the work of Meyerhold in the 1920s.

The play's context of the battle between the Holy Roman Empire and the Cathar communards alludes to the US presence in Vietnam and the Italian Communist Party, but its satire seemed unfocused. Puppa notes a didacticism, which had been held in check in previous plays, in Brechtian songs and unspoken implications and allusions. Here it was directly expressed in a speech by Brancaleone which used the play's title to express a moral condemning those who used religion, morality, political power and war to gain prestige.[43] Nonetheless the play toured 41 cities in northern and central Italy, and the company, which still included Corso, Melato and Pia Rame, subsequently took *Always Blame the Devil* and *Thieves, Dummies and Naked Women* on a long international tour to Paris, Moscow, Tel Aviv, Yugoslavia, Hungary, Romania, Bulgaria, Poland, Finland, Sweden, Norway, Denmark, Iceland, Germany and Holland.[44]

Popular music, an adaptation, and circus satire

During the run of *La colpa è sempre del diavolo,* Fo went to see *Bella ciao,* a performance of songs of popular origin by the folk revivalist music group Nuovo Canzoniere Italiano. This was a performance of peasant and working-class political songs and popular culture which immediately interested Fo. When he was approached by the group and asked to collaborate on a new show, he accepted willingly, and the result was *Ci ragiono e canto* (*I Think Things Out and Sing Them*), which played in Turin and later in Milan in 1966. Fo directed the show, and rewrote some of the popular musical material, but it was an uneasy collaboration. The musicians and singers in the group, many of them non-professionals, often resisted Fo's attempts to theatricalise the songs, and choreograph them in terms of the action of work rhythms, which Fo insisted that many of the songs were based on:

> Pausing for breath in a work song determines not only its rhythm, but also its melody. One could say that every type of work which differs from another because of its particular gestures inevitably determines a musical difference in the songs.[45]

Fo's ideas as a director led to clashes with the musical uniformity of the group he was working with, which included prominent left-wing folk singers, composers and recording artists Gianni Bosio, Ivan Della Mea, Paolo Ciarchi and Giovanna Marini. Fo's folk excavations also ran very much against the current of Italian theatre at a time when mildly outrageous figures of the experimental avant-garde, like Carmelo Bene, with his semi-pornographic rehashes of Shakespeare, and Leo de Bernardinis, with his underground jazz concoctions, were coming into prominence. Julian Beck and Judith Malina had toured Italy in 1965 with the Living Theatre and exerted considerable influence on Italian theatre in propagating research into physical theatrical forms and an emotive relationship with the audience, creating an elitist ghetto of individualistic conceptual theatre. (They were later to base themselves permanently in Italy, with both Beck and Malina working in Italian cinema with prominent directors like Pier Paolo Pasolini.) Fo, on the other hand, was researching popular theatrical forms from the medieval past. These appealed to him because they gave him the opportunity of getting across to a wider, non-theatre-going audience, as well as for their political importance in retrieving popular culture. As he stated in an interview in 1967:

> I maintain that in the theatre, the more one approaches the new by way of experimentation, the more there is a need to seek out roots in the past, by which I mean the relevant aspects of the past – above all those which are attached to the roots of the people, which derive from the people's manifestations of life and culture . . . This enables the expression of new research and new investigations on the basis of the 'new within the traditional', which is what I am concerned with.[46]

The first part of *Ci ragiono e canto* presented popular festival songs and ironic popular songs about war. The second part contained work songs, a representation of the apocryphal gospel version of Christ's passion (which Fo would later take up again in *Mistero buffo),* and the finale was the anarchist song 'Our Home Is the Whole Wide World'. This was sung in chorus with the audience, a *coup de théâtre* which Fo later used in an ironical form to conclude the first act of *Accidental Death of an Anarchist.*

In 1966 Fo travelled in Eastern Europe, the USA and Cuba, studying the new forms of theatre in these countries. He remained unimpressed by much of the new avant-garde, experimental theatre he saw, regarding it as sterile, formal and technical experimentation which too frequently used new material for its own sake. In Cuba he was impressed by the poverty of means that young theatre practitioners employed, making do with simple props and costumes, and the gestures of ritual.

On his return to Italy he was invited to adapt and direct the French playwright Georges Michel's play *The Sunday Walk* at a small experimental theatre in Milan, the Durini. As he was to do in his later adaptations, Fo completely gutted Michel's text, a gentle satire about a petit bourgeois family going through its provincial rituals without any acknowledgment of the violence and turmoil in the outside world. He also changed the play's references to the Algerian war to the Vietnam war and clashes between police and demonstrators in Italy.

As the continually changing, updated texts of his own plays prove, Fo runs completely against the grain of any literary theatrical tradition, and takes an essentially practical, pragmatic approach to texts. In this case he also used Michel's play to experiment with stagecraft: the production included a beat group on a circular platform centre stage, performing songs specially written by Fo. There were also non-naturalistic lighting effects, costumes and action, and the actors performed more than one role apiece. Fo used the play to make a savage attack on the cosy domestic security afforded by electrical appliances, a theme he was later to take up in his own plays. Most of the reviews of *The Sunday Walk* expressed uneasiness about the increasingly left-wing tendencies Fo was displaying in his work, but the critic of the magazine *Il Dramma* commented that 'Fo has saved all the intelligence of the play and replaced its delicacy with a bitter polemical thrust.'[47]

Fo's final play in the mainstream, establishment Italian theatre, *La signora è da buttare* (*Throw the Lady Out*), opened at the Teatro Manzoni in Milan in September 1967. Fo used a clown show, revue-sketch format (again reminiscent of *Oh! What a Lovely War*) to satirise pre-Kennedy America (personified by the 'lady') and the Vietnam war. The American critic A. Richard Sogliuzzo, in what was the first critical article about Fo to appear in English (in 1972), described the play as follows:

Set in an American circus of the 1860s, *The Lady is to be Thrown Out* progressed like a circus performance: acrobats, clowns, dancers, tightrope walkers, and trapeze artists rushed on and off. A hundred mechanical contraptions whirred and hummed. The pace was frenetic; the joy excessive, manic. Fo and his company sang, danced, joked, performed on the high wire, executed impressive feats of acrobatics. His verbal banter, spiced with his Milanese argot, delighted the audience, but in the end it was gesture and movement that prevailed over language. Among that gesture and movement were an avalanche of teeth pouring out of Fo's mouth, an oxygen mask that became a serpent, shoes propelled by themselves, hands flying through the air, and performers sitting in mid-air with their coat-tails folded under them, plus an endless array of surrealistic sight gags. Gradually, however, one realised that the joy was fraught with tragedy, clearly evident in the death of a dove at Dallas. The lady to be eliminated was the owner of the circus, an aged female P.T. Barnum, representing American capitalism. A moment before her death, she was elevated above a sink in a Statue of Liberty pose, and then ascended to a heaven packed with consumer goods, a touch of mock ritual denigrating both Church and State. Fo's circus was a metaphor of the industrial state, a vast bureaucracy of machines and trapezes in which man had yielded his individuality to the collective pandemonium, a puppet in a tyrannical circus of injustice, prejudice, crime, and war.[48]

Although this is a description of the updated TV version of the play broadcast in 1976, it gives an accurate picture of the play's bustling pace and circus techniques. It was an example of what Fo called 'theatre of provocation', with its form akin to that of agit-prop. Italian theatregoers in 1967, however, did not take kindly to the play's grotesque, black political satire. In one scene Fo ridicules forensic research by tracing an absurd trajectory of the bullet which kills the Bride in White (a representation of Kennedy in Dallas), hitting a stray dog, a chauffeur and an ice-cream van on its way to its target. Fo was almost arrested for 'offences against foreign heads of state' in the play's references to President Johnson, and it also satirised American imperialism, racism, justice and absurd forms of entertainment like the 'flea-tamer' who tries to take out a flea's appendix. In using a frantic, sketch-based, clown show format (the cast included I Colombaioni, a duo of circus clowns), consistency of characterisation was eliminated in a style which moved further towards the epic theatre which Fo was espousing, in which the actor plays not a character but a 'mask' (in the sense of the archetypal characters of the *commedia dell'arte*).

In the TV version of the play, Fo reprised his dwarf-puppet routine from *Always Blame the Devil*, this time as St George, as well as giving a virtuoso performance on a tuba, and Rame appeared in one scene on a horse. Sight gags with domestic appliances and medical tubes and mistaken injections anticipated his later adaptation of Brecht's *Threepenny Opera* and *Trumpets and Raspberries*. A sketch dealing with drug addiction and an 'injection juke box' anticipated a theme which was to recur in a number of Fo's plays in the 1970s and 1980s. Despite its rather sprawling, inchoate form, *La signora* received French-language productions in 1969 in Rennes and Montreal. Fo described the style of the show to an American interviewer in 1976:

> the actor must be the exclusive renderer of whatever hap-
> pens . . . he does not have to wear a robe to become a
> character, but to become a mask . . . The mask is the
> dialectical synthesis of conflicts, whereas a character carries
> with him conflicts without ever achieving their synthesis
> . . . the actor is an individual entity, while the mask is col-
> lective, because it tells of a general concern . . . it is the
> voice of the story, not the means of acting it out. It is not
> I who identify with what I present on stage. Rather, I can
> criticise, suggest conflicts, contradictions, hypocrisies, and
> comment under any circumstance. This is the epic fact, the
> estrangement.[49]

In both its 'epic' style and its political-satirical content, *La signora è da buttare* shows that Fo's theatre could no longer be contained within the structure and fulfil the expectations of the conventional bourgeois Italian theatre. The irrepressible energy and zest of Fo's plays were becoming too much for mainstream theatre's subscription audiences and predominantly safe diets of revived classics or modernised classical stories. Although the play ironically received a prize of 8 million lira (£4,000), which Fo again donated to university theatre research, it was to prove to be his last work for Milan's establishment theatre. After touring *La signora* in Scandinavia, Fo disbanded the Compagnia Fo–Rame, and set about finding his own alternative theatre outlets which could reach audiences outside the mainstream.

'For years I have been the court jester of the bourgeoisie,' Fo later told Italian journalists, in what has become a famous and often-quoted utterance, 'hurtling invective in their faces, which they responded to with ignorant laughter. Now I will become the jester of the proletariat. They will become the recipients of my invective.'[50]

CHAPTER 3

THEATRE IN THE SERVICE OF CLASS STRUGGLE 1968–1973

> My opinion of Dario Fo and his work is so negative that I refuse to talk about him. Fo is a kind of plague on the Italian theatre. I should say the worst possible things about him, but this doesn't seem an appropriate time.
>
> (Pier Paolo Pasolini in *Panorama,* after Fo's arrest in Sassari, November 1973.)

The events of May 1968 in Paris had rapid repercussions in Italy. They were compounded by the repercussions of the Vietnam war, the cultural revolution in China, and the various guerilla movements in Latin America and Africa in having a major influence on Italian intellectuals and students. Those on the left were not enamoured by the prospects of compromising with a centre-left government, and took to the streets with students and workers, initially backed by the Italian Communist Party. Franca Rame had become a member of the PCI in 1967, while Fo, though remaining outside the party, supported its tenets from a distance. He aligned himself with Gramsci's emphasis on the importance of popular culture and the guiding role of the intellectual in reaffirming that culture. Giorgio Strehler, following the example of Jean-Louis Barrault at the Théâtre de l'Odéon in Paris, resigned from the Piccolo Teatro in Milan, and set about forming his own collective theatre company outside the state structure. Fo and Rame approached the PCI, assuming that it was backing the new breakthroughs brought about by the student revolts, with a view to setting up a theatre cooperative which would operate through ARCI. This was the party's cultural and recreational wing, which could give them access to the *camere di lavoro* and *case del popolo*, PCI community centres and workers' clubs. As Fo was later to say in an interview with the French newspaper *Libération*:

> the bourgeoisie accepted even our most violent criticisms of them as long as we criticised them inside their own structure, in the same way as the king's court jester was allowed to say the most incisive things to the king, as long as he said them at court, to the courtiers who laughed, applauded and said, 'My, how democratic this king is.' This was a way for the bourgeoisie to show itself how sympathetic and democratic it was . . . But once you go outside this dimension and go and talk to the peasants and the workers, to the exploited, and tell them a few home truths, then you're not accepted . . . If your work's run by the boss, it becomes the boss's work, whereas if it's run by the working class, it's the work of the proletariat, even if it's contradictory and incomplete.[1]

This type of shift from the 'official' theatre to an 'unofficial', alternative circuit was shared by a large number of left-wing European writers after 1968. These included John Arden in the UK, who in his play *The Bagman* expressed a predicament very similar to that outlined by Fo above. *The Bagman* dealt with the necessity for self-management, and for siding with the 'thin men' against the 'fat men', in order to combat what Herbert Marcuse referred to as the 'repressive tolerance' of the establishment. Fo and Rame attempted to use the theatrical talents which had brought them enormous success in Italian mainstream theatre to support class struggle and the revolutionary process which they saw, in the heady and euphoric atmosphere of 1968, as a real and viable alternative to state reform:

> When we got involved with ARCI, it was in the hope that the spirit of 1968 was moving things in a new direction, even though we were well aware of what cooperatives involved, and who was behind the *case del popolo*, and in whose interests they were. We had the illusion that working on a grassroots level, we could change the

organisational structures, and that the PCI had adopted a revolutionary line from the pressure of the student movement and the workers. We saw it as the only possible solution, the only representative of the working class.[2]

Nuova Scena: a new theatre for a new audience

In 1967, Peter Brook's *US* had played in Italy, and had a resounding impact in theatrical circles for its earnest and thought-provoking attempt to bring home the implications of the Vietnam war to middle-class intellectuals. A young Milanese theatre group, the Teatro d'Ottobre, were so impressed by *US* that they spent several months working on an Italian adaptation of the play. They also explored forms of collective, cooperative theatre which American groups like El Teatro Campesino and the Bread and Puppet Theatre had brought to Italy. Fo approached the Teatro d'Ottobre and invited them to play a part in Nuova Scena, the new cooperative he had set up as a private club in order to avoid state censorship and discourage the presence of police in the audience.

In October 1968, Nuova Scena performed Fo's new play, *Grande pantomima con bandiere e pupazzi piccoli e medi* (*Grand Pantomime with Flags and Small and Middle-sized Puppets*). The play opened at the Casa del Popolo of Sant'Egidio in Cesena, a modest beginning for what became a historical event in the context of Italian political theatre. Almost no critics attended the first night, and the audience consisted mostly of local people and PCI sympathisers. The form of the play, with its revue-length sketches which made historical leaps in a matter of moments, and used a two-level stage with actors in black leotards who doubled a large number of emblematic roles, was a return to the 'rough theatre' (to use Brook's term) of *Il dito nell'occhio*. But there was an increase in political charge which made it resemble more the 'Red Revues' of Piscator. Characters were replaced by generalised 'masks' representing Capital, the Confederation of Industry, High Finance, the Church, the People, Rebels and Peasants. The use of puppets, masks, pageantry and masquerade elements resembled *commedia dell'arte*, which Fo affirmed in his opening stage directions. Nonetheless it is worth emphasising, as Sogliuzzo does, that the stagecraft of this and subsequent plays by Fo also stems from a popular, pre-*commedia* tradition:

> Because of his extensive use of mimicry, masks and puppets, Fo's theatre is mistakenly characterised as stemming primarily from *commedia dell'arte*. But *commedia* satirised social stereotypes, whereas Fo's political satire (broad comedy and highly presentational) originated in the period between the tenth and twelfth centuries, the post-feudal age when the Italian peninsula experienced a burst of political freedom; jesters roamed the land with a repertoire of gags and skits celebrating the end of feudalism, and ridiculing the remaining feudal overlords and the Church.[3]

Grande pantomima ridicules the Church, the Monarchy, the Army and Industrialism, representatives of which are born from a giant puppet representing fascism. The play pits these caricatures against a dragon, representing the people, in a constant duel which takes us through a potted political history of Italy from fascism to the economic boom and the age of consumerism. The play suggests that the shadow of fascism still hung over the contemporary Italian political scene. Despite its sprawling, rather inchoate form, which resembles Fo's previous play, *Throw the Lady Out*, it makes its points with wit and economy. It satirises the use of natural disasters like earthquakes to re-entrench and make political capital for the ruling class, in a way which uncannily predicts the aftermath of the earthquake in southern Italy in 1981:

> KING: Yes . . . a great disaster . . . a veritable cataclysm, with several million victims – that'll give us an excuse to organise a campaign of solidarity, fraternity . . . At times like this, everybody suddenly becomes charitable, and the people forget all their resentments in a flash . . . The king – that's me – and the queen – that's her – visit the site of the disaster and console the poor desperate survivors . . . I usually kiss a couple of orphans. Then the

queen bursts into tears, and I shed a few tears myself, in front of the television cameras – and hey presto, it's game, set and match. The nation is overwhelmed by emotion, and cleaves to their national father-figure, and zap, the revolution is put down![4]

The play also hits out at other topical targets, as in its satire of the mass media for its cannibalism of popular culture, and its creation of what the French Situationists referred to as the capitalist 'society of the spectacle' to distract people from examining their social problems and acting accordingly. Mindless advertising jingles are repeated throughout, counterpointing ironically events such as clashes between armed police and demonstrators. As well as attacking the contradictions of the political actions of middle-class intellectuals, the play also initiates a series of representations in Fo's work of the monotony and exhaustion suffered by workers on production lines. In an absurd Monty Python-like sketch, workers are tested for foot prehensility so they can work on a double production line. *Grande pantomima* is deliberately left open-ended, in order to stimulate what became known as the 'third act' in the work of Nuova Scena – debates and discussions with the audience about political issues and popular culture.

Towards the end of 1969 there was some dissension among the ranks of Nuova Scena due to a certain amount of resentment by some of its members about the dominating role played by Fo and Rame. This conflict was never satisfactorily resolved. In *Grande pantomima* Fo and Rame had begun by playing relatively minor roles, but the group soon realised that when they were not on stage the production became rather lacklustre, and their roles gradually increased in size as rehearsals progressed. This led to accusations against Fo and Rame of manipulating the company, perhaps an inevitability given their superior acting talents. The company subsequently divided into three groups. Fo formed one on his own, performing *Mistero buffo,* and another was coordinated by Vittorio Franceschini, writing and performing their own material, which included *MTM*, a satire on automatism on the production line, and *A Dream of the Left,* a portrait of the revolutionary aspirations of a young middle-class intellectual.

Franca Rame participated in a third group which performed two plays written and directed by Fo. These both had long titles – *L'operaio conosce 300 parole, il padrone 1,000: per questo lui è il padrone* (*The Worker Knows 300 Words, the Boss Knows 1000 – That's Why He's the Boss*), and *Legami pure che tanto io spacco tutto lo stesso* (*Chain Me Up and I'll Still Smash Everything*), which consisted of two one-act pieces, co-written with Fo by Franco Loi. *L'operaio* dealt with the necessity of retrieving popular and working-class culture, and included criticisms of the PCI which were not taken kindly. The play was devised for an ensemble cast of 12 actors (including Rame) who play 30 different roles, and the situation of the play is that of a group of workers who are cleaning out an old library in a *casa del popolo* which is being converted into a recreation centre and billiard room. They start leafing through the books and quoting Mao Ze-Dong, Lenin and Gramsci, and as they are stacking the books into large boxes, four scenes from the books 'come alive' and are acted out. One scene deals with Gramsci's visits to factories in Turin while he is trying to form the PCI, and through it the play expresses what has become a cornerstone in Fo's aims in reviving popular theatre:

> The worker is knowledgeable, because he's the vanguard of the people, and the people have a vast culture . . . A large part of it has been destroyed and buried by bourgeois aristocrats and religious power, but it is our duty to rediscover it.[5]

Another section of the play presents the monologue of the mother of Michele Lu Lanzone, a Sicilian activist murdered by the Mafia for encouraging the peasant farmers to appropriate their land. This became a performance vehicle in its own right for Franca Rame, and was frequently presented in Fo's and Rame's later 'direct intervention' plays. The mother, now in a mental asylum, relives her trade-unionist son's death after he discovers a spring in a region stricken by drought, and his comrades find his dead body plugging up the spring. There is also a reconstruction of the Stalinist show trial of the Czech communist Slansky. The play ends with a reconstruction of Mayakovsky's 'suicide' after his satirical plays have virtually been silenced by the Soviet state theatre, and a description of his performances in Soviet factories in which his poem on the death of Lenin becomes a rallying point. The case of Mayakovsky is clearly used as a model for the socialist satirical theatre Fo was inclining towards. The main point of the play was expressed in an old and neglected Communist Party slogan: 'If a poor man asks you for charity, give him tuppence for bread and threepence to buy a book'.[6] It ends with the workers unpacking the books and putting them back on the library shelves.

The PCI was angered by the play's exposure of a few sore points in its current party policies about culture, and saw Fo as biting the hand that was feeding him. The Communist Party newspaper *L'Unità* withdrew a positive review by one of its regular critics, who subsequently resigned, and substituted a notice by an anonymous critic who described the play as 'crude, banal and sentimental, affronting the objectivity of [historical] facts by distorting them.'[7] In a post-play discussion after one performance in Sestri Levante, a representative of ARCI attacked the play for attempting to change the structure of the PCI rather than helping the oppressed. A fiery debate followed in which a tearful Franca Rame accused the PCI of trying to sabotage their attempts to set up an alternative theatre circuit.[8]

Despite some powerful scenes, *L'operaio* suffered from the fact that Fo did not act in it. There was also very little comedy in it, it was often dryly didactic, and it lapsed into gloomy melo-dramatic sentiment on occasions. The highly doctrinaire Marxist line which it pushed also dated it very quickly. It is a prime example of what Fo later referred to as 'un teatro da bruciare' (throw-away theatre),[9] designed to assist the cause of revolution and class consciousness in the 'hot autumn' (*autunno caldo*) of 1969 when the political and cultural activities of the Italian Left were at their peak. David Hirst, whose translation of the play received a production in England by the Yorick Theatre Company in 1985, regards it as 'one of the most original, fascinating and underestimated of Fo's works,'[10] but it was long past its use-by date by 1985.

Legami pure consists of the two one-act pieces *Il telaio* (*The Loom*) and *Il funerale del padrone* (*The Boss's Funeral*). Both were very simply and functionally staged and dealt directly with working-class situations in contemporary Italy, making even more direct criticisms of the PCI. In the first, a communist family who do domestic piecework with weaving looms discover that they have to work 16 hours a day to meet their overheads. Their work is distributed to them by a PCI party official, who makes every effort to convince them to keep working and that they are not being exploited. It is a grotesque comedy of domestic chaos which culminates with the Father going berserk. Exhausted by the work and shocked by the fact that his daughter is sleeping with her boyfriend (a satire on the outmoded male-dominated attitudes present in the PCI), he smashes the looms (which are imaginary, represented by mime) and hits his wife on the head. The Mother (played by Franca Rame) remains staunch in her belief that it is important to follow the precepts to be found in the Communist Party newspaper *L'Unità* even though she never has the time or energy to read it. After she is knocked out, she dreams of a Communist Party shake-up:

> Kick out all the deviationists, whether they're politically motivated or just hangers-on makes no difference . . . This isn't a party for just anyone, pigs and dogs . . . It's not enough just to be exploited, you have to be totally and constantly committed – not just go to Mass on Sundays ![11]

These ironic references to the Catholic church as a source of comparison with the PCI, together with the play's criticisms of the Feste dell'unità (Communist Party summer festivals), led to further attacks by the PCI against Fo and Nuova Scena.

The Boss's Funeral was loosely based on the situation in an occupied factory at the time. A group of workers who have occupied a textiles factory are about to be evicted by a Police Inspector, who appears in the auditorium of the theatre. They decide to put on a play about the funeral of their boss in order to draw attention to their predicament. By showing a group of workers portraying themselves and a group of caricatured

'Influential People', as well as a pantomime Vulture, Fo uses a makeshift agit-prop street-theatre format which reflects the Carnival 'Feast of Fools'. The play-within-the-play satirises industrial pollution and the often appalling working conditions in Italian factories where explosions and accidents were a frequent occurrence. It culminates in a scene which extends the disputed meat-factory sketch in *Canzonissima*. A group of executioners are about to kill a worker, who has been chosen by drawing lots, in order to keep the factory accident figures to a constant daily average. At the last minute the actors, adapting a 'reality' device from the Roman theatre of Seneca's time, substitute a butcher who is about to kill a live goat as part of his daily work. This gives rise to an argument among the actors about the justification of this type of theatrical device (at a time when directors like Jodorowsky and Ortiz in the USA were killing live chickens and rats on stage). As a result, the play is cut short in order to pursue a debate with the audience about whether the animal should be killed.

Loose and minimal in its form, *The Boss's Funeral* shows Fo approaching the type of caricatured street theatre which he was later to use in his own idiosyncratic way in the 'roadshows' which he performed in actual occupied factories. The prominent French theatre critic Bernard Dort was particularly impressed by the play, seeing it as a multi-levelled Pirandellian exercise in theatrical metaphysics in which 'a fiction destroys itself in the course of being acted out and extends into the area of class struggle.'[12] This reading tends to over-emphasise the play's philosophical underpinnings at the expense of its more simple agit-prop purpose.

By this time ARCI were no longer prepared to tolerate the 'provocativeness' of Fo's plays, and refused to allow him to continue using the *camera del lavoro* in Milan. Meanwhile disputes within Nuova Scena on the political line of the company and its organisation along cooperative lines reached a head. The company split up, with one faction, led by Vittorio Franceschini, going its own way, taking half the company's lighting, sound and stage equipment, and retaining the name Nuova Scena. Fo, Rame and a few others were thus left to go their separate way. As Fo later recalled in an article published in 1976:

> When we were at the *camera del lavoro*, at a certain point we were kicked out with the excuse that our theatrical criticisms were dividing the working class. In actual fact it was a space which originated and developed in a way that was too autonomous, and caused trouble because thousands of people with direct connections with the working class were starting to come along ... on their own initiative because they felt it was their theatre.[13]

Although Nuova Scena continued its activities for a further two years under Franceschini, the Nuova Scena period produced little of lasting value apart from *Mistero buffo* and *The Boss's Funeral,* which subsequently received productions outside Italy. The ARCI initiative was short-lived as the PCI's policies were clearly too moderate to accommodate a writer and performer of the status of Fo, who tended to cause controversy in any theatrical context. Fo's absence from the cast of all the plays except *Mistero buffo* meant they had to rely too heavily on Franca Rame to give them theatrical life. The doctrinaire theatrical policy of egalitarian 'socialism in practice' of Nuova Scena was clearly not suited to the theatrical talents of Fo and Rame. As Chiara Valentini commented on both *L'operaio* and *Legami pure* in 1977:

> Fo was probably overcome by the anxiety of producing works of political intervention, and making as many points as possible that could be brought up in the discussions after the play (which were in fact very lively). He was also concerned with presenting critical analyses to a left-wing audience, and rather than restricting himself to exposing the flaws of their adversaries, he wanted to rub their noses in their own flaws.[14]

ARCI subsequently invited the Piccolo Teatro to put on two plays at the *camera del lavoro* in Milan, but after this it became virtually unused, while Fo and Rame sought their own outlets to get across to left-wing and working-class audiences.

La Comune and *Accidental Death of an Anarchist*

In 1970 Fo and Rame formed a new group with the musician Paolo Ciarchi and the administrator Nanni Ricordi, the Collettivo Teatrale 'La Comune'. They organised their own playing spaces within the environment of the 'extra-parliamentary' Left, which had grown along with a spreading disillusionment with the PCI. The PCI in turn was attempting to get rid of what it saw as 'revolutionary extremist' and 'Chinese style' elements. These included the group which had formed around the newspaper *Il Manifesto,* who had approached the party in the wake of the student action. After the 'hot autumn' of 1969, in which the Italian Left went onto the offensive, the student movement had begun to dissipate. Militants on the outer Left, while still claiming to maintain contacts with the working class, began to split into relatively small groups reflecting Marxist-Leninist, Maoist and other ideologies.

The year 1969 had also seen the first outbreaks of terrorism in Italy, a further incentive for the PCI to exert a 'clean-up' operation. Many of these terrorist attacks, like the bomb in the Banca Nazionale dell'Agricoltura in Piazza Fontana in Milan in December 1969, on which Fo was to base his play *Accidental Death of an Anarchist,* proved to be the work of right-wing terrorists, supported by the Italian Secret Services. In the context of this shifting ground among the Italian Left, La Comune stated its aims as 'putting our work at the service of the class movement, which doesn't mean slotting into existing set-ups, but contributing to the movement, being present in it, changing with it and its struggles and real needs.'[15] But according to Cappa and Nepoli's critical survey of Fo's plays, La Comune's new alternative circuit catered to a larger represen-tation of students and a smaller proportion of the working class than Nuova Scena and the ARCI circuit,[16] which was perhaps to be expected, given its extra-parliamentary ambience.

In October 1970 La Comune took over an abandoned workshop (*capannone*) in via Colletta, in a working-class suburb of Milan, which was to be their base for three years. They converted it into a type of community theatre which became a rallying point for various extra-parliamentary groups in Milan. Fo and Rame were careful not to become mouthpieces for any of these groups, remaining part of an autonomous cultural organisation which was involved in a Marxist–Leninist movement of class struggle in its broadest sense. In any case, Fo's work entered its most overtly political, revolutionary phase, as the first play La Comune presented at the Capannone di via Colletta showed. Entitled *Vorrei morire stasera se dovessi pensare che non è servito a niente* (*I'd Rather Die Tonight If I Had To Think It Had All Been In Vain*), it was put together and presented by a cast of six after only a day's rehearsal, as a response to the 'Black September' terrorist events in the Middle East. The title came from a poem about the Italian Resistance by Renata Viganò, and it was subtitled 'Resistance: the Italian and Palestinian People Speak'.

The first act consisted of readings, songs and mimes based on accounts by Italian partisans of their experiences, and the second act readings and performances of personal testaments by members of the Palestinian liberation movement. Highlights of the first part included a monologue by Franca Rame about Luisa, a woman from Bologna who is raped and tortured by fascists, but whose faith in Communism is unshaken, and a monologue in dialect by Fo about the partisan Angiolino Bertoli, who has to hide in a septic tank during a raid on an army barracks. The second part included two animal fables, another feature which was to refigure in subsequent Fo work. In one the Russian bear helps the weaker animals of the Middle East against the US tiger, but ends up striking a bargain with the tiger. The other pitted the rooster of Amman against the pigs of King Hussein. The play was staged in a very rudimentary way, with actors holding scripts and using microphones. It had a direct, 'living newspaper' form, in the vein of 'theatre of intervention', commenting on political events in the Middle East and relating them to historical struggles in Italy. Discussions afterwards included critiques of the USSR and more criticism of the PCI, which caused the reviewer in the PCI weekly *Rinascita*, Edoardo Fadini, to ask who Fo expected to listen to him.[17] But according to Valentini, 18 thousand spectators came to see the play in the course of a month.[18] The play typified what Fo was later to state in an interview with the Italian *Playboy* magazine:

> Our theatre is a throwaway theatre [*un teatro da bruciare*], a theatre which won't go down in bourgeois history, but which is useful, like a newspaper article, a debate or a political action.[19]

Ironically, Fo's next play 'went down in history' as his most widely performed play all over the world, and a 'classic' of twentieth-century theatre. By 1991, when *Accidental Death of an Anarchist* was revived in a new version at the National Theatre in London, it had been performed in 41 countries, including Argentina, Chile, South Africa, South Korea and Romania,[20] and had provoked controversy and police action in some of these countries. The play took 'throwaway theatre' much deeper and much closer to the root causes of Italy's political malaise, and went a good deal further than didactic documentary theatre. It exemplified Fo's view of this type of theatre:

> it shouldn't be just a documentary theatre of cold information, a theatre which, for all the respect I have for Piscator, doesn't get to the bottom of things. There must also be a vast mechanism to make people laugh about dramatic events.[21]

Morte accidentale di un anarchico (*Accidental Death of an Anarchist*) did precisely this. Described by Fo as 'a grotesque farce about a tragic farce', it opened at the via Colletta theatre in December 1970. This was almost exactly a year after the Piazza Fontana bombs had shaken the Italian public and revealed a network of corruption, intrigue and unexplained contradictions in its wake. Fo's play was a response to what had become known as the 'strategy of tension' in Italy, in which the new Christian Democrat government, having deposed the centre-left coalition, tried to crack down on the Left and dissipate its forces. Since 1969, according to statistics quoted in the play, there had been 173 bomb attacks in Italy, 102 of which had been proved to have been organised by fascists. More than half the remaining

71 appeared to have been organised by the Right with the intention of bringing suspicion and blame on the Left. In this situation, La Comune set about providing a theatre of 'counter-information' against the widespread discrediting of the Left in the press and on television. This had reached its apex in the case of Giuseppe Pinelli, a Milanese anarchist railway employee charged with placing bombs in the Milan railway station in 1969, and then charged with the bombing in Piazza Fontana, which had killed 17 people and injured 100. Pinelli had been charged together with Pietro Valpreda, a Roman anarchist ballet dancer, who languished in prison for nearly ten years (and whose prison notes were later published in Italy and in an English translation). On 15 December 1969, Pinelli died after 'falling' from a fourth-floor window of the Milan police station where he was being interrogated. As Fo wrote in his introduction to *Accidental Death of an Anarchist*:

> In the spring of 1970 the comrades who came to see our plays urged us to write a full-length play about the Milan bombs and the murder of Pinelli, discussing their causes and political consequences. The reason for this was the fearful vacuum of information about the problem. After the initial shock, the press was silent, and the official left-wing newspapers, especially *L'Unità,* hadn't put themselves out beyond the odd sporadic comment like 'It's a disconcerting business.'[22]

Shortly after this a book entitled *La strage di stato* (*The State Massacre*) appeared, published by the left-wing printing house Samona-Savelli and written anonymously, documenting all the principal facts of the Pinelli 'defenestration' and the 'strategy of tension'. This book, which was later published in English as *Italian State Massacre* by Libertaria, together with legal documents and court transcripts of the Pinelli inquiry, became the source material for Fo and La Comune for their play. Fo set out to craft 'a farce as painfully grotesque as the action of the magistrates and the contradictions in the official statements.'[23]

At the same time as the play opened, in December 1970, a lawsuit had just begun, instigated by Inspector Calabresi, who had been in charge of the Pinelli case (and who was later assassinated in 1972), against the extra-parliamentary Left's newspaper *Lotta Continua,* which had accused him of causing Pinelli's death. This meant that Fo's play became a direct source of information and a discussion point for the whole Pinelli affair, which had had a severe impact on the Italian Left. The play was constantly updated, each performance including reports on the day's hearing in the *Lotta Continua* case, and in its various versions, over a period of four years, the play was seen by more than a million people in Italy.[24] It also became Fo's most internationally celebrated work.

In *Accidental Death of an Anarchist* Fo created for himself one of his most extraordinarily comic and 'histrionic' roles, that of a 'Maniac' (*Matto*) who infiltrates the Milan police headquarters. He goes through a number of impersonations of different characters in his strategy to force the police to admit to the ludicrous illogicality of their version of Pinelli's 'leap' and to confess their responsibility for his death. As Pina Piccolo has indicated, both the play's central character and general situation owe something to Gogol's play *The Government Inspector*[25] in which a visiting inspector invokes terror in a provincial Russian government office. But Fo raises the stakes of Gogol's game considerably to strike at the heart of the Italian state. In his opinion, Gogol's play

> doesn't make you laugh. Everything resolves itself in ticklish levity, because it is totally lacking in tragedy and indignation. Everything is resolved in a joke against petty provincial power rather than imperial power. Maybe that has some sense in contemporary Russia, but it's no coincidence that the Tsar rescued Gogol, because he knew the play was satirising petty, low-grade bureaucrats from the provinces, not the capital. The Tsar enjoyed the play immensely because it satirised petty, inept, ignorant, boorish bureaucrats, and left the emperor and all his apparatus alone; striking against intermediaries is merely mediocre.[26]

Fo's Maniac ('I'm a maniac, not a fool – watch your terminology,'[27] he says at one point) combines some of the blustering farcical antics of Il Lungo's encounter with state bureaucracy in *Gli arcangeli non giocono al flipper* with the medieval figure of the disconcerting, truth-telling Madman in *Mistero buffo*. But above all he is a representation of Fo himself in his multifarious guises as clown, political pamphleteer, *giullare,* stand-up comic, quick-change artist and political satirist. In the first scene he is interrogated by an Inspector after being charged with impersonating a psychiatrist, and admits that he has got his training from being a mental patient in a number of asylums. He also reveals that he suffers from 'impersonation mania', otherwise known as 'histrionic mania':

> from the Greek 'istriones', meaning actor. Acting's a hobby of mine you see, but I never do the same part twice. I'm a great believer in living theatre, so I need a company of real people who don't know they're acting. I wouldn't be able to pay them, anyway, since I'm always broke. I did apply for an arts council grant, but I haven't got the right political connections.[28]

This thinly-veiled meta-theatrical distinction between character and actor was not a ruse to bluff Italian audiences. Nor was Fo's attempt to provide a 'historical' framework to the play in a spoken prologue which stated that the action takes place in New York in the 1920s and refers to the death by defenestration of an Italian anarchist called Salseda. This historical event is used merely as a source of ironic detachment and there is no attempt to sustain it throughout the play.

The Maniac threatens to jump out the window if the exasperated Inspector lets him go, and proceeds to impersonate a certain Inspector Pietro Anghiari – a reference to Fo's previous unperformed play about this historical character from the crusades. He also succeeds in creating an argument, which later comes to blows, between the Inspector and a 'Sporty' Inspector by joking about the latter's fascist connections. After stealing the Inspector's coat and briefcase, the Maniac impersonates an examining magistrate who has come to reopen the inquiry into the anarchist's death. In this guise, he forces the 'Sporty' Inspector and the Superintendent (who appears to be based on

Calabresi, although Fo deliberately doesn't give any of his characters' names) to act out their roles in events leading up to the anarchist's death. The Maniac acts the part of the anarchist, correcting the police's version from the transcripts of the interrogation, which he has stolen from the Inspector's office. The police's version of the anarchist's death is that it was caused by a 'raptus': 'an exasperated form of suicidal anguish which can affect psychologically normal individuals if provoked by some form of violent anxiety or desperation.'[29]

In trying to ascertain the cause of this anxiety or desperation, the Maniac proceeds to pick holes in the police's two different versions (both of which are based on actual police statements to the Italian media), pointing out their glaring inconsistencies. He intimidates them into admitting that their actions were not free of guilt, and then convinces them that the government wants both the Superintendent's and the 'Sporty' Inspector's heads, quoting 'an English saying that goes like this: "the master sets his mastiffs on the serfs. If the serfs complain to the king, the master kills the dogs to appease them." '[30] He then plays on the two policemen's despair to induce them to jump out the window like the anarchist (proving the 'raptus' theory). They are about to do so, such is the skill of the Maniac's persuasions, when they are interrupted by a Constable. At this point the Maniac says he has been bluffing them, resorting to the same 'tricks and traps' they used on the anarchist in faking a story that the Roman anarchist ballet dancer (Valpreda) had confessed he had planted the bombs. As for the English saying, 'if anything, it's the other way round − if the dog dies, the king immediately sends telegrams of condolence to the master, and smothers the dog in decorations!'[31] The Maniac then reverses his strategy and sets about trying to help the police to come through his interrogation unscathed by juggling their two versions to prove that their interrogations had no effect on the anarchist's death. In a brilliantly farcical build-up to the end of the first act, the Maniac goads the police into inventing a story which depicts them as kindly sympathising with the anarchist and trying to cheer him up and make him 'feel at home' (since the anarchist group he belonged to was infiltrated by police informers). This culminates in the Maniac, the Super-intendent, the 'Sporty' Inspector and the Constable lustily singing the anarchist song 'Our home is the whole wide world'. This ironic *coup de théâtre* would have been remem-bered by some of the play's audiences from *Ci ragiono e canto*. It pushes Fo's 'satirical licence' to the utmost in giving the police a dose of their own medicine.

In the course of helping the policemen to construct a version of the anarchist's 'fall' which exonerates them from any suspicion, the Maniac comes up with the following hilarious theory. After the Constable states he tried to save the anarchist from jumping by grabbing his foot, but was left with only a shoe in his hand, the Maniac extrapolates:

MANIAC: But in this statement here, there's clear indica-tion that when the anarchist was on the ground dying in the courtyard, he still had both his shoes on. On-the-spot witnesses testified to that, and there was a reporter from L'Unità among them, as well as a few other passing journalists!

INSPECTOR: That's odd . . .

MANIAC: It certainly is! The least this speedy Gonzales could've done in the circumstances was to rush down the stairs, get to a landing on the second floor, stick his head out the window as the suicide came flying past, slip the shoe back on his foot in mid-flight, and then shoot back up like a rocket to the fourth floor to be there at the same time as the falling man hit the ground.

SUPERINTENDENT: There you go again, being sarcastic!

MANIAC: I take your point – I just can't help it, I'm sorry. So, we're stuck with three shoes. You don't happen to remember if he was a triped by any chance?

SUPERINTENDENT: Who?

MANIAC: The railwayman, the suicide – if he had three feet, it logically follows that he'd've been wearing three shoes.

SUPERINTENDENT (*annoyed*): No, he was not a triped.

MANIAC: Please don't get in a huff – don't forget you can expect anything from an anarchist, even that! . . . It's possible that one of his shoes was too big for him, and he hadn't got any stuffing handy, so he slipped on another, smaller shoe first, and then put on the one that was too big.

INSPECTOR: Two shoes on the same foot?

MANIAC: Why not? What's so unusual about that? It could've even been a galosh – you know those rubber overshoes people used to wear?

SUPERINTENDENT: 'Used to' is right.

MANIAC: Some people still wear them – do you know what I think? What came off in the constable's hand wasn't a shoe at all, it was a galosh!

INSPECTOR: No, it's too ridiculous for words – an anachist wearing galoshes? No self-respecting anarchist would be seen dead in those antiquated, conservative things.[32]

This scene provides a climax to the absurd logic which Fo, in the guise of the Maniac disguised as an examining magistrate, uses to point out the grotesquely farcical lengths to which the Italian police went to exonerate themselves from any responsibility for Pinelli's death. It also exposed their refusal to follow up any leads pointing to the right wing in their investigations of the Piazza Fontana bombs. The bombs were in fact subsequently proved to be the work of two fascists, Franco Freda and Giovanni Ventura, who, as in the case of a number of other bomb attacks in the 1970s, were acting under orders from the Italian Secret Service. The ensuing trial dragged on for more than 12 years, with the police, with characteristic absurdity, attempting to prove that the fascists were working in collaboration with anarchists. Valpreda, who had been depicted in the Italian press as a 'monster', was never completely exonerated, and was accused of 'subversive associations' largely in order to cover up the incompetence of the Italian police and their collusion with right-wing elements in dealing with the case. (There were various unexplained incidents such as the facility with which Ventura and Freda were able to escape from custody and leave the country.)

It is important to emphasise that the police characters in *Accidental Death of an Anarchist* are no mere buffoonish caricatures or stereotypes – a factor which makes many foreign productions of the play inept. Although Fo makes them the butts of comedy and farce, this derives from the inconsistencies of their statements and behaviour, which is in fact that of devious, dangerous types who show the abuses of power the police exerted in brazenly cracking down on the Italian Left. This was frequently done without a shred of evidence, and often involved resorting to wildly trumped-up accusations. In his review in *The Independent* of the 1991 National Theatre production, for example, Paul Taylor commented: 'What hurts the drama . . . is that there is no contest. It's like watching people with no legs, so to speak, being repeatedly out-dribbled by a soccer genius, a pleasure which soon wears off . . . The drama needs some opposition.'[33] This pinpoints a structural imbalance which occurs in a number of Fo's plays, where his own and Rame's virtuoso roles are far stronger than the rest of the company's subsidiary parts. (Rame did not perform in *Accidental Death of an Anarchist*.) But it also points to a tendency in productions outside Italy to reduce the police characters to farcical ciphers, destroying the dramatic tension the play derives from its political context. As Fo has pointed out, in his production of *Anarchist*,

> I didn't have great actors, but they worked extremely well because they were all good support actors [*spalle*], and for support actors to work well they have to be cold, almost detached . . . It doesn't matter if they don't have charisma or charm. The important thing is to maintain the tempo set by the lead actor, and to be good at following the leader, like in a bicycle race.[34]

The main challenge for productions of *Accidental Death* is to maintain the play's tightly-wound spiral of dramatic tension by making the police characters credible and menacing as well as gullible and foolish, rather than simply foils and stooges for the Maniac's series of confidence tricks. As Joylynn Wing has usefully pointed out in her analysis of the play, which unfortunately refers to Gavin Richards' 1980 British adaptation rather than Fo's original text, the police cover-up becomes equated with illusionistic theatre. The illusion is exposed and subverted by the Maniac's numerous disguises and improvisations, but it is important for the actors to preserve the realistic basis of the play:

> It becomes the task of the troupe onstage (led by the Maniac in the guise of an investigating judge) to create a standard realistic representation, featuring a believable plot with which the audience can identify. The opposition/rupture lies in the fact that what they so desperately try to make believable is patently untrue: the anarchist didn't jump – he was pushed. Thus a particular mode of theatrical represen-tation (realistic) becomes inextricably implicated with its counterpart in politics (the believable cover-up).[35]

As with most of Fo's plays, this realistic basis of the play also has many affinities with Bakhtin's concept of 'grotesque realism'. As Pina Piccolo has noted, its entire situation is based on a carnivalesque 'world upside down' situation.[36] A certified lunatic who has already impersonated an army captain, a naval engineer, a surgeon and a bishop, succeeds in wreaking havoc in a police station by impersonating a magistrate, then a forensic expert, and finally a bishop, and throws a number of criminal charge sheets out the window in the process. But despite the play's anarchic situation, Fo does not show any undue sympathy for the anarchist characters. He depicts them as an insignificant group of extremists whose organisation was so chaotic that they were incapable of planning or carrying out an operation on the scale of the Piazza Fontana bombings – an operation which, as one of the Inspectors lets slip, required 'military precision'. The play's audience was aware of the serious implications of the 'strategy of tension', and it is a measure of Fo's achievement that he was able to turn the situation into a vehicle for madcap farce and popular comedy. The play distances the tragic implications of the situation in order to forestall the audience's empathy – which is one of the reasons the Maniac continually changes his disguise – and make them think seriously about the political implications of the play. As Fo later wrote in his preface to a sequel to the play:

> this monstrous tragic farce which goes under the name of 'state massacre', presented courtesy of the 'democratic' organs of the state . . . had the programmed result of a vast 'isolation campaign' of workers' struggles and the 'obliter-ation' of their more militant activists.[37]

The play's indictment of police behaviour takes a more serious turn with the entry of a woman Journalist, who is based on Camilla Cederna, a reporter for the weekly magazine *L'Espresso,* who unearthed some embarrassing facts about the Pinelli affair. (Cederna, who is referred to as 'Maria Feletti' in the play, died in 1997.) Her hard line of questioning, however, is counterbalanced by a great deal of farcical, slapstick stage business caused by the Maniac's change of disguise to hide the presence of the 'examining magistrate'. He dons a false moustache, an eyepatch (from under which he produces a glass eye), and a 'false' artificial hand and leg to become 'Captain Marcantonio Piccini from forensic research'. As Wing has commented, Piccini is

> a preposterous conglomeration of such blatantly bogus body parts that he is transposed into a virtual marionette. . . . As the scene builds, it becomes increasingly evident that the grotesquely corrupted body of the 'Maniac' and the body politic are theatrical reflections of each other.[38]

While the Journalist reveals disquieting facts like the bruise on the back of the anarchist's neck which had nothing to do with his 'fall', and the police calling an ambulance five minutes before the alleged time of this 'fall', the Maniac substantiates her interpretation of events while pretending to be protecting the police. His ruse is made more difficult by the entry of the Inspector who interrogated the Maniac at the beginning of the play, a forensic expert who brings in a facsimile of the Piazza Fontana bomb. The Inspector recognises the Maniac, and has to be gagged and even injected by his colleagues to prevent him from giving the game away to the Journalist, in a double bluff which occasions stage business deriving from Fo's earlier farces. The play uses a provocative, Pirandello-like device after the Journalist questions the police about their use of intelligence infiltrators in left-wing extra-parliamentary groups:

> SUPERINTENDENT: . . . I don't mind telling you we've got a few planted in the audience tonight, in the normal way – would you like to see them?
> *He claps. We hear voices from various points in the stalls.*
> VOICES: Yes sir! What are your orders? *The* MANIAC *laughs and turns to the audience.*
> MANIAC: It's all right, don't worry, they're only actors. The real ones are sitting tight and keeping out of sight![39]

This sequence – which was cut from both British versions of the play – emphasises in satirical form the constant threat of police intervention Fo and his company underwent during the tour of *Accidental Death of an Anarchist*. Despite the fact that it was frequently performed in large arenas like sports stadiums, which required the use of microphones by the actors in an atmosphere that emulated that of a rock concert, there were usually police searches of the audience at the door. The Flying Squad intervened more than once, and there were anonymous bomb threats, proof of both the vulnerability of La Comune and their predominantly left-wing audiences, and the disturbing impact of the play on the police and right-wing factions in Italy. The scene also showed the difference between Fo's use of meta-theatrical devices and Pirandello's. As Fo commented to a US interviewer in 1987 about Pirandello:

> The emotional climates of our plays are different. Pirandello is a pessimist. His plays wound. They pile catastrophe up on catastrophe. You leave the theatre troubled and distressed. Pirandello and I deal with the same themes but I'm an optimist. Even when I face tragedy in my plays, I face it with a positive mental outlook. It's a question of personality, not philosophy.[40]

These comments are particularly appropriate to *Accidental Death*, which also 'piles catastrophe upon catastrophe', but Fo deals with a tragic situation in terms of farce. Rather than wanting to trouble his audience, he wants to make them laugh, but he also wants them to feel indignant about the cover-ups and miscarriages of justice perpetrated by the Italian police force, as well as the surveillance and intimidation of left-wing groups by police and intelligence services.

The farcical capers of the play's situation reach a climax when the Maniac is stripped of his 'forensic' disguise, and proceeds to impersonate a Bishop who is collaborating with the police. This disguise – which was cut in the first English version of the play – enables Fo to broaden the implications of the play's situation. It satirises the church, but also discusses the implications of scandal, which, as the Bishop states, is used as 'the fertiliser of social democracy'.[41] The Bishop refers to the Profumo scandal in Britain as an example of the 'catharsis of indignation' which scandals cause. He also refers to their use by governments to re-entrench their power by creating red herrings which distract the political consciousness of the people, who are content to see the state washing its dirty linen in public. The Inspector, who has recognised the Maniac, then produces a gun, and handcuffs all the other characters so he can unmask the 'Bishop'. This ruse backfires, since the revelation of the Maniac's psychiatric record means that under Italian law he cannot be incriminated: 'Italian lunatics are like the sacred cow in India – you so much as touch them and you get lynched!'[42] The play ends with the Maniac producing a detonator for the facsimile bomb, as well as a tape recorder with which he has been recording the entire proceedings, and threatening to circulate the tape in order to 'cause a scandal ... Give Italians a chance to emulate their English and American social democrat counterparts! Then we can face the world and tell them the real reason we walk around with our noses in the air because we're up to our necks in the shit!'[43] This is Fo's definitive conclusion to the play, but as Chiara Valentini has commented:

Like *Mistero buffo*, *Anarchist* grew and developed over a period of years, enriched continually by new situations and characters, in this case taken not from medieval texts but from the current events of the strategy of tension which Italy was experiencing day by day. As a member of the audience ironically commented during a discussion after a performance at Forlimpopoli, 'What Fo has shown us this time is a *mistero buffo,* only we can understand this mystery perfectly.'[44]

It is worth describing the original ending of the play, as two different endings were mixed up, altered and re-elaborated in the first London production of the play. In Fo's first version of the play, after the Maniac produces the detonator to the bomb, he threatens to blow up the police and the Journalist and jump out the window. There is a blackout and an explosion offstage, and noise from the courtyard below indicates that the Maniac has jumped. The Journalist interviews the Superintendent and the Inspectors about this new 'jump', and they immediately come up again with the 'raptus' theory. After the Journalist rushes off to take the news to her newspaper, a man with a beard, who 'resembles' the Maniac, enters. He reveals that he is the 'real' examining magistrate, and when this indeed proves to be the case (the beard is real), proceedings begin over again before the play is thrown open to the audience for discussion. In his second version, Fo pruned this ending, since the explosion of the bomb seemed an inappropriate stage device to resolve the situation, as did the destruction of the illusionistic framework of the play by having the Maniac actor reappear. In the second version, the Maniac simply reveals his tape recording of proceedings, and announces he is taking it to the media. In leaving the ending relatively unresolved, the play avoided any sort of catharsis. As Fo later explained:

> We don't want to liberate the indignation of the people who come along. We want them to keep their anger inside them, and not be freed of it, so that they can take action on events, and get involved in the struggle . . . Anger and hatred must become conscious action in collaboration with others, and not the individual letting off steam in an impotent way. The great weapon of satire and the grotesque – a weapon always used by the people in their struggle against

the dominant classes – finds further verification in its enormous possibilities of penetration.[45]

To close the play by tying up loose ends would be mirroring the use of 'catharsis' in state scandals. Fo wanted the 'stink' provoked by the Pinelli affair and the 'strategy of tension' to remain in the air. In leaving the audience's anger and indignation without an outlet, Fo and La Comune hoped, as Brecht did in his didactic plays, to stimulate a desire for political change. Discussions after the play tended to deal with the need for a revolutionary strategy and a 'counter-power' developed on Marxist-Leninist lines against the Christian Democrat state. The play was written as a response to a political need in the Italian Left, and remains part of Fo's 'throwaway', journalistic theatre of 'counter-information', written for a specific purpose to discuss a particular and pressing political problem. It is worthy of note that Fo has never attempted to revive the play himself, although he did at one stage plan a film version which never materialised. As Valentini commented:

> *Anarchist*, like *Mistero buffo* before it, represents a form of direct political intervention, in which Fo demonstrates fully that a different, non-middle-class, popular theatre can develop outside traditional theatres and circuits. The relationship with a politically committed, alternative, revolutionary audience did not result in meaningless shorthand or a condescending intellectual operation. *Anarchist* is a work of information and propaganda, but at the same time the most effective possible response to an audience which demanded current, topical, political subjects. *Anarchist* completely refuted the accusations made by many on both the Right and the Left that Fo's plays are simply propaganda vehicles preaching to the converted.[46]

In the course of its extensive tour of Italy, the play's title was changed to *Accidental Death of an Anarchist and Other Subversives* to incorporate the news of the death of the well-known left-wing publisher Giangiacomo Feltrinelli. (Feltrinelli was found dead under an electricity pylon with unexploded dynamite next to his body which appeared to have been planted.) This was further indication of the predominantly topical, documentary nature of the play, and its attempt to engage audiences in active discussion about immediate political issues.

Political documentaries

Part of La Comune's attempt to stimulate revolutionary strategy and build a revolutionary party involved research into the history of the Italian working-class movement. They produced a couple of pamphlets on the subject, before beginning research for a new play based on a book by Renzo Del Carria, *Proletari senza revoluzione (Proletarians without Revolution)*. The result, *Tutti uniti! Tutti insieme! Ma scusa, quello non è il padrone? (United We Stand! All Together Now! Oops, Isn't That the Boss?)*, was considered by Franca Rame to be Fo's best play after *Mistero buffo* and *Accidental Death*.[47] It was first performed at the Casa del Popolo in Varese in March 1971, and subsequently toured Italy together with *Accidental Death*.

Subtitled 'Workers' Struggles 1911–1922', the play dealt with the history of Italian working-class struggle in those years, the period of the Great War, the reformist policies of the Italian Socialist Party, the activities of Gramsci and the birth of the Communist Party, and the advent of fascism. It set out to illustrate Gramsci's dictum of 'knowing where we come from in order to know where we're going to', and it is one of Fo's more didactic plays, using placards, songs and discussions. But it went beyond the somewhat arid seriousness of *L'operaio conosce 300 parole* in using comedy and farce. In dealing with the betrayal of the workers' struggles by the PSI and the trade unions during the Turin factory occupations of 1920, the play covers similar ground to that of Trevor Griffiths' play about Gramsci, *Occupations*. Historical events are filtered through a series of Brechtian chronological flashbacks involving Fo's central character, Antonia (played by Franca Rame – Fo did not act in the play).

Antonia is a dressmaker who develops from being a naive representative of the world of high fashion into a revolutionary activist. Her character is based on the *commedia dell'arte* character of the *'étourdie'* (scatterbrain), a type of vamp who, as she becomes politically conscious, uses her 'mask' in a calculated way. Her husband, Norberto, a militant in the revolutionary wing of the Italian Socialist Party, is killed by a fascist squad, and Antonia, pretending to be a police informer, inveigles her way into police headquarters. A top-level collaborationist meeting is taking place between a trade unionist, an industrialist's wife, a police superintendent, a colonel and a fascist, and Antonia avenges her husband by shooting the fascist. The body is dumped in the same rubbish tip where Norberto was shot along with 20 other comrades. The play ends with a monologue by Antonia, in which she regrets the fact that she has killed 'the dog instead of the masters', realising that killing a fascist won't change the system, and that anger without rationality is not a means of constructive action.

The play drew implicit parallels between the Socialist Party before the Livorno split (when the Italian Communist Party was formed) and the reformist policies of the PCI current in the 1970s. It also urged a divided and increasingly ghettoised Left to 'build the revolutionary party', to use the words of the Trotskyist militant in Trevor Griffiths' play *The Party,* which dealt with similar arguments to Fo's play in a contemporary 1970s setting. Despite its serious political message and the depth of its central character (Rame was on stage virtually throughout the entire play), the play used a number of farcical devices and gags to leaven the dogma. But according to Paolo Puppa, there was an imbalance between the detailed historical and bibliographical research that lay behind it, and its use of popular theatrical forms to present this material:

> All the apparently exclusively theatrical solutions derived from *divertissement* and gratuitous *pochades* were a response to the need to translate the results of the historical inventory into an elementary, but second-hand form. The detailed and systematic reconstruction of the historical period was deliberately transferred into low and banal theatrical forms: the Libyan campaigns of 1911, the Second World War, the clashes between interventionists and their adversaries, the

revolutionary movements of 1917, the factory occupations, the middle-class panic, the founding of the PCI in 1921, the march on Rome in 1922, the conflicts between the different currents of the Socialist Party, the debates in the workers' movement, the various different trade union hypotheses. All these national events (which were continually linked to external international events such as the October Revolution, the crises of the liberal regime and the explosive contradictions in the capitalist system, and the struggle of the masses against the bourgeois fascist recovery) were translated into the style of the theatrical tradition of *avanspettacolo*. This was combined with a reliance on a chorus with placards to raise the register from a *sermo rusticus* into a *sermo gravis*, in a solid binary structure which was the rhetorical antithesis of agit-prop theatre.[48]

In one scene, in which Antonio visits Norberto in prison in 1917, Norberto is represented by a saxophone, which indicates his various responses by different intonations – a gag later used (with a clarinet) in *Trumpets and Raspberries*. The play also used masks for some characters, such as carabinieri, fascists and an industrialist's wife, and Antonia anticipated Rame's later female protagonists in refusing to be a 'wife who is all house, kitchen, church and bed'. The play again antagonised the PCI, as well as the PSI (Italian Socialist Party) in its portrayals of the leaders Togliatti and Gramsci. In a discussion after one performance in Trieste attended by local PCI members, the company and the audience almost came to blows.

Between 1971 and 1972, La Comune intensified its political interventions, using the via Colletta theatre as a forum for political discussions, and continuing its criticism of the policies of the PCI. The level of these debates was taken to an extreme in *Morte e resurrezione di un pupazzo* (*Death and Resurrection of a Puppet*), an updated rewrite of *Grande pantomima*. Fo, wearing a priest's robes and a mask, played the part of the PCI leader Palmiro Togliatti, who had died in 1964. The play used puppets to contrast Togliatti's policies with those of Lenin and Mao Ze-Dong, presenting him as an epitome of the PCI's revisionism.

In an aggressively satirical style, it attacked American imperialism, the upsurge of fascism in Italy and right-wing terrorism, using a format similar to that used by the US theatre group the Bread and Puppet Theatre.

According to Valentini, the students and militants of the ultra-left were highly entertained, but the workers and agriculturalists, many of whom had fond memories of Togliatti, were not. The play was refused permission to be performed in council-run theatres and sports stadiums in cities such as Pisa, Reggio Emilia and Bologna, which had left-wing local governments. Its hard-line satire and criticism of Togliatti were later reconsidered by La Comune, who admitted that the play was a 'tactical error' in its attack on a figure who had had a considerable grassroots, popular following.[49]

In their work with Nuova Scena and La Comune, Fo and Paolo Ciarchi had continued to explore the popular, militant, peasant and worker's songs they had explored in *Ci ragiono e canto*. Nearly all of Fo's plays during this period included songs which often interrupted the action in Brechtian fashion. *Morte e resurrezione di un pupazzo* included one song in particular, 'La grande quercia' (The Great Oak), which refers to the 'great oak' of capitalism and imperialism being felled by an army of worker-ants, which became something of a political anthem. In his introduction to his 1977 collection of Fo's songs and ballads, Lanfranco Binni singles out this song as a marker of Fo's militancy, in which

> the musical direction has become unified with the words of the song, drawing on a long tradition, and carrying it a long way, into the hearts of the struggling people, and living in their conception of the world and in the conscience of the people's culture and its enormous creative force. It is no longer Dario Fo solo, with his instinctive attraction to the 'low life' that causes him to laugh at the misery of bourgeois culture. It is a Dario Fo who identifies deeply with the force of political consciousness, the process of revolutionary transformation through which the people are constructing their own unity . . . [He has shifted] from

an individual dimension to a choral, collective dimension, from an instinctively anti-bourgeois conception of the world to the understanding that in every society that is divided into classes there can be only two points of view: the bourgeois view and the proletarian view.[50]

Viewed in retrospect, Binni's rather simplistic, doctrinaire Marxist rhetoric suggests that 'La grande quercia' could be seen as something of a low point in Fo's songwriting. During this period of La Comune's work, there was a tendency for the collective ideological solemnity and solidarity of anthemic choral posturing to take over from the individuality, wit, complexity and distinctive satirical charm of Fo's earlier songwriting in the 1950s and 1960s. His shift from comic, satirical and individualistic songs to collective political solidarity songs also marks a shift from *musica leggera* (literally light music, or pop music) to *musica popolare* (people's music).

Morte e resurrezione di un pupazzo was followed by *Fedayn,* subtitled 'The Palestinian People's Struggle through its Culture and Songs', which was first performed in the Capannone di via Colletta in January 1972. This was a further development of the Palestinian documentary *Vorrei morire* in which La Comune worked directly with eight members of the Popular Democratic Front for the Liberation of Palestine (PLF), who appeared in the play. A series of autobiographical accounts by Palestinian guerillas (introduced and read in Italian translation by Franca Rame) were presented with slides, mimes and songs. The play's support of the PLF line in the interests of internationalism provoked considerable controversy among the Italian Left, especially for its criticism of the Al Fatah movement. La Comune eventually issued a statement admitting they had 'confronted the internal problems of the Palestinian resistance movement too directly, in a situation of general lack of information.'[51] This play was followed by another documentary drama about the death of Feltrinelli, *Traliccio di stato* (*State Pylon*), written and staged by La Comune and the mime Albert Vidal, in which Fo's role was that of an adviser.

At about this time La Comune's political activities extended into the area of providing help for political prisoners detained under suspicion of terrorist and related offences. This organisation, called Soccorso Rosso (Red Aid), in which Franca Rame was particularly active, had about 3,000 supporting members recruited from La Comune's audiences. Its task was to write letters and send packages and books to prisoners, and maintain contacts with their families and lawyers. Funds for the organisation were collected after performances at the via Colletta. Needless to say, La Comune did not receive any government funding, but their productions were nonetheless sufficiently popular and successful to be able to donate the proceeds of many of their performances to occupied factories and other deserving causes.

La Comune's political activities during this period tended to overshadow their theatrical output, which largely consisted of cannibalised, revamped versions of previous Fo plays. *Ordine per DIO 000.000.000 (Law and Order for God and Money's Sake!!!,* 1972) was an extended rewrite of *Il telaio (The Loom).* It expanded it into two acts, adding two extra characters, a prostitute and a revolutionary son, as well as more intensified attacks on the PCI. It was generally considered to be one of Fo's weakest plays – Valentini called it 'probably Fo's worst play'.[52] But it was praised in a review of the play by Dacia Maraini, a feminist novelist and playwright, and founder of Italy's first all-women theatre, La Maddalena in Rome. Maraini's comments indicate the unique position which Fo's work occupied in a moribund contemporary Italian theatre:

It can't be said that Fo hasn't dealt with current topics in this play. If an Italian theatre exists, it should be produced exactly like this. This is theatre which takes a stand, and uses polemics, both cultural and political, insults, revolt, gripes, falling in love, rational and reckless frenzy, self-observation and observation of others. If there were a hundred plays like this every year, one could say the Italian theatre was alive. Probably ninety-nine of these plays could be discarded ... In compensation, however, we would have the delight of feeling that inside the enormous, semi-

paralysed, gaudy but bloodless body of Italian theatre, hot
and surging blood had started to flow again. Since there are
unfortunately only two or three plays like this a year
instead of a hundred, they end up being regarded with suspicion, and viewed from the perspective of the orderliness
and refinement of museum theatre.[53]

Political repression against La Comune was growing
alongside the political controversy of their plays. In the summer
of 1972 they were evicted from via Colletta due to police
pressure on the owners of the building, and were left without a
base for two years. In October 1972 they were charged with
inciting prison revolts through their activities in Soccorso Rosso
together with a young woman militant from Lotta Continua.
This abortive inquiry into Fo's and Rame's political activities
was instigated by the Genoan magistrate, Mario Sossi, and
yielded nothing incriminating. The following year Sossi was
kidnapped by members of the Brigate Rosse, but set free after a
series of interrogations which revealed, among other things, the
Red Brigades' contempt for and total variance from the political
line pursued by Fo and Rame. Later Fo and Rame were also
evicted from their apartment in Milan by a Jewish landlord who
refused to have tenants who were sympathisers of Fedayin.

Three years after the Piazza Fontana bombs, Fo wrote an
updated version of events with the intention of continuing the
'counter-information' of *Accidental Death of an Anarchist*. *Pum,
pum! Chi è? La polizia!* (*Knock Knock! Who's There? Police!*) was
written and rehearsed in just over a week, and continued the
story of police cover-ups and corruption since the Pinelli affair,
documenting the events which had occurred since the previous
play. The sequel is set inside the Ministry of Internal Affairs, and
Fo played the part of the Chief of Confidential Affairs, in a
performance in which he remained on stage throughout the
play's two and a half hours. *Pum, pum!* lacks the fictional, farcical
mechanism of its predecessor, being more of a comic
documentary reading (in which all the actors had their scripts on
stage), and is predominantly a 'word play'. It moves at a frantic
pace, as phone calls, telegrams and telexes come into the

ministry announcing the latest turn of events. There was, this time, no attempt to fictionalise the protagonists of these events, who are referred to by name throughout. 'We want to demonstrate,' said Fo in his spoken introduction to the play, 'with this morass of news and information, that the state is criminal, and there's no getting away from it. We believe there is only one valid signpost – the one Lenin gave us when he said we have to smash the state.'[54]

It became virtually a monologue for Fo in which he drew analogies between the hypocrisy of Christian Democrat politicians and Scapino's performance in Molière's *Tartuffe*, demonstrating the thesis that Italian politics, being a form of theatre in itself, needed no theatrical mediation. But *Pum, pum!* led to further political harassment of La Comune. After opening in Rome while Valpreda's trial was going on, they moved to the Cinema Rossini in the outskirts of Milan, which they were forced to occupy after police put pressure on the owner to evict the 'subversive' Fo. The poster of the play, drawn and designed by Fo, showing a blood–spattered family (somewhat in the style of a Ralph Steadman cartoon), caused Fo to be charged with 'offences against the armed forces'.

The prominent intellectual and semiotician Umberto Eco commented favourably on *Pum, pum!* in his weekly column in *L'Espresso*, describing Fo as a 'comic [who] provides cause for alarm', and criticising the police and political repression against him. He also condemned the abduction and rape of Franca Rame by fascists, which occurred in March 1973.[55] Rame was held at gunpoint, dumped in a van, raped, beaten up, burnt with cigarettes and slashed with razor blades and then left in a park. Ten years later she used this as the basis for a monologue, *Non mi muovo, non urlo, sono senza voce (I Don't Move, I Don't Scream, My Voice is Gone)*, also called *Lo stupro (The Rape)*, which was premiered in London in May 1983. At the time, she prepared an 'intervention' play called *Basta con i fascisti! (Stop the Fascists!)*, an audiovisual piece comparing fascism past and present, which she toured around La Comune's circuit. La Comune also tried to organise anti-fascist demonstrations, including one in the Milan Palazzo dello Sport, but were refused permission by the local council.

Meanwhile, dissension within La Comune was growing, recalling the situation before the break-up of Nuova Scena. Eventually, a faction who were members of Avanguardia Operaia (Workers' Vanguard, a far-left group) accused Fo and Rame of suffocating the creative activities of the others and took control of the company. The situation reflected the inevitable conflicts caused by the contrast between Fo's and Rame's status as lead actors and the egalitarian political line of the group. This conflict was summed up in 1975 by the US translator and critic of Fo, Suzanne Cowan:

> as intensely involved in political work as the troupe is at all times, one cannot avoid the feeling that its effective communication with the masses of working people is to some extent obstructed and overshadowed by the presence of a great performer. No matter how democratic, how sincerely 'anti-status' he may be, a Star must in some ways inhibit the performance of mundane, everyday political tasks. And it is only through such unglamorous Organisation work that political change can, in the last analysis, take place. Revolutions nearly always have their flamboyant heroes, moments of pageantry, theatrical climaxes. But revolutions are not *theatre*. At times Fo seems to lose sight of this distinction, and tends to upstage both the working people who make up the majority of the mass movement of which his theatre is a part, and the members of his own company.[56]

This may well be the case, as seen from a rigidly orthodox Marxist perspective, but Fo's profession is that of an actor, director, designer and playwright, and he had become one of the most accomplished and talented members of these professions in European and world theatre. It was primarily his and Rame's performances which drew crowds and made La Comune the political force that it was, rather than the egalitarian ideology of the company. In the event, after a stormy meeting in the summer of 1973, 20 members of La Comune took possession of the theatre equipment which Fo and Rame had accumulated in 20 years of theatre activity. After this split, the former members of La Comune produced little or no theatrical work, being racked by further dissensions in the ranks, leaving Fo, Rame and two others to proceed on their own from scratch.

The 'roadshows' and Fo's arrest

Fo and Rame continued their activities in 1973 on a reduced scale, maintaining the banner 'La Comune'. They teamed up with the Sicilian *cantastorie* (traditional singer-storyteller) Cicciu Busacca, who had participated in a third version of *Ci ragiono e canto* in 1973. (A second version of this show, with a more contemporary focus, adapting industrial workers' songs, had been produced in 1969.) They were also joined by Piero Sciotto, another Sicilian, who became a key figure in Fo's company as actor-manager and musician. The group began performing a series of what Fo has referred to as '*messe da campo*' (roadshows), following the example of the Chicano militant theatre in the USA, El Teatro Campesino. They toured small-scale shows around Lombardy and Veneto, performing to local people and at demonstrations and other political events. The main play they presented, along with other stories of the wartime Resistance, was a short piece entitled *Mamma Togni*. This was a monologue performed by Franca Rame about a peasant woman weighing more than 90 kilos, whose husband and son had been shot by the Germans during the war. Mamma Togni single-handedly broke up a fascist meeting in Milan, physically attacking the speakers, and became a 'mother' to the Italian anti-fascist movement.

In September 1973, Allende was assassinated in Chile and Pinochet's military government took power. The 'new' La Comune decided to write and perform a play on the subject, at a time when fears of a similar coup in Italy (which had frequently been expressed by Feltrinelli and others) were still being expressed. The result was one of the most dramatic plays Fo has produced, not in terms of its form or even its content, which were rough and ready, in the 'roadshow' style, but in terms of the impact it had on audiences. *Guerra di popolo in Cile* (*The People's War in Chile*) was constructed along similar lines to *Vorrei morire* with performances of first-hand accounts of the Chilean situation and songs written by Fo about the Colonels, Santiago stadium and Victor Jara. The play also incorporated *Mamma Togni,* and *Cicciu Corno*, a ballad by Busacca about a unicorn who symbolises the need for revolution. There was also a monologue by Franca Rame in the guise of a Chilean Christian Democrat 'procuress' who backs the *coup d'état,* weeping and invoking the pope. The play toured extensively around Italy, and retrieved the considerable audiences La Comune had previously enjoyed, largely due to the controversy and scandal provoked by the final part of the play. Chiara Valentini has described a performance at the Palalido in Milan to an audience of 5,000:

The first sign that something was wrong was a voice with a southern accent which suddenly burst from the battery microphone Dario Fo was wearing round his neck. 'Hello, hello. This is Dragon. Orders from Dragon to move the squad north.' This interrupted Fo's monologue about Augusto Pinochet, and he blinked and tried to explain it away: 'These cops are everywhere. They even pump their radio messages through our microphones.' Then he carried on as if nothing had happened. After a while the interferences started up again. Agitated orders and coded sentences came through. Suddenly a youth shouted through a megaphone, 'The telephones aren't working.' Then a voice from the stalls said, 'The radio's gone dead.' 'Come on, comrades, it's nothing. Just keep calm,' exhorted Fo from the stage, but his voice became more and more strained as he pressed on with his lines. Someone in the audience seemed to get an attack of nerves, and started up a long monologue: 'It's not as if we're in Greece or Chile. We've got a Communist Party, the unions – a coup's impossible.' Tension spread through the audience. Suddenly a police inspector came in, and leapt on to the stage: 'I must interrupt this show. The following persons are to accompany me to the police station.' He began listing the names of the best-known representatives of the extreme Left present in the auditorium. The tension reached breaking point, and various people started muttering *'coup d'état'*. Someone started singing the 'Internationale', and immediately everyone leapt to their feet, raised clenched fists, and sang at the top of their voices in what they thought would be their last expression of freedom. (At this point the 'police inspector', another 'policeman', and the members of the audience who had started the 'incident' got up on stage and joined in the singing.) The audience were stunned for a moment, then they realised that they'd been had. In Turin a youth ate ten pages of his diary, which were full of what he thought were compromising addresses. In Merano a student tried to jump out of a window, breaking the glass. In Nuoro, where two coach-loads of Sardinian shepherds had arrived from Orgosolo, someone flashed a cheese knife when they saw the fake inspector.[57]

While the play was being performed in Sassari, Sardinia, in November 1973, Fo, who had refused to allow 'real' police to enter the theatre, was arrested for 'verbally violent resistance to a public officer'. Rame and the rest of the company organised a demonstration outside the Sassari police station until Fo was released 24 hours later. The event created considerable controversy in the Italian press and mass media, where Fo became the centre of attention, opinions about him tending to fall into two camps. Among the number of intellectuals interviewed at the time about Fo, there were those like Natalia Ginzburg and Franco Zeffirelli who saw him as a talented actor who had been led astray by revolutionary politics. As Zeffirelli stated:

Fo is a very great actor, director and clown, the last great clown of our time. I don't judge Fo's works from a political point of view; to me it's enough that his work is good, which it is, on an artistic level . . . Dario Fo's plays are liked much more by the bourgeoisie than by workers.[58]

Film director Pier Paolo Pasolini was more extreme, describing

Fo as a 'plague on the Italian theatre'. The other, more partisan, point of view was that Fo was predominantly a political animal who was becoming dangerous to the Italian political establishment. This was because of his capacity to draw enormous crowds in sports stadiums and engage them in political debates which attacked the government and state authorities. This view saw Fo as being harassed as a 'subversive'. Fo's lawyer, Sandro Canestrini, stated after his arrest:

> The fact is that Dario Fo has for some years been more than just an actor. He's a politician, a man engaged in a tough battle against the authorities. It's logical that the authorities are using all their weapons, even the most reckless and openly illegal, to silence him.[59]

As La Comune was still a private club, under Italian law the police had no right to enter the theatre in Sassari. A relatively minor incident became blown up in the Italian mass media at precisely the time when Fo, Rame and La Comune needed the free publicity. As a result, they returned to the spotlight of public attention and drew more audiences to their plays.

CHAPTER 4

POLITICAL THEATRE ON SHIFTING GROUND 1974–1983

The Palazzina Liberty and *Can't Pay? Won't Pay!*

All the revolutionaries and militant workers of Milan got into the habit of coming to the Palazzina (a theatre or a non-theatre, according to your point of view), where state authorities were . . . subjected to mass criticism, all as well orchestrated by Fo as his plays. Although the Palazzina no longer serves this purpose, due to the vagaries of the [Italian Left] movement, militant theatre continues.

(Piero Sciotto, 'Con Dario Fo', March 1977.)

After Fo had successfully toured *Mistero buffo* in France in 1974, La Comune, which had become 'Il Collettivo Teatrale "La Comune" diretto da Dario Fo' ('La Comune' for short in the remainder of this book), set about finding a base for itself in Milan. They presented a list of 20 disused buildings owned by the Milan council to a Socialist Party assessor, and obtained permission to examine them. They then chose a dilapidated, rat-infested art nouveau building which had served as a vegetable market in the middle of a public garden in Porta Vittoria, a working-class area of Milan. With the Socialist councillor's blessing, they took it over and started cleaning it up, naming it the Palazzina Liberty. Within days there was an uproar from Christian Democrat members of the council, who accused Fo of being an 'enemy of the regime' and tried to revoke the permission. La Comune decided to occupy the building, and local volunteers began helping to make it habitable.

The council replied by erecting a fence round the building, and La Comune produced a series of leaflets saying: 'The rats thank the DC'. They also organised demonstrations, rallies of up to 10,000 people, and various fund-raising activities, which included a performance of *Mistero buffo* in the gardens to 15,000 people. 'Occupying the Palazzina Liberty is one of the most important theatrical events we have ever staged,' Fo commented at the time. After a court order was brought against them by the council, La Comune obtained permission to remain temporarily in the building, and they set about turning it into a local community centre. Plans were developed which included a library, day nursery, conference centre, theatre and audiovisual workshops. La Comune also hung a red flag from the roof – a gesture which would have been inconceivable at British equivalents such as Arnold Wesker's Centre 42 or Joan Littlewood's Theatre Workshop.

La Comune's first theatrical offering at their new home, however, *Porta e Belli contro il potere* (*Porta and Belli against the Authorities*), was deemed inappropriate for the theatre's new popular audience, and taken off after a week. It consisted of a series of polemical readings by Fo of sonnets by two popular nineteenth-century dialect poets. As Fo later commented:

> they were splendid texts, and when I recited them individually they worked marvellously, but not all together in the same show . . . There was no theatrical progression, no development. But I can assure you that I knew how to recite them with the right degree of energy and rhythm, especially Porta's poems.[1]

During the summer of 1974, Fo worked on a play about a series of events which had occurred in Marghera, Turin and the south of Italy, and became known as *autoriduzione* or 'self-reduction', within a left-wing movement of civil disobedience. Fo was subsequently accused of using the play to foment a similar popular movement in Milan, since it predicted the spread of the phenomenon there. Organised groups of people had begun refusing to pay the rising prices in supermarkets and public transport, as well as gas and electricity bills, and insisting on paying what they considered to be a 'fair price'.

Italy was going through a severe economic crisis – there was a large deficit in the balance of payments, exports had diminished, and workers were being laid off all over the country. The clout of the trade unions, who had achieved a number of improvements for workers during the 'hot autumn' of 1969, was beginning to pale as employers fought back through the Confederation of Industry, claiming that labour costs were too high. In Italy, employers are responsible for paying health and social security contributions for their workers, as well as a proportion of their sickness benefit and a 'thirteenth month' salary in December. Consequently many of them were tightening their belts and putting workers into *cassa integrazione*, a system under which laid-off workers receive 80 per cent of their wages from the state until they are either re-employed or made definitively redundant.

During this time of rising prices and falling employment, the PCI was still busy pursuing a policy of collaboration with the Christian Democrats at governmental level – the famous 'historic compromise'. They had also interpreted events in Chile in terms of a need to declare war against radical, extremist elements, and pursue a moderate line of reformism which was neither anti-USA nor anti-USSR. In this context, as Antonia explained in Fo's new play, *Non si paga! Non si paga! (Can't Pay? Won't Pay!)*, civil disobedience and *autoriduzione* was a grassroots movement which was a better substitute for striking:

> Some workers who'd appeared from a nearby factory started shouting . . . 'It's your right to pay the right prices . . . It's just like a strike, but it's even better than a strike, since we workers always get our pay docked when we go on strike. In this type of strike, at last it's the bosses who have to pay for it!' . . . Don't pay! Don't pay! And that goes for all the money you've cheated us out of over the years we've been shopping here.[2]

Can't Pay? Won't Pay! is probably Fo's best-known play outside Italy after *Accidental Death of an Anarchist*. By 1990 it had been performed in 35 different countries.[3] It is his most comic and entertaining work in terms of its plot complications and reversals of situation, smoothly incorporating political points into the farcical mechanism. The sometimes 'preachy' long speeches of some of his other plays were also kept to a minimum. Like most of his plays since 1968, it was written as a response to a political need and dealt with a specific political situation. Fo and La Comune discussed the play with groups of workers before presenting it in public, in order to ensure it dealt accurately with what was a particularly working-class predicament, and several changes were made as a result of these discussions. As Fo explained in his preface to the play, even the play's farcical form (for which he was criticised from some quarters for returning to the theatrical mechanism of his 'bourgeois' plays) is connected with a basic need:

> As in old Neapolitan and Venetian popular farces . . . here the starting point, the fundamental impetus, is hunger. The initial, instinctive solution in which everyone takes care of himself in resolving the atavistic problem of appetite devel-ops into a need to work collectively, to get organised and fight together. This is not just for survival, but to live in a world where there are fewer brightly lit shop windows, fewer motorways, and no government corruption, no thieves – the real thieves, the big fish, that is – and where there is justice, justice for all.[4]

This basic revolutionary message of the play, also inherent in its plot situation, is sometimes obscured in foreign productions which obviously lack the specific, collective social background of the play's original context (including the occupation of the Palazzina Liberty). In terms of Fo's work, the play lies closest to *Zanni's Grammelot* in *Mistero buffo,* in which a starving peasant tries to eat himself, and to the gallows humour of *Accidental Death*. In terms of English farce, there is a danger of reducing it to the slick, middle-class boulevard comedy of Alan Ayckbourn rather than to the sick, outrageous, but basically working-class humour of Joe Orton's *Loot* (with which it shares a coffin as a repository for criminal deeds), a play which is also in its way about justice.

Can't Pay? Won't Pay! is set in a 'modest working-class flat' to which Antonia returns from the local supermarket after indulging in some *autoriduzione* with her fellow-housewives. This has got so chaotic and out-of-hand that it has turned into outright looting, curbed only by the arrival of the police. The play is Fo's first openly feminist comedy insofar as it deals directly with the problems working-class women have in running a household in times of economic crisis. Also, most of the far-fetched and farcical explanations used to disguise the real reasons behind the play's bizarre events have a social and political origin. After Antonia off-loads her stolen goods on to her neighbour Margherita, for example, she explains the latter's consequent 'pregnancy' by explaining that since Margherita is a Catholic, she cannot take the pill. As a result, she had to tape up her stomach to avoid being sacked by her employer on grounds of maternity. Antonia's subterfuge is a result of her husband Giovanni's legalistic, line-toeing PCI view of *autoriduzione*:

> This miserable flotsam of society, breaking the law and being provocative. They're playing right into the bosses' hands – now they'll be able to go round saying workers are thieves and the dregs of society and should be thrown into prison.[5]

He states that if he caught his wife doing such a thing he would kill her, and then take advantage of the newly passed Italian divorce law. Ironically, when the police arrive, searching the area (which contains more than a thousand working-class families), Giovanni opens the door to a Constable, who is a Maoist with a university degree, and in full sympathy with *autoriduzione*. Giovanni is taken aback, since his tolerance for the police extends only as far as the PCI MP Amendola's view of them as necessary 'sons of the people', to which the Constable retorts:

> We're no sons of the people . . . we're slaves . . . the slaves and thugs of the bosses. We're the ones who have to apply their laws, and protect their racketeering and their bombs![6]

This leads Giovanni to the paranoid conclusion that the

Constable is an *agent provocateur.* He is subsequently convinced of the economic justifications for *autoriduzione,* however, when Margherita's husband Luigi reveals that the factory where they both work is being closed down and they are being put on *cassa integrazione.* When the two men again encounter the Maoist Constable, who is present at a collision between two lorries carrying illegal bags of sugar and flour, he persuades them to steal some of the goods and 'save them from destruction'. Borrowing a stratagem from the Vietcong, they hide their stolen sacks in a coffin.

Meanwhile their wives have been caught with their 'bellies full' by the Constable, trying to stash their stolen goods. Antonia concocts a story about the fictitious feast of 'Saint Eulalia', an old woman whom God made pregnant and whose disbelieving husband was struck blind. This covering story is almost immediately substantiated by a power cut, and the Constable is struck unconscious while trying to find the door in the dark. The men hide the coffin in the same closet where the women have hidden the Constable, believing him to be dead. The situation is resolved neatly – unusually for Fo – with Giovanni confessing his own appropriation to his wife, and the Constable emerging from the closet believing he has become pregnant. The two couples witness a battle in the streets below between the police and the local women, which ends with the police withdrawing. Then in a final scene which was cut from the only published English version of the play, they discuss the political consequences of this revolutionary course of events. Giovanni sees them – at least in the original version of the play – in the Utopian contexts of 'a world where you can even see the sky and the plants producing flowers, and where there's spring, and girls laughing and singing.'

Although *Can't Pay? Won't Pay!* became one of Fo's most popular plays outside Italy, and was the first of his plays to receive a production in the UK, critical response to it in Italy was surprisingly tepid. Many critics saw a conflict between the superbly crafted farcical plot and the play's political statements and Marxist analyses, although this is far less evident than in many of Fo's other plays. Lanfranco Binni, for example, normally one of Fo's most sympathetic critics, saw it as a ponderously didactic attempt to incorporate topical political arguments:

> The play's political argument (in which the notion of 'self-reduction' is rather ambiguous and virtually amounts to a defence and justification of appropriation as an extreme measure in extreme poverty) is laboured. It is arrived at after a remarkable waste of gags and dialogue which shows among other things an obvious imbalance between Fo and the other characters on stage.[7]

But as Fo later pointed out, this apparent 'imbalance' is in the 'classic' tradition of the comic and the *spalla* (comic foil or stooge),[8] which both Fo's and Rame's characters drew on with their supporting actors, Piero Sciotto and Anna Bergamin. The complexity of the play's situation and the ingeniousness of its comic inventions make it one of Fo's best plays, but his critics were possibly becoming jaded and over-familiar with some of the gags which Fo recycled from earlier plays. They were also uneasy about the play's apparent approval of *autoriduzione*. But to see the play as an incitement to theft would be to ignore the deliberate comic and satirical exaggeration which Fo employs in virtually all his farces, particularly in the comic resolution of *Can't Pay? Won't Pay!*, which stands traditional farce on its head.

Largely as a result of the play's popularity abroad – it was in the repertoire of the Berliner Ensemble for several years as well as running for almost two years in London's West End – Fo produced a revised, updated version of the piece at the Palazzina Liberty in September 1980. At the time, 24,000 Fiat workers had been put on *cassa integrazione*, and Giovanni and Luigi became Fiat workers. Fo also added references to the political situation in Poland (where workers were literally 'on their knees') and Afghanistan, while making jokes about Pope John Paul II. Responses to this new version of the play were again far from favourable, and not helped by the lack of topical political background the original version could rely on. The new edition of the play appeared at a time when the enthusiasm and positivism of left-wing politics in Italy had eroded, whereas this had previously nourished and sustained Fo's work in a way which had given it a topical popularity and made him a major spokesman for the Italian Left. By 1980, the extra-parliamentary Left had become dissipated, due to the increase in terrorism and the widespread arrests of left-wing groups accused of sympathising with terrorism – the case of Toni Negri* being a prime example.

As *La Repubblica*'s theatre critic Ugo Volli commented, Fo's political rallying calls ran the risk of coming across as empty rhetoric:

> We listened to the same old arguments the other evening at the Palazzina Liberty, among the usual above-capacity crowd, with growing embarrassment and irritation. There was something, or rather a number of things, which made them tired and empty, the fruit of pure rhetoric without an object. The crowd was huge, yes, but different. Not the younger brothers and sisters of the audience of six years ago, nor even the same people six years on. Rather it was almost a normal audience, left-wing but not militant, mixed in with theatregoers . . . Then, obviously, there was the historical context. Mass illegality, *autoriduzione* and the like are not only all over and done with, but forgotten issues after years of bloodshed. Ideas like socialism and revolution and the working class have become much more complex (if not confused), and seeking an impetus for action has now become somewhat difficult.[9]

*Toni Negri: a writer and lecturer in Political Science at the University of Padua and the Sorbonne, and the leading figure of the ultra-left Autonomia movement in Italy. He was arrested and imprisoned, charged with 'subversion of the state' during the wave of arrests of the Autonomia on 7 April 1979. In 1983, while still in prison, he was elected a member of parliament representing the Italian Radical Party (PRI), and consequently released from prison under a law which protected Italian politicians from imprisonment. After a motion was passed in parliament (from which the Radical Party abstained) to have him re-imprisoned, he fled to France. In April 1984, he was sentenced to life imprisonment plus 30 years, under a number of charges including that of 'inspiring' various acts of terrorism.

Volli's comments are symptomatic of what had happened to the Italian Left since the mid-1970s, and perhaps further proof of the 'throwaway' nature of most of Fo's plays. Consequently the reworking of *Can't Pay? Won't Pay!* was something of an exercise in nostalgia. Nonetheless the video recording of this production which I saw indicated that the play remains one of his strongest in terms of its farcically convoluted plot, its potently comic situations and its appealing proletarian characters. Two US commentators have also indicated its strong Rabelaisian, carnivalesque nature, drawing on medieval imagery of the feast, hunger and pregnancy to outline the universality of the play's situation. Joel Schechter again invokes Bakhtin's grotesque realism:

> The grotesquery of the situations in which Fo's characters find themselves is almost Rabelaisian. Bakhtin noted that in Rabelais's world, the grotesque 'discloses the potentiality of an entirely different world, of another way of life . . . a return to Saturn's golden age . . . [requiring] bodily partici-pation in the potentiality of another world.' . . . A police officer appears to experience an hysterical pregnancy . . . several women stuff boxes of pasta and vegetables under their coats, so that they look pregnant; their husbands almost instantly accept the roles of worried, expectant fathers . . . The resulting farce offers a vision of urban Saturnalia, where instead of Rabelaisian monks, pilgrims, or scholars, we see housewives, factory workers, and police officers undergo illegal or bizarre transformations in body, and in their rela-tions to nature (vegetables, birth) and private property (unaffordable groceries) . . . Rabelais's grotesquery has given way to antic transformations more suitable for an age of inflation, shoplifting, and miracle salad dressing.[10]

Martin Walsh draws on Breughel's painting of Carnival and Lent to describe what he refers to as the revolutionary 'proletarian carnival' of the play:

> The carnivalesque is important from the very first moment . . . Plenty invades poverty or, to borrow Breughel's

images, the 'Lean Kitchen' becomes the 'Fat Kitchen'. A curious irony of the play is that, despite the enormous quantities of food Fo packs into his set by the end, no one manages to feast. The wraith of hunger continues to lurk within the carnivalesque. . . . With admirable economy of means, Fo intensifies the carnivalesque outburst. He does not continue to pile up narrative reports or attempt to portray the events themselves; rather, he dramatises the *reaction* and brings it into his one-room worker's flat. The forces of Lent invade the scene as the municipal police initiate a house-to-house search for the stolen produce . . . Both casts of characters leave the shelter of house and home, and take to the festival streets, to reunite as couples at the end of this proletarian carnival. . . . Fo's play is grounded in the notion of *festa*, which not only stokes its farcical energies, but determines its comedic outcome. The fundamental *action* of the play can thus be defined as getting 'pregnant' with the revolution through the irresponsible 'carnival' of spontaneous action.[11]

These comments suggest that although the play's immediate political context may have disappeared, its situation and characters have enough life and complexity in them to have cross-cultural resonances. The play's English title became a slogan during the protest against Margaret Thatcher's poll tax in Britain in 1990, and the play itself was a strong influence on a satirical farce about the poll tax, Patrick Prior's *Revolting Peasants*. This was performed at the Theatre Royal in Stratford East in March 1990, and indicates that Fo's play had a strong impact in the UK.

In a brief and very curious study of Fo's work published in 1984, Lino Pertile, the translator of the London production version of *Can't Pay? Won't Pay!* suggested that by the mid-1970s, Fo had 'reached an impasse' and begun a 'process of gradual disappearance from the cultural scene'. According to Pertile, Fo's plays no longer expressed any dialectical relationship either with the Italian Left or bourgeois culture. Pertile claimed Fo was preaching 'blatantly to the converted', reiterating ultra-left slogans with a 'plebeian narcissism', and merely reflecting 'the process of cultural degradation happening in Italy'.[12] His conclusions took Fo to task in no mean terms:

> We may well wonder whether Fo did not, despite himself, pander to the lowest common denominator of the farce, the belch and the raspberry, and thus promote, or at least contribute to, the blight of counter-productive vulgarity which is the bane of recent Italian popular culture – and all this despite his ambition to heighten the political consciousness of the working masses. The superficiality of Fo's propaganda became propaganda for the superficial and his theatre was its first victim.[13]

This rather splenetic evaluation of Fo's progress, which fails to provide any examples of the 'blight of counter-productive vulgarity' in mid-1970s Italian popular culture, has, needless to say, been proved incorrect by history. But even in the mid-1970s it is arguable that Fo was exerting a positive influence on 'respectable' Italian culture. In his study of theatre in Milan from 1960 to 1980, Domenico Rigotti describes Fo's theatre in the 1970s as 'the first, and, on such a sensational scale, probably the only alternative space to function in the Lombard capital.'[14] Rigotti also cites the work of the Teatro dell'Elfo, a group of young left-wing actors including Giuseppe Cederna, Antonio Catania, Paolo Rossi and Silvio Orlando (all later to become prominent film actors), directed by Gabriele Salvatores (later to become an Oscar-winning film director). This group had formed in Milan in 1973 and were in many ways influenced by Fo. They focused on the work of the actor, mounting productions on a shoestring budget and exploring the actor–audience relationship – sometimes, like Fo, without costumes or makeup, and sometimes in more avant-garde contexts. Salvatores' 1987 film *Kamikazen*, based on an Italian adaptation of *Comedians* by Trevor Griffiths (which was uncredited), is a good example of their often chaotic but energetic, farcical and popular performance style. Fo took considerable interest in the Teatro dell'Elfo's work, and has claimed 'they were too intelligent to use me as a model to copy – only to steal from.'[15]

Political pamphlets

It is ironic in the light of Pertile's comments that Fo, an exponent of journalistic, topical, documentary political theatre, was proposed as a candidate for the Nobel Prize for Literature in February 1975, while he was performing *Non si paga!* He was nominated by a group of Swedish writers and journalists and members of the Pen Club, which also included Simone de Beauvoir and Alberto Moravia – surely proof of the durability of his plays and their place in theatre history. But at the time Fo expressed his aversion to wearing a tuxedo and bowing to the king of Sweden:

> I can imagine the looks on the faces of a number of pre-fects, magistrates, police superintendents and politicians of my acquaintance, who have spent so much energy trying to shut me up and put me in handcuffs. And the Swedes go and play a joke like this on them . . . But there's no risk of my winning anything, for two good reasons. The first is that the Nobel Prize, like a number of other prizes, has a particular political guise, and it's unlikely that they'd give it to a nuisance like me. The second is that my plays are not intended to go down in history. I write and perform satire that is linked to everyday current events – the content of my plays is immediately disposable.[16]

Although Fo had to wait another 22 years to receive the Nobel Prize, his award in 1997 was also considered by many of his detractors to be a joke, but his international reputation had increased to the point that he had become a major figure in world theatre. His follow-up to *Non si paga!* was another 'throwaway' piece written as a response to the Italian parliamentary elections of June 1975. Parts of it were even used in an election TV transmission by the left-wing party PDUP (Partito Democratico per Unità Proletaria, a splinter party from the PCI), who were at the time connected to the ultra-left

Manifesto group but also attached to the PCI. In it, Fo elaborated his dwarf trick of *La signora è da buttare* in a caricature of the Christian Democrat government minister – and sometime prime minister – Amintore Fanfani.

In *Il Fanfani rapito* (*Fanfani Kidnapped*), Fo achieved a theatrical *tour de force* in his impersonation of the eponymous diminutive Italian politician, his hands in a pair of shoes, while Arturo Corso performed physical gestures behind him, enabling him to seem to fly through the air and even walk on walls. The play is an election pamphlet, exaggerating the already somewhat comic, buffoonesque antics of Fanfani in a plot in which he is kidnapped. He turns out not to have been abducted by the Red Brigades, but as part of a scheme by the then Prime Minister Giulio Andreotti to gain public sympathy and support for the Christian Democrats. As Fo stated at the time:

> [It] is not cabaret, nor is it a satire of a famous member of the government and his mannerisms and weaknesses. It is a grotesque representation of authority, and the excessive arrogance of Christian Democratic power. In other words, the play isn't intended to demonstrate that Fanfani is a villain and the DC his victim. It explains that Christian Democracy as a whole has represented a moral outrage for 30 years in its arrogance, its contempt for the people, and its embezzlements.[17]

Subjected to an interrogation by his tame captors, Fanfani offers a confession of all the 'crimes' of 30 years of Christian Democracy, and accuses his colleagues of various kinds of corruption. His kidnappers, faced with a suspicious mass media, are forced to send Fanfani's ear (J. Paul Getty style) to the Italian public to prove the kidnapping is genuine. As a result, they have to move their hideout, and Fanfani is transported, in drag, to an abortion clinic run by nuns. In a gag lifted from *Non si paga!*, an attack of nerves causes his stomach to swell up with intestinal gas and he is given a Ceasarian operation which produces a blackshirt fascist puppet. He then ascends to heaven, which is worse than earth, and undergoes a trial at the hands of a Guerilla-Madonna (Franca Rame) and a revolutionary Christ, and is kicked out for his political crimes. The Madonna predicts the defeat of the Christian Democrats and the victory of the working class, while Fanfani wakes up in his office to discover that the entire proceedings have been a bad dream. At this point, a group of real kidnappers break in and drag him away, acting on Andreotti's orders. Although the Madonna's predictions did not come true, the Left gained a considerable number of votes in the elections. Fo dominated proceedings far more than he did in *Non si paga!* but *Il Fanfani rapito* received more sympathetic critical responses, with Binni even describing it as 'a more coherent farce than *Non si paga!*'[18]

Since the kidnapping and murder of Aldo Moro in 1978 (about which Fo was to attempt another play), *Il Fanfani rapito* might appear in bad taste, which indicates the tendency of many of Fo's plays not to outlive the dramatic political situations they draw on. But *Il Fanfani rapito* is a more extreme example than most of a play written for a specific occasion, and its specificity meant it did not receive any productions outside Italy. In the first of four plays (which were later collected together in volume 10 of the Einaudi edition of his work) he wrote about kidnapping public figures – Fanfani, Fiat owner Gianni Agnelli, a fictional woman industrialist and Pope John Paul II. Valentini notes that *Il Fanfani rapito* opened simultaneously with Giorgio Strehler's production of Goldoni's *Campiello* (later done at the National Theatre in London) at the Piccolo Teatro. The contrast between Fo's makeshift political satire and the glossy, carnivalesque Venice of Strehler's stylish, lush but rather empty production, could not have been more extreme. It served to illustrate how far Fo had diverged from his earlier work with the Piccolo, which he now saw as an example of 'cultural colonialism':

It's centralism – they put on plays for the mainstream, then move around with a colonialist mentality, putting on three, four or five plays, all of them equally mainstream, not done for *that particular place,* not creating plays which people need. *The Three Sisters* has nothing to offer the people of Quarto Oggiaro, but they are interested in what we have to say about appropriation and class struggle . . .

[The Piccolo] does Brecht with tinsel . . . There's a very
intelligent lighting operator at the Piccolo . . . who used to
say, 'Well, tonight I'm off to light *The Caucasian Chalk
Cherry Orchard.*' He'd got the message.[19]

As Valentini commented, the Piccolo and the Palazzina
Liberty's audiences also provided a sharp contrast:

At the Piccolo there was the bourgeoisie, the cultural
establishment, the prestigious critics, at the Palazzina there
were all the youth and intellectuals of Milan, the supporters of the divorce referendum and full-frontal combat with
the DC, laughing and applauding the ramshackle and not
yet run-in gangster story about the DC and its leader.[20]

Almost all of Fo's plays are tried out in public performance
before they are properly 'run in', and foreign visitors are often
surprised at how 'ramshackle' the productions are, which often
play for weeks before being rewritten and tightened up. This is
another factor that separates Fo from both the mainstream
Italian theatre establishment and the avant-garde. While *Il
Fanfani rapito* was playing, Carmelo Bene, one of the leading
figures of Italian avant-garde theatre, was gaining a reputation in
Europe with his semi-pornographic *S.A.D.E.* This was an
exercise in theatrical megalomania which was to lead to a series
of unintentionally comic 'adaptations' of Shakespeare's tragedies
with Bene an overbearing protagonist supported by semi-naked
females. The Palazzina Liberty, on the other hand, had become
a community theatre which attracted non-theatregoers on a
scale at least ten times that of the Half Moon Theatre in the East
End of London, and where workers, students and local people
came for the political content of Fo's plays as much as for their
author's creative inventiveness.

In June 1975, Fo, Rame and other members of La Comune
went to China, an experience which Fo recalled with great
enthusiasm, particularly because of the examples of popular
theatre he saw. He noted in particular a Shanghai storyteller's
representation of a tram journey through the city:

A bit like me in *Mistero buffo,* he reconstructed people's comments, even if they were banal at times, and expressed their concerns – their discussions about work, wages and struggles against Lin Piao. He portrayed a character who thought Confucius was a party director, and another one who hadn't got the gist of the latest party directives. All this was done in a grotesque vein, accompanied by drum rolls which established the rhythm of the performance.[21]

Fo had a discussion with the Artistic Company of Jinan, a group of dancers, acrobats and actors ten times the size of La Comune, who performed in factories, shipyards, mines and army barracks, pursuing a Maoist cultural line. He found many points in common with the work of La Comune. On his return to Italy, he took issue with Michelangelo Antonioni, accusing the film director of reflecting only a dignified, surface view of Chinese reality in his controversial documentary *Cina – Chung Kuo* (*China – The Centre of the World,* 1974), and of presenting an unduly pessimistic, Western intellectual's view of the Chinese way of life. Fo's response to China was essentially optimistic, seeing the vestiges of the cultural revolution in terms of an ironic, satirical, anti-official popular culture which he related to his own situation in Italy. This led the prominent journalist Giorgio Bocca to suggest that Fo's trip to China had been like a pilgrimage to Lourdes.[22] Fo attempted to write a play about his experiences in China, but was unable to find a suitable theatrical form, and it was not until two years later that he was to use the theatrical material he picked up in China in his monologue *Tale of a Tiger.* In the meantime, Fo continued his research into the *giullari,* writing and directing a series of medieval and popular Sicilian sketches and ballads performed by Cicciu Busacca and his two daughters in the style of the Sicilian *cantastorie,* under the title of *La Giullarata.* This piece included *The Origin of the Giullare* from *Mistero buffo,* and is closer to the various editions of *Ci ragiono e canto* and Fo's experiments in popular musical forms than to his political plays.

In 1976 Fo returned to the political arena of the Palazzina Liberty to confront the drug problem, which, arriving later in

Italy than in most other European countries, was rapidly becoming a bigger problem than elsewhere. This was due to Mafia involvement in drug manufacturing and racketeering and perceptions that state authorities and the police were using drugs indirectly to erode the forces of the revolutionary Left. Some militant-left groups, like Avanguardia Operaia and the Movimento Lavoratori per il Socialismo, had even gone to the extent of setting up vigilante groups who went around Italian cities beating up drug dealers and mounting anti-drug campaigns. Fo saw drugs as 'a class problem: rich people consume and use drugs, while poor people are used and consumed by drugs.'[23]

In the play, *La marijuana della mamma è la più bella* (*Mother's Marijuana is the Best*), Fo again uses a farcical format, in which Grandpa (Fo) and a classic, fat, southern Italian *mamma* (Rame) pretend to be drug addicts and dealers. They do this in order to teach their son Luigi a lesson, since they have discovered that he has been smoking marijuana. Fo set out to attack the Italian press and government's 'censorship' of the drug problem, and to discuss it in social, cultural and political as well as medical and scientific terms. But he later considered the play as not having taken a sufficiently solid stand on the problem. Its main concern is to expose the complete failure of the Italian authorities to deal with the drug problem in medical and scientific terms, preferring to criminalise it, while thousands of housewives continue to resort to 'mother's little helpers'. In his preface to the play, Fo stated that he had

> tried to involve people by entertaining them, making them laugh themselves rigid if possible. We think that the intelligence that operates through satire and mockery, along with the rationality of irony, is, when all's said and done, the best and healthiest of all drugs, particularly when obtuse authorities are continually trying to repress every citizen who has any ideas about freedom.[24]

In fact the play succeeds best as comic entertainment, using devices of disguise and deception similar to those of *Can't Pay? Won't Pay!* The somewhat parochial political context of the play, however, renders it of less interest than its predecessor, even though both plays deal with relatively universal problems. In 1980 the Belt and Braces Roadshow, after their London success with *Accidental Death of an Anarchist*, commissioned from me a translation of *Mother's Marijuana is the Best*, which had also been performed in Germany. This English version was never performed, due partly to the transfer of *Anarchist* to the West End, and partly to the difficulty of making the play relevant to English audiences. It is a long-winded piece, which at one point refers directly to its own 'preaching',[25] while borrowing a lot of its slapstick stage business from Fo's earlier farces.

One of the play's most hilarious sequences, however, would appear to derive from the Shanghai storyteller Fo enthused about. Grandpa relates how he took LSD by mistake (for aspirin), and hallucinated a farcical tram journey in his wardrobe, which ends up in the Milan police station, where he meets Pinelli in mid-air. This is Fo at his imaginative, improvisational, self-quoting best, and the speech generates an ingenious train-journey metaphor which runs throughout the play. Another notable feature of the play is that the PCI Grandpa is given some convincing and sympathetic lines which describe the current situation in the Italian revolutionary Left at a time when, according to the statistics the play quotes, 65 per cent of people under 24 had been unable to find their first job.[26]

> Wonderfully united, you new left groups, aren't you? And then you complain we don't give you any credibility in the PCI! You're riddled with sectarianism – beating the shit out of one another over a load of shit![27]

The play was criticised in some quarters for being too ponderously didactic and moralistic and for neglecting the political symptoms which were to lead to a renewal of the revolutionary spirit of the Italian Left in 1977. This proved to be a watershed year for student radicalism, especially in Bologna, and there were often violent clashes between students and police throughout Italy. At the time the Autonomia movement, of which Toni Negri was a prominent figure, began to make its presence felt at a conference of 30,000 left-wing militants in Bologna.

In May 1976 La Comune performed *Mother's Marijuana* at the
Teatro Tenda, a large circus tent in Rome, in a month-long
season together with *Mistero buffo* and *Non si paga!* The cast of
Marijuana included two actors who were to become important
figures in the 'new Italian cinema' which emerged in 1988. The
Rome-based Ennio Fantastachini, who has played lead roles in
many Italian films of the 1980s and 1990s, including Sergio
Rubini's *La stazione* (1990) and Gianni Amelio's *Open Doors*
(1990) played the part of a priest. The son Luigi was played by
the actor-playwright Claudio Bigagli, who played a leading role
in the Oscar-winning *Mediterraneo* (1991), directed by Gabriele
Salvatores, and whose bedroom farce *Piccoli equivoci* (*Little
Misunderstandings*) was filmed by Ricky Tognazzi in 1988. The
music for *Marijuana* was composed by Fiorenzo Carpi, his first
collaboration with Fo since 1967. Fo and Rame were to return
to the drug problem in *The Pope and the Witch* in 1989 and in
Rame's own play *Heroine* in 1991.

Return to TV and *Female Parts*
After a 14-year absence, 1977 was the year of Fo's triumphant
return to Italian television. This was the result of a change in the
administration of RAI brought about by the Left's gains in the
elections of the previous year. Two 'cycles' of Fo's plays were
shown on the non-religious, socialist-inclined second channel of
RAI. They represented a valuable retrospective of Fo's work,
although his more politically contentious plays like *Accidental Death
of an Anarchist, Can't Pay? Won't Pay!* and *Il Fanfani rapito* were not
included in the transmissions. These plays were subsequently filmed
by La Comune in order to have a permanent record of them. The
two different versions of *Mistero buffo* which went out on TV nevertheless managed to cause considerable controversy, as described in
Chapter 1. Two editions of *Ci ragiono e canto* were also screened,
together with *Settimo: ruba un po' meno, Isabella* and a new, updated
version of *La signora è da buttare*. The latter added references to
Presidents Johnson, Nixon and Ford, and a sequence in which Fo
plays a dwarf representing St George fighting against the dragon, as
well as a virtuoso number in which he plays a tuba.

Fo and Rame also put together a new play for the TV series, *Parliamo di donne* (*Let's Talk about Women*), where for the first time they directly confronted women's issues. This was an attempt to give Franca Rame a series of roles which were not the usual 'support' roles which she had played in most of Fo's work prior to the 1970s, as well as to deal with the condition of women. Although Rame denies being a militant feminist (and the show was criticised for simply presenting female roles rather than exploring female problems), *Parliamo di donne* was a kind of women's version of *Il dito nell'occhio*. It was a collection of sketches and songs (including *Mamma Togni* and *Michele Lu Lanzone* which were lifted from two previous Fo plays) dealing with situations such as abortion, the absence of actresses in the Elizabethan theatre, the holy family and the like. In one sketch, 'The Pregnant Man', a wealthy industrialist who is president of the anti-abortion league becomes pregnant through a process of parthenogenesis. His wife and daughter are also pregnant, and he decides to have an abortion.

One piece stood out in particular in *Let's Talk about Women*. Entitled *Il risveglio* (*Waking Up*), it was a monologue dealing with a working-class mother who wakes up and goes through her morning chores with her baby before going off to work, only to discover that she has lost her key. She reconstructs her actions throughout the previous day and evening, including the argument she has had with her husband (who is asleep in bed), until she finally finds the key. At the end she realises that it is Sunday and that her entire rigmarole of actions has been unnecessary. The play presents a realistic, inside view of the predicament of many working-class mothers in Italian cities:

We slave away like pack-horses and never even get a moment to ourselves. Is this what marriage is all about? Has it ever entered your head that I might have problems too? Do you ever ask me if I'm tired, or if I'd like a hand? Who cooks your dinner? I do. Who does the dishes afterwards? I do. Who does the shopping? I do. Who does all the financial somersaults to survive until

the end of the month? And then I have to hold down a
job on top of all that![28]

This tirade avoids being rhetorical by coming in the context of
the woman's reconstruction of her argument with her husband
– an argument which is at least partially resolved. It also indicates
the near-naturalism of the piece, which is also not without its
comic aspects. The piece used minimal staging and Rame began
to perform it live with an 'epic' economy of means, miming
most of the action with a doll.

Later in 1977, the Fos collaborated on a series of five
monologues performed by Franca Rame under the title *Tutta
casa, letto e chiesa* (*All House, Bed and Church*), which indicted the
classic traditional Italian male view of women. Over the next six
years these plays were re-elaborated, transformed and
reconstructed until they were almost unrecognisable. They
provided a one-woman show which Franca Rame toured all
over Italy and Europe, achieving an acclaim which almost
paralleled that of Fo's *Mistero buffo*. The plays resulted from a
series of discussions with women in factories and research into
women's 'testimonies' throughout Italy, and were tried out in
front of a women's collective. In them Franca Rame played a
more prominent role than usual as a writer, sketching out
situations which were then put into dramatic form by Fo. They
amounted to a reversal of the relatively second-order role Rame
had always played in La Comune, and through them she was
able to identify more fully with the female characters – who
extend across different class boundaries – that she performed:

> I've understood completely what the condition of women
> and wives involves, especially that of the wife of a famous
> actor like Fo. It means always being put in second place in
> relation to a man, and being judged as incapable of any
> autonomous choice.[29]

Since she began performing *Tutta casa, letto e chiesa*, Rame
became more independent of her previous collaborations with
Fo, and the couple often toured separately (Fo with various
editions of *Mistero buffo*). It was Rame, rather than Fo, who was

the first to perform in London, at the Riverside Studios in 1982.

The first production of *Tutta casa, letto e chiesa* at the Palazzina Liberty in December 1977 consisted of five monologues, which lasted two and a half hours. These were performed on a virtually bare stage (as in *Mistero buffo*) with only the minimum props and settings required. The sparsity emphasised the 'breaking down of the fourth wall' which Fo had advocated in all his plays since 1968, as well as the 'epic acting' involved in directly presenting (rather than representing) a character. There were comments and asides to the audience, and any attempt at a naturalistic portrayal was avoided. In *Waking Up*, as we have seen, the pretext for the monologue is the woman's conversation with her baby (which the audience can clearly see is a doll).

In the second piece, *Una donna tutta sola* (*A Woman Alone*), the character is a lower-middle-class housewife whose husband locks her in the house to prevent her from sexual misdemeanours, and who converses with a new, unseen neighbour. In this longest and most comic of the monologues, this 'woman on her own', who has already survived a couple of suicide attempts, has to contend with male aggression on all sides. She has to fight off the advances of her husband's crippled brother, who watches pornographic films in the next room, a peeping Tom with a telescope, an obscene phone-caller whom she continually confuses with her husband, as he is being pursued by a creditor, and her ex-English teacher, who is in love with her and tries to break into the house. While she irons to the blaring sounds of a radio, record player and cassette recorder, her brother-in-law hoots the horn on his wheelchair for her attention, her baby cries and the phone rings, and she confides frankly in her new neighbour, discussing her sexual problems in a disarmingly comic way:

> Well, I can tell you everything's far from OK as far as me and my husband are concerned – I just can't manage to . . . You know . . . I just don't feel anything. How can I put it . . . That's it – yes – that's a word I can never bring myself to say; I really have to force it out – orgasm. It sounds like the name of some hideous animal, some sort of squat little

monkey halfway between a mandrill and an orangutan. I get the feeling I've read about one somewhere in the newspaper: 'a fully grown orgasm has escaped from the American circus . . . The orgasm was recaptured after a furious struggle with firemen.' And when people start talking about 'reaching orgasm', it sounds a bit like catching the tram after you've had to run like hell . . .[30]

For her performance of the show at the Public Theatre in New York in September 1983, Rame changed the English title to *Adult Orgasm Escapes from the Zoo,* in acknowledgment that the candid, open and basically cheerful character of this monologue is one of her finest and funniest farcical creations. The piece ends after she slams the door on her English teacher's hand, shoots the peeping Tom, pushes her brother-in-law down the stairs in his wheelchair, and sits waiting calmly, rifle in hand, for her husband to return home.

The third monologue, *La mamma fricchettona* (*Freak Mother*) dealt with a typical Italian *mamma* pursuing her son, who has left home and joined a group of 'Metropolitan Indians'. This libertarian hippie movement, which flourished briefly in Italy in the mid-1970s (the hippie phenomenon was late arriving in Italy) soon became outmoded, and the play was discarded. It is set in a confessional in a church where the Mother takes refuge after she has abandoned her family to become a 'witch mother' to the hippie movement and discovered drugs and free love. She has also been denounced to the police by her family as a result. The play's situation vaguely parallels the generation-reversal of *Mother's Marijuana* – as the mother becomes increasingly 'liberated', her son becomes increasingly conservative.

This was followed by a direct confrontation of women's sexual problems in *The Same Old Story*, which demonstrates that sexism and male domination are just as prominent in left-wing circles as they are in other environments:

> Of course I want to make love, but not like a pinball machine, where all you have to do is put your money in the slot and my lights light up and you bash your balls around ping ping pong pong. Go on then, knock me about

as much as you like. No, right, if you knock me about I go into tilt. You get the picture?[31]

The piece begins as a one-sided conversation between a woman and her lover (who is unseen), and confronts the problems of contraception, abortion, 'phallocracy' and unwanted children. The monologue then proceeds into an absurdist, scatological 'fairy tale' about a little girl with a doll who uses swearwords, which is used to prove in a roundabout way that women of all social classes have 'the same story' as far as male sexism is concerned.

The original version of the show concluded with *Medea*, which was based not on Euripides' play, but on a popular Italian version of the Medea story which originated in Magna Grecia. It was performed in the archaic dialect of that historical central Italian region, with Rame acting out different 'choral' roles as well as the tragic protagonist. In it, Medea becomes a symbol of a 'new woman' who kills her children not out of jealousy but out of a desire for liberation from the shackles of domestic servitude. This piece came under fire from English feminists, who saw it as advocating infanticide. In her study of Rame's work, Maggie Günsberg accused the piece of being 'anti-feminist':

> Not only does it lend credence to extremist anti-feminist discourses, among them that of feminists as bad mothers and second-rate women generally, but it fails to locate the true source of Medea's problems by simply reiterating, rather than deconstructing, the patriarchal ideology underpinning the original play. . . . By acting the archetypically 'bad mother', she also plays into the hands of a patriarchal society that can simply classify her as 'mad'. Ultimately, her action is one of unproductive false consciousness rather than a true *presa di coscienza* [gaining of consciousness] leading to successful self-reconstruction (*autocoscienza*).[32]

But as Fo and Rame point out in an extended comic prologue to *Medea*, which continues to be omitted from English versions of *Tutta casa*, this version of Medea is a popular Umbrian and Tuscan witch-like creation, whose story is allegorical rather than instructive. Their Medea's motivations for killing her children are not those of the angry, jealous woman of Euripides' drama, but of a woman without the ability to mediate or engage in dialectics, who is mistaken and irrational, but who achieves a *presa di coscienza* in freeing herself of the yoke her husband has imposed on her.[33] If this is not overcoming patriarchy, it is hard to see what is. As Sharon Wood has argued, Medea refuses to play the expected role of a sacrificing mother, and murders her children to ensure she will not be annihilated by a law of nature which privileges men:

> Hers is not an act of individual madness or even revenge, but an assertion of her own subjective identity and being. It is a political act which defies the assimilation of femininity to motherhood, which refuses to contemplate women as both mothers and sexual beings . . . Medea's anguish is evident, but the murder is a profoundly political act intent on breaking the chain of servitude which the patriarchal ideology of motherhood has foisted on women.[34]

Despite the difficulties of *Medea*, the monologues of *Tutta casa, letto e chiesa* were soon embraced by feminist theatre practitioners throughout Europe and the USA – where Rame performed it in 1986. By 1990 it had been performed in 35 countries, making it Fo's and Rame's second most widely performed play (along with *Can't Pay? Won't Pay!*) after *Accidental Death of an Anarchist*.[35] In an article about Rame's work published in 1985, Serena Anderlini emphasises the accessibility of Rame's brand of feminism, which could be associated with socialist feminist movements (or their US equivalent, materialist feminism) rather than radical or cultural feminist tendencies:

> Her theatre does not explore relationships among women, and it avoids the mother–daughter relationship so dear to the avant-garde of the feminist movement. If her feminism is elemental, and focuses on the issues of power in heterosexual relationships, it also goes beyond idiosyncratic anti-male positions. The plays suggest that the dynamics of

power and liberty, violence and love, conventionality and authenticity, is what really is at stake in women's issues.[36]

In her influential book *Feminism and Theatre* (1988) US feminist critic Sue-Ellen Case includes a section on Rame and *Waking Up* and *The Same Old Story*, which she sees as an example of materialist feminist theatre. Case argues that

> There is no notion of patriarchy as such in Rame's Marxist-feminist texts: instead, the privileges accorded to the male gender are seen as an extension of capitalist production modes and class privilege into the personal, domestic sphere. Women appear as an exploited class within an exploited class. The vocabulary of Marxist thought is used to describe their condition and hurled as insults at the leftist men. Though the plays dramatise a lack of understanding on the part of male Marxists, they are not intended as final critiques. Rather, they are located in the tradition of socialist realism, aimed at educating the men and women in the audience.[37]

Case's readings of these two pieces indicate how they were framed in the rhetoric of the debates of Fo's and Rame's militant work of the 1970s. But it needs to be noted that in the late 1970s Rame was moving progressively away from notions of 'socialist realism' and 'the vocabulary of Marxist thought' towards a more universal type of language and a more 'epic' performance style.

In an essay published in 1995, Marga Cottino-Jones uses the rather arid discourse of orthodox militant feminist textual studies, in managing to make Rame sound much more threatening to male audiences than she is. Downplaying the highly comic aspects of most of Rame's monologues, and her easy rapport with her audiences, both male and female, Cottino-Jones attempts to build her into a 'transgressive' feminist icon:

> While normal discourse in literature, cinema, and theatre aims at narrative closure where the male subject's desire controls the female object, Rame's stage discourse is quite different from what audiences or readers are accustomed to. Her female characters, dominating the stage as they do

with their presence and addressing the spectators in a very strongly subversive voice, strike the audience as at least unusual, often transgressive and therefore unacceptable and/or incomprehensible. The discourse of these characters constructs the female as a point of resistance to male control able to break down a centuries-old silence with a subversive voice calling attention to the unfairness of the woman's condition, especially in her role as mother.[38]

Maggie Günsberg, in a detailed study of Rame's plays in the context of a study of gender in the Italian theatre from the Renaissance to the present, also emphasises the centrality of Rame's voices and characters in terms of stage presence. Pointing out that most of Rame's impersonations involve some degree of *autocoscienza* (self-awareness and self-agency), Günsberg nonetheless finds them wanting in terms of any extended critique of patriarchy. She argues that Rame's characters sometimes reinforce traditional images of femininity, and 'her female parts remain inscribed by patriarchal definitions of femininity policed by internalised strategies of self-victimisation and powerlessness, leading to continued entrapment in circumscribed roles.'[39] In other words, they are not positive or 'empowered' enough. While acknowledging that Rame's use of comedy 'is particularly important in that it counteracts one of the dominant stereotypes of feminism as unattractively bitter and humourless,'[40] Günsberg is inclined to perpetuate this stereotype. This is evident in her judgment of Rame's performances as displaying

a feminine viewpoint still entrammelled and confined by patriarchal definitions and parameters, with a preponderance of negative dramatic closures sealing the inability of the female parts to find fulfilment in what they *do*, rather than how they *appear*, and particularly, how they appear in the eyes of men.[41]

It is worth recording that Rame herself, in a statement she made in 1977 when she first began performing *Tutta casa, letto e chiesa*, denied being a militant feminist:

For a theatre like ours, which follows hard on current events and is at the same time shaped by them, it would have been a very grave oversight to have failed to have picked up on the woman's question. The feminist problem is far too important now. These girls, or rather women, have done some extraordinary things, while, like any movement, they also have their negative and mistaken aspects. But this happens in all real movements . . . I have a lot of esteem for the feminists, especially those who are not completely antagonistic towards men, and those who are working courageously to change things, working in local communities, and with abortion, etc. I am not a militant feminist, since most of my time is taken up with theatre, Red Aid, and a thousand and one other things that have to be done to keep things afloat. But I do follow the developments and activities of the feminist movement.[42]

In the course of more than 500 performances of her one-woman shows, Rame added various other monologues. Twenty-five of these were published by Einaudi in volume 8 of Fo's collected works in 1989, including a Roman *Lysistrata*, *Ulrike Meinhof*, and a monologue about Irmgard Moeller, *Tomorrow's News*. Fo and Rame organised a petition for Moeller after the Stammheim 'suicides' in 1978, and it was signed by a number of prominent Italian writers and directors, which led to accusations against Fo of supporting terrorism in an article in the Italian magazine *Panorama* by the PCI MP (and sometime poet) Antonello Trombadori.

Accusations of supporting terrorism were to dog Fo and Rame from this period onwards, largely because of Franca Rame's involvement in Soccorso Rosso. Fo and Rame were criticised for their involvement in a campaign to release Petra Krause, a Swiss-Italian woman who was accused and charged of a series of terrorist-related offences in Milan and Switzerland in 1975. Soccorso Rosso managed to secure her temporary release from prison in 1977.

From her involvement in Soccorso Rosso, in which she wrote letters and organised legal aid to some 800 Italian prisoners, Rame wrote a monologue, *La madre* (*The Mother*), which she added to her one-woman show in 1982. Based on accounts by women who were relatives of terrorist suspects being detained in Italy's special prisons, the play is a condemnation of the Italian government's treatment of prisoners awaiting trial. Suspects could legally be held in prison for up to five years and four months before their cases first came to court, and ten years and eight months before their final trial. The protagonist of *The Mother* sees a photo of her son on the TV news, and learns that he has been arrested and charged with being a terrorist involved in a political assassination. The play takes the form of a direct address to the audience, focusing on the Mother's reactions to the news. The human issues behind terrorism are emphasised in a way which, far from being imputable as support for terrorism, comes across as a strong condemnation of it. The piece serves to highlight the repressive and inhumane laws which operated in Italy as a result of terrorism.

The Mother describes in detail the indignities and humiliations of visiting her son in a high-security prison in Sardinia. She is forced to undergo anal and vaginal searches before being allowed to see him, and she is horrified to discover he has a swollen face and broken hands as a result of being beaten up by police. The play is a chilling indictment of strip-searching, and Rame's performance of it in London in 1983 served to complement a campaign against similar practices in Armagh Jail in Northern Ireland. This provided another example of the universality of many of the political issues the Fos' plays confront in an Italian context. Rame's left-wing, liberal, tolerant Mother (but the play stresses it could happen to anyone) is outraged by 'being treated . . . like an animal', and thinks of denouncing the strip-searching to the newspapers:

'As soon as I get out of here, I'll report it. I'll write to the papers. Oh yes I will.' But then I just felt like laughing: write to the papers? But what newspaper is going to publish anything on what I am going through now?

I am only the mother of a terrorist. Sixty-five per cent of people are in favour of capital punishment . . . I . . . I opened my legs and let her get on with the job.[43]

The Mother is a representative of female rage at female impotence in a male-dominated system of repression. This aligns her with the woman who is raped in *I Don't Move, I Don't Scream, My Voice is Gone*, who decides to put off reporting the rape until the next day, as she can't bear the thought of describing her experience to the police, and with Ulrike Meinhof trapped in her fishtank-like cell in Stammheim. All three pieces are a powerful medium for the voice of oppressed women to be heard publicly, and direct cries from the heart unmediated by any paraphernalia of dramatic representation.

In 1981, a second version of *Tutta casa, letto e chiesa* opened at the Teatro Odeon in Milan. Fo and Rame had not performed at the Odeon, whose plush red velvet still housed a predominantly bourgeois audience, since *Always Blame the Devil* 16 years previously. The reasons for this return to the bourgeois theatre were partly the eviction of La Comune from the Palazzina Liberty – although they subsequently used a converted cinema, the Cristallo, as their base. They also involved a desire to demonstrate that the women's issues the plays confronted were of an 'inter-class' concern, and addressed themselves to all types of women. As Rame explained:

> I realised that in turning our backs on the so-called bourgeois theatre, we were refusing a portion of spectators who would never have come to a stadium or into a circus tent, but still have the right to be entertained, to laugh, and at the same time to see certain problems dealt with.[44]

Fo had already made something of a return to mainstream theatre in 1978, after touring *La storia della tigre* around Italy. He was approached by the prestigious Teatro alla Scala, which was celebrating its bicentenary, and asked to become a director. At first this seemed an acknowledgment of his importance, albeit controversial, as a theatrical figure both in Italy and abroad, an importance which had been consolidated by his success on Italian TV. At the time of his appointment, Fo justified his entry into one of the bastions of the Italian and European cultural establishment:

There's little to be scandalised about. La Scala is hardly the stamping ground of the conformist bourgeoisie, or monumental productions, or the academy. It's a great theatre with a history which often included satire against the authorities and periods of great political tension . . . It also put on the first theatrical representation of class struggle, in *William Tell*, whose protagonist is a highlander supported by a crowd of peasants who fight for their rights against the bosses.[45]

Plans for a collaboration between Fo and La Scala were to include his co-writing and directing a new opera by the Communist composer Luigi Nono, and some little-known Verdi operas. But his first task, and in the event, the only one which got off the ground, was a production of Stravinsky's *The Soldier's Tale*, which Strehler had also directed at La Scala in 1957. Fo set about almost completely rewriting Ramuz's libretto, politicising it and adding *grammelot*, as well as expanding it to include Stravinsky's Octet, which brought disgruntled responses from some music critics. Fo turned the work into

a kind of accusation against capitalism, which speculates on the concept of patriotism and uses the peasant, the poor devil who is eradicated from his land, and entices him with traffic, business and bogus dreams, taking away his fields and his culture.[46]

Stravinsky's soldier-protagonist became a type of *Zanni*, in a 'choral' production which used a cast of 32 (as opposed to four in the original) students from La Scala. In the process, Fo shredded Stravinsky's opera in mounting a visually spectacular 'image track' to the music. The production, which Fo wrote, designed and directed but did not act in, is a rare example of his capacities as a director of a large-scale work. It consisted of 14 'stage pictures', including the city, the stock exchange, war, a market and a 'ship of fools'. There was an ingenious use of basically simple stage props, like sticks and newspapers, to create stunning visual effects, and Fo used a giant cane puppet and a Brechtian inventiveness which would seem to illustrate the words of the Devil: 'Create the revolution with imagination.' In changing the work from a chamber opera to a 'piazza opera', Fo's *Soldier's Tale* fitted the bill for La Scala's 'decentralisation' programme. The production opened in Cremona and played in the Teatro Tenda circus tent in Rome. This was ideal for Fo's own work, but in the context of La Scala represented a type of ghettoisation, and after disagreements with the La Scala administration, Fo terminated his collaboration with them.

The cast of *The Soldier's Tale* included Paolo Rossi, a young comic actor who was to make a name for himself in the 1980s and 1990s as one of Italy's most prominent and popular stand-up stage and television comedians and film actors. Rossi developed a dialect-based satirical style of comedy monologue strongly influenced and inspired by Fo. Interviewed in 1998, he acknowledged Fo as one of his *maestri* along with popular, carnivalesque figures such as Ruzzante and Rabelais, and Fo performed with him in his television series *Scatafascio*.[47]

Confronting terrorism and *Trumpets and Raspberries*

In 1979 Fo wrote and performed a series of television sketches which were transmitted by the second channel of RAI under the titles *Buona sera con Dario Fo* and *Buona sera con Franca Rame*. These provoked little in the way of controversy, perhaps due to the fact that they were broadcast in a safe, early evening slot. *Buona sera con Franca Rame* included 'The Old Age Problem', a sketch in which old people are thrown out of windows in order to save on pensions and old people's homes, which was later recycled in 1992 in *Settimo: ruba un po' meno no. 2*. In another sketch, which was subsequently published, 'The Black Out', a paranoid woman makes elaborate preparations, including blind-folding herself, for a power cut, which throws her daughter's birthday party into total chaos.

Meanwhile Fo was working on a play about the kidnapping and murder of Aldo Moro, the former Italian Prime Minister and Christian Democrat leader, an event which had put Italian terrorism into the international news headlines. *The Tragedy of Aldo Moro* was based on the letters Moro wrote to his Christian

Democrat colleagues while in a 'people's prison', pleading with his colleagues to negotiate with his captors. Fo saw a resemblance between the tone of the letters and that of Greek tragedy, and the situation of *Philoctetes* in particular, seeing the DC government's refusal to negotiate as using Moro as a scapegoat and sacrificial victim for their own self-preservation. So he drafted the play in the form of a Greek tragedy, with Satyrs, Bacchanals, a *Giullare* Narrator, and eight Christian Democrats, as well as Moro (who was to be played by Fo). This gave it a static, wordy form, which got too bogged down in the particular details of the event, quoting extensively from Moro's letters.

Fo tried out the first act of the play once as a public reading in support of the campaign for the release of Toni Negri and the other victims of the wave of arrests carried out against members of Autonomia and other Italian far-left groups on 7 April 1979. He then discarded it, although the text of this first act (the second act was never completed) was published in *Panorama* and *Lotta Continua*. Fo found himself unable to clarify in dramatic form the confusing course of events surrounding the 'Moro tragedy' which he wanted to relate to the context of Italian terrorism as a whole, and jettisoned the project. Terrorism had become the most predominant political problem in Italy, and had been used to pour discredit on the Left so successfully that most of the 'extra-parliamentary' groups were being forced to keep a low profile, if not go underground to avoid being criminalised. Discussing terrorism from a leftist point of view became increasingly delicate in a situation in which Moro, whose overtures to the PCI had made him something of a controversial figure in the DC (despite his otherwise highly conservative views), had become mythologised into a kind of heroic martyr figure of Italian democracy. In the play, one of Moro's colleagues comments on the DC's refusal to negotiate with terrorists:

What exactly are you trying to get at, Aldo? Are you trying to claim that the tragic increase in violence is all the fault of our policy of refusing to go to the negotiating table? So we're to blame for the fact that the *brigatisti* have become so ruthless, are we? Are you trying to say that if we agreed to empty the prisons and release their so-called 'comrades', we'd now be in an idyllic state of peace? I suppose the Red Brigades would just be showering flowers and confetti on us, and helping old ladies across the street, and instead of exploding bombs, they'd be letting off fancy fireworks to thrill the kiddies?[48]

Faced with the bewildering complexities of the DC–BR stand-off of the Moro situation at a time when there was little impetus left in the grassroots Italian Left, and little opportunity to deal with events in his usual comic-satirical way, Fo was well advised to abandon this abortive attempt to deal with terrorism. But he clearly felt an obligation to go ahead with it, as no Italian writer or film director – discounting Bertolucci's dismally inadequate film *Tragedy of a Ridiculous Man*, about a terrorist kidnapping, and Leonardo Sciascia's documentary study of Moro's letters, *L'Affare Moro* (*The Moro Affair*) – seemed able to deal with the subject. Fo described the current situation as

a state of affairs in Italy where there is no longer any talk of reform, where the logic of the lesser of two evils has been discarded, where trade unionists have been forced on to their knees, and class struggle has been thwarted at every turn . . . What is needed is the courage to assess contradictions, and to strive to understand at all costs.[49]

The difficulty of maintaining an objective viewpoint, together with the problems of sorting out the morass of information and contradictory events, in a complex issue where there was no defendable party, required more distance than Fo was in a position to have. In 1983 the Spanish writer Jorge Semprun, who wrote a number of screenplays for Costa Gavras' films, completed a play about the Moro kidnapping, which indicates that perhaps it took a non-Italian writer to assess the event with sufficient detachment. But Fo was to return to the issue, confronting it in a more imaginative, fictional form, two years later.

Ironically, despite Fo's continued anti-terrorist stance, he and Rame were refused a visa to enter the United States in 1980, where they were to perform *Mistero buffo* and *Tutta casa, letto e chiesa* in the Festival of Italian Theatre at the New York Town Hall. The reasons given for this refusal by the US embassy in Rome were the activities of Soccorso Rosso in helping political prisoners in Italy, which was seen as a support of terrorist violence. In fact Franca Rame had visited some of the leaders of the Red Brigades, including Renato Curcio, in prison, at the time of the Moro kidnapping, in an attempt to persuade them to speak out publicly and advocate Moro's release, but had been unable to achieve any results.

As a result, amid accusations of McCarthyism, 'An Evening without Dario Fo and Franca Rame' was held in New York in May 1980. This was attended by Richard Foreman, Martin Scorsese, Arthur Miller, Bernard Malamud, Sol Yurick, Ellen Stewart and others. Students of New York University also presented an English version of the first act of *Can't Pay? Won't Pay!* Piero Sciotto read a letter from Fo and Rame deploring the situation and explaining the problem caused by the new law of 'repentant terrorists' in Italy, which often led to the arrest of innocent people. This event probably brought Fo and Rame more publicity than they would have received if they had been granted a visa. As one New York critic pointed out, they were in select company, as Brecht, Charlie Chaplin and Gabriel García Márquez had also been refused entry to the US.

In their annual conference, the American Critics' Association protested about the visa refusal, sending a letter to the Secretary of State Edmund Muskie. Nevertheless, in September 1983, the American Department of State once again refused Fo and Rame an entry visa to the USA, accusing them of 'belonging to organisations supporting terrorist groups'[50] and citing Soccorso Rosso. This was despite the fact that Fo had no direct involvement with the prison aid group, and that in 1983 he was the foreign author whose plays had received the most productions in the US (and world) theatre.

Fo and Rame had been scheduled to perform *Mistero buffo* and

Tutta casa, letto e chiesa at Joseph Papp's Public Theatre in New York, and to run theatre workshops in the theatre departments of the Universities of Boston, Los Angeles and Washington. *Tutta casa, letto e chiesa* was at the time being performed throughout the USA by 18 different theatre companies, including a production of the play by film director Arthur Penn with the actress Estelle Parsons. Papp promptly sent a telegram to President Reagan, appealing to him as a theatrical 'colleague', while Fo and Rame began a lawsuit against the US State Department for damages. They announced they would donate any damages received to sacked workers, occupied factories, anti-drug organisations, handicapped people, squats, and prisoners and their families. In a press conference in Milan, Fo outlined the gravity and illegality of the charge made against him and his wife by the US State Department:

> We are Italian citizens who are supposed to have committed the crime of aiding and abetting terrorists in Italy. The Italian judicial authorities, however, have never charged us or even made inquiries into the activities carried out by Soccorso Rosso, nor have they accused us of any support of terrorism: in any case our position on the subject is well known. Now the Americans arrive on the scene and decide that we support terrorists, which means either that the Italian judicial authorities aren't doing their job or that they are in complicity with us.[51]

In January 1981, *Clacson, trombette e pernacchi* (literally 'Car Horns, Trumpets and Raspberries', – a 'Carnival' title which was rendered in an American production of the play in 1983 as *About Face*) – opened at the Cinema Cristallo in Milan. Fo had finally overcome his block about confronting issues related to terrorism, in what was his first new play for five years (since *Mother's Marijuana*). The farcical form of *Trumpets and Raspberries* resembled that of its predecessor, and showed clearly that Fo's sympathies were categorically against terrorism and any violent form of political action. It incorporates extracts from Moro's letters and Fo's comments on current Italian political events. It also uses comic devices which closely resemble Fo's farces of the 1950s and 1960s, particularly the mistaken identity situation of *Aveva due pistole*, while borrowing some of its trappings from Plautus' *Brothers Menaechmus*.

The basic situation is that of a 'comedy of errors' (or 'comedy of terror'). Antonio, a Fiat worker in *cassa integrazione*, who begins where Giovanni in *Can't Pay? Won't Pay!* leaves off, saves the life of Fiat boss Giovanni Agnelli, after a road accident which occurs while terrorists are trying to kidnap Agnelli. This use of one of Italy's most prominent international businessmen, the owner of Fiat and the Juventus football team, in a fictional kidnapping, was a deliberate, open provocation. Agnelli is disfigured in the accident, and after Antonio flees, leaving his jacket over the Fiat boss, the latter is mistaken for Antonio. Agnelli then undergoes plastic surgery which gives him Antonio's face. This leads to a double-identity situation (both Antonio and Agnelli are played by Fo) when Antonio's wife Rosa (Franca Rame) takes Agnelli for her prodigal husband. This occurs after an encounter with Antonio's mistress Lucia, who is unable to reveal the 'exchange' of identities to Rosa. The real Antonio is forced to go into hiding for fear that he will be implicated in the terrorist kidnapping, since his car (a Fiat, naturally) in which he rescued Agnelli, has been spotted:

ANTONIO: I'm done for. A wanted terrorist! They probably think I'm the brains behind the whole plot! And
what's more, I've saved my own boss – the face that
sacked 40 thousand workers. I'm really stuffed.

LUCIA: Oh, come on, don't be so pessimistic. OK, the
guy's an arsehole, but as soon as he comes to and lets on
he's Agnelli and you saved him, you're in line for a big
reward.

ANTONIO: Oh yeah? You think he'd admit to having his
face saved by one of his scumbag workers?[52]

Agnelli (who is referred to throughout the play as 'The Double') has lost the power of speech as well as his memory. This occasions some variations of *grammelot* as the Doctors try to restore his power of speech so that the police can interrogate him. The situation is a farcical 'about face' in which Agnelli comes under accusation of terrorism. In the confusion of identities, both characters succeed in hoodwinking the police while stretching the credibility of the situation to breaking point, calling for theories of schizophrenia as well as amnesia to cover up the difference between Antonio and The Double. The farcical situation reaches its peak when Rosa uses a mincing machine and feeding apparatus to feed Antonio, strapping him to a chair (since The Double can only be fed through the nose) and forcing him to play his clarinet to keep him from crying out. The police leap on the feeding apparatus and use it as a torture device (since it is more sophisticated than their own methods) and force a false confession of terrorist activities out of Antonio.

In the final scene of the play, agents from rival sections of the Italian secret political police – DIGOS, SISDE, SISMI and UCIGOS – take up hiding places behind various articles of furniture in the room to await the outcome of the situation. This satirises the efforts of the various factions of the Italian police to cover themselves in glory by capturing terrorists. It is then revealed that Agnelli has plagiarised Moro's letters to government ministers, who have responded differently this time, calling for an amnesty on political prisoners in exchange for Agnelli. This proves the latter's claim that he is more important than Italian politicians:

> I represent the real centre of power . . . Don't you see that? Haven't you read your Karl Marx? Yes, I know. Nowadays it's only we top-level industrial management people who bother to read *Das Kapital*, especially the bit where it says that 'the true source of power is economic and financial, public holdings, the stock exchange, banks and merchandising – in short, capital'. I am the state! The capital I represent is the state! You've got no choice but to save my dignity, even if you die in the process![53]

This speech, which is delivered while Agnelli is standing aloft on all the previously mobile furniture which has now been arranged into a kind of staircase, exemplifies one of the play's defects. There is a tendency to make lengthy political statements which come across as lectures, as in The Double's previous three-page potted history of recent Italian political events. In it he accuses the Italian government of using terrorism as a pretext to avoid problems like unemployment, inflation, education, hospital reform and the Mafia.

Trumpets and Raspberries also seemed to take a backward step in its treatment of its women characters. There is a virtual cat-fight between Rosa and the radical-chic Lucia in the hospital. The deception of Rosa, who, unlike Antonia in *Can't Pay? Won't Pay!*, is presented as a repressed, working-class housewife, blissful about being able to do her husband's washing and ironing again, also comes across as needlessly cruel. This is even despite her unwitting 'revenge' on Antonio with the feeding device. Not surprisingly, Franca Rame was dissatisfied with the role of Rosa, which was definitely retrogressive in comparison with the characters she was portraying in *Tutta casa, letto e chiesa*. Although it played to 50,000 spectators in 34 performances in Milan, *Trumpets and Raspberries* toured only sporadically over the course of the next year, and was then dropped.

The play opened at a time when another terrorist kidnapping, that of the judge D'Urso, was in a dramatic phase, and this gave it considerable topicality. But its opening night was marred by inaccurate press reports of an incident which led to further accusations against Fo of supporting terrorism. In an extra-theatrical practice by now customary in performances of Fo's plays, relatives of prisoners in Trani, in Apulia, where there had been prison riots, read the text of a report they had filed against the prison director, mentioning violent incidents against prisoners after the revolt. The fact that many of the prisoners in Trani were terrorist suspects was misconstrued as support on Fo's and Rame's part for not only the prison revolt but also terrorism. The episode highlights the 'bad press' Fo had been getting in the Italian media. But in the context of continuing smear campaigns against the Italian Left, Fo had spoken out on a problem which was becoming increasingly difficult to put into perspective. As Valentini commented:

Enormous courage is needed to speak about current events at the present time, and no one up to now has been up to it. Dario Fo has tried, without pussyfooting around, choosing the path of political theatre, taking equal risks on both aesthetic and legal fronts. The tabloid press has realised this, and when it hasn't ignored him, it has attacked him hypocritically, without having the courage to get down to the point. Young and theatreless audiences have also realised this, and queued for hours at the Cristallo box office in Milan, hoping that at last here was someone talking about ourselves and our history.[54]

Although in Valentini's view *Trumpets and Raspberries* was less accomplished than even *Grande pantomima* or *Il dito nell'occhio,* she acknowledged that Fo was the only Italian author to confront the most vital and disturbing Italian political issue of the 1980s. The play, despite its *longueurs,* was a unique example of contemporary political theatre, which made its points forcefully in suggesting that the connections between high finance and terrorism may not be as far-fetched as they would seem.

Ed Emery has made the interesting point that Fo's use of carnival and *commedia dell'arte* masks and kerchiefs in the play (as in a scene when a cafe waiter enters in a Pulcinella mask, and in the central idea of plastic surgery and mistaken identities) connects with the use of face masks and handkerchiefs as disguises by the Italian revolutionary Left in street demonstrations. This 'streetfighter's kerchief' was later taken up by Benetton as a fashion motif. Emery also notes the play's use of 'the injection-in-the-bum-of-the-wrong-person routine', which Fo lifts wholesale from an earlier play of his, *Gli imbianchini. Clacson* also makes use of a mobile window, as in a number of Fo's other plays, which virtually becomes a character in its own right. The play's highly structured sense of situation and its 'reworking *Commedia* within a framework of radicalism' leads Emery to suggest it 'deserves to be taken a lot more seriously than it has been.'[55] Stuart Hood has suggested that it was Fo's last major political work,[56] but in his review of the play, Franco Quadri indicated that Fo was losing his capacity to keep ahead of the political *Zeitgeist*:.

Six years ago, in *Fanfani Kidnapped*, Dario Fo was ahead of

the times; with this grotesque scenario of a terrorist kidnapping of Gianni Agnelli he is merely keeping abreast of
current events in dramatic form. But the weapon of laughter has great difficulty in taking advantage of a tragic
situation which affects us daily and has scant possibility for
the imagination. It is no coincidence that *Clacson* . . . has
been through a tortuous gestation. Not even the latest
stage version succeeds in working perfectly . . . The context suffers from a mania for explanation and a cumulative
vagueness, because in the course of the play almost every
target is aimed at, except for ideological clarity.[57]

Nonetheless, Fo's work was now immensely popular outside
Italy, and productions of the play were immediately planned in
15 different countries. These included the Yale Repertory in the
USA in 1983, and in London it opened in the West End in
November 1984 with Griff Rhys Jones in Fo's double role. But
the London production proved to be something of a toothless
tiger – Irving Wardle in *The Times* describing it as 'an
entertainment for those who know little about Italian justice
and care less.'[58]

Adapting Brecht and *The Open Couple*

In 1981 Fo became the most widely produced Italian playwright
in the world. Productions of his work had been performed in
Japan, India, Australasia, and even (despite his pro-PLO stance)
Israel.[59] He was invited by the Berliner Ensemble to do an
'updated' adaptation of Brecht's *Threepenny Opera*. But after
completely rewriting the play, and adding his usual satire on
domestic consumer products (in the wedding scene between
Polly and Macheath scores of electrical-appliance wedding gifts
arrive on a conveyor belt) Fo found his version rejected by
Brecht's daughter Barbara and it was never performed at the
Berliner Ensemble. Fo claimed to be following Brecht's own
example in showing a healthy disrespect for the classics, and also
to be making a statement against the reverence shown towards
Brecht's plays as classics in the European bourgeois theatre. He

also claimed to base his version more on John Gay's *Beggar's Opera* than on Brecht's reworking of Gay, and cut all of Brecht's and Kurt Weill's songs. Using the somewhat dubious and risky form of a rock opera, he added 24 pastiches of songs, rewritten by Fiorenzo Carpi, by the likes of David Bowie, Patti Smith, Frank Zappa, Janis Joplin and Jimi Hendrix (suggested by Fo's son Jacopo) which became totally unrecognisable in their Italianisation.

In December 1981 Fo's adaptation was taken up by the Teatro Stabile di Torino and the Teatro Il Fabbricone of Prato, and with the title of *L'opera dello sghignazzo* it opened at the latter theatre. The title literally means 'The Opera of the Sneering Laugh', and expresses a concept Fo had used frequently in his previous plays, that of pouring scorn and contempt on the authorities through laughter. It has been translated by Ed Emery as *The Opera of Guffaws*, which does not quite convey the same idea. Il Fabbricone had developed a highly aesthetic, refined and lush house style from the productions of Luca Ronconi, a director who had made his name in the 1960s with a highly 'rough', knockabout version of Ariosto's *Orlando furioso*. Since then he had become a highly stilted, formalised, conceptual director of workshop productions similar in concept to those of Peter Brook, but resulting in visually impressive, somewhat 'deadly' classical revivals. In this context, Fo claimed that, in choosing the 1980s form (although it is in fact more akin to the 1960s, as the musical models suggest) of a rock opera, he was

> respecting historical progression. Gay's *Beggar's Opera* used popular music of the 1700s, the irreverent, scurrilous music of inns and festivals, the pop of the time, in other words . . . *The Threepenny Opera* also used the popular music of its period: waltzes, tangos, ragtime, variety and German cabaret. For the 1980s, rock was inevitable, and we've recreated everything, without making any reference to Weill's music.[60]

What this meant was that 'Mack the Knife' was substituted by an instantly forgettable rock song about 'plastic cosmetic culture' and 'Pirate Jenny' became a 'futuristic' electronic number about a 'Blue Metal Starship'. As he had done in his adaptation of Michel's *The Sunday Walk,* Fo placed a rock band on stage, but the outdated, hybrid rock songs detracted from a play in which not a single line of either Brecht's or Gay's versions was retained. In using an impressively visual, modular set capable of accommodating any number of scenic actions, Fo claimed to be following Piscator's idea for staging *The Threepenny Opera*, but the result was more a Ronconi-like glossy veneer. Fo's use of professional actors from the establishment theatre (his having by now disbanded La Comune as an acting company) also caused the play to steer dangerously close to the 'plastic, cosmetic culture' it was satirising.

Fo's role in the production was originally restricted to director and designer (as in the more fortunate *Soldier's Tale)*. After a poor critical reception, which found other things to criticise in the play apart from the rather dubious charge of sacrilege against Brecht, Fo took over the role of Peachum in a salvage operation at the Teatro Nazionale in Milan in April 1982. This new version added topical references to the Falklands War, and the case of the Mafia boss Cutolo, who became a model for Macheath. This meant that the play became another political performance vehicle for Fo's comic and topical improvisations in an example of epic acting which outdid Brecht. It also meant that when Fo was not on stage, the play became very lacklustre. Peachum became a crooked lawyer who organises a racket of fake drug addicts whom he uses to 'fiddle' the state system, and the role reflected Fo's constant battle against the theatricality of Italian political reality. As Peachum states in Fo's version:

This job is a theatrical job . . . and the theatre is fiction. Only great fiction manages to outdo reality . . . If you have a duodenal ulcer and describe it in real terms, you achieve a nauseating, repellent effect. As Diderot said – and also Bertolt Brecht, who stole it from him: 'The worst stage drunk is the actor who drinks for real.'[61]

A more insidious symptom reflected by *L'opera dello*

sghignazzo is the widespread tendency of contemporary Italian directors to adapt existing texts to their own frequently self-indulgent concerns – as in Ronconi's stifling and tedious three-hour rendition of Ibsen's *Ghosts* at the Spoleto Festival in 1982. Eduardo de Filippo commented on this phenomenon of adaptation in a lecture to students at Rome University in 1982:

> I will curse down to the seventh generation anyone who changes a single line or word of a play of mine. I've had enough of adaptors, revisers and re-elaborators . . . I would like to incriminate anyone who uses the preposition 'from' – as in 'from Shakespeare' – for theatrical fraud.[62]

The problem of adaptation – ironically compounded when de Filippo himself later accepted a commission to write a Neapolitan version of Shakespeare's *Tempest* – is one which also applies to foreign versions of Fo's own plays. They often require extensive adaptation due to their detailed, topical references to Italian political issues which non-Italian audiences cannot be expected to understand. But in the case of *L'opera dello sghignazzo,* there have been almost no productions of the play outside Italy, and none in English.

In 1982, Fo continued to demonstrate his consummate skill as an adaptor and performer of medieval texts in *Il fabulazzo osceno*. This was another example of his exhumation of little-known popular texts which he uses as vehicles for his dazzling improvisatory abilities as a solo performer, and his scathing political sallies at figures of authority. The following year, he returned to the format of the clown-show revue-sketch in *Patapumfete*. This was a series of short pieces which he wrote and directed for the clown duo I Colombaioni, confronting contemporary social problems such as drugs, violence, video games, factory production lines and TV quizzes in an essentially physical, slapstick way. The aim was to highlight the dehumanising, brain-damaging high-tech trappings of an increasingly epileptic contemporary culture.

Patapumfete also included a two-handed version of *The Morality Play of the Blind Man and the Cripple* from *Mistero buffo,* which proved only how much more imaginative, suggestive and consummately theatrical Fo's own solo performance of the piece is. Fo appeared to be experiencing something of a crisis as a playwright in the early 1980s, at a time when there was a widespread crisis of creativity in the Italian cinema and theatre at large. But he remained unique as an actor and mime, and continued to make his presence felt increasingly outside Italy. The same was true of Franca Rame, who continued to perform *Tutta casa, letto e chiesa* throughout the world to considerable acclaim.

In the early 1980s, Fo and Rame began to have increasing difficulty organising their schedules to accommodate what they saw as a fundamental commitment to touring their work in Italy with the ever-increasing pressures of invitations to tour abroad. Fo alternated performances of *Il fabulazzo osceno* in northern Italy with *Mistero buffo* and *La storia della tigre* in Sweden and Germany. Rame took her latest version of *Tutta casa, letto e chiesa* to Montreal, Sweden and Germany, and both had to turn down offers from as far afield as Australia and Majorca. At the end of 1983, the couple were considering going to Cuba – an interesting choice after being refused entry to the USA – and Fo had definite commitments in Germany. The consistently lower profile they were given in the Italian press since their success abroad coincided with the *riflusso* or decline in the optimism and militancy of the Italian Left, for reasons outlined elsewhere, which led to a downward curve in the Fos' popularity at home.

In November 1983 they began work on a new play, *Coppia aperta, quasi spalancata (The Open Couple – Almost Wide Open)*. This was a two-hander in which Fo directed Rame and Nicola de Buono, an actor who had worked with them several times previously, most notably in *Isabella*. The play tackles a theme which at first sight seems more the domain of a boulevard *farceur* such as Alan Ayckbourn – the ironies and contradictions of a couple who have agreed to pursue an 'open relationship', but continue to discuss their extra-marital affairs. But *The Open Couple* is no made-to-measure farce, and nor does it necessarily reflect the Fos' own private predicament as performers who are frequently working in different cities or even countries. 'It's not a thesis play,' Fo stated during rehearsals. 'Almost every line is taken from conversations we've had with our friends. It's an autobiography of the intellectuals we know, with an added surrealistic charge.' He also pointed out that the apparently private concern of the piece was no new departure for him, as many of his plays, including *Female Parts* and the Agnelli play, have had marital relations at their core. 'The problem exists for everyone, including the working class – it's universal. The woman's role in the family situation is always one of subjugation, like the proletariat, while the man plays the role of the bourgeoisie.'[63]

Any suspicion that the Fos had even temporarily retired from political theatre are put paid to by the Brechtian form of *The Open Couple* – much more evident than in *The Opera of Guffaws* – which consists of a series of flashbacks of a couple's disastrous attempts to live separate lives. They frequently step out of character to comment on events, criticise each other's inconsistencies, and wryly observe each other's semi-serious suicide attempts which express the emotional torment of their situation. As de Buono commented, 'The play shows a private situation which becomes public and political.'[64] The idea of the 'open couple' is shown to be a fallacy because, as Fo explains the sexual politics of the situation, 'it works from the husband's point of view as long as he has other relationships, but when his wife does likewise, he breaks down and wants to go back to the conventional couple situation.'[65] In the final scene the husband appears to commit suicide in the bath with a hairdryer (an idea adapted from the James Bond film *Goldfinger*) when his wife's lover, a whizz-kid nuclear scientist and rock musician whom he had believed she has invented, makes an appearance. Such a complicated interplay of deception and play-acting has been built up between the couple that we are unsure whether his suicide is real or simulated. In rehearsals, Fo insisted on the tragic vein of the play, constantly calling for more dramatic tension. 'The wife really does want to kill herself, and her husband actually shoots her in the foot during a scuffle at one point – if you don't play the tragedy it'll turn into a light comedy or a *pochade*, which it isn't. There's a tragic basis to the play which turns into comedy through the situation.'[66]

Nevertheless the play is predominantly a light comedy which contrasted with one of two companion monologues with which Rame toured it, *The Rape*. But it became clear why Fo was not playing the part of the husband himself when he stepped in to demonstrate a gag which in his hands was so hilarious it toppled the quasi-serious balance of the play. The husband and wife are playing cards when she drops a clanger about her new relationship with the nuclear physicist. Fo showered the pack of cards into the air to underline the fit of self-recrimination in which the husband storms across the stage. 'Snow effect,' commented Rame laconically, and the line was added to the play. After a week's rehearsal, they were already well into a second version of the original text, and lines were being added, cut and re-discussed continuously.

The Open Couple contains a number of echoes of *Accidental Death of an Anarchist*, like its fourth-floor setting, and the wife's attempts to throw herself out of the window – again a window occupies a central position. These and other running gags which resurface from previous Fo plays, emphasise its undiminished political charge. But they also demonstrate what has changed in Italian left-wing politics over the past decade. As Fo commented:

> In *Accidental Death* I talked about the 'liberating belch' caused by scandal, where people's imagination creates a catharsis which distracts attention from the real political problems. In this play there's a line saying that now there's not even that belch left any more – there's no more indignation. A lot of the political militants of the '60s and '70s have drifted into the orange people, or got into macrobiotic food, or played about with the 'open couple' idea. In the face of the failure of revolutionary ideals, the basic problem is how people relate to one another.[67]

At one point in *The Open Couple*, the wife describes how she and her new lover decide to go to Comiso, a town in Sicily where there were ongoing protests about a nuclear reactor – a kind of equivalent to Greenham Common in the UK. The husband paints the scene scathingly as a desire to join up with a bunch of clapped-out hippies, Communist Party tenderfoots, geriatric ex-partisans and arthritic left-wing MPs. In fact the couple only get as far as Parma in central Italy, as it became more important for them to consummate their sexual relationship. 'I deal only indirectly with the nuclear problem in the play because it's riddled with speculation,' Fo stated. 'The Socialist Party and the government are involved in all sorts of dirty double-dealing with the USA and the USSR. It's not a question of making the masses aware of the nuclear threat. I think people are sufficiently aware. What is needed is an autonomous popular movement.'[68]

Fo and Rame rehearsed *The Open Couple* in the cold, dingy Teatro Cinema Cristallo, an ex-music hall and converted cinema which they had made their occasional base in Milan since losing the Palazzina Liberty. At the same time, the Piccolo Teatro was housing a lush, lavish production by Giorgio Strehler of a play with a similar theme, Lessing's *Minna von Barnhelm*. But this light, romantic and luxuriously lit production, which Strehler described as 'a search for the real couple in which the maternal code forms a dialectic, based on love, with the paternal code'[69] could not contrast more, in its frivolous conventionality and aestheticism, with *The Open Couple*. Fo's play relied on rudimentary staging, a Brechtian form, a primary focus on the actors to convey the situation, and an emphasis on gender and power. *Minna von Barnhelm*, in contrast, was all style. With military-style music provided by Fo's old collaborator, Fiorenzo Carpi, and lighting and set design in a dazzling sepia black and white, it was poles apart from the functional utilitarianism of Fo's approach to stagecraft. Fo later described Strehler's production as

a classic case of how to destroy actors' skills and talents. And it's not as if [Strehler's] actors aren't good, but you can never see their eyes or their faces because they're in constant darkness, because the aim of the direction is to insist on a chromatic, atmospheric effect, which is perhaps a magical counter-light, which is the best effect there is. The director has absolutely no interest in showing their expressive intensity, their facial expressions, their laughter or their anger. Frequently we don't even see their bodies, and as a result their gestures are completely artificial, because at that moment it was important for the window to be featured, and a fractured ray of light to illuminate the stage. . . . these expedients reduce the actor to a decorative, aleatory presence, stifle their energy and obliterate the character which the actor is trying to present.[70]

Rame later performed *The Open Couple* in tandem with *Coming Home* (*Rientro a casa*), a monologue written in collaboration with Fo, in a double bill which opened in Trieste in December 1983 and in Milan in February 1984. Using back-projected slides to set the scene, the latter play deals with a mother returning to a squalid, grimy and anonymous apartment block in south-east Milan after a day of protest and misadventure. She has left her husband in disgust at his using her as a sexual convenience, taking 21 seconds to complete the sexual act, and ended up spending the day in a hotel room with a colleague from her office, who has been in love with her for years. In the evening, drunk, bewildered and exhausted, she arrives home, and is reconciled with her husband in the darkness of the bedroom. The following morning she discovers she has got the wrong apartment and the wrong family – a story-line which aims to bring home the universality of the sexual problems Fo is exploring in the play. Stuart Hood has noted that Rame subsequently made over a thousand textual emendations to this play. As with her other monologues, she constantly rewrites, revises and updates, making them an example of what Hood calls 'open texts'.[71]

In 1983 Rame added a prologue to *The Open Couple* in which she played on words for sexual organs and activities such as 'vulva', 'vagina' and 'orgasm', as well as including her monologue *The Rape*. This was a blow-by-blow account of her abduction, rape and torture by three men in a van in 1973, performed in a detached, almost flat style, allowing the events to speak for themselves. As a result the play was subjected to a restriction to audiences over 18 by the Italian Ministero dello

Spettacolo. Rame wrote a letter of protest to the Ministry in December 1983, suggesting that there was far more direct portrayal of rape and violence openly available to viewers of Italian television than there was in her play, which was a relatively unemotive and non-visual description of her assault. But the ban on *The Rape* remained and can be seen as another attempt to censor Fo's and Rame's work by the Christian Democrat government. Writing in the *Corriere della Sera*, the critic Roberto De Monticelli commented on the absurdity of the restriction, describing Fo and Rame as

> unique in the context of Italian theatre both for their subject matter and the style they adopt. These plays, at a time when the theatre is either escapist or going back to the past, connect us forcefully with the present, the ideas and behaviour of today, and to an image of our society.[72]

A similar sexual misunderstanding and confusion of identities as in *Coming Home* lies at the basis of *Il candelaio* (*The Candlestickmaker*), a monologue written by Fo for Rame in 1983. This play reflected the renewed interest Fo had taken in the English Elizabethan theatre since coming to London. Its basic situation reflects the sexual substitution of Shakespeare's *Measure for Measure*, although it is in fact based on a play by the sixteenth-century Neapolitan playwright Giordano Bruno. In Fo's version, a costumist announces to the audience that the actress about to perform the piece is indisposed, and ends up performing it herself in a theatrical image of the art of disguise and dissemblance. The Candlestickmaker has grown tired of his wife and begun to frequent a prostitute, whom the wife approaches to learn the art of sexual attraction so she can win back her husband. The prostitute obliges, and trains the wife in her art, and the husband is taken in. The wife concludes 'he's rediscovered me as a whore, and I've rediscovered him as a whorer. We've thrown convenience and respect to the winds, and perhaps now some real respect has grown between us.'[73]

Rame revived *The Open Couple* in 1986, with Giorgio Biavati, an actor who had performed in *Trumpets and Raspberries* and other Fo plays, replacing Nicola de Buono. She added the monologue *The Mother* to it, and gave the pieces the general title of *Parti femminili* (*Female Parts* – probably derived from the original title of the London production of *Tutta casa, letto e chiesa* at the National Theatre). She also performed *The Open Couple* with other pieces from *Tutta casa, letto e chiesa* in the USA, at Covent Garden in London and in the Assembly Rooms at the Edinburgh Festival in 1986. In October 1986 she added another monologue, *Una giornata qualunque* (*A Day Like Any Other*), after only 12 days of rehearsal. This was premiered at the Teatro Nuovo in Milan, where, as she told the audience, she had last performed 33 years previously in 1952 in a revue called *The Fanatics*.

In *A Day Like Any Other* (also known as *An Ordinary Day*) a woman makes a video tape to send as a letter to her husband, who has left her for another woman, warning him she has decided to commit suicide. She is continually interrupted by telephone calls from women who have dialled her number, which has been printed by mistake in a medical magazine, in the belief that she is a famous psychoanalyst. They all ask her for advice, ignoring her attempts to explain their misunderstanding. She is eventually telephoned by a woman doctor on the verge of suicide, whom she is forced to counsel, even as she is being carted off to an asylum. The production used a large video screen on which Rame's image was projected, and its farcical treatment of suicide made it an appropriate companion piece for *The Open Couple*. Both plays toured widely and were favourably reviewed, with many reviewers emphasising the importance of Franca Rame's work as an actor and co-writer with Fo. *The Open Couple* also proved to be highly popular in Germany, where it remained in production in various cities over a 13-year period, with 633 performances in the 1987–88 season.[74] It also received a production in Minsk, in Belorussia, in 1994, but proved less popular in the UK and the USA, where it was seen as something of a 1970s period piece.

CHAPTER 5

FROM *ELIZABETH* TO *THE POPE AND THE WITCH* 1984-89

The Tricks of the Trade

Fo began a series of teaching performances at the beginning of the 1984–85 Italian theatre season, after he was invited to open a special all-Italian project at the prestigious mainstream Teatro di Roma, under the title 'From the *commedia dell'arte* to Variety'. Fo outlined his didactic aims for the project in an interview in the newspaper *La Repubblica*:

> I'll explain and demonstrate, along with extracts from *Mistero buffo*, how the allusive power of gesture is faster than that of writing. It is the audience which influences the mould, the weave, the charge and the physiognomy of a performance, by the way in which they react. Certain things won't work if they're only written in advance, which is why I regard myself as a performer of texts that are compiled in a pentagram including rhythm and sound.[1]

These comments indicate the gap which exists between Fo's plays in their written form, and his own performances of the plays – a gap which is widened considerably further in translations of the texts into another language. At the Teatro di Roma Fo performed a series of extracts from *Mistero buffo*, *La storia della tigre* and *Il fabulazzo osceno*, frequently freezing and analysing them on the spot, explaining his movements and mimic techniques. The results, a fascinating self-analysis of his own performance, were televised in six one-hour parts on Channel 3 of RAI in February and March 1985, under the title *The Tricks of the Trade*. In them he demonstrates how, for example, he changes from one character to another in *The Resurrection of Lazarus* in the course of representing an entire crowd of people. He also explains how, in *Tale of a Tiger*, the performer can create different angles of perspective similar to close-ups, tracking shots, pans or cross-fades in the cinema. In 1987 he published a book based on these lecture-performances, *Manuale minimo dell'attore* (*A Short Manual for the Actor*). This was a summation of 35 years of performance experience and 10 years of workshops and teaching seminars, as Chiara Casarico commented in her brief biographical study of Fo in 1998:

> As well as being a study of his own art, *Manuale* . . . repre-sents a first attempt to present his research in an organic and systematic form: from medieval theatre to the *Commedia dell'arte*, from the use of the body in performance to the use of masks, from techniques of *mise en scène* to writing tech-niques. After 35 years of experience in the theatre and 10 years of teaching, Dario Fo found he had a great deal of cultural baggage. The manual was developed from the thousands of hours he had recorded with students and aspiring actors, and was rich in observations and advice. Its intention was also to discuss theatre and to unravel all its clichés and commonplaces, such as the claim of a hierarchy of drama, tragedy and comedy.[2]

Fo's minimalism of means in his solo performances creates curious resonances in a mass-media society. Eugenio Barba, for whose International School of Theatre Anthropology Fo has done a number of performance-seminars, has reported how the Japanese sculptor Wakafuji was struck by the similarity between some of Fo's movements in *Tale of a Tiger* and the karate gesture known as *neko hashi daci*, or 'standing on cats' feet'. Barba himself has compared a 'synthesis' of Fo's movements in the same piece to those of a Schultz *Charlie Brown* comic strip.[3] Barba's observations show how Fo's performances cover a wide range of visual techniques which stimulate an audience's imagination. His is very much a 'theatre of the eye', to use the title of an exhibition in Rome devoted to Fo's drawings, designs, paintings, costumes and posters. This exhibition, *Dario*

Fo: Il teatro dell'occhio (Dario Fo: The Theatre of the Eye), opened at the Palazzo Braschi at the same time as Fo's lecture-demonstrations at the Teatro di Roma. This acclaim for his work by the 'higher' Italian cultural institutions suggested that his success and popularity outside Italy was beginning to be acknowledged within mainstream Italian culture.

Another interesting feature revealed by the TV programmes *The Tricks of the Trade* is the way in which Fo had embellished his pieces in the course of their repeated public exposure. In *Tale of a Tiger*, for example, the roaring lessons which the tigress and her cub give to the Chinese villagers to help them intimidate the Japanese invaders were expanded from a couple of simple roars in the early performances of the piece to a fully orchestrated sequence. They had become a series of aural and physical demonstrations, imitations and reactions involving extraordinary vocal modulations and timing. Fo also explained how one piece from *Il fabulazzo osceno*, 'The Butterfly-Mouse', had similarly expanded from its original format of a 15-minute sketch to a performance vehicle lasting 40 minutes, largely through 'the accumulation of pauses, digressions, interpolations and stage business.'[4]

In November 1984, the world-renowned Neapolitan actor-playwright Eduardo de Filippo died. Fo, as the only other Italian actor-playwright of comparable stature, was asked to speak at his funeral, and gave a speech which, he claimed, was censored by the Italian national TV networks.[5] But Fo regarded the extensive media attention given to de Filippo's death as a vindication for past discrimination against the 'non-literary' aspects of de Filippo's theatre. He also emphasised his use of dialect, his espousal of popular forms of theatre, his use of a 'theatre of situation' and his continual modifications of his text as a result of performance. These are all features which Fo has in common with him.[6] Fo had known de Filippo since the time he lived in Rome in 1956, and they had often talked about collaborating. But Fo had had to withdraw from a project in 1984 in which he was to act with his old collaborator Franco Parenti in a production by Giorgio Strehler of de Filippo's play *La grande magìa*. The news of de Filippo's death broke shortly before the news that Fo and Rame had finally been granted an entry visa to the USA, after two refusals. This enabled them to attend the Broadway opening of *Accidental Death of an Anarchist* at the Belasco Theatre.

Fo and Shakespeare, Rame and *Elisabetta*

After Fo and Rame returned to Italy from New York at the end of 1984, they began work on *Quasi per caso una donna: Elisabetta* (*A Woman Almost by Chance: Elizabeth*). In this play Rame played Queen Elizabeth I of England, and Fo her transvestite cosmetic adviser. The play is full of references to Shakespeare's plays, and shows evidence that Fo's exposure to English culture had had an influence on his work. Fo described the new play in an interview with the critic Ugo Volli:

> The action takes place in 1601, but its theme is very topical. It's about the commitment of the intellectual, and the need to participate in world events and take a position. It's worth emphasising that it's a political play, but it's also moral, and makes a statement about the function of theatre . . . The theatre shouldn't be regarded in an idealistic way, as if it dealt with stories that have no relation to reality.[7]

Fo began the play in his usual way with a prologue, without his costume, giving a quasi-history lesson explaining the play's setting and historical background. He also incorporated his English *Grammelot* from *Mistero buffo*, 'The English Lawyer'. He then reappeared in long skirts, ruffles and a maid's cap as La Donnazza (Dame Grosslady in the English version, Mama Zaza in the US version), a character partly based on Celestina from the novel by the sixteenth-century Spanish writer Rojas. Fo described La Donnazza as 'a villainess who dabbles in intrigues and plots, and comments on the action. She is a figure of the people, a plebeian figure even, lowly and full of ingenuity. A bit like a Shakespearian fool.'[8] The plot of *Elizabeth* involves a *coup d'état* which the Duke of Essex, an ex-lover of the Queen, has plotted against her, with the assistance of Shakespeare's impresario, Southampton. There is thus a good deal of talk about Shakespeare in the play, although he does not appear as a character, and Elizabeth begins reading his plays, finding strong resemblances between herself and Richard II, Cleopatra and Hamlet. This occasions a reworked reprise of one of Fo's earliest comic routines from *Poer nano* in the early 1950s, a brief elaboration of the plot of Hamlet. Rame portrays Queen Elizabeth as what Fo described as

> a terrible woman, who speaks Greek and French at court, and then proceeds to crack dirty jokes. She has her skin stretched in an extremely painful sort of facelift, and has applications of leeches, who eat up her fat. She also has her breasts stung by bees to give them an uplift . . . Hers is the first modern state. She invented the secret service and modern politics. There's even a sort of Moro affair, when three lords are kidnapped and held to ransom by rebels. She, naturally, doesn't give in to this, and maintains a hard line.[9]

Although the play would no doubt raise a few eyebrows among Shakespearian scholars, Rame's dramatic role as Elizabeth was compared by some Italian critics to her role as the Spanish Queen Isabella in *Isabella, Three Sailing Ships and a Con Man* more than 20 years previously. There were also thematic aspects of *Elisabetta*, notably the role of the intellectual in power politics, which linked it with the earlier play. One critic who made this comparison was the playwright Carlo Maria Pensa, who also noted:

> The idea . . . is wonderful. In the English court at the turn of the seventeenth century, the sluggish and sluttish sovereign battles against conspiracies, disguises, amorous intrigues, betrayals, hard-line revolutionaries, and cellulitis. She is aided and abetted by the radical cosmetic remedies of La Donnazza, a sort of court jester in petticoats. This clumsy character, who speaks in a reinvented Padano dialect, is brought to irresistible comic life by Dario Fo.[10]

The idea, however, Pensa concludes, is not sustained by the play's dramatic structure, which is fragmentary, disconnected and unbalanced. He also thought it was too reliant on Fo's and

Rame's apparently unconnected solo performances, which distorted any attempt at dramatic shape. What this suggests is that both Fo and Rame may have 'outgrown' the conventional dramatic structures of the pre-written play through their extensive work in a solo, *canovaccio* (improvised) tradition.

The text of *Elisabetta* was first published at the end of 1984 in a special issue on Fo of the Italian theatre magazine *Ridotto*. This included translations of a number of British press reviews of *Mistero buffo*, *The History of Masks* and *Tutta casa, letto e chiesa* (*Female Parts*). It indicated that Fo's and Rame's critical reception in the UK had been taken very seriously in Italy, and been a major factor in giving them a more respectable profile at home. Similarly, the subject matter of *Elisabetta* reflects the results of Fo's acclaim in the UK. In his spoken introduction to *Elisabetta*, Fo suggests that there is a political motive for choosing its particularly English historical subject. He refers to the birth of the secret police and the institution by Edward VI of the possibility of 'supergrassing' and giving Queen's evidence as political features of Elizabethan England which have particular relevance to the 1980s. This relevance, however, tends to be stated rather than demonstrated in the play.

Elisabetta is set in 1601, after the execution of Mary Stuart, whose decapitated head keeps recurring in Elizabeth's nightmares. It could be seen as a sequel to Schiller's *Mary Stuart* – a play which had had considerable impact on Italian theatre in the 1980s. In 1983 it was revived in a particularly lush, glossy and saccharine production by Franco Zeffirelli, in an attempt to rekindle a fashion for romantic drama. Earlier, the feminist playwright Dacia Maraini – another Italian playwright whose plays are widely performed outside Italy – had written a modern, all-women adaptation of Schiller's play. Maraini reduced it to a ritualistic encounter between Elizabeth and Mary, backed up by the two queens' respective ladies-in-waiting, with all of the play's four roles actable by two women. Similar in concept to Jean Genet's play *The Maids*, Maraini's *Maria Stuarda* created considerable interest outside Italy, most notably in a touring Dutch production which was set in a boxing ring. Her version of the play was also an attempt to make its subject matter accessible and relevant to contemporary women, and in doing so used simple, direct and unelaborate language. As Maraini stated:

> What language can we put in the mouths of people on stage who are representing reality, even if it is imagined? We are too used to the hybrid Italian of translations, which is so poor. I think the language of normal Italian today is completely lacking in sensuality. It's grey, uniform and pretty monotonous and abstract. So when you write, you have to bear in mind the way people speak, and use a language which is close to them and comprehensible.[11]

In Fo's work this need for a direct, accessible but also colourful language is expressed through dialect. In *Elisabetta* his invented transvestite character Donnazza speaks in the Veneto dialect, mixed with what was described as 'a ragbag of argots and dialects'.[12] Franca Rame's Elisabetta uses a gutsy, earthy form of speech more appropriate to a prostitute than a queen, but also more appropriate to Elizabethan parlance than Schiller's elegant verse. At one point in Fo's play, Elizabeth's lady-in-waiting, Martha, reprimands Donnazza for her vulgar speech. 'I pick up my way of talking from being in the company of queens,'[13] is the response.

The action of *Elisabetta* also has an earthiness and vulgarity which links it firmly to popular theatre and satirises the historical pageantry and gentility normally associated with the play's subject. Fo borrows the situation of his earlier monologue, *The Candlestickmaker*, in casting himself as Donnazza, Elizabeth's beautician. Donnazza is employed to make Elizabeth look more sexually attractive to her ex-lover, Essex, as part of her attempt to thwart his coup against her. As well as giving her leeches to lose weight, and high-heeled clogs to improve her walking, Donnazza administers bee stings to the queen's nipples to make them more prominent. In a grotesque climax to this 'treatment' the queen ends up literally pissing herself. This beautification is linked to one of the play's main themes, expressed in its subtitle, of transvestism and dressing up to play a part in power politics and history. In what is probably a cheeky reference to an incident which happened at Buckingham Palace in 1983, when a young Irishman found his way into the Queen's chamber, Fo's play has a hired killer discovered climbing the walls of the palace. In the ensuing alarm, Elisabetta has to get rid of her young semi-naked lover, Thomas, who turns out to be the intruder's son. In the following sequence, most of which was cut from later versions of the play, the queen dresses him up in her gown and ceremonial wig:

DONNAZZA: That's classy. Very tasteful indeed. Real theatrical.

ELIZABETH (Rame): If you he-men were forced to wear dresses like that in battle instead of armour, there'd be no more wars, I warrant you. How does it feel?

BOY: Like being squashed inside a cage in hell. Oh, the shame. Don't breathe a word to a soul. I beg of you.

DONNAZZA: Why don't you try on these high-heeled clogs for size?

ELIZABETH: Good idea. Come on, jump to it! See if you can walk in them. Come on, chin up – quick march! Mind you don't topple over – you look like a paralytic duck. Clumsy clod.

BOY: It's hard with high heels . . .

ELIZABETH: Come on, chin up. Kidneys in – wiggle your hips – that's it. Splendid. Isn't he a treat, Martha? Lovely! You haven't played little girls' parts before, have you? You know I'm the patron of a boys' theatre company.

BOY: Yes ma'm. The Queen's Boys.

ELIZABETH: Not one of them makes a convincing girl. You do though.

BOY: You're making fun of me again.

ELIZABETH: Oh no I'm not. I was just about to let you in on a secret, Thomas. I'm too embarrassed now.

MARTHA: Come now. Don't you think it's time you turned your attention to more serious matters?

ELIZABETH: Oh get off my back, Martha. See, Thomas, she doesn't want me to talk about it.

BOY: You can be perfectly frank with me, ma'm.

ELIZABETH: You won't go blabbing about it?

DONNAZZA: Spit it out, ma'm. Drop your clanger!

ELIZABETH: Right. I'm not a woman. In the complete sense.

BOY: What? Not a woman?

DONNAZZA: What a sob story!

ELIZABETH: Oh come on. I bet you've heard all the gossip already. It's a big topic of conversation at court. That blabbermouth Ben Jonson was even going to write a play about it until someone burned his theatre down and he had second thoughts.

MARTHA: I should think so.

DONNAZZA: Oh yes, I know him, the bastard. He was going to put that play on in his theatre. What was it called again?

ELIZABETH: *Perforce a virgin.*

DONNAZZA: That's the one . . .

ELIZABETH: The virgin perforce was me.

DONNAZZA: The queen played by a transvestite!

BOY: How vulgar!

ELIZABETH: Vulgar? What do you mean? Don't be so impressionable, Thomas! What would you say if I told you I was born a boy and my mother passed me off as a girl so my father wouldn't strangle me in my cradle?

BOY: You've got to be joking.

DONNAZZA: It's no joke. It's all true. All because her mother Anne Boleyn was in her husband Henry the Red's bad books. He roared at her – 'Anna, you slut!' Oops, sorry ma'm. 'If you bear me a son, I'll beat you black and blue, and the bastard bairn'll never get to be the King of England.' Right?

ELIZABETH: Exactly. And when I was born a boy –

BOY: A boy? You?

ELIZABETH: That's right. My mother hollered out 'It's a girl!'

DONNAZZA: And hid his little willy!

MARTHA: Stop it, Elizabeth. You're driving me mad.

ELIZABETH: Shut up! Why should I hide it? I'll tell him straight from the horse's mouth – yes, that's right, I'm a male homosexual! They raped my brain day after day and inverted my nature. I'm a man-woman. Go on, laugh. Queen Elizabeth – what a hoot![14]

Like Maraini's *Maria Stuarda,* Fo's play deals with the dilemma of a woman assuming what is traditionally a male role in power politics. *Elisabetta,* however, treats this theme in terms of grotesque farce and burlesque, and although it has some fine farcical moments, as a text it frequently seems over-written and convoluted. Fo's Donnazza lines are often little more than one-line repetitions of what has already been said by other characters, and the character seems little more than a comic choral figure at times. Fo's claims for the play's contemporary political relevance are also difficult to substantiate in the text. The implied parallel between the kidnapping of four of Elizabeth's lords by Essex, who offers them in exchange for the release of 24 political prisoners, and the Aldo Moro kidnapping, is a subject which Fo dealt with far more comprehensively in *Trumpets and Raspberries.*

Rame found performing the play something of a burden, and according to David Hirst, the final performances of the play in Turin were cancelled and substituted with *Mistero buffo* and *The Open Couple* – which immediately drew full houses. Hirst maintains that the play 'advanced neither the feminist cause nor the reputation of the partnership'[15] and sees it as evidence that Fo had returned to his 'bourgeois period'. Hirst goes on to suggest that, by the mid-1980s, Fo had become 'a writer with little political centre, with a minimum commitment to involve his audiences in political debate . . . an irresponsible satirist who takes a delight in swiping out at an indiscriminate range of targets.'[16] Harsh judgments from a critic who subsequently produced a whitewashed hagiography of the elitist, aesthete director Giorgio Strehler, Fo's main ideological rival for four decades.[17]

Harlequin and *Kidnapping Francesca*

Fo's and Rame's major project in 1985 was *Hellequin, Harlekin,*

Arlecchino. Fo developed this into a two-act play, based on *lazzi* (improvised stage business) from the *commedia dell'arte* compiled by the scholars Delia Gambelli and Ferruccio Marotti. But Fo's and Rame's recreation of the *commedia dell'arte* involved a large degree of invention and improvisation rather than any 'arch-aeological' attempt to reconstruct its techniques and methods. Fo had always considered his performances as being re-enactments of the role of Harlequin, particularly in the sense of his anarchic destruction of conventions,[18] so it was perhaps inevitable that he would eventually attempt the role. Although he considered the *commedia* to be an institutionalised form of the more subversive, independent traditions of the *giullare*, he was interested in the demonic origins of Harlequin and his dis-ruptive qualities.

In contrast with the two most famous postwar Italian portrayals of Harlequin, Mario Moretti and Ferruccio Soleri in Goldoni's *Harlequin: Servant of Two Masters*, both directed by Strehler – which Fo has claimed to have seen more than 30 times – Fo was more interested in the improvisational origins of Harlequin's repertoire. He also wanted to explore the character's anarchical, amoral and transgressive aspects. When he was invited by Marotti and the critic Franco Quadri to do a laboratory workshop on Harlequin for the 1985 Venice Biennale to celebrate the 400th anniversary of the publication of the first text about Harlequin in France, he accepted willingly.

After doing research on the *commedia* scenarios given to him by Gambelli, Fo started his laboratory at the 'Free University of Alcatraz', an informal summer theatre school he had established with Rame and their son Jacopo in the country in Santa Cristina di Gubbio in Umbria. The improvisations and *lazzi* which he developed over a six-week period from the scenarios were filmed and a written record was kept of proceedings, as well as photographs. The English academic Christopher Cairns also took part in the proceedings, and his account and analysis of the development of the play is a useful document (Cairns, 1993). Fo used sketches to visualise his performance of Harlequin, which was built out of a series of short farcical situations of 10 to 20 minutes' length. He also drew on his own repertoire of gags and sketches, as well as adapting techniques from farce, pantomime, the circus and music hall.

The resulting play, which Fo and Rame (reprising her role of Marcolfa from one of Fo's farces in the late 1950s) first performed in Venice in October 1985, was considerably modified as it toured between October 1985 and March 1986. As usual, Fo began with a prologue, which took the form of an illustrated lecture about the *commedia dell'arte* complete with costumes and slides of masks. (This was adapted from the seminar *The History of Masks* which Fo had given in London, Edinburgh and other parts of Europe the previous year.) As Cairns records, one notable claim Fo made in this prologue was that Harlequin used to defecate on stage, and then throw his excrement at the audience to bring them good luck.[19] This is consistent with the Rabelaisian, carnivalesque scatology elsewhere in Fo's work. ('Shit' is a common expression for 'good luck' in the Italian theatre.) As Fo stated in an interview:

> [Harlequin] is really a wild animal without any sense of honour, an anarchist. You could say that Harlequin totally rejects this society, but not because he has another one in mind. He is simply, totally, anti-social. He refuses to compromise in the face of basic human physiological needs – eating, shitting, pissing, making love. He goes ahead blithely, destroying everything: honour, logic, common sense, good taste . . .[20]

He illustrates Harlequin's celebration of obscenity in a sketch entitled 'Phallicthropic Harlequin', in which his penis grows to a gigantic size after he drinks his master's love potion. In order to hide it from female passers-by, he disguises it as a cat and then a baby. Fo also draws analogies between *commedia* characters and Italian politicians before ending the prologue with a fanfare of music and acrobatics. In the first monologue, Rame as Marcolfa is discovered mopping the floor of the stage. The curtain is stuck, and a ladder has to be brought in to fix it, which occasions a series of visual gags. She then performs a monologue loosely based on Giordano Bruno's *The Candlestickmaker*, about a woman who takes lessons from a prostitute to regain her husband's interest. This is interrupted on occasions by Harlequin. 'The Gravediggers' is a longer sketch in which Harlequin and Ruzzello are digging a grave for a suicide, whom Harlequin claims has drowned himself in a vat of wine. Resulting antics involve Harlequin pissing on a skull, and skulls and a skeleton emerging from the grave (echoing puppet and marionette effects from previous Fo plays), as well as a chaotic funeral. This sketch involves what Cairns has described as 'a systematic dismantling of conventional taboos; death, the Church, the family, with surreal touches.'[21]

The second act opens with 'The Lock', an extended sexual joke in which Harlequin encounters Franceschina, he polishing and fondling an enormous key, she polishing an enormous lock. Harlequin asks if he can turn his key in her lock, but she refuses, eventually succumbing when Harlequin produces a picnic lunch. But Harlequin then discovers his key has been replaced by an inflatable rubber one. In the final piece, 'The Donkey', Harlequin is terrorised by two dogs who turn out to be his friends Razzullo and Scaracco in disguise. Franceschina laughs at his cowardice, and he has a long conversation with a donkey, who turns out to be his two friends in disguise again. He then tames an escaped lion, believing it to be his two friends again, impressing Franceschina. There is a final dance of animals, celebrating the fact that the *commedia* masks and the movements and mannerisms of its characters were all based on animals. As Fo has stated, 'The rite of dressing up in animal skins is linked to the culture of almost every race on earth.'[22] Fo wore a costume covered with patches made out of red and yellow leaves to emphasise the wild-life, forest origins of Harlequin, and he has stated that his mask is a mixture of a cat and a monkey.[23]

But despite Cairns' claim that Fo's Harlequin was 'a liberating of his stage personality, not a caging of it,'[24] the historical costumes and masks of the play seemed an encumbrance. Some of the elaborate visual gags seemed ponderous, and despite *tours de force* of performance like 'The Lock' and 'Phallicthropic Harlequin', which were reprised in other contexts, it did not display Fo's or Rame's writing or performance skills at their peak. Fo's facial expressions, which Rutlin has described as a mask in themselves, consisting of 'bulging eyes, large squashy nose and huge, elastic mouth',[25] are an essential part of his performances, and concealing them behind a mask is like tying his hands behind his back. The importance of *Harlequin* lies more in the opportunity it gave Fo to explore the historical roots and improvisational traditions of Harlequin and the links it provided with his own performance style.

The year 1986 saw Fo and Rame's triumphant tour of the eastern states of the USA with *Mistero buffo* and *Tutta casa, letto e chiesa*, and Rame also performed *The Open Couple* at the Edinburgh Festival. As a result, their work became more widely known in the English-speaking world, and particularly in the USA, where a number of productions of their plays began to be mounted. In July, Fo went to Montalcino to perform *Mistero divino*, a title punning on 'wine' and 'divine', which originates in *The Marriage at Cana*. This was a compendium of four pieces from his repertoire involving both Dionysian and spiritual features. *Zanni's Hunger* and *The Marriage at Cana* from *Mistero buffo* were combined with *Phallicthropic Harlequin* and *The First Miracle of the Boy Jesus*. Rame's tour of Italy with *Parti femminili*, which included a new version of *The Open Couple* and *A Day Like Any Other*, saw Fo and Rame returning to the 'official' Italian theatre circuit, ETI (Ente Teatrale Italiano), for the first time since they broke away from it in 1968. The end of the year saw a return to Fo's contemporary political farces with *Kidnapping Francesca*, which expanded on the ideas behind *Trumpets and Raspberries*, exploring the superior importance given to economic power over political power in Italy.

In *Kidnapping Francesca* Francesca Bollini de Rill, a prominent and wealthy woman banker, who is regularly featured on magazine covers such as *Vogue*, *Manager* and *Capital*, stage-manages her own kidnapping in order to deflect attention from her imminent arrest for bankruptcy. As in *Trumpets and Raspberries*, there is a mistaken-identity plot. The Francesca who is kidnapped by a group of rather inept abductors disguised as firemen, who break in on her as she is attempting to seduce a young man (after giving him an AIDS test), turns out to be Francesca's look-alike secretary. (Both roles are, of course, played by Franca Rame.) She has already told this to the young man – who turns out to be one of the kidnappers – but manages to convince them that it is a trick: her look-alike secretary is an invention. After the first scene, there is a lengthy monologue by Rame explaining that the play is in defence of rich people, and recounting tongue-in-cheek some of the difficulties and burdens they have to endure: 'now that the workers have abandoned the class struggle, the only ones who keep it going, undaunted, with great difficulty and all alone, are the employers.'[26] Francesca is then taken to a disused dairy farm and held hostage by the kidnappers, who wear masks of current prominent Italian politicians Andreotti, De Mita, Craxi and Spadolini (later substituted by Ronald Reagan) – further contributing to the theme of mistaken identity. Francesca's double tries to outwit her kidnappers, convincing them that the kidnapping has been organised by her lover, a lawyer, whom she has told to give them two billion lire. While three of the kidnappers are collecting the money, she succeeds in turning the tables on the fourth member and terrorising him.

The subsequent course of events in Act Two follows a series of complicated twists and turns. Francesca's mother, a medium, arrives on the scene, along with a priest, who performs an exorcism on the terrorised kidnapper. The walls of the building begin closing in on them as the kidnappers return with the money, locked in a suitcase along with a bomb. Francesca is the only person who knows the combination of the suitcase lock, but she refuses to divulge it until her kidnappers tell her who their leader is. This turns out to be Francesca's mother, in collaboration with Francesca's husband, with whom her mother is having an affair. He in turn is revealed to have disguised himself as the priest, and takes possession of the money at gunpoint. At this point the 'real' Francesca appears, and reassures everyone that the 'other' Francesca is in fact her secretary, and that she has been monitoring events with the help of the young man. She attaches the suitcase-bomb to the ceiling, and exits with the young man, as the other characters count down to the explosion. Francesca then reappears to assure the audience there will be no explosion and that she will sustain the play's thesis in defence of rich people with an alternative ending. The play then ends with her distributing the money among her mother, her husband and the kidnappers, whom she offers jobs as her bodyguards, followed by a song in praise of the rich.

Much lighter in tone than Fo's other political farces, *Kidnapping Francesca* is nonetheless entertaining, and intricately plotted. Although he directed it, Fo did not play a role in it, leaving Rame to dominate proceedings. While its satire of the rich is a little strained at times, it makes up for its shortcomings in political critique with its clever and complicated plot mechanism. It was later effectively adapted in 1994 by Stephen Stenning into an English version, *Abducting Diana*, in which Francesca becomes Diana, a British media magnate. Rame and her company continued touring the play throughout Italy in 1987, after she and Fo had directed the US premiere of *Archangels Don't Play Pinball* at the American Repertory Theater in Cambridge, Massachusetts.

Fo then went to Amsterdam to direct and design Rossini's *Barber of Seville* for the Amsterdam Musiktheater in March, adding a *commedia dell'arte* troupe, numerous sight gags and visual effects and using political placards to enhance the libretto based on Beaumarchais' play. While he was working on this and doing performances of *Mistero buffo*, Rame announced in a television interview with the blonde Sardinian personality Raffaele Carrà that she was divorcing Fo on grounds of desertion. This immediately hit the headlines in Italy and it came as a shock to Fo, as the couple had not previously discussed the issue. While they did not go through with the divorce, they continued working separately, with Rame going to San Francisco to perform *The Open Couple, The Rape* and *Medea*, and Fo continuing with his one-man shows. Fo also published his collected writings on theatre, *Manuale minimo dell'attore* (*A Short Manual for the Actor*).

Fo was then appointed as a professor of Drama at the University of Rome, and gave a number of seminars there on Harlequin, the *commedia dell'arte* and other subjects. He wrote a new series of monologues in the manner of *Mistero buffo*, *La rava e la fava* (The Radish and the Bean), which remain unperformed. He also performed a series of his one-man pieces at the Festa dell'Unità in Bologna under the title *The Lion's Share* (*La parte del leone*). Rame returned to television, acting in *A Hare with a Little Girl's Face* (*Una lepre con la faccia da bambina*) a historical mini-series directed by Gianni Serra for Channel 2 of RAI.

At the end of 1987, Fo was again surrounded by controversy, when he performed *The First Miracle of the Boy Jesus* for the first time on Italian television, watched by 13 million viewers. This took place on a Christmas variety-lottery show, *Fantastico*, compèred by the popular Roman Catholic actor-singer Adriano Celentano, with whom Fo also duetted in a song in front of a Christmas crib. There were hundreds of telephone calls to Italian newspapers – *Il Messaggero* in Rome claimed it had received more than 600 – protesting against Fo's 'blasphemous' portrayal of the boy Jesus performing miracles with bolts of lightning to protect local children from a bully. There were also protests from the Vatican, and Fo admitted he had performed the piece as an act of provocation. Celentano, on the other hand, claimed that the performance was 'the greatest demon-stration of faith that an atheist could ever give. What he performed that evening is worth more than the thousands of sermons given by priests in the churches.'[27] The previous week, Rame had also provoked controversy when she performed *The Rape* on the same show – the first time it had been seen on Italian television.

Return to TV and *The Pope and the Witch*

In 1988 Fo reprised *La parte del leone*, his compendium show of performances from his repertoire of monologues, in Palermo. Fo and Rame then went back to working together in Italian television, for the first time in 26 years (with the exception of transmissions of their plays). *Trasmissione forzata* (*Forced Trans-mission*) was a series of eight 90-minute variety shows transmitted on Channel 3 of RAI in April and May. It included numerous sketches and songs, some performed with Fo's old collaborator, the singer-songwriter Enzo Jannacci. Beginning with a cheeky song which proclaimed 'It's always a holiday at RAI/What a ball at the RAI/RAI is carnival country/They never censor us,' the shows also reprised some of Fo's and Rame's old material from *Mistero buffo*, *Obscene Fables* and *Can't Pay? Won't Pay!* There were also satirical sketches and songs directed against the RAI, Italian politicians and other topical political issues, interspersed with dancing girls and parody news broadcasts. Extracts from *Canzonissima* and Rame's previous TV show *Buona sera con Franca Rame* were also included. There was a ballet about Palestine and an appearance by Celentano and the Witz Orchestra of Trieste dressed up as butterflies. Rame performed 'Italian Rape Weather Forecast', a satirical 'weather report' about rape statistics in Italy. This was followed by a fashion parade of rape-safe clothing and a campaign to collect signatures in support of the law against sexual violence being discussed in the Italian senate at the time. Fo reprised his *Grammelot* about the defence of a rapist from *Mistero buffo*, 'The English Lawyer', to add support to the argument. Other pieces performed by Rame included 'I Had Plastic Surgery' in which a grandmother records a secret video for a close friend about her humiliating experiences after undergoing rejuvenating surgery. In 'The Pregnant Grandmother' a middle-aged woman becomes a 'rent-a-womb' for her daughter and a wealthy industrialist's wife. These were both later included in the Einaudi volume of 25 monologues for women as part of Fo's collected works. Fo and Rame were given carte blanche to do what they wanted in their TV show, although their contract included a 'penalty' clause of a billion lire fine in case of 'accidents'. The result was mixed, with the strongest pieces being those from Fo's and Rame's existing repertoire, while their attempts to satirise Italian TV variety shows and news and current affairs programmes were sometimes amusing.

In the same year, Fo acted the part of a retired professor in *Musica per vecchi animali* (Music for Old Animals), a film directed by his friend, the satirical writer Stefano Benni. This was Fo's first film role since 1958, but it was not a success. He also played the role of the lawyer Azzeccagarbugli in Salvatore Nocita's television mini-series based on Manzoni's classic novel *I promessi sposi* (*The Betrothed*). This performance showed his essentially theatrical gestures and mannerisms tended to overwhelm the more restricted requirements of realistic character portrayal in television drama. In 1988 Fo also recreated his Amsterdam production of *The Barber of Seville* at the Teatro Petruzelli in Bari. This production later toured Brazil, where Fo also performed *Mistero buffo* and Rame did *Female Parts*.

The year 1989 saw the fall of the Communist regimes in eastern Europe, as well as Tiananmen Square, which dealt crushing blows to the Communist-inclined Left in Europe. Fo responded to the events of Tiananmen Square with a performance of an updated version of *Tale of a Tiger*, adding a prologue about Tiananmen Square, to 30,000 people at a solidarity rally for Chinese students in Milan. He later wrote two short monologues about Tiananmen Square, *Letter from China* and *The Story of Qu*, which were performed by Rame, the latter at the Festa dell'Unità in Modena.

In *Letter from China* a young Chinese student militant reflects on the violence of the massacre, after all the foreigners have disappeared from Beijing. She recounts a visit to one of her professors, who is hiding out in the country. He explains that the authorities' backlash was so violent because the students dared to discuss their rights and demands for freedom directly with the emperor without intermediaries. This caused a public spectacle which had never been seen in China since the days of the Long March. As she watches her comrades being arrested, she decides not to try to escape. The radio broadcasts warnings to the students to give themselves up and to others to denounce them. She concludes with a plea to foreign observers not to forget the Chinese students, and to sing the 'Internationale' in memory of them.[28] The piece recalled Fo's directly militant plays of the late 1970s like *Ulrike Meinhof* and *Tomorrow's News* in its simple and direct denunciation. He wrote another unperformed play in 1989, *Il ricercato* (The Wanted Man), about the Mafia, before returning to contemporary political farce with *Il Papa e la strega* (*The Pope and the Witch*), which was first performed at the end of October.

The Pope and the Witch starts from the bold premise of confronting Pope John Paul II with the realities of drugs and birth control in Italy. The Pope is not named as such in the play, but is easy to recognise in Fo's flamboyant portrayal, which includes some mock Polish *grammelot*. The play was a response to an Italian law which criminalises any use of proscribed drugs and which makes an estimated 600,000 drug addicts in Italy liable to be thrown into prison. Fo clearly relished the opportunity to play a contemporary Pope, which he had frequently done in improvised sketches about Popes Paul VI and John Paul I in prologues to *Mistero buffo*. In a prologue to the *Pope and the Witch*, Fo recounts how the present Pope had begun to get under his skin to the extent that he found himself performing papal gestures at home. He also suggested that Pope John Paul II (who has of course written plays himself) had begun to be influenced by the play, and even to borrow lines from Fo's play. This was evidenced by his refusal to involve himself in a demonstration for stricter laws against drugs in St Peter's Square, and his recent visit to drug addicts in prison in Volterra.

In the play proper, as cardinals and nuns manoeuvre about the Vatican with mobile phones, it is revealed that thousands of children from the Third World are gathering in St Peter's Square. This demonstration has been organised by a group called the International Movement for the Defence of the Abandoned Child. The Pope begins suffering from a phobia about being attacked by these children, and to cure it a famous specialist is sent for. The specialist arrives with a woman disguised as a missionary nun (Franca Rame), who reveals that she is a healer, hypnotist and Witch. She delivers a monologue telling the story of Pisellino, who is born from a dried pea as a result of a vow of celibacy. This story is a variation of the *Tom Thumb* folk tale, and Antonio Scuderi has described it as 'a saturnalian vehicle for an invective against the Church's stance on birth control.'[29] The Witch succeeds in curing the Pope's phobia by subjecting him to an imaginary 'child hunt'. But the Pope then succumbs to an attack of arthritis, which leaves his arms raised and locked in a blessing. After further therapy, which involves the Pope swinging from a chandelier, this is also cured. But when the Pope is informed of the real identity of the fake nun, as well as her activities in support of legalising drugs and birth control, he throws her out of the Vatican. As a result, he is immediately paralysed once again.

In Act Two the Pope, still afflicted, is forced to visit the Witch in disguise in her clinic, where she dispenses low-priced drugs to addicts. During a series of 'low life' incidents involving drug dealers attempting to sabotage the Witch's clinic, the Pope is forced to inject himself with heroin, and undergoes a 'conversion' to the anti-prohibitionist cause. As a result, when he returns to the Vatican he issues a papal encyclical calling on the governments of the world to decriminalise drugs and to legislate for birth control. He declares that 'the condom is not the devil's raincoat'.[30] The church is in turmoil, and a number of foreign governments fall. There is a series of botched assassination attempts against the Pope (with a toy car, a poisoned parrot and a Brazilian nun) by the Mafia and other interested parties. He attempts to avert these by disguising himself as a captain of the Swiss guards, raving in 'Slavic grammelot'. He is eventually shot dead as he experiences a spiritual vision.

The play suggests that in aligning itself with the prohibition of drugs, the church is also aligning itself with organised crime. This is further explored in the Pope's references to Calvi's suitcase, to Sindona, Marcinkus and the Banco Ambrosiano (all involved in a Vatican-supported money-laundering scandal in 1981) while under the influence of heroin, during which he suggests the Vatican organised Calvi's death:

Marcinkus, Sindona. Sindona was great friends with Calvi. Calvi used to often go to London, and to pass the time he used to do balancing acts on Blackfriars Bridge. To keep perfect balance he always put two bricks in his left jacket pocket and held a heavy briefcase full of explosive documents in his right hand. To avoid falling into the filthy water of the Thames, he kept a coil of rope around his neck as a precaution. But alas, he slipped and hanged himself.

They found the bricks in his pocket, but not the briefcase – it had disappeared! Problem: where was Calvi's briefcase?[31]

Later in the play, after the Pope's 'explosive' encyclical, a hooded monk delivers Calvi's briefcase to him. It of course turns out to be 'explosive', and the Pope throws it offstage in the nick of time.

Having re-entered the 'bourgeois' theatre circuit of subscription audiences, Fo and Rame were once again enjoying playing the roles of provocateurs. Reviewing the first-night performance in Novara in November 1989 for *Corriere della Sera*, Giovanni Raboni described the audience's reactions as 'in perfect equilibrium . . . between entertained, embarrassed and sympathetic.'[32] He went on to speculate whether anyone had been converted to the play's anti-prohibitionist cause. But as Franca Rame told English director and critic Albert Hunt in an interview, 'We have a conviction . . . that by a tiny little bit we do succeed in educating people and changing society by our kind of theatre.' Hunt was unstinting in his praise for the play's outrageous ideas and comic inventions, and he described it as 'the kind of show you'll see, if you're lucky, half a dozen times in a lifetime of theatregoing.'[33] His response echoed those of a number of Italian critics, who were also overwhelmingly enthusiastic about *The Pope and the Witch*. Anna Bandettini, reviewing it in *La Repubblica*, claimed it 'seemed to strike all at once the most sensitive chords of contemporary political, social and religious issues.'[34] Maria Grazia Gregori in *L'Unità* placed Fo's Pope among 'the gallery of crazed, surreal characters of the best plays of this Italian actor-playwright, who stops at nothing,' invoking *Accidental Death of an Anarchist* and *Il Fanfani rapito*.[35] The play went on to win the 'Golden Ticket' (Biglietto d'oro) award for the production seen by the most spectators in Italy in the 1989–90 season. Unfortunately this did not prove to be the case with the play's English production – the last West End performance of a Fo play in London – in 1991. But Fo and Rame continued to perform *The Pope and the Witch* into 1990, updating it for its performance at the Teatro Lirico in Milan on 20 January, and spanning the new decade with this strong and very funny ensemble piece.

CHAPTER 6

INTO THE 1990S: MOLIÈRE, COLUMBUS, RUZZANTE AND THE NOBEL PRIZE

Molière at the Comédie Française

In April 1990 Fo was invited by the artistic director of the Comédie Française, Antoine Vitez, to direct a Molière play at the Salle Richelieu in rotating repertoire with Brecht's *Galileo*, Sartre's *No Exit* and Beaumarchais' *Figaro* trilogy. As John Towsen has pointed out in his account of this project, this was a bold move for such a traditionally conservative institution as the Comédie Française. But they were beginning to become more adventurous and seek more contemporary relevance under the directorship of Vitez, who had been appointed by the dynamic French Minister of Culture Jack Lang. (Vitez, who had produced *Mistero buffo* in Paris in 1974, died at the end of April 1990, while Fo was still in rehearsal.) Towsen argues such a project threatened French tendencies to play down Molière's Italian roots in the sixteenth-century Italian *commedia dell'arte* troupe based in Paris and to favour a strictly text-based, high-culture approach to his plays.

Fo chose to direct a double bill of early Molière plays, both involving the *commedia*-derived character of the trickster Sganarelle: *The Flying Doctor* (*Le médecin volant*) – for which there was no complete text, but rather a sketched-out scenario – and *The Doctor in Spite of Himself* (*Le médecin malgré lui*). Towsen records that the former had received only 113 previous performances at the Comédie Française, which indicated its obscure status in Molière's canon, while the latter had had

2,136.[1] Fo used sketchbooks to devise storyboards for the plays – a technique which had by now become his stock-in-trade. *The Flying Doctor* is a light-hearted romp about the servant Sganarelle attempting to prove he is the twin of a doctor, which involves 'flying' between a balcony and the ground in order to appear beside his own double. *The Doctor in Spite of Himself* is a more complex and biting satire on the medical profession in which Sganarelle, a woodcutter who beats his wife, impersonates a doctor and deceives a number of patients.

Fo added a carnivalesque, acrobatic chorus of five towns-people to both plays, in order to give them a more community-oriented focus, and to give Sganarelle's individualistic, sub-versive antics a more class-oriented perspective. *The Flying Doctor* opens with Sganarelle being pursued as a thief (with the French word 'voleur' punning on both flying and thieving), and includes a Harlequinesque routine in which he drinks his own urine. In *The Doctor in Spite of Himself* Fo emphasises the rage, indignation and grotesque aspects of Molière's attack on the medical profession. Both plays involved direct address to the audience, and used the auditorium as part of the playing area, as well as a considerable amount of stage business with flying harnesses, ropes, trapezes and song and dance and acrobatics. The technical aspects of the production were so complicated that the other repertory productions had to be cancelled for three days before the Molière plays' opening night.

Fo worked intensively with the Comédie Française actors on physical business and *lazzi* from the *commedia*, using a *commedia* script, *Arlecchino, the Flying Doctor* to recreate gags, as well as drawing on his own extensive repertoire. Consequently, both plays became very free adaptations with a great deal of additional boisterous stage business. The physical and scatological elements Fo introduced seemed to be a direct challenge to the highbrow principles of the Comédie Française audiences, but the produc-tion was revived again the following year. As Towsen noted, 'It was hard not to notice the pleasure Fo and the supposedly staid audiences of the Comédie Française took in bawdy and scatological humour.'[2] Although, according to Towsen, some French critics found the production 'too Italian', and others not

Italian enough, and many found more of Fo in it than Molière, it was a 'palpable success' for the company.[3] Given Fo's nomination of Molière as one of his *maestri* in his Nobel Prize address, this was a satisfying outcome for all concerned.

AIDS and genetic experiments

The technical complexities of the Molière plays were again present in Fo's next play, *Hush! We're Falling! (Zitti! Stiamo precipitando!)* which opened at the Teatro Nuovo in Milan in November 1990. Dashing it off over a ten-day period in the previous summer, Fo addressed the issues of AIDS and genetic research. He also made topical references to the Gulf War, racist attacks in Italy, the Mafia and a number of other political events, without ever focusing clearly on any of them.

The play is totally dominated, even overwhelmed, by its complex, freewheeling plot mechanism and its elaborate mechanical gadgetry and special effects. With a cast of 12 (including Fo and Rame) in 27 different roles, it opens in a mental asylum where the inmates take part in a series of elaborately costumed *Grand Guignol*-styled psychodramas organised by the director, a former cinema special-effects expert. The asylum is being investigated on suspicion of using its patients as guinea pigs for genetic experiments. This investigation plot, which recalls the *Government Inspector*-like story-line of *Accidental Death of an Anarchist*, is quickly dropped after the arrival of the wealthy engineer Riversi (played by Fo, neatly attired in a business suit and tie). Riversi has test tubes full of mosquitoes containing his family's blood, which he wants tested for AIDS. He is obsessed with women, but also has a phobia about AIDS. He discovers the director of the hospital, known as Madame Curie (Franca Rame), has in fact been carrying out illegal experiments on her patients, but has also discovered an antibody which destroys the AIDS virus in the process. He sets about courting her, as the antibody can only be transmitted through seven bouts of sexual intercourse. His seduction and deception of Madame Curie is obstructed by her phobia about sex, her blood poisoning and her belief that she is being pursued by extraterrestrial beings, which involves her getting about with an elaborate panoply of drips and helmets. After a simulated sexual encounter in a swimming mime (in order to deceive the extraterrestrial beings), Riversi offers to finance Madame Curie's research, and invites her to move into his high-security mansion in the country.

The second act opens at Riversi's house, where his family and friends are betting on the number of daily Mafia and Camorra murders that will be reported on the evening news. Madame Curie sets up her elaborate experimental machines there. Riversi, with the collusion of his wife, family and friends, fakes the news of a crash on the stock market which has left him virtually bankrupt, as Madame Curie is known to have a compulsion to care for victims of misfortunes. This deception enables him to sleep with her, and he discovers she also has a menagerie of snakes and lizards. But in the meantime the other male characters both at the hospital and at Riversi's house have discovered Madame Curie's sexual powers, and they all begin to court her in various ways. The hospital superintendent arrives to inform Riversi that a woman doctor who has experienced a similar 'cure' to him has begun to be afflicted by a strange kind of St Vitus' dance which involves spraying water everywhere. Riversi is also afflicted, and attempts to hide it from the others, who are too busy attempting to seduce Madame Curie. She in turn reveals that she is in love with Riversi. She then produces a solar-powered engine which she has invented, disguised as an organ. Riversi is horrified by its implications, which will cause economic disaster. He quotes what he claims is an old adage: 'If shit produced marketable energy, poor people would be born without arses.'[4] A space ship then descends from the flies, and Madame Curie's extraterrestrial beings spirit her away with her engine. Her disembodied voice bids everyone farewell in an echo of the final line of *Accidental Death of an Anarchist*: 'You idiots don't even know how to hide the avalanches of crap you produce to make a buck. Crap you are slowly drowning in. Goodbye!'[5]

Some of the incidental aspects of the play – such as the *grammelot* Rame speaks to her machines and the dwarf played by Nicola de Buono with shoes on his hands, in the style of *Fanfani rapito* – are imaginative. Fo's and Rame's characters and the asylum setting are faintly reminiscent of their 1964 play *Seventh Commandment: Steal a Bit Less*, while Rame's witch-like character has overtones of *The Pope and the Witch*, but tends to be encumbered by too many tics and eccentricities. Other aspects – like the black jokes about burning a *vu' cumprà* (African migrants who sell trinkets on the streets and beaches in order to survive in Italy), cooking and eating vaginal fungi, and Madame Curie pissing herself – seem in dubious taste. Riversi dressing Madame Curie up as 'Barbie's aunt' and her sexual harassment by a gang of men are also of doubtful comic value.

Hush! We're Falling! is by no means one of Fo's best plays, but it did not entirely deserve the scathing review its Milan production received from Della Couling in *The Independent*. Couling, whose review coincided with the opening of the National Theatre production of *Accidental Death of an Anarchist* in January 1991, found the staging of *Hush! We're Falling!* 'of a standard any provincial rep company would have been ashamed of'. She also suggested that Fo's company was full of young actors 'who find it useful for their careers to bathe for a while in the master's glory.' Contrasting the fur-coated audience at the Teatro Nuovo with the factory- and non-theatrical audiences they performed to in the 1970s, she accused Fo and Rame of 'hogging most of the dialogue' and concluded 'the court jester has become emperor, and this particular emperor hasn't many clothes on any more.'[6] Fo's and Rame's productions do often have a rather ramshackle, work-in-progress feel to them, especially in the early days of their run, indicating their preference for content over style, which their audiences are accustomed to. It is also arguable that most of the audiences they had performed to in the 1970s would not be out of place at the Teatro Nuovo two decades later. *Hush! We're Falling!* does take a very unfocused, scattershot approach to AIDS, genetic experiments and a number of other subjects, and its ponderously detailed plot and cumbersome stage machinery tend to obscure any clear satirical perspective, but it still has characteristic flashes of ingenuity from both Fo and Rame.

It is interesting to compare Couling's review with the report on the play by *La Repubblica*'s theatre critic Ugo Volli. Conceding that the play is vulgar and offensive in places, Volli compares its farcical, nonsensical structure to buildings by the Spanish architect Gaudí:

There is always something dizzying, clearly unfinished, programmatically improbable, and therefore disturbing in Dario Fo's plays: an excessive construction, full of buttresses, protub-erant pinnacles, curves which contravene the laws of gravity, and excessive drops, which remind me of certain of Gaudí's buildings. His plots cannot be dismissed as unimportant, because he always chooses to talk about reality, but they are hidden under so many layers of games, jokes, diversions, comic stereo-types and improbable statements of verisimilitude that they become totally immersed in theatricality, without any mimetic logic. The great attractions of Dario Fo as an actor ... and his indomitable desire to bring polemics into the theatre ... have prevented most Italian critics and most of our cultural world in general from recognising his greatness as a playwright, despite it having been recognised all over the world. Fo is, together with Pirandello, the only Italian theatre practitioner this century of international status, and he achieves this more as a playwright than as an actor.[7]

Apart from invoking Fo's training as an architect, Volli's comments uncannily anticipate debates which occurred after he was awarded the Nobel Prize – the first Italian playwright since Pirandello to receive it. In particular they anticipate Umberto Eco's statement that it was Fo's international status as a playwright rather than his prowess as an actor and *giullare* that had earned him the prize.[8] It is indicative of both Fo's uniqueness and his relative lack of recognition in Italy in the 1990s that such a re-evaluation of his work should be prompted by one of his weakest plays.

Let's Talk about Women and *Johan Padan*
In 1991 Fo and Rame launched separate projects, one of which involved Rame's first foray into solo playwriting with two one-act pieces reprising the title of Fo's and Rame's 1977 television

show, *Let's Talk about Women* (*Parliamo di donne*). In *Heroine*, Rame plays Carla, an ex-Latin mistress and 'Mater Tossicorum' (Mother of Addicts) who has become a street saleswoman, trading in pornographic videos, fake mobile phones, contraceptives and other gadgets and stolen goods. She waits on the fringes of a public park in the outer suburbs of Milan in fog and rain, for a drug dealer to sell her heroin to administer to her daughter, who is an addict, and whom she keeps chained to the bed. She is armed with a pistol, and has various encounters with a gallery of low-life and disabled characters, drug addicts, a police inspector and armed robbers, as well as holding conversations with God. She has already lost two sons, who subjected her to physical abuse, and who died of heroin overdoses and AIDS. She dreams of taking her daughter to Liverpool, which she thinks is a good environment to get her daughter off drugs, and because she likes the Beatles.

A drug dealer eventually arrives, but he has been shot in the stomach and she cannot find any drugs on him, as there is a scarcity. A police inspector turns up and finds drugs concealed in the dealer's wig. A drug addict entrusts Carla with two bags full of stolen money. In a long conversation with a girl, she also reveals she works as a prostitute to support her daughter's habit. At the end of the play, she realises that the preceding events, including the bags of money, have been a dream. Two armed robbers burst into the park, and one throws a bag of money under her vendor's stall. She is then killed in the crossfire between the two armed robbers, one of whom snatches the bag of money. Carla, amateur therapist and Good Samaritan to drug addicts, is something of an extension on Rame's witch character in *The Pope and the Witch*, and *Heroine* shares the earlier play's concern with the plight of Italy's criminalised drug addicts. But its tendency to rely on exaggerated, melodramatic events and characters makes it rather heavy going.

In *The Fat Woman* – also referred to as *Fat is Beautiful* – Rame plays Mattea, a 50-year-old woman separated from her husband, who has gone off with another woman. Mattea has achieved economic independence by patenting an electronic invention, but is suffering from obesity due to a compulsive eating disorder brought on by a lack of human affection. We first encounter her one morning in a darkened bedroom in an amorous dialogue with a man whom we do not see. She then has a telephone conversation with a woman at an employment agency called 'Fat is Beautiful'. She has breakfast, and after the unseen man makes a few more amorous comments, we realise that his voice is simply a tape recording, which she switches off.

She is then visited by a man under the mistaken impression that she is his estranged wife, and whom she tries to get rid of by playing her tape recording. But he persuades her to let him in, and she listens to his problems from behind a screen. He discovers her exercise bicycle and 'electronic boyfriend', and she finally consents to let him see her. He is overwhelmed by her size, and she gets rid of him by threatening to take her clothes off. A young man arrives and, while Mattea is in the bathroom, tells her that her invention of an alarm clock with amorous tape recordings has made her a lot of money. Mattea's married daughter Anna arrives and joins her mother in the bathroom. The young man watches their silhouettes from the next room until Mattea discovers him and shoos him into the kitchen. Anna tells her mother about the problems she is having with her lover, a married man, and how she has been beaten up and put in hospital by her husband. She then plays a tape recording of her encounter with her lover's wife in disguise as a travel agent. Mattea castigates her daughter's 'Brazilian soap opera' behaviour and accuses her of being un-liberated. They have an argument, and Anna reveals that Mattea's ex-husband is remarrying and having a child with his new wife. The young man takes Anna home, leaving Mattea to reactivate her 'electronic boyfriend'.

Wearing padding to make her look obese, and appearing as an oversized silhouette, Rame's portrayal of Mattea is more plausible than that of Carla in the previous play. *The Fat Woman*, in its treatment of separation and sexual relationships, is closer to the emotional territory of previous Fo–Rame plays like *The Open Couple*, *A Day Like Any Other* and *Coming Home*. Fo's absence as a writer – although he directed both plays – is less noticeable than in *Heroine*, and Mattea's description of her electronic invention makes a telling point about relationships:

All those poor deluded people buy my cassettes with voices of false lovers because they are afraid of real voices. A real relationship involves commitment, and forces you to bend over backwards for the other person. So it's better to immerse yourself in a tape recording of the words and maybe even the images of an uncomplicated, prefabricated lover who you can turn off with a remote control.[9]

The play's treatment of fat as a feminist issue has come under criticism from Maggie Günsberg, who argues that Mattea is not a positive or empowered enough character, being still subject to patriarchal conditioning about body image:

Despite her understanding of the perception of body size as conditioned by cultural and historical context, she still assumes thinness as the ideal, and her work is geared to the goal of losing weight. While Mattea's deliberations about fatness and food are comical, she remains trapped in the position of victim to poor self-image . . . She is ultimately problematized in her body not only in terms of size and its assumed negative implications for sexual attractiveness, but also in her reproductive power, in which she has also been supplanted by another woman.[10]

But as the colour photographs of the production which accompany the published text of the play make abundantly clear, Rame's Mattea is almost a puppet-like creation in the manner of Fo's dwarfs, and any realistic identification with her character is difficult. The play's theatricality is foregrounded in other ways, such as the use of a screen and the use of silhouettes, making it more of a Brechtian 'epic' demonstration in the manner of *The Open Couple*. *Let's Talk about Women* was denied access to two theatres in the north of Italy, the Teatro Concordia in Bolzano and the Cinema Teatro Rosmini in Roveretto, both of which were run by priests. Clearly both did so on moral grounds, and as a result Rame made accusations of censorship in the Italian press. But despite this publicity, the plays did not generate as much interest as Rame's other solo performances. Fo has stated that audiences were uncomfortable with the issues raised by *The Fat Woman*:

> It's a bitter play which many people liked and were moved by, but people had difficulty seeing it calmly, and often found its constant anguish too heavy . . . I think it became an exercise which people rejected, because it is about suffering a condition which people avoid at all costs, even when it is provoked by a play.[11]

Fo's *Johan Padan*, which he toured in tandem with *Let's Talk about Women*, is a theatrical *tour de force* on a par with *Mistero buffo* in which Fo narrates and acts out the epic tale of a lowly Venetian hanger-on in Columbus' discovery of the Americas. A response to an invitation from Expo '92 in Seville to do a play for the quincentennial celebrations of Christopher Colombus' first voyage to the Americas, Padan is a fugitive *zanni* figure from the *commedia dell'arte* who finds himself part of Columbus' fourth voyage. In it Fo claims to speak a dialect made up of elements of Catalan, Castilian, Brescian, Bergamesque, Venetian, Provençal, Portuguese, Neapolitan and *grammelot*, but in reality it is mostly Padano, as in *Mistero buffo*, with a few Spanish words thrown in for good measure.

Fo also uses a large book of his own paintings and drawings of key elements in the story mounted on a lectern as a prompt as he performs the adventures of his eponymous picaresque hero who escapes from the Inquisition in Venice on a fishing boat bound for Spain. On the fishing boat, Johan recalls a youthful love affair with a witch who is able to read the moon and predict a storm at sea which floods Venice and washes a ship into the nave of St Mark's. After 25 days' sailing, he reaches Seville, where he sees four heretics being burnt: 'I've escaped from flames burning my arse only to find flames right under my balls!'[12] He gets a job making and setting off fireworks – which occasions some gestural bravura from Fo – and observes Columbus' return to Spain from his first voyage to the Indies with a worthless cargo of monkeys and parrots. Johan is invited to go on Columbus' second and third voyages, which bring back a cargo of precious stones and Indian slaves, but he declines.

While working as a banker's scribe writing fraudulent letters of credit, he is discovered by the Spanish Inquisition, and escapes on Columbus' fourth voyage. He is put in the hold and forced to look after the mules, asses, cows and pigs that are being transported to the Indies. The ship arrives at the idyllic San Domingo, where the crew sleep in hammocks and enjoy the amorous favours of the Indian women. But after Indians are taken on board for transportation back to Spain, other Indians fire arrows at them and are massacred by the Spaniards. Johan begins to learn the Indians' language, and becomes an interpreter for the Spaniards, who instruct him to try and persuade the Indian chief to part with his gold. After a few months, the ship loads up a cargo of Indians, who are used as bait for fishing when they begin to die. A storm breaks out, and Johan and four other animal attendants are left behind with the Indians when the rest of the crew take off in lifeboats. They attach themselves to the pigs, who tow them through the sea to the coast, where they discover the smashed remains of the lifeboats. Other Indians discover Johan and the other survivors and make a series of bonfires to warm them up, treat them kindly and provide them with exotic food, women and hammocks. After this feast, they are sold as slaves and carried off by another group of Indians in canoes to Florida.

Johan begins acting like a clown to keep his new masters happy, and one full moon he is taken away, painted in different colours, and plucked of all his hair like a turkey. He realises he is being prepared to be eaten, refuses to eat any more food and is force-fed. He comes down with jaundice, and to save his comrades, suggests they drink his urine and become jaundiced as well. The natives discover their ruse and are angry, pissing on them and tying them up. Johan manages to escape into the forest, preferring to risk death from wild animals. But as he is escaping, he sees a group of Indians attacking the village, and raises the alarm. In the ensuing battle, the village shaman is disembowelled, and Johan cauterises him and sews him up, saving his life. He does likewise to the other wounded Indians, and is invited to be the guest of honour at the banquet where his comrades will be eaten. Looking up at the moon, Johan predicts a terrible storm, which destroys the village and surrounding countryside. The villagers proclaim him a saint and ask him for advice. He suggests they move south, in the direction of his home.

After two days' forced march and starvation, Johan, his comrades and the villagers come upon a friendly but distressed tribe of bald Indians who are refugees from a Spanish invasion. Johan, wanting to go home, offers to take them to the Spaniards and to intercede for them. After at first refusing, the 400 natives decide to follow their shaman-saint. In the forest, Johan helps them capture some horses – which the Indians have always been afraid of – tame them and ride them. After two months, they meet a group of Incas, who refuse to acknowledge Johan's saintly authority because he is too similar in appearance to the Spaniards. Nonetheless, Johan performs two miracles – a 'fishleap' in a lake at full moon which provides fish to eat, and a comic rain dance which turns a drought into a flood. Then Johan and his entourage of a thousand Indians come upon 30 Spaniards on horseback dragging 100 Indians in chains. They ambush the Spaniards with improvised spears and capture their horses, and the Spaniards are led off in chains by a group of Indians.

Johan realises that Christianity is the only cause for the Spaniards' persecution of the Indians, so he decides to teach the natives – with great difficulty – the basic Christian precepts. Due to the climate and conditions of the Americas, he substitutes a mango for Eve's apple, a prickly pear leaf for a fig leaf, and a pigeon for the holy ghost. He also creates an affair between Christ and Mary Magdalene in case the Indians suspect Christ and the apostles of homosexual activity. When he tells them about Christ's resurrection, the Indians celebrate by getting drunk, making love and snorting hallucinogenic powder up one another's nostrils, and Johan has to teach them a happy Easter hymn to satisfy their desire for celebration.

On 21 March 1513, seven years after his escape from the shipwreck with the pigs, Johan and 8,000 Indians reach the Spanish headquarters at Catchoches in Florida. Johan grooms a group of Indians to encounter the Spaniards with crucifixes and gifts, singing hymns. The Spanish governor sets them to work

unloading ships, cutting corn and picking cotton. Overnight, the
Indians disappear and the governor threatens to hang Johan if
they do not return. The Indians return and ask for a pardon for
Johan, but the governor refuses, claiming he has transgressed the
authority of the king. As Padan is about to be hanged, thousands
of Indians appear carrying torches, and threaten to burn down
the city. When they discover the Indians have sabotaged their
cannons and horses, the Spaniards are forced to surrender, and
are sent back to Spain on their ships. They threaten to return
with an army, but after Johan consults the moon, they are
shipwrecked in a storm. Johan remains in Florida for another 40
years, occasionally feeling nostalgia for his home in Venice, and
witnesses a number of subsequent unsuccessful Spanish invasions,
until King Carlos declares Florida a no man's land. The play ends
with him singing the Easter hymn about the Resurrection, a
populist celebration of Christianity.

Lasting over two and a half hours, regularly breaking the
'fourth wall' and shifting the perspective of its imaginary world
for the audience, with its imaginary cast of thousands and huge
historical sweep of events, *Johan Padan* is in many ways the apex
of Fo's carnivalesque solo performances. It combines elements
of all of them, while introducing new aspects to the
oppressiveness of Christianity and colonialism, and embodying
animals, miracles, shipwrecks, fireworks, battles and episodes of
cannibalism. The irreverent, desperate, Dionysian figure of
Padan bears some resemblance to the subversive Christ of *The
Marriage at Cana* or the *First Miracle of the Boy Jesus* in *Mistero
buffo*. But there are also more pagan, shamanistic, fantastical
aspects which are pre-Christian, and might be traced to Fo's
childhood experiences of the *fabulatori*.

Antonio Scuderi has described Padan's lessons to the Indians on
the precepts of Christianity as 'one of the most memorable
episodes in all of Fo's theatrical corpus in terms of the humour and
irony it directs at religion.' He also invokes Bakhtin's notion of
bringing the spiritual down to earth in commenting on the play's
'saturnalian sub/inversion', and finds the Rabelaisian-grotesque
element of *Johan Padan* much more prominent than in any other
Fo play. Scuderi, who edited and subtitled a video version of the

piece in the USA, also notes that given Fo's age in 1991 (he was born in 1926), *Johan Padan* was likely to be 'his last major solo piece'.[13] It is fortunate that this video record of it exists, as, given the enormous amount of energy it required to perform, and Fo's failing health at the time – he began to suffer from heart palpitations – it did not remain in his repertoire for very long.

As in all of Fo's one-man shows, *Johan Padan* was accompanied by a lengthy prologue relating the themes of the play to current events. In this case Fo alluded to the corruption scandals that had decimated the ruling Christian Democrat party, but, as Ron Jenkins has recounted, he also referred to the rise of neo-Nazism in Germany. Fo describes Queen Isabella of Spain as 'the first Nazi' in expelling the Jews from Spain in 1492. He also recalls the shocked response of the Spanish audience to this observation when he performed the piece in Spain, at a time when there was a campaign to have her declared a saint by the Pope.[14]

But as Scuderi has noted, Fo's portrayal of the Spanish occupation of the Americas is not always 'politically correct', as he criticises the Indians' cannibalism and their treatment of human beings like animals, as in the scene when they prepare Johan for the slaughter. This combines with what Scuderi identifies as a strong element of 'zoomorphic symbolism' in the play, which can be linked with both the carnivalesque and the *commedia dell'arte*. When the Indians first encounter the Spaniards on their horses, they believe that they are strange beasts, a belief supported by the Spaniards' bestial behaviour towards the Indians. Padan and his comrades' rescue by riding on the back of pigs, and the Indians' belief that the pigs are another race of Christians, is also a strong carnivalesque symbol, which is reproduced on the cover of the text of the play. As Scuderi has commented:

> this image iconographically displays the function that zoomorphic symbolism has in the play. First, by playing with the icon of the equestrian statue, the horse/pig substitution signals an ironic inversion to the notion of noble endeavours on the part of the Europeans. Second, the overriding message of the play is signalled by the ensemble

of man and beast: human beings devoid of their humanity are no better than animals.[15]

Scuderi argues that the combination of the play's animal imagery with its Bakhtinian scatology – as in the scene where Johan's comrades drink his urine in a mood of festivity, in order to obtain the symptoms of jaundice and escape being eaten – provides a grotesque 'cosmic overview' which unifies the human and the natural and trivialises human power and cruelty.[16] Scuderi's view of the play, along with its epic complexity and awareness of cultural diversity, is affirmed by Marisa Pizza in her 1996 book about Fo's solo performances:

The attention given to humanity in Fo's narrative and performative research reaches its highest level in *Johan Padan*. The object of this research places the actor at the centre of an infinite plurality of references. The spaces the action takes place in are immense, and the theme of the voyage which the narrative and performative event is based on is developed on a vast scale, delineating the epic aspects of all possible planes of the action: relations with nature, the construction of knowledge, the physical and mythical presence of animals, fantastical arrangements of food, the fascination and power of the supernatural, religion, liberated sensuality, rebellion against power, and the play's foremost evocative aspect and central thematic nucleus: relations with the other, and encounters with cultural diversity. On this point in particular, any risk of facile rhetoric is overcome through a strong critical awareness that demolishes any egotism in the text.[17]

Johan Padan, then, is 'total' theatre on an epic scale in which Fo confronts issues of colonialism, imperialism, cultural plurality, freedom, scatology, sex, the supernatural, laughter and the grotesque and displays his most complex and sustained performative achievement.

'Clean Hands' and Ruzzante

In 1992 Fo was engaged in two foreign productions. A revival of *Isabella, Three Sailing Ships and a Con Man* was performed at the Centro Dramático Nacional in Valencia, Spain, and a re-mounting of his 1987 Amsterdam production of Rossini's opera *The Barber of Seville* took place at the Opéra Garnier in Paris, for Rossini's bicentennial. Fo also played the narrator in his own adaptation of the text of a production of Prokofiev's *Peter and the Wolf* in Lanciano in July, and this was later broadcast on Italian radio and released as a CD in 1996.[18]

Later in the year, Fo and Rame collaborated on *Seventh Commandment: Steal a Bit Less No. 2* (*Settimo: ruba un po' meno no. 2*). This was a long, topical monologue about Italy's corruption scandals of the early 1990s, which they updated almost daily from newspaper reports. The play was performed by Rame in front of a triptych of 108 photographs of politicians, businessmen and state officials who had been implicated in the Milan 'Tangentopoli' (bribe city) scandals, and there was a trolley stacked with newspapers, magazines and books. The photos, newspapers and magazines were added to daily during the run of the play, as more and more prominent figures were implicated in the growing corruption scandal. The title derives from an incident reported in newspapers in which a group of nurses in a Milan hospital were trafficking in corpses. Fo and Rame found the situation reminiscent of Fo's 1964 play *Seventh Commandment: Steal a Bit Less*, which was referred to by the use of snippets of songs from it.

A 'deliberately ramshackle and chaotic show, but only on the surface,'[19] the play starts by referring to Robert Graves' book on Greek mythology to illustrate the prevalence of political corruption throughout history. Sketches deal with corrupt officials' secretaries committing suicide in sympathy with their bosses, and the activities of Mario Chiesa of the Socialist party, who tried to flush 37 million lire down the toilet after being caught accepting a bribe from a cleaning company. Chiesa, whose ambitions included wanting to stand for mayor of Milan, was the first victim of magistrate Antonio di Pietro's 'Mani pulite' (clean hands) operation in February 1992. After he began confessing and naming names in March 1992 there was an avalanche of arrests of the highest ranking Milanese politicians and businessmen, exposing a network of corruption which spread all over Italy. One of the play's sketches dealt with the daily TV news reports of 20 or more arrests on corruption charges, which prompted fashion magazines to start printing articles about what to pack in your suitcase when you go to prison. The play also lampooned the grotesque trivia of TV chat shows. The nihilism of the 1990s was contrasted with the naive political activism of the 1960s and the Feste dell'Unità, and the inability of the Italian Communist Party to base itself on theft and greed like other political parties. ('Tangentopoli' led to the collapse of the Christian Democrat party, which had ruled Italy since the Second World War, and paved the way for the election victory of Silvio Berlusconi's Forza Italia party in 1994 and the left-wing Olive Tree alliance in 1995.)

After a satirical sketch about pornographic films, Andreotti and other corrupt government politicians were satirised, as well as the new mood of festivity and excess which the scandals had generated. Act Two of *Settimo* began with a catalogue of long-standing frauds and obsolete state organisations, and proof of the cultural basis of theft in Italian popular and religious tradition. 'A Tragedy of Jealousy' recounted a news story of a family where the son is having an affair with his mother-in-law and the father and daughter discover them and kill them. Rame also told stories from her adolescence and about her marriage and her son's adolescent sexual activities. She then satirised the Northern League* and the prospects of the world being taken over by black races because of the holes in the ozone layer. She constructed a hell full of corrupt politicians, where the Pope pays a visit, followed by a Utopian 'happy end' where Italian political scandals of the previous three decades are all resolved and redressed. These included the Piazza Fontana bombings, the passenger plane mysteriously shot down at Ustica, the bribery

---

*A fanatical, separatist, free market political movement (Lega del Nord) founded in the north of Italy by Umberto Bossi in 1991, advocating autonomy for a newly created northern Italian state (known as Padania).

scandals, the squalid conditions in hospitals, the dominance of the country by industrialists and the Mafia, and the political partitioning of RAI TV and other mass media.

Tongue in cheek, Fo and Rame conceded that the realities of current affairs in the 'Clean Hands' unveiling of fraud, bribery and corruption amongst high-ranking Italian politicians, businessmen and state officials were more imaginative and far-fetched than any satirical inventions they could create. Consequently they contented themselves with a kind of rambling, living newspaper 'chronicle theatre' which was part stand-up comedy and part political burlesque. The play, the text of which was published in the November 1992 issue of the theatre magazine *Sipario*, opened in Carrara in the north of Italy at the Teatro degli Animosi. The first-night audience consisted of subscribers, provincial officials and local politicians and an array of women in fur coats, who were greatly amused by Rame's accounts of the fate of some of their friends, colleagues and associates. In one performance, a lawyer was so incensed by the play's implications that he stormed out of the theatre, and was himself arrested for corruption two hours later.

Nineteen ninety-three was a year of celebration of the tricentennial of Goldoni, whose plays were being performed all over Italy and the rest of Europe. Fo had never been greatly impressed with Goldoni's text-based incorporation of *commedia dell'arte* into a middle-class mercenary Venetian context which celebrated trade and commodity above all else. He chose instead to celebrate the sixteenth-century actor-author Ruzzante, also known as Angelo Beolco. Fo had long regarded Ruzzante as one of his *maestri*, and had studied his work in detail since his first encounters with him with Gianfranco De Bosio in Turin in 1958. Fo originally planned and made sketches for *Dialogues from Ruzzante,* a large-scale spectacle with 15 actors, which placed Ruzzante in the context of a crowd of Venetian people inside an enormous skeletal structure. This was to be a joint production between Fo's and Rame's company and a publicly-funded group called Teatro dei Incamminati. As Joseph Farrell has pointed out, this collaboration was prevented, well after rehearsals had begun, by a ministerial letter citing 'an obscure law forbidding co-productions between public and private companies.'[20]

Fo was consequently restricted to performing a reading of some of Ruzzante's texts with Franca Rame and two other actors. The result, *Dario Fo Meets Ruzante*, (spelled with one 'z', in the more acceptable, cultivated way), opened at the Spoleto Festival in July 1993. The four actors read from lecterns in a static performance set-up which seemed to have become standard with Fo's plays in the 1990s. In a prologue, Fo describes Ruzzante as 'a revolutionary, as well as the greatest actor of the Renaissance in all of Europe', an illegitimate son, and the only actor-playwright of his time not to be tied down by the dictates of a court, which enabled him to be an independent representative of the peasant and the dispossessed. He also explains the origins of the name 'Ruzzante' as meaning 'butting' like a goat or bull, as well as having sexual overtones (*ruzzare* meaning 'to romp').[21]

In 'The Oration' Fo performs an anarchic address given by Ruzzante to Cardinal Marco Cornaro in 1521. In it he asks the church to change its laws demanding that peasants fast, since they are hungry enough as it is, and requiring them to wear clothes, since it is more natural to go around naked, and to make love in moderation, since making love is also natural. Ruzzante also asks the church to legislate against poets and writers using refined language, since they do not have to experience hunger and hard work, and to allow priests to take wives, since they take the peasants' women. He then asks them to make new laws eliminating the discrimination against peasants by the citizens of Padua, and allowing peasant men to have four wives and peasant women to have four husbands, so they can 'increase and multiply'.

In 'Betìa' Nale is married to Tamìa (Franca Rame) but in love with Betìa, who is married to Zìlio, Nale's best friend, and Tamìa is in love with Meneghèllo. Zìlio discovers Betìa's relationship with Nale and stabs him. They all believe Nale is dead, but he is not, and he appears to a distraught Tamìa to tell her about life in hell, which is as bad as their lives as peasants. Tamìa realises that Nale is alive, and Nale, moved, makes peace with Zìlio. The two women, Nale and Zìlio decide to live together as a foursome, leaving Meneghèllo, who resolves to join them. Fo has described the character of Betìa as 'a peasant woman who has always lived in the country, who arrives in the city but is still bound to the roughness and coarseness of her village.'[22]

The second part of *Ruzante* begins with 'Life', a short and witty philosophical treatise. This is followed by 'Bertevèlo the Fisherman's Dream', reminiscent of the tales of the *fabulatori* of Lake Maggiore. The eponymous hero finds a woman's handbag full of gold, silver and precious stones after a storm at sea, and dreams of all the food and sexual activity he will indulge in now that he is rich. His dream ends with him drowning in a sea of love and luxury.

In the final piece, Beolco's best-known play, 'Ruzzante returns from Battle', a soldier ravaged by the experiences of fighting for the Venetian republic returns to Venice in a miserable state, looking for his wife Gnua. He meets his friend Menato, who is appalled by his physical condition, and after Ruzzante tells him some of his adventures, Menato eventually tells him that Gnua has found another man. Gnua arrives to keep an appointment with her new man, and Ruzzante declares himself. She asks why he has not brought her a present as proof of his love for her, and explains that she needs a man to provide for her so she can eat. She and Menato also cast doubt on Ruzzante's valour at war, suggesting he is a coward. Gnua's beau arrives and beats Ruzzante with a stick, leaving him lying on the ground as Menato and Gnua watch. After attempting to convince Menato he has been attacked by 100 men, Ruzzante then tries to laugh about his situation. Menato suggests it has been 'like a comedy', which makes Ruzzante laugh even more.

While Ruzzante's often grotesque view of the world is anarchic, and inclined towards free love, Fo emphasises that his gritty, warts-and-all portrayal of the grim realities of hunger and peasant life leaves no room for populist sentimentality. Fo has commented that the character of Gnua, rather than being callous, is primarily concerned with survival:

She makes sure she receives gifts in exchange for sex, and eats regularly, and feels desired every day. She's scared of nobody. She has a clear idea about what she wants. She already talks with the sophisticated detachment of a prostitute. . . . She describes cruel and violent things casually, with a slightly nasal, feminine intonation which is not a shout, but shows awareness of her profession. She treats her man with contempt not because she doesn't love him but because she doesn't want to be poor any more.[23]

It is not difficult to see the appeal Ruzzante has for Fo. His concern with creating grotesque comedy out of the hunger, misery and infidelity of peasant life aligns him with the *zanni* and the *villano* in *Mistero buffo*, while his imaginative concern with the cosmos and the philosophies of life links him with the *giullari* and *fabulatori* who have been Fo's primary influences.

While *Dario Fo Meets Ruzante* was rather static, lacklustre and roughshod in performance, it was also, like *Harlequin* and the Molière production, an important 'excavation' by Fo of one of his primary sources. He returned to it in 1995, performing it as a solo piece in the manner of *Mistero buffo* under the title *Dario Fo Performs Ruzzante*. Restoring the 'z' to his mentor's name, he added a lengthy prologue in which he makes his usual reference to current events. He also added 'Galileo Galilei', a dialogue ascribed to Galileo and influenced by Ruzzante, in which a doctor and the peasant, Nelo, discuss the cosmos and the universe. The peasant claims it is much bigger than scientists have imagined, and describes it in terms of a moveable feast of cheese or a huge omelette (the earth), polenta (the sun), a chestnut tart (Mars), chickpeas (Venus), and God as capable of crushing humanity with his thumb.

In October 1993 Fo and Rame produced another topical play about the 'Tangentopoli' corruption and bribery scandals, but set it in the eighteenth century, following Fo's tendency to make historical parallels. Initially entitled *A Country in the Dustbin (Un paese nella patumeria)*, it was later retitled *Mamma! I sanculotti! (Mummy! The Sans-culottes!)* in reference to the revolutiony group of the French Revolution. Describing the play as a 'mechanical farce in the manner of Feydeau', Fo explained the *sans-culottes* reference as invoking the way in which the formerly uncommitted, corrupt individuals of the 'Mani pulite' (clean hands) scandals had suddenly discovered a revolutionary zeal:

> Respectable people who had never even noticed a bomb until it was put right under their noses; respectable people who break out in a rage because they have to pay their taxes for the first time ever. And members of the Northern League, who are quick to make the most perverse pro-nouncements, but also to run away at the first signs of any serious revolt.[24]

The play had a cast of eleven, including three actors playing newsreaders, and at one point actors planted in the audience stand up and comment on the action. Fo took the role of an investigating magistrate who stumbles over the truth about the organisers of the 'state massacres' of Piazza Fontana and a number of other bomb explosions in the 1970s. Rame played a mad policewoman who is in charge of the magistrate's bodyguards. With music by Fiorenzo Carpi, and collaboration from Fo's long-time assistant director Arturo Corso, it was a wild, extravagant thriller-farce incorporating songs, dances and grotesque clown-show effects. It also included a scene about the surgical transplant of animal body parts on to humans, an issue that Fo had become increasingly concerned about, with an operation performed on a banquet table with a man substituting for a calf. Focusing on the collusion between the Mafia, terrorists and state politicians, the play involved a series of complex Mafia executions and explosions performed with special effects and complex gadgetry. One explosion filled the auditorium with smoke, and plates of *palliata* (spaghetti with a sauce made from sheep intestines) were offered to members of the audience. Fo and Rame also indulged in a continuous bickering match which brought them out of character at times. Fo performed a part in drag, complete with high heels, and a large Buddha figure dominated proceedings.

Building on the themes already explored in *Seventh*

Commandment: Steal a Bit Less No. 2, the play's elaborate farcical mechanisms and extravagant comic effects were an attempt to outdo what Fo and Rame saw as the wild improbabilities of current events during the 'Tangentopoli' and 'Clean Hands' bribery scandals. Antonio Scuderi, who attended rehearsals of the production, has described what he calls 'a dialectic of written text and creative spontaneity in action, and a conscious attempt on the part of Fo to continue the Italian comic tradition.'[25] As with most of Fo's plays, rehearsals go through three phases: Fo writes a draft of the play and does sketches of the set and costumes; the cast have their lines read by a prompter, and together with Fo begin the chaotic process of changing and reshaping the play, and performances begin, with further alterations to the text based on audience response. Only after this does a definitive text emerge. In the case of *Mummy! The Sansculottes!* the final text was not published, and only the 'copione di scena' (performance script) exists.

Sex, devils, Sofri and the Nobel Prize

August 1994 saw Fo directing another Rossini opera, *An Italian Girl in Algiers*, for the Rossini Opera Festival in Pesaro. This production was later also staged at the Amsterdam Musiktheater, and subsequently broadcast on Dutch television. He also directed another long, rambling, living-newspaper-styled monologue performed by Franca Rame, *Sex? Thanks, Don't Mind If I Do!* (*Sesso? Grazie, tanto per gradire!*). This was a collaboration between Rame, Dario and Jacopo Fo, basing the play on material from a book published in 1992 by Jacopo Fo, *Zen and the Art of Fucking* (*Lo Zen e l'arte di scopare*), which had sold more than 70,000 copies. The original title of the play was the same as the book, but it was changed in order not to provoke controversy, which it nonetheless still managed to do. It was conceived as an educational comic performance-lecture about sexual repression, AIDS, contraception and sex education, and played in front of a backdrop representing the garden of Eden, with giant phallic wax candles based on those used at the Easter festival in Gubbio. As Rame said of the play:

We turned Jacopo's book into a play, in which basic aspects of sexual relationships are explained, and love is celebrated as the expression of pure feeling based on affection. Our aim was also to inform young people and adults about the dangers of AIDS. We thought that in a politically squalid, dark and confused period like this it was indispensable to go back to the personal and start off with the essential things of life: love, feelings and pleasure.[26]

'The Old People' is a grotesque sketch, based on one of Rame's short television pieces, enacting a proposal ascribed to the Berlusconi government of getting rid of old people by throwing them off balconies to save on pensions. A re-enactment of Loreena Bobbit's castration of her husband leads into a chronicle of the follies of the Berlusconi government, who are described as not even worth satirising, and provide justification for the importance of talking about sex. 'Adam and Eve's First Sexual Encounter', in which the couple discover sexual pleasure at the same time as they discover guilt and the devil, is based on a passage from Boccaccio. 'Mazzapegol' presents a little sex-maniac demon who is kept in a sack. 'The Abortion' recounts Rame's first sexual experiences and her abortion, leading into an extended comic sketch about American gymnastic lessons in faking orgasms. There are also passing illustrations of promiscuity, frigidity, post-coital sadness, impotence, pornographic films, Jacopo's adolescent sexual insecurities, ways of avoiding premature ejaculation, and the importance of Zen in the sexual act.

In the second part of the show, 'Where We Came From' traces the transition from ancient matriarchal societies to patriarchal societies and woman's subsequent loss of superiority. 'Virginity' debunks the myth of the intact hymen. 'The Clitoris' uses paintings by Fo of flowers to demonstrate the topology of the female sexual organs (referred to generically as 'Florida') and the 'G spot'. 'The Male Sex Organ' uses the wax candles of Gubbio to demonstrate the modalities of the penis and penetration. Rame also demonstrates the need for pelvic gymnastics. The final piece is 'The Story of the Three Desires', a sexual fable translated into the Padano dialect of *Mistero buffo*, about a couple granted three wishes by a goldfish who discover that discovering new forms of love is not the same as exploring new forms of sexual adventure.

Due to the explicit nature of the sexual material in the play, it was restricted to audiences aged over 18 by the Berlusconi government's Department of Entertainment censorship commission. Although the department did not see the play, it issued the following rather comical pronouncement:

> The text, despite its didactic purpose, could in fact, due to its crude and not always scientific language, cause offence to the common decency which requires respect for spheres of intimacy, and provoke distress among adolescent spectators, with possible effects on their behaviour in relation to sex, which is not simply a detailed list of anatomical parts and tubes.[27]

The theatre magazine *Sipario*, which published the text of the play in their December 1994 issue,[28] appealed against this censorship, and launched a solidarity campaign and petition. Supporting the Fo–Rame company's 'extraordinary contribution to Italian theatre over the past 30 years in terms of civil and cultural commitment,'[29] the petition was signed by audiences and a number of prominent Italian and foreign intellectuals. A group of left-wing MPs of the 'progressive' tendency also raised the matter in the Italian parliament, bringing the play considerable publicity, but it was still denied access to the secondary-school audiences it was primarily aimed at.

The production toured to Naples, where it was performed on international AIDS day. Free tickets and condoms were handed out to the first hundred students in the audience, and a group of teachers asked the company to tour it around schools. In Rome, bookings by 3,000 school students had to be cancelled because of the age restriction. The play was also performed the following year in Milan, Bologna, Florence, Turin and Genoa, receiving favourable reviews which emphasised the play's educational aspects in most of these places. The censorship restriction was eventually withdrawn, but not before some theatres had cancelled the production and its effect on the box office had been felt. The censorship commission subsequently released the following comical revocation:

> The staging of the play, which employs a necessarily theatrical language which is free of any vulgarity of action or gesture, and pervaded by the affection of a deep maternal love, does not provoke the distress anticipated among adolescents.[30]

One of the play's defects, which was indicated by Aggeo Savoli in a review in *L'Unità*,[31] was its exclusive focus on heterosexual relations. There was only one passing reference to homosexuals in the entire piece, intended to imply that homosexual problems and dilemmas were the same as heterosexual ones. In 1997 Jacopo Fo performed his own monologue based on *Zen and the Art of Fucking* with some degree of success in Milan and Rome, and later released an educational video version of the piece, complete with performances by Fo, Rame, Paolo Rossi and others.

At the beginning of 1995 Fo toured his monologue version of *Dario Fo Performs Ruzzante*. On 17 July he suffered a stroke and lost 80 per cent of his eyesight. Nonetheless he made a quick recovery, and managed to conduct a few seminars in schools and universities later in the year. In March 1996 he celebrated his seventieth birthday with performances in Milan of a series of monologues with Franca Rame under the title *The Emperor's Bible and the Peasants' Bible* (*La Bibbia dell'imperatore, la Bibbia dei villani*).

This was later performed at the Benevento Theatre Festival in September 1996, and conceived as a 'supplement' to *Mistero buffo*. It consisted of *The First Miracle of the Boy Jesus* and *The Massacre of the Innocents* augmented by new material based on a re-edition of a lavish bible owned by the Emperor Charles the Bald (nephew of Charlemagne). In 'Pigs without Wings' a pig asks God to give him wings, and then romps about heaven with a sow, causing God some amusement at first. But God eventually punishes the pig, who falls into a sewer, making such a big splash that it reaches heaven. *Abraham and Isaac*, one of Fo's oldest performance pieces, dating back to *Poer nano* in the early 1950s, was also reprised. 'The Shepherd's Cantata' is a piece in Neapolitan dialect about a miracle performed by the Madonna, with two *zanni*, originally included in the 1985 play *Harlequin*. 'Adam and Eve's First Sexual Encounter' and other material from *Sex? Thanks, Don't Mind If I Do!* performed by Rame was also included. There was also the usual lengthy prologue by Fo containing references to current political events. The play was performed in other parts of Italy later in the year. Fo also did a voiceover for the villain Scarafoni in Enzo D'Alò's successful, if rather moralistic and sentimental animated feature film *La freccia azzurra* (*The Blue Arrow*).

For the remainder of the 1996–97 theatre season, Fo and Rame revived *Mistero buffo* and *Sex? Thanks, Don't Mind If I Do!*, performing pieces from them together in a single show which toured around Italy. In common with his practice of writing at least one new play every summer, Fo wrote *Leonardo: The Flight, the Count and the Amours*, a play about Leonardo da Vinci in Urbino in 1502, in the summer of 1996.

In 1997 Fo's production of Rossini's *An Italian Girl in Algiers* was remounted in Cagliari, Sardinia. He also wrote and directed (with Arturo Corso as assistant director) *Il diavolo con le zinne* – literally, 'The Devil with Tits'. This play became widely known as 'The Devil with Boobs', a title given it by US journalists after Fo won the Nobel Prize, but it is perhaps more appropriately titled *The Devil in Drag,* in Ed Emery's English translation.[32] A play about corruption and the law written for the Taormina Festival in Sicily in August, it was performed by a company which included Franca Rame and the prominent Italian Shakespearian actor and Taormina Festival director Giorgio Albertazzi. Albertazzi may have appeared an odd choice for the leading role of a corrupt judge in a Dario Fo play, given his reputation for right-wing views. But it was he who in 1981 had directed Franca Rame in a television production of George Bernard Shaw's *Mrs Warren's Profession*, and who had commissioned the play for the festival. After venue problems, the production opened at the Teatro Vittorio

Emanuele in Messina in August, which was far from full on
opening night, and the play was clearly still at a 'running in'
stage, with prompters visible and Fo shouting instructions to
the actors.

Inspired by *commedia dell'arte* and Renaissance comedy, *The
Devil in Drag* is set in the sixteenth century in the Po valley
during the Inquisition. Albertazzi plays Judge Alfonso de
Tristano, a magistrate, perhaps loosely based on the 'Clean
Hands' protagonist Antonio di Pietro (although Fo played down
any parallels), who is investigating an arson in a church. He
comes into conflict with a cardinal, who is making profits from
burning down churches and getting rid of the witnesses. A
squadron of devils come on the scene, and one of them is
transformed into a suppository-devil intended to inhabit and
corrupt the magistrate, but who possesses his old housekeeper,
Pizzocca Ganassa (Rame) instead. As a result, she sprouts
luscious breasts and buttocks, and seduces the magistrate when
he comes home drunk. They are discovered and the magistrate
is tried for immorality. But the key witnesses in the case are all
eliminated before they can testify. Finally the judge is absolved
of the main charges against him but sentenced to five years'
imprisonment as a galley slave for heresy. Fo described the play
as:

> A Machiavellian comedy, a gigantic late sixteenth-century
> intrigue, with judges and devils, housekeepers possessed by
> devils, hermits, gendarmes, torturers and even a monkey.
> . . . It is inspired by events in post-[Paris]-Commune
> [European] cities, when everyone suffered from a constant
> phenomenon, fires. There were fires in lepers' colonies,
> churches, hospitals, and in their place banks and palaces
> were built. Even then there was rampant speculation and
> corruption, and magistrates who carried out enquiries . . .[33]

The Devil in Drag received very unenthusiastic reviews.
Masolino D'Amico in *La Stampa* found it 'disappointing' and
suggested that Fo had put too much of his creative efforts into
developing the array of different, partly invented, partly archaic
dialects – including Neapolitan – spoken by the devils and

Rame's character, and not enough into the plot or the play's political perspective.[34] *La Repubblica*'s reviewer called it 'a devil with blunt horns', and, although anticipated as 'the theatrical event of the summer', saw the result as 'a rehearsal rather than an opening night' and a 'sorry exhibition' barely rescued by Rame's central performance.

The text appeared to have been written solely as an entertainment vehicle, with 'undistinctive' songs – including a homage to Fo's long-time musical collaborator Fiorenzo Carpi, who died in mid-1997. There were also puppets, a choreographed final scene of galley slaves, a shadow theatre, and a scene in which a Berlusconi-like prelate eats a plateful of excrement. According to *La Repubblica*, Albertazzi, apart from a moment of comic brilliance in the sex scene, seemed 'ill at ease' in a comic role more suited to Fo himself.[35] The production later moved to the Teatro Carcano in Milan, where it was playing on 9 October 1997, when Fo was awarded the Nobel Prize for Literature.

News of the Nobel Prize came while Fo was driving from Rome to Milan with the young television personality Ambra Angiolini, recording a mobile television chat show entitled *Roma-Milano*. A reporter for *La Repubblica* held up a placard informing him of the news, and the following day's issue of the newspaper devoted seven pages, including the front page, to Fo. Fo's response to the prize, in which he described himself as 'flabbergasted' (*esterefatto*), was thus also recorded on Italian television. The Swedish Academy's press release stated:

> For many years Fo has been performed all over the world, perhaps more than any other contemporary dramatist, and his influence has been considerable. He if anyone merits the epithet of jester in the true meaning of that word. With a blend of laughter he opens our eyes to abuses and injustices in society and also the wider historical perspective in which they can be placed. Fo is an extremely serious satirist with a multifaceted oeuvre. His independence and clear-sightedness have led him to take great risks, whose consequences he has been made to feel while at the same

time experiencing enormous response from widely differing quarters . . .

Fo's strength is in the creation of texts that simultaneously amuse, engage and provide perspectives. As in
commedia dell'arte, they are always open for creative additions and dislocations, continually encouraging the actors
to improvise, which means that the audience is activated in
a remarkable way. His is an oeuvre of impressive artistic
vitality and range.[36]

Citing *Accidental Death of an Anarchist, Can't Pay? Won't Pay!*,
Trumpets and Raspberries and *The Devil in Drag*, the press release
emphasised Fo's debt to the jesters of the Middle Ages. It also
cited his and Rame's works about women's issues, and the
difficulty translators have in rendering his use of topical
references and *grammelot*, singling out Ed Emery's decision to
remain close to the original version of *Accidental Death of an
Anarchist* in his English version of the play. Italian reactions to
the news of the Nobel Prize predictably polarised left- and
right-wing factions, but were united by an overwhelming sense
of surprise. The leader of the right-wing National Alliance
party, Gianfranco Fini, described the award as 'shameful', while
his colleague Marco Zacchera claimed it was 'a joke and an
insult to Italian culture'. The Vatican newspaper *Osservatore
Romano*, a constant critic of Fo throughout his career, seized on
the Swedish Academy's use of the word 'jester', and observed:
'Fo is the sixth Italian Nobel Prize winner after Carducci,
Deledda, Pirandello, Quasimodo and Montale; after all these
wise choices we get a mere jester. . . . Giving the prize to
someone who is also the author of questionable works is beyond
all imagination.'[37]

On the left, deputy prime minister and arts minister Walter
Veltroni described Fo as 'one of the most incisive and disturbing
authors since the war', and the award as an acknowledgment of
politically committed theatre 'of social condemnation of
injustice and marginalisation'.[38] Fo's publisher since 1966,
Giulio Einaudi, compared Fo with Fellini, while Umberto Eco
was pleased that the award had gone 'to an author who does not

belong to the traditional academic world.' Eco, interviewed in *La Repubblica*, saw the award as proof of the 'enormous popularity' of Fo's plays outside Italy, where they could not rely on Fo's presence as a performer. A rather tight-lipped Giorgio Strehler, also quoted in *La Repubblica*, stated that the award 'could only bring greater prestige to Italian literature and theatre. We feel honoured as Europeans and as theatre practitioners.'[39]

Other responses were less generous. A previous Italian Nobel Prize winner for science, Rita Levi Montalchini, stated she had never heard of Dario Fo and didn't know who he was: 'Is he Italian?' The crime writers Fruttero and Lucentini described the award as 'laughable' and 'a farce', and accused Fo of making 'benevolent allusions to the Red Brigades'. The Italian poet Mario Luzi, who had also been nominated for the prize, reacted to the news of Fo's victory with 'great bitterness'.[40] It was subsequently revealed that the Accademia dei Lincei, which is the only Italian organisation empowered to nominate Nobel Prize candidates to the Swedish Academy, had nominated Luzi in 1997 for the seventh year running. In protest against Luzi's failure yet again to win the prize, the Accademia dei Lincei refused to make any nomination for the prize in 1998.[41] An article by Franca Zambonini entitled 'Sorry, Wrong Prize', appeared in the former Christian Democrat magazine *Famiglia Cristiana* arguing that the award was for literature, which had to be readable in schools, and that Fo's use of *grammelot,* clowning and improvisation, not to mention his political campaigning, disqualified him from this category.[42] These sentiments were echoed by the prominent right-wing Peruvian author and former politician Mario Vargas Llosa, who expressed his doubts whether Fo was 'a first-rate author. Even the Nobel, like any other prize, can make mistakes.'[43] Reactions such as these prompted Fo to describe himself ironically as 'the Nobel thief',[44] while pointing out that he had been congratulated by former Nobel Prize winner Gabriel García Márquez.

Reactions in the USA ranged from condemnation of the award in the *Wall Street Journal*, to amused approval from playwright Tony Kushner, author of the acclaimed play *Angels in America*, in *The Nation*. In an article entitled 'Fo's Last Laugh', Kushner summed up the controversy surrounding the award, maintaining that Fo

> deserves to win the Nobel Prize for his life of theatrical activism [and] his dedication to progressive politics . . . because he's made the wicked old men of the Vatican angry enough to denounce him in terms that recall the church's anathematising of actors in the Middle Ages . . . because his winning forced the [*New York*] *Times* to translate the title of his new play as *The Devil with Boobs* . . . because he writes *debatable* texts. He has dedicated his genius to making everything he touches debatable. Awarding him this Solemn Honour is brave and perhaps even reckless because it subjects Literature, and prizes, and Newspapers of Record, to the Fo effect. . . . with Fo winning, the debate becomes fun because it's forced out of the big-yawn area of 'literary merit' (for which we should read long-term market value). The prize augments and amplifies Fo's dangerous silliness. Fo in return graciously augments and amplifies the prize's essential silliness. Both in the process are ennobled. . . . there's an absolute need to blow a big juicy wet raspberry in the direction of the Clubhouse of Greatness, and I like to think that's what the Nobel board, perhaps guided by 'a tragic sense of life', has done, wittingly or unwittingly, this year. They couldn't have found a raspberry-blower more mighty, more worthy, than Dario Fo.[45]

In the UK, responses were also primarily of surprise, at least according to an article in *The Times*, which suggested that Arthur Miller and Salman Rushdie had been on the short list for the prize. *The Times* quoted theatre critic Benedict Nightingale describing the award as 'quite a surprise' and Fo's London publisher, Michael Earley, as being 'shocked' by the news.[46]

Fo immediately dedicated the prize to Rame, and in typically polemical and controversial fashion, announced his intention of using the prize money to campaign for the release of three imprisoned former left-wing activists from the group Lotta Continua, Adriano Sofri, Ovidio Bompressi and Giorgio Pietrostefani. These three had been sentenced to more than 20 years' imprisonment in January 1997 for the murder of police inspector Luigi Calabresi in 1972, after long and torturous legal proceedings, including the legal maximum of three appeals. They were condemned on evidence given by a 'repentant' terrorist, Leonardo Marino, in 1988, and sentence was passed four months before the case would have been subject to a statute of limitations. The examining magistrate for the case was Saverio Borelli, who had taken over the head of 'Clean Hands' investigations from Antonio di Pietro, who, after undergoing a series of legal and other attacks on his integrity, had resigned and later gone into politics. All the evidence in the case, such as bullets and the getaway car, had long been destroyed, and Marino's evidence was full of inconsistencies. These included an account of a three-minute conversation with Sofri in which the latter proposed killing Calabresi – a piece of evidence which Fo made great play with, using *grammelot* to emphasise the high speed at which the conversation would have had to proceed. Marino, ironically, was released from prison because the statute of limitations had expired in his case. A petition was started up to request a pardon for Sofri, and was signed by more than 150,000 people, but it was refused by the Italian president Oscar Luigi Scalfaro in October 1997. A widespread campaign was mounted among the Italian Left in support of the case. In June and October 1997 Sofri, Bompressi and Pietrostefani held three-week hunger strikes to protest their continued imprisonment, and Sofri published two books and numerous newspaper articles about his predicament. He also demanded a new trial, as a pardon implied he was guilty of the crime. This case, which involved events in Italy's political history which were linked to those of *Accidental Death of an Anarchist*, became the subject of Fo's new play.

On 10 December 1997, dressed in a tuxedo and bow-tie for the first time in his life, Fo received the Nobel Prize from King Charles XVI of Sweden to shouts of approval and a standing ovation. Some Italian newspapers subsequently made ironic reference to the title of a satirical song Fo had written for Enzo Jannacci in 1969, 'Ho visto un re' (I've seen a king). Three days previously, dressed in a conservative black suit and tie, he had delivered an address entitled 'Contra jogulatores obloquentes' (Against Jesters of Irreverent Speech), which he turned into a bravura performance. The title was an allusion to a law passed in 1221 by the Emperor Frederick II allowing people to insult, beat, and even kill jesters. Instead of a printed text of the address, Fo, in his by now customary way, provided 25 pages of coloured paintings and handwritten key words which outlined his main themes. He described the award as the 'Oscar of all Oscars', and emphasised his role as a jester (*giullare*), and the history of oppression by kings that jesters had been subjected to. He also noted that his award had caused 'sublime poets who fly high to come crashing down to earth' (a possible reference to Luzi) and complimented the Swedish Academy on having given the award to a black writer 11 years previously, followed by a Jewish writer, and now a jester. He spoke of the influence on him of the glass-blowers and *fabulatori* (storytellers) of his childhood near Lake Maggiore. He acted out one glass-blower's story about a town called Caldé which gradually slid down the slopes of a hill into the sea, without its inhabitants being aware of it. He also expressed his debt to Ruzzante and Molière:

> my mentors, both of them authors, actor-managers and directors of their own plays, who were treated with arrogance and contempt by the authorities and their literary lackeys, and hated because they used their stages to fight against hypocrisy and violence by making people laugh: as everyone knows, people in power don't like laughter.[47]

He then went on to talk about his visits to universities, during which he observed that young people's heads seemed to be full of nonsense generated by the mass media, and they appeared ignorant of recent history or current events, and bereft of any sense of political commitment. He noted as instructive examples of political repression the recent burning to death in Siva in Turkey of 37 writers, actors and dancers by religious fanatics, and the Sofri case in Italy. He also acted out transplant and cloning experiments, which he regards as creating 'Franken-stein's pig brother', and attacked the patenting and copyrighting of gene modification and human cloning, in a general condem-nation of 'genetic manipulation'. He spoke of the need for young people to be informed about the 'state massacres' in Italy in the 1960s and 1970s, along with the deliberately misleading judicial inquiries carried out into them, and the farcical court cases they led to. He resolved to continue 'singing' about Italy's political history to arouse the indignation of young people. To conclude, he launched into a eulogy of Franca Rame, without whom, he stated, he would not have won the prize, and recalled their work together in occupied factories and the violence they were subjected to. He ended with an 'epic' re-enactment of his arrival at the theatre where Rame and Albertazzi were performing in Milan after hearing news of the prize. This involved portraying the crowds who engulfed them, Franca embracing him in her costume, a tram stopping so that the passengers could get out to congratulate them, and an impro-vised band of 40 people playing trumpets, trombones and drums. The applause and celebration he acted out spread to the audience at the Swedish Academy for what Jim Heitz of the Associated Press described as a 'manic, unorthodox . . . lecture, . . . a torrent of words, burlesque gestures and noises and the sense that madness is overtaking the stage, followed by the realisation that Fo is a craftsman with icy control.'[48] Fo's performance also included a poem by Mayakovsky, which he later admitted to making up on the spot, and an extract from Ruzzante done as an encore.

After receiving the prize, Fo immediately set to work on the Sofri play. This involved reading thousands of pages of court transcripts, compiling documentary material, reconstructing the murder of Calabresi and doing a series of sketches, paintings and drawings of the principal events and characters involved in the case. On 21 December he had an hour-long meeting in Bologna, where *The Devil in Drag* was being performed, with the left-wing Italian prime minister Romano Prodi, during which he discussed Sofri, Bompressi and Pietrostefani. Fo and Rame were clearly enjoying the celebrity the Nobel had brought them, and were regularly making headlines in Italian newspapers. Fo was offered the Ambrogino prize, an award given each year on the feast of St Ambrogio, by the Mayor of Milan, Gabriele Albertini, a member of the separatist Northern League. He snubbed this award, which was offered on the same day as he gave his Nobel address, causing considerable offence. In January 1998 Fo and Rame received more appropriate awards at the carnival celebrations in Viareggio: the 'Burlamacco d'oro' (Golden Jest) and the 'Ondina d'oro' (Golden Wave), 'confirming the value of satire, irony and mockery against the power of bad faith, which the two artists have devoted themselves to with invaluable skill.'[49] At the 1998 Venice Carnival, a huge puppet-like effigy of Fo was displayed.

In early 1998, Fo announced he was working on a play about St Francis of Assisi, who is often referred to as 'God's jester' (il giullare di Dio). Provisionally entitling it *Mistero buffo 2*, he performed extracts from the play on RAI television. Based, like its predecessor, on obscure texts from local folklore and popular sources, as well as a recent book by Chiara Frugoni, *Vita di un uomo, Francesco d'Assisi*, (The Life of a Man, Francis of Assisi), it would present an alternative perspective to the official version of St Francis' life. Fo wished to concentrate on the saint's sense of humour, his refusal to beg alms, and his radical, audacious side.[50]

Fo also launched his Neapolitan version of Molière's play *Don Juan*, based on a translation by Delia Gambelli, which was published in December 1997, with another attack on cloning and genetic manipulation. In February 1998, he gave another address-performance about genetic manipulation at the European Parliament in Strasbourg, in support of a campaign by the European Green Party to ban cloning and the patenting of genetic inventions in Europe. Also in February, Fo wrote a widely publicised letter to the Italian president, Oscar Luigi Scalfaro, after evidence had come to light in a statement by a 'repentant' terrorist, Biagio Pitarresi. Pitarresi claimed that the *carabinieri* division of the Pastrengo district of Milan had ordered the abduction and rape of Franca Rame in 1973. Rame's case had come under the statute of limitation, despite similar evidence being presented by the neo-fascist Angelo Izzo in

1987. Fo asked Scalfaro to call for a new inquiry into the case. Scalfaro's reply – which Fo refused to make public – expressed sympathy for Rame, but did not acknowledge the responsibility of the Italian state in the case.

Shortly afterwards, documents belonging to the Italian Secret Service were released that revealed that information given them in April 1974 by an informer known as 'Anna Bolena' indicated that Fo had been suspected of being the leader of the Red Brigades. Despite its comic overtones, the revelation was a reminder of the more dangerous aspects of the prejudice and condemnation that both Fo and Rame had undergone, and that they continued to be associated with terrorism by their detractors. This was indicated by the only feature article about Fo winning the Nobel Prize to appear in an Australian newspaper, by Desmond O'Grady, who claimed: 'Even if Sofri had supported terrorism, probably it would not discourage Fo, who has expressed sympathy for many imprisoned terrorists, from the Italian Red Brigades to the Basque ETA movement.'[51] O'Grady also reiterates the smear campaign conducted against Fo after the Nobel by members of the post-fascist Italian Right, who accused him of being a member of Mussolini's Republican armed forces in 1943. These charges eventually led Fo to a further rebuttal, explaining in a weekly magazine that he had briefly joined up with an artillery battalion in Varese in order to avoid being forced by Mussolini to work in Germany, but that he had discovered that the battalion was also being sent to Germany to assist the German army, and had deserted.[52]

The Sofri play, ironically entitled *Free Marino! Marino is Innocent!* (*Marino libero! Marino e innocente!*) was presented publicly as a work in progress at the Teatro Puccini in Florence in January 1998. This was followed by an 'open rehearsal' in Turin in March, which was repeatedly interrupted by a group of young squatters. One of them, a young woman, accused Franca Rame of being a fascist, causing her considerable distress, especially since her abduction by fascists had been in the news recently. The squatters, who had been involved in a demonstration after being evicted from a *centro sociale occupato* (occupied social centre) in Turin, had asked Fo if they could present their cause to the audience after the play. Fo invited them to the play, and they joined the audience members sitting on the stage – a common feature in Fo's productions – smoking, drinking, heckling and jeering as the play went on. Fo, who had a few years previously offered his support for the evictees of the famous Leoncavallo social centre in Milan, asked them to stop interrupting, without success. They were evicted from the theatre with the audience's full support, and some of them apologised to Fo in the interval. The incident was proof of the importance of Fo's campaign, and the play's objective, to inform Italian young people about the political history of the past 20 years. Rame later accused the media of exaggerating the incident, and issued a statement in which she expressed sympathy for the young people involved in the *centri sociali occupati*, offered them support and attacked their criminalisation, and spoke out about youth unemployment.[53]

Marino at Large (as the play is called in Ed Emery's translation) opened at the Teatro Nazionale in Milan on 16 March, at a time when the Sofri case was at the centre of public attention. A book by Daniele Biacchessi and others, *Il caso Sofri*, was published on the same day, and an article about the case by Umberto Eco appeared in the French newspaper *Le Monde*. Fo's play consisted of the customary prologue, followed by eight 'chapters' dealing with the Sofri case, entitled 'The Time of the "State Massacres" ', 'The Police Investigation', 'Marino Prepares', 'Luigi! Find Luigi!', 'Marino has no Interest', 'Penitence', 'Coup de Scène' and 'The Final Con-Trick'. The play was essentially a monologue by Fo, with assistance from Rame with back projections of Fo's drawings, a ventriloquist-style dummy of Marino, puppets, cut-out figures and other props.

The opening performance was televised on RAI 2 on 18 March, after initially being programmed for 17 March. The earlier date coincided with the decision to be announced by the Court of Appeal as to whether the Sofri case would be reviewed, and RAI decided to delay it as a result, a decision which angered Fo. In the event, the request for a review of the trial was denied by the panel of three judges, and Fo expressed anxiety as to whether his play had damaged Sofri and the others' case. An appeal against the court ruling was filed, but without much hope of success, and plans were made to take the case to the European Court of Justice. The text of the play, which included more than 100 of Fo's brightly coloured drawings and paintings, was rushed into print by Einaudi and appeared on 27 March, along with the text of *The Devil in Drag*.[54]

On 6 April 1998, Fo wrote a lengthy letter to *La Repubblica* protesting about the 'shameful judicial solution' to the Sofri case, 'which has provided journalists all over Europe with a big laugh.' Citing a summary of the case by John Hooper in *The Guardian*, he states that in order to understand why the three suspects were not freed after the Court of Cassation reversed their guilty verdict, 'one has to move away from the world of Dickens and Orton into that of Lewis Carroll (the author of *Alice in Wonderland*).'[55] Fo's use of these English frames of reference is interesting, suggesting that he wished to place the case in a broader European context, but also draw on English concepts of justice and 'fair play'.

Marino at Large is set on the last night of December 1999, with Sofri, Bompressi and Pietrostefani represented, like the other characters, by cardboard cut-out profiles. The characters assemble in prison with the magistrates who carried out investigations and sentenced them, and the informer who gave evidence against them with '120 lies', Leonardo Marino. Marino is represented by a ventriloquist's dummy manipulated by Fo, who plays a judge. One scene analyses the evidence found after Calabresi's murder, which included reports of a blue Fiat 125 driven by a woman, a line of inquiry which was dropped after Marino confessed to the crime.

The play also gives a résumé of the long series of contradictions and untruths involved in the case. Fo's paintings and drawings were projected as slides, and the play covers 30 years of Italian political history, from the bombs in Piazza Fontana which *Accidental Death of an Anarchist* dealt with, to the present. It also traces the involvement in these events of the secret services, neo-fascists, corrupt magistrates, the ultra-left newspaper *Lotta Continua*, the *carabinieri* and journalists. Resembling the documentary plays Fo and La Comune performed in the

1970s, the play demonstrates Fo's continued commitment to a politically engaged theatre which deals with current events and issues relating to social justice.

In the summer of 1998, an exhibition of Fo's and Rame's performances and memorabilia opened at Cesenatico, the seaside town where they generally spend each summer, under the title *Pupazzi con rabbia e sentimento – La vita e l'arte di Dario Fo e Franca Rame* (Puppets with Anger and Feeling – the Life and the Art of Dario Fo and Franca Rame). Fo and Rame continued to make regular pronouncements in the Italian press on issues such as genetic manipulation, squatters, and even the rights of street performers, who are forbidden by a 1927 Italian law from holding public shows. At a buskers' festival in Modena in September 1998, Fo gave improvised performances along with 200 musicians, painters and street performers and criticised the law. And in October 1998, Fo was inevitably asked for his comments when the Nobel Prize for Literature was awarded to the Portuguese novelist José Saramago. Saramago had been a front-runner for the prize the previous year, and Fo had met him in Stockholm. Citing the themes of Saramago's novel *The Gospel According to Jesus* as 'similar to mine: becoming politically aware, struggling, refusing to accept any compromise with the regime or regimes', Fo described the 1998 award as a 'continuation from the previous year: they have given the prize to a writer for his civil battles as well as his quality as a writer . . . an excellent choice, because it continues to award not literature for its own sake but writers who attempt to create a civil conscience.'[56]

CHAPTER 7

FO AND RAME IN THE UK

Translating Fo

> Our own work has always managed to survive, at least up
> to now, because of the fact that we have always taken situ-
> ations of struggle as our point of reference.
> (Dario Fo interviewed in London, May 1983.)

Dario Fo's plays were beginning to be produced in translation
outside Italy as early as 1960, but it was not until 1978, with
Robert Walker's production of *We Can't Pay? We Won't Pay!*
at the Half Moon Theatre in London, that his work began to
become known in the UK. By this time Fo was already one of
the most widely performed playwrights in world theatre.
European directors and theatre groups, like the Belgian theatre
collective NewsScene, which dedicated itself exclusively to
producing Fo's plays over a period of four years, had already
performed translated versions of most of Fo's adaptable plays.
The Dario Fo Theater in Vienna performed his plays exclusively
between 1979 and 1995, and they were also widely performed
in France, Spain, Germany, Denmark and Sweden in the 1960s
and 1970s. One reason for this was probably the relative cultural
proximity of these countries to Italy, and the fact that Fo and
Rame had toured there. The traditionally provincial, parochial
English theatre culture is more isolated, and slower to respond
to cultural events – particularly those of a highly 'unofficial'
nature – in the rest of Europe.

In an article written in 1981, Jørgen Stender Clausen listed
productions of 16 different plays – some in multiple productions

– by Fo in Denmark between 1962 and 1980. These included relatively obscure plays like *The Worker Knows 300 Words*, *The Boss's Funeral*, *He Who Steals a Foot*, *Seventh Commandment: Steal a Bit Less*, *Throw the Lady Out*, *United We Stand! All Together Now!*, *Mother's Marijuana* and even *Law and Order for God and Money's Sake!!!*. Clausen argued that Fo's plays were better known in 1980 in Denmark than anywhere else in the world except Italy. He attributed this to the fact that the Italian theatre practitioner Eugenio Barba, who had been based in Denmark since 1966, invited Fo and Rame to give seminars there in 1968. In the same year Fo also directed a production of *Throw the Lady Out* at the Danish National Theatre, Det Kongelige Teater. Fo and Rame returned to perform *Mistero buffo* and *Tutta casa, letto e chiesa* in Denmark in 1980, and Clausen claims that they were a strong influence on a number of experimental Danish theatre groups, including Solvognen (Sunwagon). He suggested Fo's influence was as strong in contemporary Denmark as the *commedia dell'arte* had been in the seventeenth century:

> The Danes were attracted to and conquered by Dario Fo's theatre because it was a popular, satirical and politically engaged theatre, non-formalist and full of common sense behind its apparent farcical demeanour – qualities which have always distinguished the best Danish theatre. It was also popular, in the sense of being produced in places derived from the people and based directly on their traditions. This final aspect presented a new dimension for Danish culture.[1]

Fo's work found a place primarily in the repertoires of alternative, experimental Danish theatre companies. Clausen also points out that the first substantial full-length critical analysis of Fo's work outside Italy, *The World Upside Down: Dario Fo and the Popular Imagination*, was published by the Danish critic Bent Holm in 1980. Holm drew on Bakhtin and semiotics and provided an extensive analysis of *Seventh Commandment*, which was published at the same time in his translation, and was used for a number of subsequent Danish productions of the play. Fo's work had a similarly popular reception in Sweden, where the

Italian director Carlo Barsotti, who had been based there since the 1970s, produced a number of Fo's plays as well as a television documentary about Fo and Rame. This provides cause and context for Fo's Nobel Prize.

The most immediate difficulty which held up the arrival of Fo's work in the UK (and the USA, and the rest of the English-speaking world) was the specific political content of most of his plays. Largely written as a direct response to particular Italian political situations, their reference points are difficult to translate into an English context, even when their implications are universal (as in the case of price increases in *Can't Pay? Won't Pay!*). Understanding *Accidental Death of an Anarchist* without any knowledge of the Pinelli affair, the 'state massacres' and the 'strategy of tension' is difficult, although the play's exposure of police incompetence, corruption and brutality certainly have universal applications. The problems of how to cope with specific topical and cultural references in Fo's plays, such as his repeated criticisms of the Italian Communist Party, were also apparent. Frequently these reference points could not simply be cut without disrupting the entire dramatic logic and structure of the plays. This is not, however, tantamount to saying that there was any lack of a comparable tradition of working-class and popular culture in the British theatre, but appreciation of these factors in Fo's work was difficult. Fo's own comments on this subject, as reported in an interview with Catherine Itzin in London in 1980, reflect that there may have been a reciprocal lack of understanding:

> Left intellectuals in Britain seemed to have created a strange cult of the working class, glorifying the people and worshipping their lack of culture. Left theatre people here, he thought, didn't really know much about working-class culture and even seemed proud of the fact.[2]

This is to ignore the work of, to name three British theatre groups and playwrights of the 1970s, John McGrath and 7:84, Red Ladder, and Belt and Braces. Plays like Trevor Griffiths' *Comedians* also drew heavily on working-class culture, and John Arden had used popular ballad forms and medieval popular theatre. There also appeared to be a reciprocal ignorance of most of these writers and groups in Italy. In 1990 Fo expressed an awareness only of the work of Shaw, Pinter and Osborne, whom he described as 'an author with a great talent for humour'.[3] But he was also familiar with Griffiths' *Comedians* and Nigel Williams' *Class Enemy* through productions of Italian adaptations of them by the Teatro dell'Elfo in Milan.[4]

Rather than lacking any equivalent cultural context for Fo's plays (with the exception of the Catholic church), what British adaptors and directors had to confront was the need to find an English equivalent for the specifically Italian cultural and political references they contained. These then had to be placed in the theatrical context of English working-class and popular culture. This often involved a need for extensive rewriting and adaptation, which ran the risk of losing sight of the author's original political and institutional targets and aims. In changing the often specific reference points of Fo's plays, there was a danger of obscuring their reasons for being written. Some English adaptations completely anglicised the plays – Stuart Hood's version of *The Open Couple* transports us from Comiso, Parma and Piacenza to Molesworth, Lincoln and York, and the version of *Archangels Don't Play Pinball* by James Runcie (son of the Archbishop of Canterbury) broadcast on BBC radio in 1986 relocates the play in Glasgow. But as David Groves has noted, there is usually a need to 'replant' the plays in their Italian setting to gain their full political impact.[5]

The US adaptor and director of Fo's plays R.G. Davis has suggested that there are three stages in the process of what he calls a 'culture-to-culture transmigration'[6] of Fo's plays. A word-to-word literal translation should, he argues, be followed by a 'sense-to-sense' version which searches for the 'humour, bite, idiomatic flavour and even imagery of the original' in the target language. This in turn, he argues, should be preceded by 'an analysis of the play in its new socio-political context.'[7] This formula is useful as far as it goes, although there is no reason why all three stages cannot be present in equal force simultaneously in a good translation. Where a word-to-word rendition is not possible in the idiom and social context of the target language, be it UK English, Australian English or American English, a sense-for-sense substitute can usually be found for Fo's jokes or political references. In their detailed linguistic comparison of four different translations and adaptations of *Accidental Death of an Anarchist*, Tim Fitzpatrick and Kzenia Sawczak argue that Fo's translator is faced with 'non-equivalences between linguistic structures, social phenomena and the social and ideological frames by which phenomena are "read" ' as well as differing 'theatrical frames'. This means that any translation involves 'various degrees of slippage . . . towards adaptation', even when it is attempting to be 'literal'. Their analysis usefully illustrates how these four factors lead to additions, subtractions and variations to the 'original' text.[8]

In an article about translating Fo's work into French, Valeria Tasca has enumerated some of the more specific linguistic problems involved in translating Fo. His tendency to use the regional dialects of Veneto and Lombardy, his use of the invented onomatopoeic language *grammelot* to mimic foreign languages, and his specific use of insults, swearwords, sexual terminology, blasphemies and obscenities all pose dilemmas for the translator. It is also important to distinguish between Fo's use of a highly colourful range of insults and 'obscene' expressions and the vulgar expressions and expletives which creep into many English versions. Stuart Hood has rightly identified in a number of English productions of the plays 'a lamentable tendency on the part of some directors to beef up the text – as one might say – by vulgarisms, four-letter words and crudities which are apparently thought to give the text a certain robustness but of which the original is either innocent or when it includes them does so with calculated effect.'[9] Hood also suggests that some attempt should be made to find an equivalent to the dialect used in plays like *Mistero buffo*, such as Lallans (Lowlands) Scots or Afro-Caribbean dialects. He suggests this because dialect is an essential part of the richness of Fo's texts and 'the audience should derive part of its pleasure from having to work at understanding what is being said.'[10] Tasca concludes with an apt summing up of the translation process:

we find a piecemeal solution for each page, and the result,
I am well aware, is a patchwork of familiar turns of phrase,
archaisms, regionalisms, more or less outmodish slang,
more or less hip slang, and hesitant neologisms.[11]

Such problems are usually solved in the UK – with varying
degrees of success – by the expedient of commissioning a
practising playwright to make an adaptation from a literal
translation. But Tasca rightly emphasises that Fo's texts are
essentially the result of an oral and gestural process which is
finalised only in performance, and that the plays' rhythm is their
most vital feature. As a former prompter in Fo's company, she
is ideally placed to follow this rhythm; as she states, 'I write in
French but I hear in Italian.'[12] Ed Emery, who has translated
more of Fo's plays into English than anyone else, uses a tape
recorder to try and find a spoken English equivalent for the
Italian text. When I have translated Fo's and Rame's work I find
it impossible not to hear their voices speaking the lines.

Hood, who has done simultaneous translations for Fo's one-
man shows, identifies another difficulty: 'by editing and printing
the version of the text as it stands today one is fixing, as an
entomologist fixes a butterfly or a moth, a theatrical event
which ought not to be subject to a closure of this kind.'[13] This
also exposes the fact that Fo's and Rame's texts are often continually evolving; some have been published in three or four
different versions, and the topical political references they
include often go quickly out of date. The 11-volume Einaudi
editions of Fo's plays represent a 'definitive' version of most of
their plays, but Fo and Rame usually urge translators and
adaptors to look for equivalent topical political references to
those in the plays in their own countries. But this can lead on
occasion to the sloppy and arbitrary expedient made towards the
end of Gavin Richards' adaptation of *Accidental Death of an
Anarchist* – a bowdlerised version regrettably still circulating.
Here the actor playing the Maniac is instructed to 'give detailed
examples of political murder and state oppression in Britain.'[14]
This, as David Hirst has pointed out, is 'diametrically opposed
to the very precise, mounting argument of the original, which

moves from analysis of specific issues and their consequences to a call for more radical political activity.'[15]

As a result of such inappropriate adaptations, Fo and Rame insist on approving production scripts for performances of their plays in other languages. This usually involves drawing on the services of an accredited editor in the respective language. As Emery, who also works as a printer and sub-editor and is closely familiar with the procedure of publishing plays, has pointed out, this can sometimes be infuriating and frustrating for the translator, since 'the only authoritative version [of any play] is the version that exists or is being performed at that moment in time; all preceding versions are superseded.'[16] For my translation of *Mother's Marijuana is the Best*, I was given a tape recording of Fo and Rame's most recent performance of the play and asked to translate from that – which proved to be far preferable to working from a printed text.

But as Emery has also suggested, despite the difficulties and frustrations experienced by translators of Fo's plays, there are a number of advantages: Fo and Rame are 'alive . . . and strong, active personalities with definite ideas about how their work should be presented to a public'. They also write in an extremely wide range of theatrical genres and language registers from tragedy to farce and archaic to modern. They are authors who perform their own material, giving every line of text 'a whole language of gesture, of facial and bodily movement which is utterly inseparable from the word on the page'.[17] This is reaffirmed by Fo's main US translator, Ron Jenkins, who has also worked as a simultaneous translator for Fo and Rame, and has noted that

> Their work cannot be translated without reference to their performance technique, and translations of their work should not be performed without taking their performance style into account. It is delicately balanced between detachment and passion, tragedy and comedy, intimacy and showmanship. These elements lose their equilibrium if the language, style and rhythms of a production do not take Fo's theatrical politics and poetics into account.[18]

Jenkins has also made an analogy between the intricacies of translating Fo's onstage performance, where the audience's responses have to be built into the timing, and Fo's portrayal of Johan Padan's difficulties in climbing into a hammock, which is 'a question of balance, of equilibrium, and dynamics'.[19] Both Emery and Jenkins acknowledge that no translation can do Fo's plays justice. As Emery puts it, 'what a poor thing is the written text of *Mistero buffo* when abstracted from the corporeal genius of Fo as he performs the piece.'[20] Nonetheless it is often in adaptation, production and performance that the translation process breaks down. Translators may be able to reproduce Fo's and Rame's performances of a play in their heads, and embody them in the texts of their translations, but the director and performer face a much more difficult task.

Adapting Fo (1) – *(We) Can't Pay? (We) Won't Pay!*

We Can't Pay? We Won't Pay! translated by Lino Pertile, adapted by Bill Colvill and Robert Walker, and directed by the latter, opened at the Half Moon Theatre in London in May 1978. It subsequently transferred to the Criterion Theatre in the West End of London in July 1981 in a revised version. This pruned the title down to *Can't Pay? Won't Pay!* and cut a number of the play's more overt political references, presumably to make the play more palatable to West End audiences. The Half Moon was a small, 100-seat theatre in the East End of London, which had gained a reputation for being one of the few alternative Fringe theatres in London to put on politically 'relevant' plays. Many of these were directly concerned with the problems of the local working-class community, and performed to audiences who included as many local, non-theatregoers as regular theatre frequenters. One of the theatre workers who was involved at the outset with the development of the Half Moon in the mid-1970s was the playwright Steve Gooch. Three of Gooch's plays were produced there: *Female Transport*, about women prisoners being deported to Australia, *Will Wat?*, about Wat Tyler and the 'first English revolution', and *The Motor Show* (written with Paul Thompson), about industrial strife at the

Ford car factory in Dagenham. These were all subjects which could be said to parallel the political, documentary and historical concerns of Fo's work. In an interview in 1983, Gooch recalled that

> The early days at the Half Moon represented to me a way to work as a playwright which was not totally circum- scribed by the conventional relationship of the playwright to the theatre; what I was interested in was a way of com- municating more directly to an audience which had a more intimate relationship to the theatre I was working with. The early days at the Half Moon were very like that in the sense that it was people who were living in that area and working in the area, who got the place started. . . . I believe that in working-class life there is a culture and there are values which are not adequately celebrated in estab- lished theatre. I was looking for that kind of context in which to write, looking for the places where people were actually getting to grips with the problems of trying to reach a working-class audience in the theatre.[21]

The similarities between Gooch's concerns and those of the Palazzina Liberty do not need to be underlined. But there were vast differences between the 'intimate' social structure which the Half Moon enjoyed, a factor which also affected its house style, and the audiences of often more than 3,000 people whom Fo performed to, necessitating a far more out-flung, public style of theatre which had to rely on communicating to a crowd. The difference in theatrical mode is akin to that between an orderly meeting and a mass rally, but a number of Fo's plays were housed at the Half Moon, including *Accidental Death of an Anarchist*, *Mistero buffo* and *Elizabeth*.

It was apt that it was Robert Walker who 'discovered' and pioneered Fo's work in the UK. Walker, who directed a number of experimental plays on the London Fringe before moving into television in the 1980s, had in the early 1970s introduced the radically new theatre of the Austrian playwright Peter Handke to English audiences. He also did a number of productions of Brecht at the Half Moon, and directed the world premiere in English of *Mayakovsky*. This was a highly political play about the Russian poet who had influenced Fo by the East German playwright Stefan Schütz. Together with the young working-class playwright Bill Colvill, Walker transformed *We Can't Pay? We Won't Pay!* into a colloquial and slangy London idiom which fixed it firmly in an appropriate English context. Nonetheless they maintained the Italian setting, names and references essential to the play's plot and situation. One example of the anglicisation of their version occurs in one of the few speeches they interpolate into the play. The Maoist police sergeant (whose character is indexed more obviously by having him quote from Mao's *Little Red Book*) encourages Luigi and Giovanni to take the contraband goods they are helping him to load up:

> Do you want to know what'll happen from here? I shall write a full report, a model of brevity and procedure, the result of which charges will be laid. A brief item on *News at Ten* will allude to a brilliant police operation where contraband has been seized and men are sought. Duly alerted by the said item the industrialists will take a quick fortuitous trip over the border. Having laid my evidence before the judge, he will, with a pained expression, because it's a bit like welching on your own kind, sentence them to four months. The industrialists will hear about this whilst sunning themselves on the beaches of St Tropez and will immediately appeal to the President who will commute the sentence to a stiff fine.[22]

This crisply cynical parody of glib 'official' police language is directly in the vein of a number of contemporary British playwrights who write political satire. It is also appropriate to Fo's own mode of debunking judicial procedures in plays like *Accidental Death of an Anarchist*. It illustrates Walker's and Colvill's often terse, economical but witty transposition of the original. But it has to be said that *We Can't Pay? We Won't Pay!* and Walker's and Colvill's subsequent revised version of the play, *Can't Pay? Won't Pay!* ultimately bear little resemblance to Fo's original play. Both adaptations make extensive cuts to the second act, omitting Fo's 'revolutionary' ending in which the wives of the sacked workers along with the local women of the area fight a pitched battle with the police and drive them out of the neighbourhood. They also cut the final song which the characters sing to the audience about 'a better world . . . with less neon lights and less motorways, maybe, but with less corruption and less crime too.'[23] Some reviewers of Fo's original production commented on the sentimentality of this song, but the West End production of *Can't Pay? Won't Pay!* substituted it with the rather clichéd Italian women workers' song 'Sebben che siamo donne' (Although we are women).

David Hirst is ballistic about the defects of the Colvill–Walker adaptation, misspelling both their names in his eagerness to discredit their version, and claiming 'the original is virtually unrecognisable' in their version.[24] To Hirst, the language of their adaptation is 'a sign not so much of a working-class idiom as of bourgeois theatrical language posing as – and patronising – working-class speech.' He also argues that the women characters are weakened as 'the adaptors simply cannot make up their mind whether Antonia is a dizzy cow or an astute and knowing freedom-fighter.'[25] He concludes:

> The Walker version invents instead [for the ending] a series of personal reconciliations between the four principal characters and rewrites the dénouement around this sentimental situation. It represents the essence of bourgeois theatre. One begins to see why the play, in this version, has enjoyed such commercial success. That it represents, however, a complete betrayal of Fo – to say nothing of Marx or Gramsci – and has nothing whatever to do with serious political theatre may be judged against the 'need to operate collectively' – Fo's approach.[26]

While it is hard to disagree with many of these points, it is remarkable how resilient Fo's plays can be to this kind of shredding and adaptation. I have to admit that when I saw *Can't Pay? Won't Pay!* at the Criterion in 1981 I still found it very funny as well as biting in its satire. But one particularly curious distortion in both Colvill–Walker versions is Antonia's offer to sell some of the goods she has taken to the supermarket to Margherita, whereas she offers to give them to her in the original. Italian generosity seems to have become British parsimony, and it is a detail which cuts strongly against the *autoriduzione* themes of the play. Another regrettable cut is a long and hilarious dialogue between the two men about the effects of advertising on their ideas of women and sex, which they try to apply to their wives. An unnecessary addition is the short scene at the end of Act One which complicates the swift exit line in the original by having the two husbands haggle over their paternity rights to a pregnancy transplant. But the play's basic farcical situation of the 'pregnancies' is ultimately what drives it and makes it a successful farce, and this is essentially retained. Fo's political preaching, on the other hand, can simply hold up the action and browbeat the audience. Having done my own translation of the play for two Australian productions – and had differences of opinion with a director who tried to reduce my version to a potpourri of the Colvill–Walker version, with a few appropriations from Davis' US version – I can sympathise with Hirst's point of view. It is also unfortunate that the Colvill–Walker version is still the only published version of the play available in the UK, and that the original Italian version of the play has long been out of print and not been included in the Einaudi collected works. (At the time of writing, Ed Emery is working on a faithful translation of the play, which will become available from Fo's English agent, Rod Hall.) It was a particularly satisfying experience to see most of Fo's original text retained in Australian English in a production of my translation of the play in Canberra in 1985. The reviewer of the *Canberra Times*, however, claimed that 'Aussie allusions lacked the rich supply of EEC surpluses and 50 per cent inflation in European versions of the play I have seen.'[27] The Colvill–Walker version had thus supplanted Fo's original play in this reviewer's understanding of what another critic referred to as a 'classic'.

Despite the relevance of the play's themes – fighting price increases – to English audiences, the original Half Moon production of *We Can't Pay? We Won't Pay!* passed relatively unnoticed in London. No national newspaper sent a first-string critic along to review it. Even *The Guardian*, normally sympathetic to left-wing theatre, dispensed with play and production in three paragraphs. This review, although reasonably favourable, also managed to omit Fo's surname. Although *Can't Pay? Won't Pay!* had already proved to be Fo's most popular and successful play throughout Europe (before it was overtaken by *Anarchist*), this first venture to secure the author long-overdue recognition in the UK was insufficient. But by the time it had transferred to the West End with a new cast three years later, Fo had become a London success. Encouraged by the commercial success of their production of *Accidental Death of an Anarchist* in London in 1980, the West End producer Ian Albery and his production company, Omega, invited Robert Walker to re-mount his Half Moon production of *We Can't Pay? We Won't Pay!* at the Criterion Theatre, where it ran for almost two years.

This re-mounting (retitled *Can't Pay? Won't Pay!*) was hampered by a pastel pink and blue set, which was apparently based on the idea of Neapolitan ice cream, and in no way corresponded to any notion of a working-class apartment in Milan. It also went through a number of cast changes, and added comic business which took it further away from Fo's original play. But in its early stages, with Alfred Molina playing Giovanni as a Fiat worker (and appearing to incorporate some of Fo's 1980 updating of the play), and the comic actress Maggie Steed playing Margherita, it managed to put across a distinctly Italian spirit. It also avoided resorting to the demeaning Italian stereotyping of the West End production of *Accidental Death*. But it pruned a lot of the play's political jokes along with the title, and added a few innocuous, gratuitous gags like a 'Where did you get that hat?' routine, a police sergeant swinging on a drainpipe, and a cuckoo clock collapsing. The universal nature of the play's theme, together with its smooth proficiency as an almost well-made farce, made it easier for West End audiences to enjoy the comedy without pondering unduly on its radical political message of appropriation. It exemplified a problem inherent in assimilating Fo's plays into the commercial, establishment structure of the West End, and expressed by Lloyd Trott:

the danger is that once West End theatre managements have sucked the sugar off Fo's plays they will quickly spit out the pill. As long as our alternative companies make their main aim transfers to the West End, we are unlikely to see the commitment to mounting Fo for his own sake, in a way that it can reach large audiences.[28]

John Barber's review of *Can't Pay? Won't Pay!* in the *Daily Telegraph*, which described Fo's 'ever-bubbling onrush of comic ideas and a natural liking for anyone in a desperate fix. He makes you glad to be alive,'[29] was used in the play's West End publicity pamphlets. It aptly summed up the process the play had gone through from a carnivalesque, politically barbed farce about hunger and poverty to a frothy and slightly risqué romp for the Brian Rix and Ray Cooney set. The September 1983 issue of the Italian theatre magazine *Sipario* profiled Fo's and Rame's success in London in the early 1980s, and stated that 'after Shakespeare, Dario Fo competes with Andrew Lloyd Webber as the most frequently performed playwright in England.'[30] (Although Andrew Lloyd Webber can hardly be described as a playwright, *Sipario*'s irony at Fo's mainstream London success was clear at a time when his fortunes in Italy were perhaps at their lowest ebb.) In an interview in the same article, Franca Rame commented on the West End production of *Can't Pay? Won't Pay!*:

> The motivations for putting on these plays are different from ours. When we did *Non si paga! Non si paga!* we started from a real situation, just as the work we did on women was very precise, both theatrically and ideologi-cally. Here *Non si paga!* is taken just as a play, without any real starting point.[31]

But although it lacked the original impetus and political context of *Non si paga! Non si paga!*, *Can't Pay? Won't Pay!* managed to create political resonances in the UK and Ireland. There were more than a dozen productions of the play in provincial theatres in England and Wales between 1980 and 1985, and two in Dublin. Its English title began to appear around London as graffiti, and during the Thatcher government poll tax protests and riots of the early 1990s it became a widely used slogan. The play seemed ripe for revival during the poll tax riots, but the production by Alexander Bridge which opened in London in March 1990 at the Lyric, Hammersmith, on a bright orange set, contained only a single reference to the poll tax right at the end. This production was universally lambasted by reviewers, with Michael Wright in *Time Out* describing it as a 'flaccid revival' of 'numbing mediocrity', and suggesting that 'David Roper's corpsing performance of Giovanni ought to attract an Equity inquiry.'[32] Jeremy Kingston in *The Times* found it 'antiquated, lightweight and . . . horribly acted,'[33] while Martin Hoyle in the *Financial Times* thought it 'entirely misconceived'.[34] Paul Arnott, reviewing it in *Time Out* for a second time, deplored its 'accents that are very much spaghetti à la Basingstoke, and histrionics suggestive of AC Milan meets 'Allo 'Allo.'[35] It seemed that the director of this revival had made the mistake not only of treating the Colvill–Walker *Can't Pay? Won't Pay!* 'just as a play', but of trying to turn it into xenophobic boulevard British farce.

Concurrent with the Lyric travesty of *Can't Pay? Won't Pay!* another play dealing directly with the poll tax, Patrick Prior's *Revolting Peasants*, was running at the Theatre Royal in Stratford East. This former Joan Littlewood-directed theatre also has, of course, a strong working-class-oriented history. Judging from the reviews, *Revolting Peasants* was strongly influenced by *Can't Pay? Won't Pay!* in its farcical confrontations between Newham poll tax rioters and riot police. Benedict Nightingale commented in *The Times* that 'Prior is still a scattershot farceur, yet to acquire Fo's blend of wild inventiveness and scrupulous logic.'[36] But *Revolting Peasants* was proof of the durability and influence of Fo's play, and its potential to be 'replanted' in a British context.

Adapting Fo (2) – *Accidental Death of an Anarchist*

The Half Moon Theatre was also the venue of the second of Fo's plays to be seen in London – the Belt and Braces version of

Accidental Death of an Anarchist. This was adapted and directed by Gavin Richards from an English translation by Gillian Hanna. It opened at the Half Moon in October 1979, although the first performance of the play had been at Dartington College in January 1979, and it had toured Liverpool and other cities in the north of England before coming to London. Belt and Braces described itself as 'a touring theatre company, founded in 1973. Its primary aim is to entertain, but with material and forms which are articulate, progressive and created from the viewpoint of working and oppressed people.'[37] These aims seemed consistent with those of La Comune, but as with the difference in scale between the Half Moon and the Palazzina Liberty, however, there was a similar difference in management and support. This was illustrated by the company, threatened with cuts in their Arts Council subsidy, asking audiences at the end of their performances of *Accidental Death* to donate money to help them survive. La Comune only received any state subsidy at all from the Italian government after the mid-1980s, and then only the minimum allowance. Prior to that they had been able to raise millions of lire from their audiences for extra-theatrical causes such as occupied factories, laid-off workers and political detainees, as well as supporting their own company. This indicated the relative health of self-managing political theatre in the two countries. Belt and Braces' appeal for money was commented on acidly by Sheridan Morley, the theatre critic of *Punch*:

> True, the threatened Arts Council cutbacks ... are appalling; but it ill behoves a company having achieved such an anarchically good box-office hit to turn around and demand public money for it. Belt and Braces does after all indicate some form of self-support.[38]

In the event, the company went on to achieve enormous commercial success with the play, which transferred to the West End, and became a 'hit' for almost two years.

The Belt and Braces adaptation of *Accidental Death of an Anarchist* had the potential to be a reasonably accurate transposition of Fo's play to an English music hall, popular theatrical vein, and of maintaining its incisive and excoriating political perspective. Richards had formerly been a member of John McGrath's 7:84, for whom he had directed one of Arden's most politically overt plays, *The Ballygombeen Bequest*, about land expropriation in Northern Ireland. This production had had to be taken off after an estate agent took legal action against it. Gillian Hanna, a member of the feminist theatre group Monstrous Regiment, had previously translated and adapted Dacia Maraini's *Dialogue between a Prostitute and a Client*. Alfred Molina, a London-born actor of Italian extraction, played the part of the Maniac. Richards' adaptation and the style of his direction of the piece, however, distorted the original text, cutting it extensively and adding speeches and stage business which often went completely against the grain of Fo's play. Richards' production used a highly non-naturalistic, agit-prop form of staging, in keeping with Fo's generally minimal use of sets and props, and frequently broke the 'fourth wall'. But it also simplified the play's police characters into buffoonish caricatures who were manipulated like dummies by the Maniac. Since this version became the most successful English production of any of Fo's plays (and was broadcast in a version for television by Channel Four in September 1983), its faults need to be enumerated. But as popular, music hall-derived comedy in a particularly English vein, it had considerable comic merit and entertainment value. Richards indicated his approach to the play as a presentational, open-form mode of popular theatre:

> The most important point about the play is that it is what popular theatre is about, not only in Italy but also in this country. What we haven't really succeeded in doing is adapting a popular form successfully for a larger audience without writing something which either condescends to sexism or racism, or which falls back on the easy jokes, the extremely vicious anti-people edges of humour. Fo is an important lesson for us [in left-wing political theatre] because, effortlessly, he destroys the invisible fourth wall and creates live theatre again.[39]

But by incorporating English forms of popular theatre like pantomime and music hall, Richards' approach to the play, where direct address, asides, and exaggeratedly slapstick stage business are at a premium, results in putting Fo's play across almost in inverted commas. And despite his disclaimer, Richards' adaptation is riddled with 'easy jokes' which often reduce the characters to caricatures. Walker's production of *Can't Pay? Won't Pay!* – with which Richards' *Anarchist* shares a tendency to use too many four-letter words – could perhaps be faulted for attempting to be too naturalistic. But Richards' version of *Accidental Death* goes to the opposite extreme, reducing the police characters to almost racist Italian stooges, and even breaking into snatches of doggerel Italian. (It comes as no surprise that as an actor, Richards later graduated on to the xenophobic television sit-com *'Allo 'Allo*.) He even calls one of the police characters 'Inspector Pissani' (Pisani in the original, although Fo does not give names to any of his dramatis personae), an unfortunate creation who at one point is made to resort to rosary beads. Fo's essential point about the police characters in the play is missed: despite being bumbling, incompetent buffoons, they are always capable of maintaining an aggressive, threatening front. They are also dangerous both for their right-wing political convictions and in their capacity to perpetrate not infrequent 'accidents' in which innocent people lose their lives. But Richards, trying to update and broaden the political perspective of Fo's piece, has the Maniac state glibly, 'These four were there torturing students at the CBS HQ in Paris in May 1968, in the USA at Attica, at Kent State. . . . All this in the name of "justice" and "democracy".'[40] Even in his most discursive, long-winded speeches, Fo never descends to this type of vague, po-faced, melodramatic leftist rhetoric, and his political allusions are usually argued through rather than blandly stated. Fo did not expend undue sympathy on the police characters, but they were at least three-dimensional comic figures. As Franca Rame commented on the West End production of the play:

I think the image of Italy as seen from abroad is often ridiculous – in the London production of *Anarchist* the characters looked like nineteenth-century Mafioso types, with long sideburns. It was a very glossy production, with stock characters who were like dummies – they reduced the play to a simple farce.[41]

Fo's play concentrates on the stubborn, insidious illogicality of the police, and reduces onstage police violence to harmless fisticuffs among themselves. Richards, on the other hand, adds a scene in which the Superintendent enters with a blackjack after beating up a suspect, in a simplistic attempt to make the police compendium political villains. Such crass simplifications of the police characters' behaviour also contradicted the complicated political background detail of the play, which Fo could rely on his audience's knowledge of. In an attempt to remedy this problem, Belt and Braces produced an admirably researched, lengthy programme in the form of a newspaper. This explained the background to the play's situation and related it to events in Northern Ireland and the recent death of the teacher Blair Peach at the hands of London police in an anti-fascist demonstration. But its painstaking explanation of the play's political relevance both in Italy and in the UK relegated Fo's arguments to an extra-theatrical context. Richards' version also mangled some of Fo's most effectively political comic business, especially in its extension of a dropped-glass-eye sequence to ludicrous extremes. He also cut the Maniac's bishop disguise altogether, as well as the police agents who appear in the audience at the Superintendent's command (despite Belt and Braces' assertion that they feared police interruption of the performance at Wyndham's Theatre). And he pruned the hilarious sequence in which the Maniac puts forward the 'three shoes' theory to explain the Constable's claim that he caught one's of the anarchist's shoes as he fell out the window.

In their detailed comparison of four different English versions of this sequence with Fo's original text, Fitzpatrick and Sawczak work from a premise taken from Hirst that actors tend to judge the play by the number of laughs it yields.[42] They note that Richards is at times primarily concerned with doing this. But despite the cuts he makes to the play, they argue that 'while Richards' adaptation has justifiably drawn criticism due to the overwhelming influence of theatrical frames on the choice made by the adaptor . . . at times it succeeds better than the other translations in encapsulating details from the original.'[43] This conclusion, however, is predicated on comparisons with the linguistic structures of the original text which assume that Richards' version is a 'translation' and that he has knowledge of Italian. His version was, however, a rewriting of Gillian Hanna's translation with an eye for theatrical solutions with comic potential and English political references. This error appears to be perpetuated in Jennifer Lorch's critique of the two English versions of *Anarchist*, which also incorrectly claims that the Hanna-Richards version was based exclusively on the 1973 Italian version of the text. (Part of the explanation for the confusion of the two endings of the Richards version is that they mixed up both versions of Fo's text. It is also worth noting that Richards also appropriated phrases from my translation of the play, including my rendition of Il Matto as 'The Maniac', who had been 'The Loony' in Hanna's translation.)[44]

In his introductory comments to the published edition of Belt and Braces' *Accidental Death*, Fo was understandably restrained in his comments about its differences from his original text:

> I am aware . . . that certain moments in the play which were of obvious theatrical and political importance at the time had necessarily to be replaced because of their limited reference – that is to say, because an English audience would be unaware of their background and, above all, because it is impossible to restate them in a theatrical context with sufficient pithiness and immediacy.
>
> So I have the impression – more than an impression – that some passages which have been skipped in Gavin Richards' version may have produced some erosion at a satirical level, that is to say in the relationship of the tragic to the grotesque, which was the foundation of the original work, in favour of solutions which are exclusively comic.[45]

But it is not only the removal of the play's tragic background – and the entire logical mechanism of the play still depends on Pinelli's defenestration – that cause many of Richards' 'comic solutions' to ring false. Some of them work against the comic tension which Fo builds up in terms of his stagecraft. Having the Superintendent grabbing the Inspector after the latter has actually jumped out the window, for example, destroys the delicately wrought farcical intrigue with which the Maniac has driven both characters to the point of almost willingly jumping from the window. It also destroys the comic moment when they are both surprised and embarrassed standing precariously on the window ledge by the Constable. Likewise, passing guitars in to accompany the Maniac and the Police singing the anarchist song at the end of Act One is an excessive and unnecessary 'breaking of the fourth wall'. It also undermines what in Fo's play is a gradually built comic *tour de force*. Having the Maniac carry his costume changes in a plastic bag reduces the element of surprise in having him change his disguises offstage, and destroys the plausibility of his duping of the police.

Other comic expedients in the Belt and Braces version, like revealing the Maniac's identity as that of a 'Paolo Davidovich Gandolpho, Prose Pimpernel of the Permanent Revolution, notorious sports editor of *Lotta Continua,* and the organ of the Jewish conspiracy'[46] reduce the play's situation to bathos. Jokes like the continual reference to the anarchist's body as a 'jam sponge' also detract from the serious basis of the farce. One extended joke at Fo's expense (which was greatly enjoyed by Franca Rame) attempts to justify the liberties Belt and Braces took with the text:

PISSANI: This is unheard of distortion of the author's meaning!

MANIAC: He'll get his royalties. Who's moaning?

PISSANI: Get back to the script!

SUPERINTENDENT: This is an insult to Dario Fo!

FELETTI: Good. I've got a bone to pick with him. Why is there only one woman's part in his blasted play? I feel marooned!

MANIAC: The author's sexist?

FELETTI: He's pre-historic!

BERTOZZO: Then why are we bothering?
MANIAC: He's a pre-historic genius! On with the dance![47]

This exchange indicates the distance from which Richards' version approaches Fo's play, with its equation of accusations of distortion of the original text with the point of view of the police characters. Despite his assault on the Colvill–Walker *Can't Pay? Won't Pay!* and his admission that Richards' adaptation's 'resemblance to Fo's original is ... shadowy,'[48] Hirst is otherwise relatively untroubled by Richards' version. He finds, curiously, that 'the vibrancy of its sexual slang' makes it 'more lively than the Italian original' and detects an 'increased sophistication in the Maniac's language'.[49] His summation of its literary virtues seems to have been infected by some of its more ludicrous excesses:

> The sophistication and complexity of the linguistic idiom employed in the British version of *Anarchist* points to a theatrical heritage which goes back to the Restoration and encompasses representative figures from Wilde and Coward through to Pinter, Orton and Bond. Witty social satire has been a distinctive element of British comedy and has always been a powerful weapon in the fight against hypocrisy and social injustice.[50]

Reviewers of the production tended to take Richards' additions, alterations and distortions as Fo's own words, which led to further confusion and misunderstanding when Richards' text was put on school and university syllabuses in the UK and Australia. Later productions of the play also used Richards' version as a starting point from which to add further 'embellishments', while reproducing its blatant misrepresentation of the play's final scene. Catherine Itzin, reviewing the Belt and Braces production in *Tribune,* described and commented on Richards' ending:

> The cops are handcuffed, and a bomb is ticking away. Does the journalist escape with her story (yes, it's a woman) leaving the corrupt cops to be blown to the fate their immorality deserves, or does she let liberal humanitarian principles

prevail and let them go? The play presents both alternative endings, so perfectly dramatised as to leave the conclusion inescapable that, with the time bomb of fascism ticking away, the fascists will take advantage of liberal dithering and blood will be shed.

In the aftermath of the terrorist murder of Airey Neave, it is profoundly unnerving to have the terrorist argument put so persuasively.[51]

The two different endings which Fo used for the play (as published in the 1973 and 1974 Italian texts) were never presented as alternatives, but correspond to two different versions of the play performed at different times. They also tell a different story, which make it clear that Fo never had any intention of presenting 'the terrorist argument'. In the first ending, the Maniac appears to blow himself up offstage, in an ironic replay of the police version of the anarchist's death, only to reappear as the 'real' examining magistrate, reverting to the play's opening situation. In the later version, he merely uses the bomb as a threat so that he can escape with his tape recording of his interview with the police. In neither version does the Maniac confront the Journalist with making the decision of whether to free the police from their handcuffs or let them be killed in the bomb explosion. Richards' own comments on his ending indicate that Itzin's response was justified: 'Actually we were right – she should have let the policemen blow up. If you're down to a choice and you're down to thirty seconds, you let them blow up.'[52]

Neither of Fo's endings put forward any argument for blowing up the police. The central argument of *Accidental Death of an Anarchist* was that the police should be exposed publicly for their responsibility for the death of Pinelli (although this was later proved not to have been the case). The play also exposed their collusion with the fascist group responsible for the Piazza Fontana bombing, and called for them to be brought to justice. In the light of subsequent, wrongful accusations against Fo of support of terrorism, Richards' additions to the play's ending does him a double injustice.

But despite its distortions, Belt and Braces' production of *Accidental Death of an Anarchist* became an unprecedented success in both left-wing English circles and in the London establishment theatre. Tariq Ali, reviewing the Half Moon production in *Socialist Challenge,* described the play as

> the best that I have seen in this country for the last 15 years (and for two of these I had to see five plays a week as the theatre critic of a bourgeois magazine) . . . Fo, close to the bone in Italy, would saw through it in Callaghan's Britain. Don't just go and see the play. Take all your friends as well.[53]

Ali's advice was clearly heeded by London's Left. The Half Moon was packed out for two separate runs of the play. At the same time Ian Albery, faced with declining audiences and profits in the West End, had been pursuing a policy of importing productions from London Fringe theatres and the Royal Shakespeare Company directly into the West End, rather than trying to mount costly new productions. He invited Belt and Braces to transfer *Accidental Death* directly to Wyndhams Theatre, stating his policy in the following terms: 'If one factory can make shoes so cheaply, I'd be crazy to put up another at twice the cost.'[54] Hedging his bets on this politically explosive commodity, he transferred it in tandem with another Fringe product. This was the Richmond Orange Tree's production of a relatively innocuous American comedy, Israel Horowitz's *The Primary English Class.* The two plays opened under the bland umbrella title *Two Farces.* The decision led Belt and Braces into a political dilemma: whether to risk accusations of a political sell-out into what they described as 'the minefields of commercialism' or, alternatively, to use the commercial channels of consumerist entertainment to attack the political values they are founded on, and reach for a mass audience. The second option was clearly more attractive, and the company boasted they were 'the left Fringe company that has kept its integrity best over the last five years and gone into the West End.'[55]

Consequently, Richards took over the part of the Maniac from Alfred Molina, who was booked to appear in another production at another West End theatre. Molina had received the *Plays and Players* Most Promising Actor Award for the part in 1980, and Richards was later nominated for a Society of West End Theatres award for the role. Albery's 'cheap shoes' policy paid off for *Accidental Death*, but not for *The Primary English Class*, which was taken off, leaving Richards and Belt and Braces to continue their production for almost two years. Concessions on ticket prices were made to the unemployed, and according to Richards, in the early months of the run, up to a third of the audience may have consisted of people who could otherwise never have afforded to go to a West End theatre. The strange political ambience of the production was commented on rather snobbishly by a theatre critic of *The Observer*:

the ultimate in absurdist West End first nights: a mob of be-parka'd, dungaree'd supporters and usherettes touting the *Socialist Worker* and *Socialist Challenge* along with the programmes and ice creams. With the aid of several excellent players, Gavin Richards, the adaptor, director and lead clown of this essay in Italian agit-prop, turned the auditorium into a fair simulacrum of left-wing pub theatre with all its good humour and camaraderie, but also with its complacent conviction of being right in being Left.[56]

In many respects the production may have paralleled Fo's own achievement in bringing his political satire to popular audiences in Italy and throughout Europe, and creating a sense of community with his spectators. This made it all the more unfortunate that so much of *Accidental Death* was misrepresented in the London production. Fo himself, after he saw it, not understanding English, confined his criticisms to the fact that it was overplayed and excessively crude and slapstick:

overloaded, verging terribly on the grotesque . . . with the excessive buffoonery they introduced into it. For us this buffoonery is 'anti-style' . . . not 'style' in some vague sense, but 'style' in the sense of a satirical form of theatre that seeks to wound, to disturb people, to hit them where it hurts.[57]

For a time, because of the liberties it took with the play's content, he sought to stop any further productions of Richards' version. According to Ed Emery, 'For a good while, Fo was so angry at what he saw as distortion of his text that he was prepared to block production of the play until certain changes were made.'[58] But Richards' adaptation was being requested in a number of British provincial theatres, as well as in Australasia and South Africa (where he rather curiously refused permission for it to be used). The Broadway producer Alexander Cohen also bought an option on it, due to the West End success, and Fo eventually relented. He justified his decision by arguing: 'if nothing else it enabled people to see a style, theatrical language and technique, a conception of theatre, which otherwise they might never have seen. And not only the *technique*, but also the *content*, the politics of it.'[59] Jennifer Lorch, who edited and introduced the Italian text of the play for Manchester University Press in 1997, argues that Richards' version of *Anarchist* 'became not only assimilated into British culture but was an influence on that culture.' She claims that its success in the West End, however, along with a number of other 'alternative' British plays, led to a loss of Arts Council subsidies, and 'contributed to the economic crisis of alternative theatre in Britain.' She also adds that Richards' version 'is characterised by a lack of faith in Fo's words which are either rammed home by vulgarisms or substituted by visual gags.'[60]

Between 1981 and 1983 there were six productions of *Anarchist* in the English provinces, and one in Edinburgh and five in Ireland. In March 1983, by which time there had been 24 productions of the play around the world, it opened at the Théâtre La Bruyère in Paris, in a production by Jacques Echantillon, translated by Valeria Tasca. Echantillon, whose production of *Non si paga!* had toured Europe for two years, did the play in a *commedia dell'arte* style, setting it in a French context, with Jean-Jacques Moreau in the lead role. When Fo saw it, he was by all accounts well pleased. In November 1988 Richards' version of the play was revived at the Bloomsbury Theatre in London. This was a low-key production by Andy Arnold featuring alternative cabaret comedian John Sparkes as the Maniac, sporting an Einstein hairstyle and using a wide range of British regional dialects. Judging from the few reviews this production gathered, it milked the play for laughs at the expense of the political satire.

The adaptation of *Anarchist* which Alan Cumming and Tim Supple made for their National Theatre production of the play in 1990 and 1991 (directed by Supple, with Cumming as the Madman, as they called him) went back to Fo's original 1970 text. It restored the correct ending and 'resolved to retain the open, uncharacterised language and to preserve the alien, rambling form.'[61] This guaranteed a certain accuracy, although they set the play in England and took a number of liberties with the text, such as having the Madman in his disguise as Marcantonio Piccini imitate Prince Charles' accent. Fo attended rehearsals and made a number of suggestions, including substituting the 'Internationale' for the anarchist song at the end of Act One, which had also been done in the Broadway production. The result was, by most critical accounts, a rather lacklustre version of the play. It played in 33 regional British theatres as a National Theatre Education Department touring production, opening at the National's Cottesloe Theatre in January 1991. It also subsequently won Supple, a TV comedian known for his role in the Victor and Barry cocktail comedy duo, a 'Best Comedy Actor' award.

Cumming and Supple took care to avoid caricaturing the characters, and to retain the subtlety of Fo's satire as well as its anger and indignation. They updated the play's political context to include references to the Guildford Four and the Birmingham Six. They also hung a picture of British Police Chief Sir James Anderton in Inspector Pisani's office, and took up Fo's suggestion to replace the anarchist song at the end of Act One with the 'Internationale'. But otherwise they made relatively few alterations to Fo's text. Most of their changes were in the spirit of Fo's notion of 'continuous substitution',[62] adapting political and cultural references to fit the context of the production.

Nonetheless the London *Evening Standard* reviewer Melanie McDonagh, in the most enthusiastic notice the production received in London, stated that 'Monstrous liberties have been taken with the original text to make the production an indictment of present abuses of authority.'[63] (Her knowledge of the 'original text' is questionable, as, like that of most of the other reviewers, it is probably based on Richards' version.) According to Benedict Nightingale in *The Times*, Fo found the Cumming and Supple version of the play 'too solemn and didactic'. Wardle, reviewing *The Pope and the Witch* 16 months later, contrasted Cumming and Supple's lack of 'satiric bite and bile'[64] with Richards' version, a judgment which differed from those of a number of other reviewers. Nightingale found it 'not as relentlessly burlesque as Richards's . . . [and] not as funny . . . marooned in some no-man's-land between knockabout and realism.'[65] Michael Billington in *The Guardian* found the police characters were 'corrupt boobies rather than Mafioso monsters'. He also thought the production was 'far less funny but politically more potent' than Richards', and 'shrewdly updated but without [Fo's] carnivalesque danger.'[66] John Peter in the *Sunday Times* described it as 'simply a batty farce' and 'essentially a harmless, jolly English production.'[67] This view was echoed by Hilary Hutcheon in *Tribune*, who found its 'British filter' was not 'Italian enough'.[68] All the reviews, then, found something wanting, and Nightingale suggested the production's lack of impact might be largely due to the historical and cultural gap between Italy in 1969 and Britain in 1991.[69] (The production attempted to bridge this gap by playing the Sex Pistols' 'Anarchy in the UK'.) This is also in spite of Fo's own suggestion that the play might be more applicable to a contemporary British context than an Italian context.[70] But given Fo's involvement in 1998 in writing a play about the Sofri case, a sequel to *Anarchist* related to the murder of Police Superintendent Calabresi, the repercussions of the events behind the play continued to drag on in 1990s Italy. Lorch concludes:

> it is not possible to produce a version of this play which aims both to be faithful to the author's intentions of the period and to make of it a viable play for the English stage, whether fringe or mainstream. The gulf between the two political cultures is too great.[71]

In 1992 Ed Emery's accurate, literal translation of *Anarchist* was published in Methuen's first edition of selected plays by Fo, *Dario Fo Plays: One*. This finally gave adaptors and directors a chance to see a faithful English version of Fo's original text, and Emery's text was subsequently used in a production of the play at the Contact Theatre in Manchester.

But undeterred by this, in April 1994 the prominent Australian actor-director Robyn Archer did a production of her own Australianised version of the Cumming and Supple version for the State Theatre Company of South Australia in Adelaide and Sydney. She cast a couple of television comedians – one of whom, Vince Sorrenti, was at least Italian-Australian – as the Madman and Pisani in an attempt to popularise the production, and a black woman journalist and television presenter with little acting experience as the Journalist. In synchrony with the set, which presented a distorted, tilted perspective of the police interrogation room, Archer dressed the police characters in green-and-black bicycle shorts and outsized jackets, reducing them to crude, crass Australian caricatures in the process. While her version was full of Australian references to police corruption, she literally put the Madman on a soapbox at the end of the play to deliver a speech about political corruption and Aboriginal deaths in custody. Reviewing Archer's production in the Sydney *Sun-Herald*, Pamela Payne noted its 'gallery of crudely executed caricatures' and its 'glib, superficial' acting style, concluding it was 'a sorry production – structurally scrappy, its rhythms askew, and rarely achieving the pace, the punch or the sharp-edged comedy that is intrinsic to Fo.'[72] Archer's production built on what has appeared to be an entrenched Australian tradition of taking British translations of Fo and reducing them to gross, broad buffoonery.

But as with *Can't Pay? Won't pay!*, *Anarchist* has survived its travesties to become a modern political 'classic' and has had considerable impact on world theatre. One example of this, as Mary Karen Dahl has pointed out in a book called *Terrorism and Modern Drama*, occurs in a play by South African playwright Ronald Harwood, *The Deliberate Death of a Polish Priest*. This play, which deals with the abduction and murder of Father Jerzy

Popieluszko in October 1984 by the Polish Interior Ministry, was performed in London in October 1985. Like *Anarchist*, it was based on trial transcripts featuring the police officers responsible, dealt with state intimidation of dissidents, and was structured as '[an] investigation of [an] investigation'. Dahl notes the similarities in the two plays' titles, and a more general intertextuality which 'suggests a purposeful restructuring by Harwood of Fo's political–theatrical concept. Such a dialogue transcends the boundaries of a single theatrical event.'[73] The specific context of Fo's counter-information about a particular event in Italy in the early 1970s proved to have global applications.

Adapting Fo (3) – *Female Parts*

After the success of *Accidental Death of an Anarchist*, the National Theatre, in line with its policy of putting on occasional plays by European writers, decided that Fo's work was a marketable proposition. They opted for an English version of *Tutta casa, letto e chiesa* which opened in June 1981. This was accurately translated by Margaret Kunzle, a regular collaborator with Fo and Rame and an interpreter for them in Milan at the time. It was adapted by Olwen Wymark, a prolifically experimental Fringe and radio playwright whose work had begun to espouse feminist themes. Perhaps uncertain of the monologues' viability in one of their large auditoriums, the National chose their smallest, most 'intimate' theatre, the Cottesloe, to mount the pieces. There being no colloquial equivalent in English such as the German 'Kinder, Küche und Kirche', the play's Italian title was changed to *Female Parts*. But the National, fearing this title's sexual implications might offend their patrons, subsequently changed it to *One Woman Plays*. This led to the usual confusion by reviewers between the adaptation's additions and alterations and the authors' text, as in *The Times* critic Irving Wardle's review:

> The authors have found the right title for these four pieces, but they could not be called 'one character plays'

. . . It is some small comfort that Fo and Rame are writing about Italy which gave the word *machismo* to a grateful world . . .[74]

Such cultural misunderstandings (*machismo,* of course, is a Spanish word) indicate the readiness of critics and audiences to regard Fo's plays as taking place in a remote country. This provides an argument for a total anglicisation of the plays, as Franca Rame has suggested. In the case of *Medea*, the final piece in *Female Parts*, the authors were completely misrepresented. Transferring the Magna Grecia dialect of the original into a bland and stilted modern English, and omitting Fo's and Rame's essential introduction to the piece, laid it open to interpretations such as Wardle made, of its being 'a feminist justification for child slaughter'. One of the principal problems of the adaptation of *Female Parts* was its failure to find a suitable English idiom for each of the four characters. This was particularly evident in the protagonist of *Waking Up*, who speaks a tame, middle-class approximation of a working-class idiom:

> Your dirty socks . . . who washes them eh? How many times have you washed my socks? We should talk to each other, Luigi! We never talk. I mean it's okay with me that your problems are my problems but why can't my problems be your problems too instead of yours being ours and mine being only mine. I want us to live together . . . not just in the same place. We should talk to each other ![75]

This speech, appearing in the context of a blazing domestic row which is being recalled, seems woefully convoluted and weak. Likewise, the protagonist of *A Woman Alone* is repeatedly tripped up by a lack of grit in her language. This means that added impetus was thrown on the actress playing the parts, and the South African-born Yvonne Bryceland coped admirably, making up in tone and emphasis for what she lacked in lines. Michael Bogdanov's production used a detailed, naturalist setting for *Waking Up* and *A Woman Alone*, whereas in Rame's performances the first piece was frequently done without any set or props, and the second with only the minimum props necessary on a virtually bare stage. This in itself indicates how the National Theatre processed the plays into a predominantly sterile, mechanical house style. The coyness of their approach was aptly illustrated by *The Same Old Story*, which resorted to Americanisms to reproduce the obscenities uttered by the little girl's doll. As a result, the improvisatory, farcical aspects of the pieces tended to become more sober, which helps to explain Franca Rame's reservations about the production:

> The English actress was very good and the direction was very accurate. However, it got a lot fewer laughs than it did in Italy, and less applause. This I think is because it was a different type of theatre from ours – it was a more natural-istic type of acting and direction. We always try to eliminate the superstructure, the excess, because the most important thing is the content. This is a theatrical choice which is epic rather than naturalistic.[76]

This 'non-epic' aspect of the National production, together with its more forbidding social ambience, tended to reduce the political impact of the pieces. But *Female Parts* remained in the National Theatre's repertoire for two years, in no small way assisted by Yvonne Bryceland's incisive performance, which she later toured successfully in South Africa. Olwen Wymark's adaptation was also subsequently performed throughout the UK and Australasia. London audiences were able to assess Franca Rame's own performance of the pieces when she performed them herself in Italian with English subtitles at the Riverside Studios in May 1982. But the most predominant aspect of her performance to strike London reviewers was her apparent glamour. Sharon Wood noted

> the shock to feminist sensibilities in Britain and America of seeing Rame appear on stage in scanty negligées; while Italian feminists have never been as suspicious of fashion as their counterparts elsewhere, Rame makes a forceful cri-tique of a culture which would have women instantly available to the male gaze.[77]

In March 1983 an English version of four of the lesser-performed monologues from the first published edition of *Tutta casa, letto e chiesa* were performed at the Drill Hall in London by the feminist group Monstrous Regiment, in a translation by Gillian Hanna. This production, entitled *The Fourth Wall*, was directed by Penny Cherns, designed by Hildegaard Bechtler, and performed by Paola Dionisotti in tandem with Maggie Nicols. It opened with *Ulrike Meinhof*, and included *Tomorrow's News*, one of the Fo's and Rame's most abrasive political monologues. It was based on Red Army Faction member Gudrun Ensslin, the sole survivor of the Stammheim prison 'suicides', for whom Fo and Rame had campaigned in the late 1970s. The Monstrous Regiment production also included two other pieces which were discarded by Franca Rame soon after she first began touring *Tutta casa, letto e chiesa*. The English group's rendition of these was described unsympathetically by Rosalind Carne in *The Guardian*:

> *Alice in Wonderless Land* is a heavy-handed attempt to over-reach the original by turning the White Rabbit into a sex-exploitation movie mogul. *The Whore in the Madhouse* presents a questionable analysis of the ethics of prostitution, making the offensive assumption that the prostitutes have lost their self-respect.[78]

But the retrieval of these pieces for an English production was clearly worthwhile, and the monologues were adapted into duologues with cabaret elements and musical accompaniment. Despite attracting little attention from press and public and having only a short run, the Fringe context of the production and the care and dedication exerted on it made it one of the few English productions of Fo's and Rame's work which did some justice to its originals both politically and theatrically. But it also illustrated the different context in which it was received. As Fo commented in 1983:

> I've been told that [the London] productions have unearthed a sort of current which has affected writers as well as performers. They've been forced to use quite different

techniques from what they normally use. The same thing happened in France. It took years to find a company who could perform our plays, and there were terrible gaps. The point isn't that we aren't performed well, but that the plays are experienced in a different way.[79]

In 1991 Methuen published *A Woman Alone and Other Plays*, an edition of 20 of the 25 Fo–Rame monologues for women which had been published by Einaudi in 1989, in lively and accurate translations by Gillian Hanna and Ed Emery. Many of the pieces had dated, and the important Prologue to the Italian text, which provides a context and perspective for the plays, as well as being an hilarious performance vehicle in its own right, was omitted. (The important Prologue to *Medea* was also omitted.) But in other respects it was a reliably definitive English version of the monologues. Hanna re-casts *The Same Old Story* in an English setting, adding details about abortion in the UK, and manages to retain the scatological force of the original. As a performer as well as a translator, Hanna was aware of 'the vital importance to find the voice of each character,'[80] and reported that a number of English-speaking women performers had incorporated a number of the pieces into their repertoire.

Mistero buffo in London

Fo's performance of *Mistero buffo* in London in May 1983, together with Rame's second edition of *Tutta casa, letto e chiesa*, brought about a belated recognition in the UK of Fo and Rame as perhaps the world's most important contemporary exponents of popular political theatre. They also held theatre workshops with English actors and actresses which were recorded, transcribed and later published. Billed in London as a 'classic', 14 years after Fo had first performed it, *Mistero buffo* won over the English audiences and critics who managed to get seats in the small Riverside Studios to the warmth, humour and grotesque comedy of Fo's performance. Fo's appearance in London was largely due to the efforts of David Gotthard, the artistic director of the Riverside Studios, which had housed Franca Rame's performance of *Tutta casa, letto e chiesa* the previous year. When the Riverside was threatened with closure due to a reduction in its grant from Hammersmith Council, Fo gave them a long-term 'loan' of £7,000 – a rare case of Italy helping Britain out economically. But despite Gotthard's entrepreneurial foresight, he was unceremoniously sacked by the Riverside board (which was backed by the Greater London Council) in 1985. Unsuccessful attempts were also made to lure Fo into a West End theatre after his three-week run at the Riverside.

Whereas French critics in 1974 had immediately found points of comparison between Fo and Chaplin and Jacques Tati, British reviewers invoked a vast array of Anglo-Saxon cultural reference-points in which to encapsulate the spontaneous, chameleon-like ease of Fo's performance range. Steve Grant of *Time Out*, after meeting the Fos in Milan, wrote, 'As a couple they have the status, charisma and attendant problems of a cross between Miller and Monroe, John and Yoko, John Arden and Margaretta D'Arcy, and Richard Briars and Felicity Kendall . . . He's rather like a souped-up Gypsy Dave Frost cum Tommy Cooper with a bit of Ken Campbell rolled in.'[81] Jim Hiley in *The Observer*, after meeting Fo and seeing *Il fabulazzo osceno*, wrote, 'It's as if Terry Wogan had suddenly acquired the technique of Marcel Marceau, the charisma of Richard Pryor, the intellectualism of Jonathan Miller and the politics of Ken Livingstone.'[82] Michael Billington in *The Guardian* invited us to 'Imagine, if you can, Dick Gregory crossed with Billy Dainty and Jacques Tati . . . Like many soloists (such as Ruth Draper), Fo can also evoke a crowd.'[83] To Michael Coveney of the *Financial Times*, *Mistero buffo* 'is like a Ken Dodd special scuppered by a cheerfully left-wing blasphemer . . . Fo himself is a physical blend of Barry Humphries and Jacques Tati.'[84] Brian Glanville, reporting on Fo's workshops in the *Sunday Times*, made the inevitable comparison with John Cleese's silly walks, adding that 'Like Max Wall or Tommy Trinder, he'll make use of a latecomer . . . Like Roy Hudd, he may crack a "difficult" joke, and pretend that one part of the audience has got it, the other hasn't.'[85] John Barber in the *Daily Telegraph* described Fo as possessing 'an impertinent Lombard nose and John

Betjeman's mouth.'[86] Giles Gordon in the *Spectator* saw him as 'a kind, gentle man, as if Alan Ayckbourn took to writing political texts . . . with teeth which, when he grins, which he does a lot, recall Cardew Robinson.'[87]

These excursions into cultural anthropology suggest that Fo is something of a polymath who can represent all things to all people, of all political persuasions. Apart from the first two, they are all based on seeing performances of *Zanni's Grammelot*, *The Raising of Lazarus*, *Boniface VIII*, *The American Technocrat*, *Scapino's Teaching Lesson* and (in the workshops) *The Morality Play of the Blind Man and the Cripple*, and Fo's improvised, topical sketches introducing the pieces. These represent only a small proportion of Fo's solo performance repertoire. But the general conclusion of most British critics was that Fo was a likeable and brilliant performer, and that his tendency to revolutionary politics was a by-product which could be taken with a pinch of salt. A fair proportion of the comparisons made were to music-hall and TV comedians who propagate a rather cosy, reactionary form of popular English humour, including smut. This indicates a rather narrow reduction of the abrasive, grotesque, frequently scatological and mocking nature of Fo's political satire. In suggesting that the English could never produce a clown like Fo because in *Mistero buffo* he relies on a historical background of papacy and religious repression, Michael Stewart in *Tribune* attempted to pigeonhole Fo's satirical targets into a cultural category remote from British concerns. But this overlooks the fact that the visit of Pope John Paul II – a constant source of Fo's topical lampoons – to the UK caused the Falklands war to recede into the background of the British public conscience. He also overlooks Fo's constant barrage of scorn directed at a vast range of Italian political contradictions.

Fo's influence had begun to be felt on political theatre in Britain, and was reflected in the Dario Fo/Franca Rame Theatre Project which was held at the Riverside Studios in London in January 1984. Conceived as a British response to Fo's and Rame's performances at the Riverside the previous spring, this event consisted of a rehearsed reading of Fo's most recent play, *Clacson, trombette e pernacchi* (literally, *Car Horns, Trumpets and Raspberries*). There were also performances of the three monologues *I Don't Move, I Don't Scream, My Voice is Gone*, (the Riverside title) *The Mother* and *Michele Lu Lanzone*, which received their English premieres, along with responding monologues by English women playwrights, including Pam Gems and Michelene Wandor. The 1982 Theatre Company's ensemble English version of *Mistero buffo* was also performed, and there was a discussion forum on the subject 'Is political theatre alive and well in Britain?' This cross-fertilisation between Fo and English feminist and political theatre seemed an admirable way of approaching their work both politically and theatrically, and probably helped to clear up a number of Anglo-Saxon misconceptions about it. These continued to proliferate in press reports about Fo, if Irving Wardle's assumption in *The Times* that Agnelli's kidnapping in *Clacson* is based on an actual event was any indication. Most of the play's comedy for an Italian audience derives from the fact that its central situation is a colossal political joke, for which Fo deliberately chose Agnelli rather than Moro. Wardle did describe Fo's visit to London in retrospect as 'a revelation comparable to London's first sight of the Berliner Ensemble'[88] – high praise indeed, and evidence that Fo's importance was beginning to filter through into Anglo-Saxon theatre.

Some attempt to provide a fuller picture of Fo's work to English audiences was made in Dennis Marks' 50-minute BBC *Arena* television programme, *The Theatre of Dario Fo*, which was transmitted on BBC2 on 28 February 1984. TV and video with subtitles are ideal media for Fo's and Rame's solo work, which relies predominantly on body movement and facial expression, and largely abandons costume, makeup, props and settings. Marks' programme included large chunks of *Boniface VIII*, but little of this performance, filmed in a circus tent during the 1983 Venice carnival, was shot from close up enough for television audiences to gain its full benefits. *Boniface VIII* was also described as 'the most popular' of the numerous pieces that make up *Mistero buffo*, which led some of the newspaper previews of the programme to assume that *Mistero buffo* was entirely about Boniface VIII.[89] The programme also included an uncredited extract from *The Resurrection of Lazarus*, but confused the issue by stating that Fo had been performing *Mistero buffo* for 20 years. The preview of the programme in *The Times* even claimed that Fo 'became a television star, performing for 20 years in his own show that consistently topped the ratings with viewing figures of around 20 million'![90] A long and rather irrelevant sequence of the Neapolitan performer Beppe Barra in the guise of the 'sad eyed' *commedia* character Pulcinella was intended to illustrate the influence of the *commedia* on Fo, but Harlequin would have been more apposite.

No examples at all were given of Franca Rame's work; she made only one, brief and unannounced, appearance in the entire programme, in which she came across as little more than an appendage to her husband. She recounted her often-told story about La Comune's benefit performance for an occupied factory in Bologna, when audiences bought more than 10,000 glasses made by the workers. There were also a number of inaccurate claims, like the suggestion that in plays like *Isabella, Three Sailing Ships and a Con Man*, 'the satire was comfortably cushioned by the sixteenth-century setting and costumes.' (The fact that the play was charged with offence against the Italian armed forces, and the censorship problems it ran into, suggest that this was far from the case.) Fo's and Rame's work outside of *Boniface VIII* was dealt with only in a rapid and confusing montage of their 1977 TV cycle. Some rare footage of *Ci ragiono e canto*, with an uncredited appearance by Cicciu Busacca, was also included, along with an extract from Gavin Richards' adaptation of *Accidental Death of an Anarchist*. What emerged from the programme was a sometimes misleading and incomplete approximation of Fo's work which did little to expand on his already known performance repertoire and provided little background information to his (or indeed Rame's) work.

It might be argued that such a task was beyond a 50-minute TV profile, but comparison with Birgitta Bergmark's and Carlo Barsotti's 1977 Swedish TV programme, *Gott folk, här kommer gycklaren: Dario Fo e Franca Rame (Good People, Here Come the Jesters . . .)* does not bear this out. This clear, imaginatively filmed programme provided extracts from *Zanni's Grammelot*,

The Same Old Story, *Waking Up* and *The First Miracle of the Boy Jesus*, as well as improvised pieces by Fo about the Italian police and Pope Pius VI. These are interspersed with cogent interviews with Fo and Rame about their early work, popular theatre, the Italian Communist Party, farce, Rame's solo performances, and Soccorso Rosso. There was also illuminating footage of the couple rehearsing *The Same Old Story*, and a powerful sequence of one of Rame's performances of *Waking Up* at an occupied factory, followed by a discussion with the audience of workers. Almost all the salient theatrical and political information about Fo's and Rame's work up to 1977 is adequately covered, while the comedy and the political force of their work is captured with an impact which Marks' programme does not even begin to achieve.

Teaching praxis

Some of the restrictions of the BBC *Arena* programme could be attributed to the fact that it was made at a time when Fo and Rame were peripatetic. It also had to make the most of the Venice carnival as a somewhat forced example of elements of popular culture and *commedia dell'arte* reflected in Fo's work. It dealt briefly with the summer school where Fo and Rame taught theatre seminars in Santa Cristina di Gubbio, showing Fo demonstrating the *commedia* character of Il Magnifico using masks made by Donato Sartori. This school, known as the 'Free University of Alcatraz', and run by Jacopo Fo, became an international alternative study centre in theatre, music, literature, journalism, pottery, aerobics, Italian for foreigners and numerous other subjects. Workshops were held there by prominent figures like the novelist and playwright Dacia Maraini, singer-songwriters Lucio Dalla and Enzo Jannacci and the Colombaioni brothers clown duo.

Fo's role as a teacher of *commedia* forms differs greatly from his role as a performer. The *commedia* half-masks restrict vastly the rich range of facial expressions which are his stock-in-trade. The stylised, stereotyped movements of *commedia* characters like Il Dottore also differ greatly from the fluid, supple and unrestricted movements Fo employs in fleshing out the multitude of characters he plays in his own solo pieces. A case in point is his portrayal of Zanni, a servant prototype of Harlequin. The *lazzo* (improvised stage business) in which Zanni chases, catches and eats a fly is one of the best-known of the *commedia*, and a prominent feature of *Mistero buffo*. In the *Arena* programme we see Fo doing a similar piece in a mask, obscuring the facial expressions ranging from mock irritation to delight which are precisely the most comically appealing aspects of Fo's performance of the piece. Fo's use of *commedia*, then, might be compared to the way a musician uses scales.

In April 1984, Fo and Donato Sartori held a seminar on *commedia* masks at the Projektgruppen Sartoris Masker in Copenhagen. Fo brought the resulting teaching-demonstration, *La storia delle maschere* (The History of Masks), to the Riverside Studios in London a few months later. This 'master class', translated by Stuart Hood, consisted of a demonstration of the various *commedia* masks and the voices and movements traditionally associated with them. It culminated in a performance of *The Marriage at Cana* from *Mistero buffo*. Robert Page, writing in *The Times*, was unstinting in his praise of the workshop and in profiling Fo's rise in the UK:

> Dario Fo, impresario of the left, maestro of comic communism, is fast becoming the kind of cult star in England that he is in his native Italy. Perhaps he cannot quite fill a football stadium here – yet – but he can draw sell-out audiences at the Riverside.[91]

After *The History of Masks*, Fo and Rame performed *Mistero buffo* and *Tutta casa, letto e chiesa* in the 1984 Edinburgh Festival Fringe. The visiting Berliner Ensemble appeared in the main festival drama programme – an apt positioning of the two groups *vis-à-vis* official culture. It is interesting to note that *Mistero buffo* created resonances for at least one Edinburgh reviewer with the sixteenth-century Scottish satirist Lindsay, whose work has exerted considerable influence on the discomforting political plays of John Arden. Allen Wright, reviewing *Mistero buffo* in *The Scotsman*, suggested that Fo trades in satire of classic quality – the medieval Italian equivalent of the comical passages in Sir David Lindsay's satire of *The Thrie Estaites*. Both 'The Resurrection of Lazarus' and 'Boniface VIII' bear some resemblance to the Scots satire's remarks on the sale of indulgences and vanity and corruption of the clergy.[92]

English reviewers had sought equivalents for Fo's works in contemporary TV comedians, and then questioned the relevance to Britain of his satire of church authorities. Wright's comments suggest that the traditional roots of *Mistero buffo* might have stronger resonances in Scottish Renaissance and medieval theatre.

Adapting Fo (4) – *Trumpets and Raspberries*

In January 1985 *The Open Couple* received a production at the Sir Richard Steele Pub Theatre in a translation by Ed Emery, directed by Simon Usher. According to Hirst, this was 'a fringe lunchtime show, and as such proved to have as little bite as a revival of a Coward play. The audience for the British fringe has little taste for this style of theatre.'[93] Nonetheless the play was revived on the London fringe in 1993, this time in Stuart Hood's anglicised translation, by the Last Theatre Company at the Camden Studio theatre, directed by Paul Plater. Performed as a 1970s period piece on a turquoise set, it was described as 'predictable' and 'cute'[94] by Paula Webb in *Time Out*, while Robert Hanks in *The Independent* found the anglicisation unconvincing and the play implausible.[95] Caroline Rees in *What's On* found it 'cleverly constructed' and the characters recognisable, but the relationship 'skin deep' and 'unconvincing'.[96] On its own, without the company of *An Ordinary Day* or *The Rape* or *The Mother*, as when Rame performed it, the play's lightness was exposed, along with its pre-AIDS dissection of a sexual relationship.

The third West End production of a Dario Fo play was *Trumpets and Raspberries*, which was the pruned-down title given to Fo's play about Fiat boss Gianni Agnelli, *Clacson, trombette e pernacchi*. This opened at the Phoenix Theatre on 15 November 1985, in the same week as the ill-fated Broadway production of *Accidental Death of an Anarchist*. It was directed by Roger Smith and translated and adapted by Roger McAvoy and Anna-Maria Giugni, with television comedian Griff Rhys Jones in the double role of Agnelli and Antonio Berardi. This production was also a transfer, having originated at the Watford Palace the previous month.

The subject of *Trumpets and Raspberries* depends a great deal on the key role of Agnelli, who was no doubt unfamiliar to many English spectators. Hirst even suggests that 'British ignorance of Italian politics renders *Trumpets and Raspberries* innocuous, even meaningless.'[97] The play's specificities pose problems in transferring it into an English context, and the adaptor wisely chose to retain the Italian setting of the play as much as possible. In a very useful programme note to the play, Stuart Hood explained the most important facts about Agnelli. But he made no mention of the fact that he was honorary president of the Juventus football team, and the English text of the play likewise cut Fo's references to Juventus. Leaving aside the fact that the club was to hit international headlines due to the massacre of some of its supporters in a European Cup final in Brussels by Liverpool supporters in May 1985, this seemed a curious omission. Football fanaticism is one strong cultural attribute (although not, perhaps, to middle-class theatre audiences) that Italy and the UK have in common. (Indeed, in his particularly ill-fated adaptation of Fo's 1989 play *The Pope and the Witch*, Andy de la Tour went to the ridiculous extreme of naming all the characters in the play after the 1990 Italian World Cup football team. Fo consequently insisted that he change their names.) More knowledge of Italian football could be assumed than a knowledge of Italian politicians like Spadolini, Rognoni and Valiani, who were retained in the English version along with a number of Italian places and events, requiring 14 footnotes in the Pluto Press edition of the text.

Attempts to contextualise Agnelli seem to have proved difficult. Hood's programme note compared him with Michael

Edwardes of British Leyland, a comparison which was changed to Ian MacGregor of the National Coal Board in the published version of the text. In the publicity leaflet about the production, Antonio's rescue of Agnelli is described as being 'like Arthur Scargill rescuing Ian MacGregor'. These references to the miners' strike were apt, if skin deep (Antonio is an active union member, but in no way corresponds to a union leader like Scargill). Michael Billington, in his *Guardian* review of the opening-night performance at the Phoenix, reports how Agnelli was described as 'a cross between John de Lorean and the Duke of Kent'[98] which indicates that the adaptation was continuing to grope for political equivalents.

The McAvoy and Giugni version of the play was edited by Franca Rame, and a number of cuts (including the three-page résumé of recent Italian political history in Fo's text of the play, and passages from Aldo Moro's letters) certainly improve its flow. Some of the later changes made to the first published edition of the Italian text, which arguably weaken it in some respects, were also transferred into the English version. Other additions to the McAvoy and Giugni version which were made during production also contrast sharply with the sense of the original:

> DOCTOR: Maybe he was knocked down by a car . . . Some hit and run driver. In fact the person who handed him over to the Red Cross promptly – poof – disappeared!
> ROSA: Poof was he aye? May God strike him down! . . .[99]

The banal anti-homosexual joke is incidental to say the least, while Rosa's speech is given Irish Catholic attributes which have no equivalences in the original. Most of Fo's work satirises the Catholic church in one way or another, but *Trumpets and Raspberries*, interestingly, does not. Other gags interpolated in production and added to the text, like having the Doctor break into German (while Antonio's speech inflexions faintly suggest an Irish brogue) seem equally inappropriate. A reference to a game called 'terrorist bingo', and an anti-terrorist squad leader using 'oo8½ Fellini' as his radio code are other interpolated 'jokes'. But in other respects, the McAvoy–Giugni translation/

adaptation was an accurate version of Fo's play – much more so that the Colvill–Walker *Can't Pay? Won't Pay!* or the Richards *Anarchist*. Hirst goes so far to describe it as 'the most genuine translation of a Fo play into English.'[100]

The use of the play as a vehicle for the comic performance of Griff Rhys Jones, its political remoteness for English audiences and the commercial nature of the whole enterprise gave it a rather toothless quality. Rhys Jones, unlike his predecessors in the West End in roles created by Fo, Alfred Molina and Gavin Richards, who both had backgrounds in politically militant theatre, belongs to a more politically innocuous English television comic tradition. This was indicated by the title of a film script he wrote, *Morons from Outer Space*. Graduating from radio light entertainment, he rose to prominence in politically escapist, 'alternative' comedy shows like *Not The Nine O'Clock News* and *Alas Smith and Jones*. His commitment to a new series of the latter programme caused *Trumpets and Raspberries* to close in May 1985, after a six-month run.

Reviews of *Trumpets and Raspberries* were tepid, with Michael Billington finding it 'not vintage Fo' but 'still a deeply subversive farce of a kind that lies outside the British tradition'.[101] Wardle in *The Times* was more scathing, seeing the production as another example of the weakening of Fo's political bite:

> What is lacking from Roger Smith's production is a sense of the cruel reality behind the gags. This is very much an entertainment for people who know nothing about Italian justice and care less. Griff Rhys Jones makes a beaming first entry to explain Agnelli's identity in words of one syllable, and thereafter farcical business takes over to the exclusion of any line of thought.[102]

This process of reduction to light entertainment was increased when the play was performed at the Melbourne Theatre Company in Australia in 1985, where it ran in Christmas repertory with Alan Ayckbourn's *Season's Greetings*. Working on a common but often risky assumption that West End products could also be successful vehicles in Australia, the director, John Sumner, made some very confused claims for *Trumpets and Raspberries* in the Melbourne *Age*:

> It is far less political, probably, than anything Fo has writ-
> ten . . . I think his politics have probably become wider
> and he is actually looking in a much broader sense at the
> political spectrum, not particularly, in the end, being
> greatly full of approval for either side . . . That is why I
> think it is a play of greater maturity than his earlier plays.[103]

Not surprisingly, this production was a commercial and critical failure as well as a political non-event, proving that Fo's 'subversive farce' lay outside certain Australian as well as British theatrical and cultural traditions.

Adapting Fo (5) – From *Elizabeth* to *Abducting Diana*

Before the closure of *Trumpets and Raspberries,* Rhys Jones and the playwright John McGrath recorded a programme about Fo for Channel Four. McGrath's work with 7:84 in both Scotland and England was in the 1980s probably the closest political and theatrical equivalent to Fo's in the UK. In the programme they commented on videotapes of performances of *Mistero buffo*. McGrath has noted the differences between Fo's *giullarate* and the popular working-class forms of theatre used by 7:84 in a way which throws light on some of the problems of transposing Fo's plays to an Anglo-Saxon context:

> I was very struck by the fact that the root of Fo's comedy
> is peasant, and essentially all the stuff about the body and
> eating and gluttony, and the wonderful outrage he gets, is
> a peasant thing. I was also very struck by the fact that our
> comedy, and our kind of radical entertainment, is indus-
> trial, and goes back through variety and vaudeville to
> industrial roots. But I think there is a way in which we can
> in a sense 'call up' the peasant, which is through the
> mystery plays, and Shakespeare, who encompassed that
> sort of peasant tradition within his rather more urban
> comedies. I don't think we've lost it completely, but we

don't have that kind of through-line contact with medieval
buffoonery and peasants that Dario Fo certainly has.[104]

McGrath's comparison of Fo's cultural roots with Shakespeare is apt given that Fo's 1984 play *Elizabeth*, which he
wrote after spending time in London and doing research into
Elizabethan theatre, was about Shakespeare. An English
production of *Elizabeth*, translated by Gillian Hanna, who also
played the lead role, opened at the Half Moon Theatre in
November 1986, directed by Michael Batz and Chris Bond.
Hanna transformed the seventeenth-century hybrid dialect-
grammelot of Fo's Donnazza into a startlingly rich and varied
amalgam of Italian, Shakespeare, Cockney rhyming slang,
spoonerisms, obscenities and Stanley Unwin-styled patter,
performed by Bob Mason. Adding English jokes and
frequently departing from Fo's text (the published version
included an appendix of literal translations of the passages
which were changed), it managed to capture the complex
word play of Fo's original:

> Tis terril-ay! I comprehensive his stratagemical acts and
> monuments! Questo Shakespeare dicket to the rabble-
> ment: 'What do you fadge? Shift your ways! Go to! You
> perfect to be put upon like slaveys, like dumbo bruttoes –
> pimply on account of your terrorizzato of tripping off to
> hell? Arseholes! Dandiprats! hell be here, here sopra terra
> . . . not underbeyant. Divven be frit. Be a bravery! Arise!
> Shuffle off this governo of turd. Batter it to a tripes!'[105]

This was the first real attempt to render Fo's *grammelot* into
English, and cast its net considerably wider than Fo's dialect
inflections, also incorporating anachronisms. As a result it
frequently seemed over-laboured, transforming the comedy
Fo produced from sound, intonation and gesture into
semantic word play. It was also, as Ed Emery commented, 'in-
accessible to many in the audience'[106] and very difficult to
follow and understand when spoken. (Emery also noted that
the English playtext of *Elizabeth* had been copy-edited and
typeset before it was discovered it was based on a pre-

rehearsal text which had subsequently been substantially changed, and it had to be redone).[107]

Compounded with the very static nature of the play, its perfunctory references to the Moro kidnapping and other Italian political events, and its reliance on monologues and scatological humour that skirted dangerously close to vulgarity, the production was not a success. The *Sunday Times* reviewer described it as 'the most terrible bilge', and found the allusion to Moro 'naive and offensive', and Dame Grosslady's speeches 'stupefyingly tedious'.[108] Paul Chand in *The Independent* was more positive, describing it as 'fairly sparkling, non-vintage Fo, that nevertheless outstrips most other writers.'[109] Martin Hoyle in the *Financial Times* saw it as reflecting a 'current Italian fascination for Englishwomen in power', but thought its political comments were 'desperately superficial' and its focus on the vulnerability of women in power anti-feminist.[110] This was echoed by Alex Renton in *The Times*, who suggested the play revealed that Italians were more misogynistic than the English, and described the production as 'bawdy', 'vulgar', 'fatuous' and 'unfocused'.[111] Given Rame's discontent with the play, and the rather cool reception Fo's and Rame's original performances had in Italy, these responses were perhaps hardly surprising.

Elizabeth was revived in London in 1991 at the Battersea Arts Centre, in a new production by Anna Farthing, an award-winning young director. Sarah Hemming, reviewing it in *The Independent*, found it 'bold and entertaining',[112] despite its losing pace in the second half. Farthing's production added bursts of period music, and Clare Bayley in *What's On* praised its restraint, but found it too 'mechanical'.[113] Suzi Feay, on the other hand, described it in *Time Out* as 'exuberant fun and dazzlingly well translated'.[114] Running for only ten days, the production attracted little attention, but indicated there was still some life in the play.

A few weeks prior to the production of *Elizabeth* at the Half Moon, an English production of *Archangels Don't Play Pinball* opened at the Bristol Old Vic. This was largely due to the efforts of artistic director Leon Rubin, late of the Liverpool Everyman, who had just taken over at Bristol, and *Archangels* was his first production. It was directed by Glen Watford from a translation by Roger McAvoy and Anna-Maria Giugni, who had also done *Trumpets and Raspberries*. Despite being subjected to the ministrations of Franca Rame, who had begun to learn English so she could oversee translations of the plays, this version was accurate. The substitution of music by Simon Slater for the original song settings by Fiorenzo Carpi was less successful. (In May 1986, the same translation of *Archangels* was broadcast on BBC Radio 3 in a Glaswegian version, adapted and directed by James Runcie – son of the Archbishop of Canterbury. This Scottish version, which was very lively and energetic, but retained little of the play's Italian origins, used *a cappella* music by Harvey and the Wallbangers.)

In the Bristol production Il Lungo became Lofty Lovelyweather (employing the main character's other names, 'Sereno Tempo'), and was played by Roger Rees. Rees gave an acrobatic performance, which included leaping into an audience box, throwing chocolates around the auditorium and threatening to cancel the interval unless the audience paid attention. A group of anti-smoking campaigners dressed as angels picketed the theatre before the performance, which was sponsored by Players cigarettes, who provided programme covers in black and gold. There was a sculpture with flashing lights specially built for the occasion in the foyer. The set consisted of a giant pinball machine with interlocking cages, and a statue of an archangel above it. The cast were mostly veterans of fringe and alternative theatre, and the predominant style of the production was an appropriate combination of street theatre and pantomime.

Noting the play's 'more generalised farcical world of haves and have-nots', Wardle in *The Times* found Lofty's overcoming of his obstacles a little too easy. (This echoes criticisms made about the Maniac's dominance of the police in *Anarchist*.) But Wardle also described the play as a 'collector's item' and 'a wonderful piece of legerdemain and also a defiant gesture'[115] which anticipated *Can't Pay? Won't Pay!*. Michael Billington in *The Guardian*, on the other hand, found it a 'genial but toothless

. . . whimsical political harlequinade' and that 'Fo's good nature swamps the social and political protest.'[116] This indicated that British critics' expectations of political satire in Fo's work were getting increasingly – and perhaps unreasonably – high.

Archangels is indeed 'a wonderful piece of legerdemain,' as I discovered in a production of my own translation of it which I directed with students at the University of New South Wales in Sydney, which opened a week before the Bristol production. In my Sydney adaptation of the play, the street kid characters became Italian Australians, and the play's satire on state bureaucracy, institutions and social status, which is somewhat tame in the 1959 original, was slightly sharpened by being applied to second-generation working-class Italian immigrants. The play's lunatic energy, gusto, continuous breaking of the fourth wall, doubling of roles and complicated sight gags make it ideal for young performers and a delight to work on. But I had to discard about a third of the original text, which would otherwise have run to three and a half hours.

In March 1987 I attended a conference on Dario Fo and Franca Rame – the first ever in the UK – at the University of Essex. This 'Fo–Rame Festival' was attended by a number of translators of Fo, academics and actors. Ed Emery, Stuart Hood and I gave papers on translating Fo, and Joe Farrell, John Francis Lane and others talked about Fo as a playwright and performer. Events at the conference included the first British production of *The Boss's Funeral* in a translation by David Hirst, directed by Chris Adamson. The final scene – in which the actors pretend to prepare to slaughter a goat (in this case a sheep), in a parody of 1960s avant-garde theatre – provoked considerable discussion.

Nonetheless the play's political perspective appeared dated, as I had discovered in a production of the play I did in Sydney in 1984. Its street-theatre performance style, however, gave it an appealing cartoon-like, agit-prop style, but the discussions between the striking workers came across as rather earnest and dogmatic. Being based on a factory occupation which occurred in Milan in 1969, its topical references were very dated, and the best solution to the play appeared to be a complete adaptation to a local situation.

The conference also presented a low-key performance of *Tale of a Tiger* by Chris Adamson in Ed Emery's translation, and a performance of Franca Rame's monologue *Coming Home*, also translated by Emery, by Teresa Asquith. Both were British premieres. Anna Ziman's performance of *I, Ulrike, Cry Out* was also included, and was part of a production in the same month of Justin Gregson's translation of *Obscene Fables*, receiving its British premiere at the Young Vic in London. This was presented by the Yorick Theatre Company in a double bill with Garcia Lorca's *Comedy Without Title*. Most of the reviews suggested that Fo's monologues, which were directed by Michael Batz, and performed by Nick Bartlett, Simon Davies, Josephine Welcome and Anna Ziman, were more rewarding than Lorca's play in an over-taxing evening. The next Fo play to be performed in Britain was the Fo–Rame monologue *An Ordinary Day*, translated by Joe Farrell, in a touring production by Borderline Theatre Company in Scotland in May and June 1988, directed by Morag Fullerton.

Andy de la Tour's version of *The Pope and the Witch*, which opened at the Comedy Theatre in April 1992, was the fourth and final Fo play to reach London's West End. Transferring from the West Yorkshire Playhouse, and directed by Jude Kelly with Frances de la Tour in Franca Rame's role as the Witch, it is in my opinion by far the worst English adaptation of a Fo play. Working from a reliably accurate translation by Ed Emery, de la Tour, who had played the part of the Superintendent in the Richards version of *Anarchist*, outdid Richards in his distortions of the play. He also expanded on the Richards *Anarchist*'s use of Italian stereotypes and caricatures, as well as adding expletives and vulgarisms to the dialogue. His renaming all the characters after the players in the 1990 Italian World Cup football squad was done 'for no reason whatever'. (The Methuen edition of the play consequently had to include an erratum stating that Fo had requested the first letters of all these names to be changed.)

In his 'Adaptor's Note', de la Tour explains how he invented a character of his own, Cardinal Schilacci, 'to embody the corrupt and violent side of Vatican city politics in the hope of making this side of the play more accessible.'[117] 'Schilacci' is a

New York Italian in charge of Vatican security, and de la Tour makes him speak in an unbelievably crass parody of New York parlance: ('Y'know what I got? I got a gross of meddling scumbag trouble-making interfering pinko scumbag journalists downstairs, that's what I got, y'hear me?'[118]) This makes Martin Scorsese's Mafioso caricatures seem highly realistic by comparison. There are crude references to the church's connections with the Mafia – something which Fo would never state so bluntly – and a puerile joke about the Pope going blind. 'Schilacci' also asks Elisa the Witch if she was 'ever a hooker in Brooklyn'. De la Tour turns 'Baggio', a Vatican press officer, into an inane parody of a yuppie with a mobile phone. He also adds Tom Lehrer's song 'The Vatican Rag' to proceedings – which Michael Coveney in *The Observer* found 'the only physically enjoyable and coherent sequence'[119] in the entire pro-duction. The Pope makes jokes about his infallibility, and assumes a caricatured Swiss accent when he disguises himself as a Swiss guard. There is a joke, repeated several times, about a nun from Brazil who attacks the Pope and is referred to as a 'Brazil nut'.

This woeful, amateurish version of the play, which also cut a number of scenes willy-nilly from the original, should never have seen the light of day and was roundly rebuked by reviewers. Sheridan Morley in the *Herald Tribune* detected 'increasing desperation on the part of adaptor and director'.[120] Ian Dodd in the *Tribune* found 'the jokes are too often sub-*Carry On*',[121] and Nicholas de Jongh in the *Evening Standard* thought the production 'gross'.[122] Benedict Nightingale in *The Times* claimed it 'aspires to be little more than funny in a bumbling English way, and even that is beyond its pedestrian powers. Of bite, bile, astringency, wit and other such virtues, there is little on show.'[123] John Gross in the *Sunday Telegraph* even suggested the production may have 'served a useful purpose' in making people 'have second thoughts about the absurdly overrated *Can't pay? Won't Pay!* and *Accidental Death of an Anarchist.*'[124] These sentiments were echoed by Charles Spencer in the *Daily Telegraph,* who turned his ire on de la Tour, describing him as 'one of the unfunniest comedians on the alternative cabaret circuit, a chap with a black hole where his sense of humour ought to be.'[125] Keith Stanfield in *City Limits* concurred with the 'chorus of disapproval', finding the production 'vapid'.[126] Michael Coveney in *The Observer* described it as 'a series of plonking pratfalls and unfunny low-level pantomimics'.[127] Compared to the overwhelmingly positive reviews the play had received in Italy, where it was seen as a welcome return to form by Fo and Rame, these reviews say a great deal about the quality of this British adaptation and production. More alarmingly, they indicate that it appeared to have seriously damaged Fo's reputation in the UK, and there were no further West End productions of his plays.

In contrast, Stephen Stenning's adaptation, *Abducting Diana*, from Fo's 1986 play *Kidnapping Francesca*, reads as a lively, tight and very funny anglicised version of the play, which deserved to be seen more widely than its Edinburgh Fringe Festival production in 1994. Working from a translation by Rupert Lowe, Stenning turned the industrialist Francesca Bollini de Rill in Fo's version into Diana Forbes-McKaye, a media magnate. This was perhaps a questionable transformation, given the lack of female media magnates, but it works in dramatic terms and allows for plenty of topical references to the British media. Diana retains most of Francesca's clever, scheming nature, convincingly outwitting her kidnappers and asserting her sexuality without resorting to vulgarity. She sums herself up in the play's opening scene:

> As chief executive of a television station and owner of three national newspapers, I'm obliged to justify media intrusions into people's private lives. It is therefore essential to keep the grubbier side of my own life secret.[128]

The play is completely anglicised, with the masks of Italian politicians which Francesca's kidnappers wear in Fo's version becoming masks of John Major, Saddam Hussein, Margaret Thatcher and Prince Charles. Stenning's adaptation is very free, with the renovated dairy farm in which Francesca is held by her kidnappers becoming an ice-cream warehouse. The kidnappers use ice-cream flavours as their walkie-talkie codes, and the mysterious priest is accompanied by an altar boy called 'Rupert'.

Fo's often prolix dialogue is pruned down to crisp, colloquial London English, and the 90-page text of the original is reduced to 75 without losing any essential details. Rame's four-and-a-half page 'intermezzo' in the first part of the original text is reduced to a few lines which the actor playing Diana is invited to extend into a 'topical stand-up comedy routine'. The final 'Rich People's Song' is cut, along with a disposable rock song in the first act. Stenning's version ends with a blackout and an explosion – shades of the Richards *Anarchist*. While there is talk of an explosion in Fo's original, Francesca reassures the audience there will not be one. A number of very English jokes are grafted onto the dialogue, but they are mostly funny and the basic farcical kidnap situation – the essence of Fo's play – is allowed to flow briskly and smoothly. 'This isn't a Ray Cooney,'[129] cautions one of the kidnappers in the first act, when the dialogue risks becoming vulgar. Although the complete loss of the play's Italian context is regrettable, Stenning's version manages to work as a moderately successful English political farce. It certainly seemed more deserving of a West End transfer than de la Tour's version of *The Pope and the Witch*.

Irving Wardle, a consistent observer of Fo's plays in the UK in *The Times*, has suggested that the main difficulty English productions of Fo have is in finding the balance between the comedy and the barbed satire. Too many productions, he argues, settle for being 'exclusively comic', while others become 'too solemn and didactic'.[130] The first point is affirmed by Fo when he describes how some directors of *Anarchist* 'are concerned with producing pure entertainment, remove the realistic sense of conflict, and exaggerate the comedy with clown effects.' This results in turning the play into 'a kind of surreal *pochade* which causes the audience to split its sides laughing, and then come out of the theatre released of any sense of indignation or anxiety.'[131] Although a number of the other plays (such as *Archangels*, *The Open Couple*, *The Pope and the Witch* and *Kidnapping Francesca*) contain this sense of indignation to a far lesser degree than *Anarchist*, most English productions have understandably lacked the sense of urgency and political outrage that caused Fo to write the plays. This is particularly evident in the two most commercially successful English productions – *Can't Pay? Won't Pay!* and *Anarchist*. Some critics have suggested, like Malcolm Rutherford in the *Financial Times*, that 'the English never did understand Italian style'[132] and are thus incapable of doing justice to Fo's plays. But many of the most important aspects of the plays have managed to survive in varying degrees in a number of productions. When compared to some productions of the plays in the USA, this becomes increasingly evident.

Despite Fo's Nobel Prize, there have been almost no productions of Fo's work in the UK since the mid-1990s. One rare exception is the National Theatre's nationwide youth theatre project's selection of *The Devil in Drag* as one of the ten plays to be performed as part of 'BT National Connections' in 1999. This used Ed Emery's translation, which he adapted into a shortened version of Fo's original. Some indication of the perhaps scant regard for Fo and Rame in the UK in the 1990s was given by a survey of the 20 most important plays of the twentieth century by Nicholas de Jongh in the London *Evening Standard*, in September 1998. Anticipating the National Theatre's selection of extracts from 100 of the most important plays of the twentieth century, de Jongh asked ten prominent British theatre directors, critics and academics to list what they regarded as the key plays of the century. The result of an overwhelmingly anglocentric selection yielded only one vote for Fo – *Accidental Death of an Anarchist* was chosen by the artistic director of the Hampstead Theatre, Jenny Topper. But Fo's compatriot and fellow Nobel Prize winner Pirandello's *Six Characters in Search of an Author* proved to be one of the three most admired plays. It and Tennessee Williams' *A Streetcar Named Desire* both received seven votes, and Chekhov's *The Cherry Orchard* received six. Brecht, Beckett, Chekhov and Pinter were the most frequently listed playwrights.[133] But despite inaccuracies and distortions, *Accidental Death of an Anarchist, Can't Pay? Won't Pay!*, *Mistero buffo* and *Tutta casa, letto e chiesa* have undoubtedly had an indelible impact on British theatre.

CHAPTER 8

FO AND RAME IN THE USA

We Won't Pay! We Won't Pay!

It could be said that Fo was 'discovered' in the USA long before
he became known in the UK. The earliest known production
of his plays in English was in New York in August 1969 at an
Off-Broadway theatre called the Cubicolo, where Maurice
Edwards directed his own translations of Fo's 1950s short farces
Marcolfa and *The Virtuous Burglar*. More than a decade later,
R.G. Davis did the first productions of both *We Won't Pay! We
Won't Pay!* (as it was titled in Davis' own version of the play)
and *Accidental Death of an Anarchist* in Canada in 1980. Davis also
directed *Female Parts* in San Francisco in 1982, and was the first
director to proselytise Fo's plays in the USA. His production of
We Won't Pay! We Won't Pay! was the first US production of
the play Off Broadway at the Chelsea Theater Center in New
York in December 1980. Davis, the founder of one of the only
US theatre groups to produce political farce in a similar vein to
Fo, the San Francisco Mime Troupe, has done at least seven
productions of *We Won't Pay! We Won't Pay!* in North
America. These include a production with an all-black cast at
the Los Angeles Actors' Theatre in Los Angeles in 1982, and a
version in Spanish with an Hispanic American cast in New York
in 1983. He also did a touring production of the play in 1982 in
Detroit, co-directed by Martin W. Walsh, who later published
an interesting study of the carnivalesque aspect of the play.[1]

Davis has also written extensively and very anecdotally about
his productions of *We Won't Pay! We Won't Pay!*[2] and
chronicled his dissatisfaction with the actors he worked with,
whom he considers did not sufficiently appreciate its Marxist
basis. But according to Ron Jenkins, in one of Davis'

productions of the play he instructed the lead actress to stand 'on the edge of the stage and wav[e] a spoon at the audience as she lectured them on the evils of capitalism.'[3] More worrying was Davis' description of himself as 'translator' of the play, given his lack of Italian – he repeatedly refers in his writings to 'Il matto' in *Anarchist* as 'Il motto', for example. Nevertheless, Walsh claims that Davis' version of *We Won't Pay! We Won't Pay!*, which was the first play by Fo to be published in the USA, by Samuel French in 1984, was 'in many respects . . . a much closer translation than the British *(We) Can't Pay? (We) Won't Pay!*'[4] This is true, as the text follows Fo's original text reasonably faithfully, retaining his original ending, which was cut from the only British version of the play. Davis adds a number of songs to his version of the play – including the Communist Party anthem 'Bandiera Rossa' (The Red Flag), the anarchist song 'Addio Lugano' (Farewell Lugano) and the partisan folk song 'Bella Ciao' – all rather hackneyed examples of 1960s Italian political songs. But in other respects his play is considerably closer to the original than the British version.[5]

The *New York Times* critic Mel Gussow reviewed Davis' New York production of the play favourably, describing Fo as 'a social reformer with a fractured funnybone', and the play as 'a madcap travesty of kitchen-sink comedies, which also manages to shoot satiric darts at the police, government bureaucracy, unions, the welfare state and masculine domestic privilege.'[6] *Variety* found it 'among the season's funniest plays, and should result in US productions of other plays by Dario Fo.'[7] The success of the New York production proved *Variety*'s prediction to be true, although it was to be four years before a Fo play made it to Broadway.

The Eureka Theatre in San Francisco did *We Won't Pay!* in 1981, adapted and directed by Joan Holden – another former member of the San Francisco Mime Troupe. Eureka went on to do three other plays by Fo – *The Open Couple*, *About Face* (a version of *Trumpets and Raspberries*), and *A Day Like Any Other* in productions which were largely successful in adapting the plays to a US context. The American Conservatory Theater in San Francisco also did *The Pope and the Witch* in 1992 in a translation by Holden directed by Richard Seyd. There were productions of *We Won't Pay!* in Seattle and Toronto in 1981, and Davis did his production of the play in Spanish (entitled *No Se Paga*) at the Teatro Cuatro in New York's Spanish Harlem in 1983. This production, according to Alisa Solomon, was able to 'engage [its] audience in the play's issues . . . and to send them home arguing over the different characters' contradicting ideological explanations of the play's events.' She also claimed that Teatro Cuatro 'did not have to adapt *No Se Paga* to make it applicable to the barrio audience,' who cheered when Giovanni agreed to steal the sacks of grain. But Solomon remained apprehensive about the reception of Fo's plays in the USA, and the difficulty of doing them justice within the commercial structures of urban and regional theatres.[8]

Accidental Death of an Anarchist on Broadway

Accidental Death of an Anarchist opened on Broadway on 15 November 1984, produced by Alexander Cohen, 14 years after its first performance in Italy. The production, like all the London West End productions of Fo's plays, was a transfer, in this case the Washington Arena Stage production, which had done well at the box office. Cohen had initially tried to import Gavin Richards' version of the play, but when Richards, unknown in the USA, insisted on playing the leading role, Cohen sought other alternatives. The US version was adapted by the playwright Richard Nelson from a translation by Suzanne Cowan originally published in the Yale-based journal *Theater* in 1979 – the first play by Fo to be published in English. Directed by Douglas Wager, it had opened at the Kreeger Theatre in Washington nine months earlier. For Broadway, it was almost completely recast, and the English actor Jonathan Pryce took over the main role (here called 'the Fool', alias 'Antonio A. Antonio') from Richard Bauer. Alterations were also made to Nelson's adaptation by Ron Jenkins and Joel Schechter, who were called in as 'script doctors', working in collaboration with Fo and Rame. According to a 'Note on the Text', their changes included 'some new political references, and dialogue closer in meaning to that of the original Italian text.'[9] Nelson's adaptation had transposed the play from Milan to Rome (for no clearly apparent reason), and included a good many topical American references, in accordance with a note by Fo published in the Washington Arena programme:

> The American public, seeing this play in its present adap-tation, obviously cannot feel the real, tragic, tangible atmosphere which the Italian public brought with them when they came to the performance. It can share this only by the act of imagination or – better still – by substituting for the violence practised by the powers in Italy (the police, the judiciary, the economy of banks and multinationals) equally tragic or brutal facts from the recent history of America.[10]

But it is debatable whether the adaptor had found suitably 'tragic or brutal facts' with which to localise the play. References mentioned in reviews of the Broadway production include a fiasco at a Beach Boys concert, government cheese giveaways and Jimmy Carter's debate briefing book. Lines like the Fool's 'Jesus! – no, I was him last week,'[11] and his summation of the past 20 years of American political history as non-stop spectacu-lar entertainment suggest trivialisation. Also questionable was the substitution of the anarchist song 'Nostra patria è il mondo intero' (Our homeland is the whole wide world) with 'Look for the Union Label' (later changed to 'Arise Ye Prisoners of Starvation'), which the Fool induces the police characters to perform wearing women's wigs. At the end of this version, the Fool threatens to blow everyone up unless they all recite 'Peter Piper picked a peck of pickled peppers.' He also invites anyone in the audience who believes in the 'raptus' theory to clap their hands. Such transpositions suggest a complete lack of any tragic, violent or dangerous political context for the play. Mel Gussow, writing in the *New York Times*, thought the Broadway *Anarchist* was not as funny as the Richards version, and that there had yet to be a 'true . . . adaptation' of the play in the USA.[12] Elinor Fuchs in the *Village Voice* was far more damning:

Can the killing of *Accidental Death of an Anarchist*, at the
Arena Stage in Washington, be an accident? The answer to
that question could go to the bone of American politics if
such a sweeping view wouldn't seem to exonerate adaptor
Richard Nelson, director Douglas Wager, and producer
Zelda Fichlander from responsibility for the loss of nerve,
intelligence, and focus that has occurred in their adaptation
of Dario Fo's 'tragic farce'. . . . Nelson has ruthlessly
Simonized it, substituting random gags for forceful satire.
Fo never writes gags, hit-and-run jokes grabbing laughs.
Nelson's utterly deflect the play's political urgency.[13]

The casting of Pryce on Broadway seemed an attempt to
emulate Richards' role in the West End version of the play.
Reviews of the Broadway production, which closed after only
a few months, suggested that Pryce's high-powered
performance almost turned the play into a one-man show. Pryce
was nominated for a Tony Award for the role, but prominent
US theatre critic Robert Brustein suggested that casting him in
the role was 'a sign of our national cultural inferiority complex'.
Brustein provided a list of US comic actors he thought more
appropriate for the part, and blamed Pryce's 'self-conscious'
performance for causing the Broadway production to be
dismissed as 'tame'. He also criticised what he regarded as the
miscasting of Patty Lupone as the Reporter, whose performance
he described as 'based on a long-departed, entirely sexist,
absolutely lovely burlesque convention: the well-stacked broad
whose ample anatomy serves as the focus for the top banana's
attention.' In Brustein's view, the Broadway production
'dissipates Fo's energies and turns the evening into a tiresome
charade.'[14] The timing of the production, with its references to
Reagan's electoral campaign coming after the president's
comfortable re-election, was also unfortunate, and critical
consensus appeared to indicate that the play's satirical force was
too soft. This consensus was borne out by Fo's own brief
comments on the production in an article he wrote for the
Italian popular weekly magazine *Oggi* after his and Rame's trip
to New York:

Jonathan Pryce is really formidable. His timing is good, he
gets the most out of the gags, and he's very likeable. But
Franca and I couldn't help noticing how some of the more
aggressive passages in the play had been softened, and some
of the more brutal political jokes had been replaced with
euphemistically innocuous stuff.[15]

Fo concluded that he found US theatre 'xenophobic' in its
tendency to distort and transform foreign plays into American
ones, but Fo and Rame nonetheless enjoyed their first visit to
the USA. They relished all the publicity and red-carpet celebrity
status they were given, and promised to return there as soon as
they could to perform. Fo turned his speech of thanks to the
first-night audience at the Belasco theatre into a performance
vehicle:

> Our most sincere thanks go to your president, Ronald
> Reagan, for the magnificent publicity campaign he organ-
> ised for our Broadway debut. Yes, only now can I reveal
> to you that it was our friend Ronald's idea to refuse us
> entry visas twice. He did it in cahoots with us, so we could
> get to be famous in the USA. He rang us up in person in
> Italy: 'Hello? This is Ronald. Listen, I've had an idea. I
> won't let you have a visa just yet. That way there'll be one
> hell of an outcry, and people will start asking "Who are
> these two actors? What are their plays like? How come
> they're so dangerous?" Public interest will mount, and
> then to cap it all, the day before I'm sworn in for another
> term – kerpow! I'll give you a visa. That way people will
> think I'm being real democratic. Even though I am a
> Republican. And you'll get yourselves standing ovations!'
> Well, that's exactly what happened. Reagan's never for-
> gotten his youth, when he was an actor. He just wanted to
> make a show of solidarity with two of his colleagues.[16]

In a letter to *Theater*, the distinguished US critic, playwright
and translator Eric Bentley suggested that Fo's text of *Anarchist*
itself was at fault for the poor Broadway production, and that
without Fo in the main role, the play was a 'disaster area'.

Unlike other reviewers, Bentley claimed that the Broadway production was an example of 'a bad play exposed in all its nakedness.'[17] But it is clearly Nelson's adaptation which is at fault, not Fo's original play. Right from the first page of the published text of Nelson's version something is wrong. Instead of the opening dialogue between the Sergeant and the Suspect about the latter's impersonation mania, the Suspect (The Maniac) opens the play with the line 'The demonstrators appear to be rather tense today.' The Sergeant (played on Broadway by the noted 'New Vaudeville' comedian Bill Irwin in a very low-key performance) then states, 'It's only one week since that anarchist we were interrogating jumped out the window.'[18] This unbelievably clumsy expository dialogue made nonsense of the play's opening scene, where the situation involving the anarchist's death emerges only gradually, and there is no mention of any demonstrators in Fo's original text. Elsewhere, Jenkins and Schechter's additions introduce very literal elements into the play, such as retaining the titles of Italian newspapers, and even translating *Lotta Continua* into 'The Struggle Continues.'[19] The published version also prints an 'alternative ending' – a translation of the first ending of Fo's original text which he later abandoned, which was used holus-bolus in the Broadway production. The US political references, mostly to Reagan, sound clumsy and self-conscious, and the dialogue is frequently turgid and limp, as in the discovery of the Fool's 'false' false leg:

BERTOZZO: But it's all a trick; it's tied to his knee!
(*Tries to unbuckle the straps*)
CAPTAIN: Let him go, you stupid fool! Are you trying to take him apart?
FOOL: No, leave him alone. Let him go ahead and unbuckle me. Thanks, my whole thigh was beginning to prickle.
REPORTER: Oh, for goodness' sake, why are you always interrupting him? You think you'll manage to discredit him in my eyes simply because he doesn't have a wooden leg?

BERTOZZO: No, it's to show you he's a bragging wind-
bag, a 'hypocritomaniac', that he's never been either
mutilated or a captain . . .[20]

The patched-up text, like the patched-up production, with an
act curtain consisting of headlines from *Il Giorno* and painted
comic-strip flats, made for a very awkward and clumsy rendition
and its short run was unsurprising.

In his article 'Seven Anarchists I Have Known', Davis
compared the Broadway *Anarchist* to other US productions of
the play. He concludes that none of the six US productions of
the play between 1980 and 1984 – including his own – managed
to match Fo's intentions, understand the play's structure, or cast
a 'recognisably political actor in the lead.'[21] (Davis himself tried
to mount a production with Abbie Hoffman in the lead but was
refused permission by Cohen, who had the US rights to the
play.) He also claims that none of the US productions came
close to Richards' London version in making the play politically
relevant for anglophone audiences.

The first US production of *Anarchist* was an adaptation of the
play by the prominent theatre critic John Lahr from Suzanne
Cowan's translation, which Davis claims was performed to
'critical drubbings and small houses'[22] at the Mark Taper Forum
in Los Angeles in January 1983. Panned by all eight Los Angeles
critics, Lahr's version put US electoral politics into the play,
and was approved by Fo, but according to Davis, the director,
Mel Shapiro, tried to turn the play into a 'banana peel
comedy'.[23] A production at the Eureka Theatre in San Francisco in November 1984, adapted by Joan Holden and directed
by Anthony Taccone, met with more success. With Geoff
Hoyle – who was to play the lead in Fo's and Rame's US
production of *Archangels Don't Play Pinball* in 1987 – in the
protagonist's role, the play ended with a long diatribe against
the local Bay Area newspapers. But according to Davis, this
production also 'seemed clearly focused for laughs at the
expense of any potential political satire.'[24] Davis tends to over-
emphasise the importance of foregrounding the political
context of Fo's plays, and his insistence that productions

employ known politically-committed actors tends to be somewhat unreasonable. His view tends towards the solemn,
polemical and didactic side of the requisite balance between
Fo's farces and their politics. Dan Sullivan, on the other hand,
reviewing the Eureka production of *Anarchist* in the *Los Angeles
Times*, thought Holden's adaptation had finally got the play's
balance right, as it 'knows that the first thing that people's
theatre has to do is be entertaining . . . the message snaking in
underneath.'[25]

Orgasmo Adulto

Franca Rame's monologues first reached the USA in two small-
scale productions in 1982. The first major production of them
was Estelle Parsons' version of nine of the pieces in two separate
editions at the Public Theater in New York in July 1983.
Taking Rame's suggested alternative title from a line in *A
Woman Alone*, *Orgasmo Adulto Escapes from the Zoo*, Parsons'
adaptation of the pieces from her own translations was published
in 1985. Parsons, who had won an Academy Award in the late
1960s for her supporting role in the film *Bonnie and Clyde*, is
probably best known for her role as Roseanne's mother in the
US TV sit-com *Roseanne*. She had previously performed two of
Fo's and Rame's pieces in the Kunzle-Wymark English versions
at the summer arts festival in Purchase, New York in 1982. But
she was dissatisfied with them, deciding to consult with Fo and
Rame and do her own versions, learning Italian especially for
the purpose.

Parsons' version includes the prologue punning on the names
of sexual organs, as well as the prologue to *Medea*, both omitted
from the published UK version. Parsons approached the plays as
if 'Italian women are playing them and speaking a fluent second
language,' throwing in an occasional Italian word for good
measure.[26] This was a sensible approach, as attempts to
Americanise the plays would have foundered, given the
specifically Italian social and political context of most of them.
While Parsons' performances didn't meet with Rame's
approval, they were at least reasonably accurate renditions of the

plays. Three of Parsons' adaptations, *A Woman Alone, Dialogue for a Single Voice* and *Freak Mommy*, were revived successfully by Shelley Mitchell at the San Francisco Fringe Festival in September 1998. They subsequently transferred to the Exit Theater in November 1998, retaining the title *Orgasmo Adulto Escapes from the Zoo*.

From *About Face* to *The Story of the Tiger*

The importation of *We Won't Pay! We Won't Pay!* and *Accidental Death of an Anarchist* into the USA had been influenced to some extent by those plays' commercial success in London. But the third Fo play to be produced in the USA – a version of *Clacson, trombette e pernacchi* called *About Face* – was first performed in April 1983, more than a year before it opened in London. Translated by Dale McAdoo and Charles Mann, two Rome-based US journalists on the English-language newspaper the *International Daily News*, *About Face* was also published in *Theater*. *Theater* went on to publish *The Open Couple, The Story of the Tiger* and *Elizabeth* and its editor, Yale drama professor Joel Schechter, was one of the main US supporters of Fo. Schechter acted as dramaturge for the production of *About Face*, which was directed by Andrei Belgrader, a Romanian émigré, at the Yale Repertory Theater in New Haven. Andreas Katsulas, a Peter Brook protégé, played the dual roles of Agnelli and Antonio. McAdoo's and Mann's version of the play worked from the 1981 text of the original play, which Fo later substantially revised, and thus starts in the car wrecker's yard rather than in the hospital.

This earlier version of the play is in many ways superior to the later version, but Dale and McAdoo manage to sound a number of jarring notes. The character of Rosa – played by Karen Shallo, who had been Antonia in the New York *We Won't Pay!* – is considerably cruder, louder, fatter and more vulgar than she is in the original play. Although it is a reasonably accurate translation, the grafting on of US references – like Agnelli's comment 'I am the state! I own you all! Like my asshole buddy, David Rockefeller'[27] – often seems crude and perfunctory.

Other Italian political references are cheapened, like Fo's line 'So Aldo Moro was sacrificed to save the respectability of the financial state, not support services which nobody gives a damn about.'[28] This becomes 'So Aldo Moro gets 15 bullets in his gut to protect me, not the bullshit props nobody gives a damn about.'[29]

In her review of the production, Alisa Solomon suggested that it had 'returned Fo to the role of "jester of the bourgeoisie" ' by not 'radically re-working the script into an adaptation that would fulfil the satirical spirit of Fo's play.' She also suggested that 'Fo's political critique is more complex and sophisticated than an American audience may be used to.'[30] But Gussow gave it a very positive review in the *New York Times*, describing Fo as 'a cross between Bertolt Brecht and Lenny Bruce,'[31] and some local reviews were also positive. In an article published in 1989 about Fo's reception in the USA, Mimi D'Aponte was able to say that

> Despite the ongoing need for constant revision, *We Won't Pay!*, *Accidental Death* and *About Face* are, thanks to multiple American productions, 'here to stay'. These three plays appear to have graduated from the stage of 'experimental' or 'alternative' theatre and will, I believe, be accepted as an integral part of contemporary international repertory desirable in American theatre schedules. Fo has in essence, during the period 1979–1988, established a base, a modest body of dramatic literature which is recognised by the collective American theatre mind.[32]

Finally granted a visa to enter the USA in 1986, Fo and Rame embarked on a sell-out tour with standing ovations for *Mistero buffo* and *Tutta casa, letto e chiesa*. They performed at the American Repertory Theater (ART) in Cambridge, Massachusetts, the Yale Repertory Theater in New Haven, the Joyce Theatre in New York and the Kennedy Center in Washington DC. With Ron Jenkins and Maria Consagra in attendance as simultaneous translators, they also received Off-Broadway Obie awards in New York, performed to students at

New York University, and played in Baltimore. Fo concluded *Mistero buffo* with an impersonation of Reagan, and reviews were overwhelmingly favourable. Fo's and Rame's performances also led to more productions of their plays in the USA. According to Ron Jenkins, Fo had become the most widely performed Italian playwright in the USA by 1986.[33] (Hardly a staggering achievement, as Pirandello, Eduardo de Filippo and Dacia Maraini are virtually the only other Italian playwrights to have been performed in the USA.) Fo in *Mistero buffo* was compared to Jacques Tati, Richard Pryor and Jackie Gleason,[34] while Gordon Rogoff in the *Village Voice* invoked Ben Jonson and Molière.[35] Rame was compared to Mae West.[36]

The couple returned to the ART in spring 1987 to direct *Archangels Don't Play Pinball*, a production keenly observed by a number of US directors and actors. Working with Jenkins as translator and interpreter, Fo rewrote the play in rehearsal, adding a homeless hobo who delivers a monologue to a cardboard cutout of President Reagan. References to TV evangelists, garbage barges and current US politicians were also interpolated, and the dog pound scene included a real dog. Sam Abel summed up the production as 'a curious blend of sensibilities, somewhere between 1950s Italy and 1980s America.'[37] The published text of Jenkins' translation, however, is an accurate version of the play which does not include these additions, or make any of the cuts that are usually made in productions of the play, the text of which runs to some 150 pages.[38]

Almost concurrently with the ART production of *Archangels*, Anthony Taccone's production of Jenkins' translation of *Elizabeth* opened at the Yale Repertory Theater in New Haven. This featured African-American actor Joe Morton as Mama Zaza, Jenkins' rendition of Donnazza. Fo added a prologue to the play which consisted of a letter to President Reagan asking him not to draw parallels between the character of Elizabeth and his own presidency. (By this time his constant references to Reagan were beginning to wear rather thin.) According to Jenkins, the production also drew parallels with events at the

Iran/Contragate hearings which were going on at the time.[39] Mama Zaza's speech in Jenkins' version was far plainer, simpler and more comprehensible than Gillian Hanna's hybridised, scattershot rendition, with Jenkins relying mainly on alliteration, assonance and onomatopoeia for effect. This can be seen by comparing the following speech with Hanna's version of it quoted in Chapter 5:

> Outrageous. Now I see what he's up to. This Shakespeare is telling people: 'What's up? Why don't you move your asses? Why do you let yourselves be treated like slaves and animals? Just because you're afraid of burning in hell? Don't you motherfuckers realise that hell is here on earth? Not down there. Don't be afraid to stand up for yourselves. Beat the shit out of your screwed up government. (*Begins singing a protest song.*)[40]

Although the over-reliance on expletives is questionable, and the protest song an odd interpolation, the language is accessible and easy to understand. Markland Taylor in the *New Haven Register* found the play 'outrageously subversive' and 'rich with raunch and scatology' as well as humane and 'unmalicious' in its satire.[41] The Yale School of Drama in New Haven also mounted a production of *The Pope and the Witch*, directed by Stephen Genn, in 1996.

In October 1989, Tommy Derrah performed *The Story of the Tiger* in a translation by Ron Jenkins at the Charlestown Working Theater in Boston, in front of a backdrop of Chinese written characters and a picture of a tiger. It included a prologue devised by Jenkins and Derrah after consultation with Fo, giving background information about the play and mentioning Fo's performance of it in Milan at a rally in support of the students of Tiananmen Square. Derrah's performance was also dedicated to the Chinese students, and he noted that

> the first students to be arrested were members of a group of couriers who had carried messages back and forth between the student leaders. The messengers called themselves the Flying Tigers. Every time I imagine the tiger

roaring in Dario Fo's play, I hear the voices of the demonstrators in Tiananmen Square.[42]

In her overview of Fo's and Rame's theatrical impact on
the USA, D'Aponte concludes that Fo had an influence on
the development of 'improvisational group theatre' work in
the USA as well as the 'New Vaudeville' brand of 'solo,
mimetic clowning', of which Geoff Hoyle is a prime
example. She also claims he had an effect on 'our renewed
awareness of a need for theatre which speaks frequently to
social and political concerns.' She cites the Eureka Theatre
Company's federal grant in 1988 to develop new US plays on
social themes, after four productions of Fo's plays, as a direct
example of this.[43]

In 1998 there was a month-long 'Fo Fest' held in San
Francisco to celebrate Fo's Nobel Prize. Coordinated by Pina
Piccolo and organised by the San Francisco Italian Institute
of Culture, it involved a number of local directors and performers as well as academics, including Joel Schechter, Ron
Jenkins, Joan Holden, Anthony Taccone and Walter Valeri.
It consisted of a series of 12 events between 17 April and 12
May, including video screenings of *Johan Padan* and a recent
documentary film about Fo and Rame by Filippo Piscopo
and Lorena Luciano. (Videos of *Mistero buffo* and *Johan Padan*,
presented by Walter Valeri, were also screened in a special
evening dedicated to Fo at the Massachusetts Institute of
Technology's Italian Association in November 1998.) There
were performances of scenes from Fo's and Rame's plays that
had been produced in the Bay Area in the 1970s and 1980s,
and a 'Dario Fo/Franca Rame Variety Revue' of monologues, sketches and songs performed in English and Spanish.
These included the US premiere of extracts from *Sesso?* (here
translated as *Sex? Thank You, As You Like It*). A special
Mother's Day event involved performances by a multi-
cultural group of Bay Area actors of monologues from
Orgasmo Adulto Escapes from the Zoo. The Fo Fest was
evidence that Fo's and Rame's influence had been stronger
in the San Francisco Bay Area than anywhere else in the

USA, due to the promotion and production of their plays by Eureka Theatre and the American Conservatory Theatre. It also showed that his Nobel Prize had more impact on the US theatre community than it did in the UK.

PART TWO

CHRONOLOGIES OF THE WORKS OF FO AND RAME

CHAPTER 9

A BIOGRAPHICAL
CHRONOLOGY

1926 24 March, Dario Fo born in Leggiuno Sangiano, in the province of Varese, near Lake Maggiore in Lombardy, northern Italy. Eldest child of Felice Fo, an employee of the railways and member of the Socialist Party, and Pina Rota, from a peasant family.

1929 Franca Rame born in Lombardy, and makes her theatrical debut in her mother's arms at the age of eight months in her family's travelling theatre troupe. 'All the political arguments which Dario and I have developed had already been put into practice by my family 100 years ago. They "immersed" themselves in every town they toured. My grandfather, father and uncle Tommaso arrived in a city or a town, informed themselves about the history of the place, and then put it on stage.' (Franca Rame, *Domenica del Corriere*, 26 Sept 1981, p. 61.)

1940 Fo moves to Milan to study Art at the Brera Art College. He starts improvising stories and sketches, influenced by the *fabulatori*, or travelling storytellers, around Lake Maggiore. Mussolini takes Italy into the Second World War, against Britain and France.

1942 Fo helps his father in the Resistance, and deserts from the army.

1944 Fo writes his first (unperformed) play, *A Master Drives a Servant Mad, Then the Servant Drives the Master Mad*.

1945–51 Fo returns to Milan and studies Set Design at the Brera Academy, and Architecture at the Milan Polytechnic. Organises a fake visit by Picasso to Milan. Leaves before completing seven of the final examinations required for a degree.

1948 Rame moves to Milan and performs in a number of variety shows, films and revues.

1949 Fo directs, designs and performs in his farce *But the Tresa Divides Us*, in Luino.

1950 Fo suffers a nervous breakdown, and is advised by a doctor to pursue a career he enjoys. Approaches the actor Franco Parenti, and takes part in his touring outdoor variety show.

1951 Fo's solo radio series, *Poor Dwarf*, is transmitted. He takes part in *Seven Days in Milan*, a summer revue with the Nava Sisters, where he meets Franca Rame.

1952 Fo performs *Poor Dwarf* at the Teatro Odeon in Milan. Acts in the revue *Cocoricò* with Giustino Durano. Writes and performs in two further radio shows, *Cock-a-doodle-doo*, with Durano, and *Man Cannot Live on Bread Alone*, with Parenti.

1953 Fo forms The Stand-ups (I Dritti) with Parenti and Durano. Their satirical revue *A Finger in the Eye*, with lighting by Giorgio Strehler and choreography by Jacques Lecoq, opens at the Piccolo Teatro in Milan and breaks box-office records.

1954 Fo and Rame are married. The second revue devised and performed by the Stand-ups, *Fit to be Tied*, runs into censorship problems and the group disbands. Fo and Rame move to Rome to work in the cinema.

1955 Fo's and Rame's son Jacopo is born.

1956 Fo writes and acts with Rame in *The Screwball*, directed by Carlo Lizzani. He collaborates on other film screenplays, while Rame acts in a number of films. Fo also writes, directs and performs in a number of television commercials.

1957 Fo co-writes and acts in Antonio Pietrangeli's film *It Happened in Rome (Souvenir d'Italie)*.

A Biographical Chronology

1958 The Compagnia Fo–Rame is formed in Milan, and *Thieves, Dummies and Naked Women* opens at the Piccolo Teatro.

1959 Fo acts in *Five-Lire Coins*, a television play by Paolo Emilio D'Emilio. *Women Undressed and Bodies to be Despatched*, from *Thieves, Dummies and Naked Women*, is his first play to be transmitted on Italian TV, live from the Teatro Gerolamo in Milan. *Comic Finale* is based on plays performed by Rame's family. Fo's 'bourgeois period' begins with *Archangels Don't Play Pinball* at the Teatro Odeon.

1960–61 *He Had Two Pistols with White and Black Eyes* and *He Who Steals a Foot is Lucky in Love* performed at the Teatro Odeon. *Archangels Don't Play Pinball* is Fo's first play to be produced outside Italy, in Zagreb in 1960.

1962 The second channel of the Italian national television network, RAI, is inaugurated with a broadcast of *Corpse for Sale* from *Comic Finale*. Other Fo–Rame farces are transmitted over a five-week period. Fo is appointed artistic director of the popular TV programme *Who's Seen Them?* He also writes sketches and songs for the TV variety programme *Canzonissima*, watched by 15 million spectators. Fo and Rame terminate their involvement with Italian TV for a period of 14 years after refusing to accept censors' cuts to their political sketches.

1963 *Isabella, Three Sailing Ships and a Con Man* tours Italy. Fo and Rame are attacked by fascists in Rome. Fo is challenged to a duel by a cavalry officer, and the play is charged with slander against the Italian armed forces.

1964 *Seventh Commandment: Steal a Bit Less* is performed in 51 cities in Italy. Fo is the most widely performed Italian playwright in Europe.

1965 *Always Blame the Devil* tours Italy, Europe and Scandinavia.

1966 Fo directs *I Think Things Out and Sing Them* with the folk revivalist music group Il Nuovo Canzoniere Italiano. Travels to Eastern Europe, the USA and Cuba.

1967 Fo adapts and directs Georges Michel's play *The Sunday Walk. Throw the Lady Out*, a satire on America, is the last play of the 'bourgeois period', and the Compagnia Fo–Rame disbands. `We were fed up with being the court jesters of the bourgeoisie, on whom our criticisms acted like an Alka-seltzer, so we decided to become the court jesters of the proletariat.' (Quoted in Chiara Valentini, *La Storia di Dario Fo*, p. 8.)

1968 Nuova Scena is formed, operating through ARCI, the cultural and recreational division of the Italian Communist Party. *Grand Pantomime with Flags and Small and Middle-Sized Puppets* is performed in community centres, labour halls and workers' clubs.

1969 First performance of Fo's one-man show *Mistero buffo*, inspired by the medieval *giullari* (itinerant performers). Rame performs in *The Worker Knows 300 Words, the Boss Knows 1,000 – That's Why He's the Boss* and *Chain Me Up and I'll Still Smash Everything*. Both plays criticise the Communist Party and lead to a split between the party and Nuova Scena. First US production of Fo's work – *The Virtuous Burglar* and *Marcolfa* – directed by Maurice Edwards at the Cubicolo, Off Broadway.

1970 Fo and Rame form the Collettivo Teatrale 'La Comune'. *I'd Rather Die Tonight If I Had To Think It Had All Been In Vain*, a comparison between Italian partisans and Palestinian freedom fighters, performed in La Comune's new space in Milan, the Capannone di via Colletta. This is followed by *Accidental Death of an Anarchist*, 'a grotesque farce about a tragic farce'. The play is written in response to audience demands for a play about the 1969 Piazza Fontana bombs in Milan, the 'defenestration' of the anarchist Giuseppe (Pino) Pinelli, and the repressive, state-orchestrated 'strategy of tension' against the Italian Left. It goes on to be performed in more than 50 countries over three decades.

1971 *United We Stand! All Together Now! Oops!, Isn't That the Boss?* is followed by political documentaries about the Communist Party and Palestine.

1972 La Comune is evicted from via Colletta. *Knock Knock! Who's There? Police!*, a sequel to *Accidental Death of an Anarchist*, closes at the Cinema Rossini after the owners refuse to extend the lease due to police pressure. Rame starts Red Aid (Soccorso Rosso), a support group for prisoners. Fo and Rame are subjected to a judicial investigation for allegedly 'subversive' activities.

1973 Rame is abducted and beaten up by a group of fascists. La Comune perform *Stop the Fascists!* Fo is arrested in Sassari, Sardinia, for refusing to allow police to enter a club performance of *The People's War in Chile*. La Comune splits up.

1974 'Il Colletivo Teatrale "La Comune" diretto da Dario Fo' occupies a disused vegetable market in Milan, the Palazzina Liberty. *Can't Pay? Won't Pay!*, which becomes Fo's second most widely performed play, opens there.

1975 *Fanfani Kidnapped*, a political burlesque, is performed for the parliamentary elections. Fo is nominated as a candidate for the Nobel Prize for Literature and visits China.

1976 *Mother's Marijuana is the Best* deals with the drug problem in Italy as 'a class problem: rich people use and consume drugs, while poor people are used and consumed by drugs.' (Fo, quoted in Valentini, *La storia di Dario Fo*, p. 167.)

1977 Fo and Rame return to Italian TV in a retrospective of seven plays transmitted on Channel 2 of RAI. These include *Let's Talk about Women*, which later develops into Franca Rame's one-woman show *All House, Bed and Church*. The transmission of *Mistero buffo* provokes an outraged response from the Vatican, which describes it as 'the most blasphemous show in the history of television'.

1978 Fo is the most widely performed Italian playwright outside Italy. He adapts and directs Stravinsky's *The Soldier's Tale* with students at La Scala. He also writes and performs *Tale of a Tiger*, his second one-man show. *We Can't Pay? We Won't Pay!* is Fo's first play to be performed in Britain.

1979 *The Tragedy of Aldo Moro* is abandoned after a rehearsed reading. *The End of the World*, written in 1963, is performed for the first time in Rome. *Buona sera con Franca Rame* is transmitted on Italian TV. Fo and Rame perform in Germany, Sweden and Denmark. The 'Dario Fo Theater' is founded in Vienna, and presents a continuous repertoire of plays by Fo until 1995.

1980 Fo and Rame are refused visas to enter the USA, allegedly because of their involvement in Red Aid. 'An Evening without Dario Fo and Franca Rame' is held in New York and attended by a number of prominent American writers and intellectuals. *Accidental Death of an Anarchist* begins a two-year run in London's West End. Rame gives the first performance of *The Rape*, in London.

1981 *Trumpets and Raspberries* tours Italy. Fo receives the Danish Sonning Prize and the New York Other Critics' Circle Award. *The Opera of Guffaws*, Fo's adaptation of Brecht's *Threepenny Opera*, is commissioned but then rejected by the Berliner Ensemble, and opens in Prato and Turin. *Can't Pay? Won't Pay!* runs for over a year in the West End in London. *Female Parts* is performed at the National Theatre (as *One Woman Plays*).

1982 Fo performs his third one-man show, *Obscene Fables*. Rame performs *It's All Bed, Board and Church* (aka *Female Parts*) at the Riverside Studios in London. Fo and Rame hold seminars at the 'Free University of Alcatraz', organised by Jacopo Fo in Santa Cristina di Gubbio.

1983 The clown show *Patapumfete*, written by Fo, is performed by the Colombaioni brothers. Fo and Rame are refused entry visas to the USA for the second time, but perform in London and hold the Riverside workshops. *The Open Couple* opens in Milan, and is subjected to a restriction to audiences over 18 by the Ministry of Tourism and Entertainment. *Accidental Death of an Anarchist* is performed in three different cities in Ceausescu's Romania.

1984 Fo and Rame perform at the Edinburgh Festival and in London (Fo in *The History of Masks*). Fo holds performance-seminars *The Tricks of the Trade* at the Teatro Argentina (Teatro di Roma) in Rome. *Dario Fo: The Theatre of the Eye*, an exhibition of videos, costumes, puppets, masks, paintings and drawings by Fo, tours Italy. *Accidental Death of an Anarchist* opens on Broadway, and Fo and Rame are permitted to enter the USA to see it. *A Woman Almost by Chance: Elizabeth* is performed in northern Italy. *Trumpets and Raspberries* opens in London's West End. *The True Story of Piero Angera, Who Wasn't at the Crusades*, originally written in 1960, is produced by the Teatro Stabile of Genoa. Fo gives the funeral oration for Neapolitan playwright Eduardo de Filippo, and writes an unperformed play about the Mafia, *God Makes Them and Then Wipes Them Out*. Rame edits the book *Don't Tell Me About Arches, Tell Me About Your Prisons*.

1985 *The Tricks of the Trade* is transmitted on Italian TV. *Hellequin, Harlekin, Arlecchino* is performed at the Venice Biennale and throughout Italy. Fo is awarded the 'Biglietto d'oro' (Golden Ticket) at the Taormina Theatre Festival. 'The criterion wasn't audience figures but box-office takings; we've always had a policy of very low ticket prices, because we want a popular audience. Even under those conditions they had to give us the prize.' (Fo, in *Europeo*, 19 Oct. 1985, p. 66.) Writes *The End of the World II* (unperformed), and directs *Elizabeth* in Finland.

1986 Fo and Rame embark on a successful tour of the eastern states of the USA with *Mistero buffo* and *All House, Bed and Church,* and receive an Off-Broadway Obie Award. Rame performs *The Open Couple* and other monologues at the Edinburgh Festival and premieres *A Day Like Any Other* in Italy. Fo receives the Eduardo (de Filippo) prize at the Taormina Festival. *Elizabeth* opens at the Half Moon, London, and the British premiere of *Archangels Don't Play Pinball* opens at the Bristol Old Vic. *Kidnapping Francesca* opens in Trieste. The Compagnia Fo–Rame is re-formed and re-enters the ETI (Ente Teatrale Italiana) Italian theatre circuit for the first time since 1968.

1987 Fo and Rame co-direct *Archangels Don't Play Pinball* at the American Repertory Theater in Cambridge, Massachusetts. Fo directs Rossini's *The Barber of Seville* for the Amsterdam

Musiktheater. Rame announces in a television interview that she is divorcing him. She tours Italy with *Kidnapping Francesca*. Fo publishes *A Short Manual for the Actor* (based on his lecture-performances, *The Tricks of the Trade*). Fo performs *The Lion's Share* at the Festa dell'Unità in Bologna: 'a free-wheeling talk-show containing performed monologues chosen, as it were, at random from my 20-year-long repertoire of *Mistero buffo*, *Tale of a Tiger* and *Obscene Fables*. The decision to choose one piece rather than another will be based on the atmosphere created each evening.' (Fo, in *Il Piccolo*, Trieste, 2 Jan. 1988.) He accepts post as professor of Drama at Rome University. Fo's and Rame's performances of *The Rape* and *The First Miracle of the Boy Jesus* to 13 million viewers on an Italian Christmas TV variety show provoke hundreds of complaints from viewers, newspapers, politicians and the Vatican. Fo writes an unperformed series of monologues, *The Radish and the Bean*.

1988 Fo and Rame write and perform in an eight-part TV variety series, *Forced Transmission*. Fo acts in Stefano Benni's film *Music for Old Animals*, his first film since 1958, and in Salvatore Nocita's television mini-series based on Manzoni's *The Betrothed*. Fo reprises his production of *The Barber of Seville* at the Teatro Petruzelli in Bari; this production later tours Brazil. Fo's plays are performed in Russia for the first time.

1989 *The Pope and the Witch*, a farce about drugs, birth control and Pope John Paul II, tours northern Italy, and wins another 'Golden Ticket' award for the most popular theatre show of the season. *Twenty-five Monologues for a Woman*, a collection of Franca Rame's solo pieces from 1968 to 1984, including some never performed, is published. A version of *Female Parts* (comprising *The Open Couple* and *A Day Like Any Other*) is transmitted on Italian television. Fo performs an updated version of *Tale of a Tiger* (with a prologue about Tiananmen Square) to 30,000 people at a solidarity rally for Chinese students in Milan. Fo later writes and Rame performs a short monologue, *Letter from China*, about Tiananmen Square. Another short piece about China, *The Story of Qu*, is performed at the Festa dell'Unità in Modena. There are 250 productions of

Fo's plays in 40 different countries in 32 different languages, including Japanese, Finnish and Indonesian.

1990 Fo adapts and directs two Molière plays, *The Doctor in Spite of Himself* and *The Flying Doctor*, at the Comédie Française in Paris. Fo and Rame produce *Hush! We're Falling!* a comedy about AIDS, loosely based on Machiavelli's *The Mandrake Root*. *Can't Pay? Won't Pay* is revived in London, and its title becomes a slogan of protest against the Thatcher government's poll tax. *Mistero buffo* is performed by Robbie Coltrane in Scotland.

1991 *Johan Padan Discovers the Americas*, a massive one-man show, is Fo's response to the Euro-American quincentennial of Christopher Columbus' first voyage, and an invitation to present a play at Expo '92 in Barcelona. Fo performs *Mistero buffo* at the festival of Italian Theatre in Moscow. Rame writes and performs two one-act plays, *Heroine* and *The Fat Woman*, directed by Fo, under the title *Let's Talk about Women*. A new English version of *Accidental Death of an Anarchist*, by Alan Cumming and Tim Supple, tours 33 British theatres as a National Theatre Education Department touring production, winning Supple a 'Best Comedy Actor' award. *Seventh Commandment: Steal a Bit Less* and *Mistero buffo* are reprised on Italian television.

1992 Fo directs *Isabella, Three Sailing Ships and a Con Man* at the Centro Dramático Nacional in Valencia, Spain, and *The Barber of Seville* at the Opéra Garnier in Paris for Rossini's bicentennial. *Seventh Commandment: Steal a Bit Less No. 2*, a monologue in two acts about the 'Tangentopoli' (bribe city) scandals in Milan, performed by Franca Rame, opens in Carrara. *The Pope and the Witch* opens at the Comedy Theatre in London. Fo is awarded an Ubu Prize for best actor in Milan by a committee of 40 theatre critics. He performs the role of the narrator in his own adaptation of the text of Prokofiev's *Peter and the Wolf* in Lanciano, and this is later broadcast on radio and released on a CD in 1996.

1993 Fo and Rame perform a reading of *Dario Fo Meets Ruzante*, a tribute to his sixteenth-century mentor, at the Spoleto

Festival. *Mummy! The Sans-culottes!* satirising the corruption scandals, tours Italy.

1994 Fo's production of *An Italian Girl in Algiers* opens at the Rossini Opera Festival in Pesaro, and is later performed at the Amsterdam Musiktheater, and broadcast on Dutch television. *Sex? Thanks, Don't Mind If I Do!*, a monologue performed by Franca Rame and adapted by Fo and Rame and their son Jacopo from the latter's book *Zen and the Art of Fucking*, tours all over Italy. It is restricted by the Berlusconi government's Department of Entertainment to audiences aged over 18. Fo and Rame and the theatre magazine *Sipario* launch an appeal against this censorship, which is signed by a number of prominent Italian and foreign intellectuals. A group of progressive MPs raise the matter in the Italian parliament, and the restriction is revoked. *Abducting Diana*, a free adaptation of *Kidnapping Francesca*, is performed at the Edinburgh Festival. Fo and Rame begin writing a regular weekly satirical column about political issues in *Il Venerdì,* the Friday supplement of the newspaper *La Repubblica.* Fo's plays have by now been performed in 70 different countries, including Bangladesh, China, Greenland, Kenya and Yemen.

1995 Fo reprises and augments his Ruzzante show as a solo performance, under the title *Dario Fo Performs Ruzzante.* He suffers a stroke, losing 80 per cent of his eyesight, but nonetheless manages to give a number of seminars in schools and universities.

1996 Fo and Rame receive *Sipario* Theatrical Awards in celebration of the magazine's 50th anniversary at the first Festival of Italian Theatre in New York. They perform *The Emperor's Bible and the Peasants' Bible* in Milan in March to commemorate Fo's seventieth birthday, and at the Benevento Festival in September. Fo does a voiceover for the successful animated feature film *The Blue Arrow*, and is awarded an honorary doctorate at the University of Westminster, London. Fo and Rame tour Italy with a combination-show of *Mistero buffo* and *Sex? Thanks, Don't Mind If I Do!*

A Biographical Chronology

1997 *An Italian Girl in Algiers* opens in Cagliari, Sardinia. Jacopo Fo performs his own monologue based on *Zen and the Art of Fucking*. *The Devil in Drag*, a play about corruption and the law, written and directed by Fo for the Taormina Festival with Franca Rame and Giorgio Albertazzi, opens in Messina to tepid reviews; it transfers to Milan. Fo is awarded the Nobel Prize for Literature, causing controversy in Italy and around the world. He delivers what is described as a 'manic and unorthodox' Nobel Prize lecture in Stockholm entitled 'Against Jesters of Irreverent Speech'. In it he pays homage to the *giullari*, Ruzzante, Molière, the *fabulatori* of his childhood and Franca Rame. Fo and Delia Gambelli publish a translation of Molière's *Don Juan* into Neapolitan dialect.

1998 Fo and Rame present a new play, *Marino at Large* in Milan in March. The play is about three former left-wing political activists, Adriano Sofri, Ovidio Bompressi and Giorgio Pietrostefani, from the extreme-left newspaper *Lotta Continua*. They were imprisoned, after three lengthy trials, for the murder of police inspector Luigi Calabresi, who investigated the Pinelli case, on which *Accidental Death of an Anarchist* was based, in 1972. They were convicted on evidence presented by Leonardo Marino in 1988. Fo also announces he will devote his Nobel Prize money to securing their release, and discusses their case with Italian Prime Minister Romano Prodi. Fo announces he is working on *Mistero buffo 2*, a one-man *giullarata* about the life of St Francis of Assisi, extracts from which he performs on RAI TV. Fo writes a much-publicised letter to Italian President Oscar Luigi Scalfaro asking him to reopen an inquiry into the involvement of high-ranking officers of the Pastrengo division of the *carabinieri* in Milan in the abduction, torture and rape of Franca Rame in 1973, after new evidence comes to light. Italian Secret Service documents released from 1974 reveal that Fo was suspected at that time of being the leader of the terrorist group the Red Brigades.

CHAPTER 10

STAGE PLAYS

A Finger in the Eye (*Il dito nell'occhio*)

A revue in two acts by Franco Parenti, Dario Fo and Giustino Durano.
First production: Piccolo Teatro, Milan, June 1953 (dir. the authors).

A satirical history of the world in 21 sketches. In a blackout, an actor bangs his head against the wall and shouts 'lights!' to represent the creation of the world. The construction of Cheops' pyramids is shown as a sacrifice of the lives of the slaves who built them. The Trojan horse is shown to be the idea of an unknown soldier, but Ulysses gets the credit. The battle between the Horatians and Curatians is presented as a baseball match, with a commentator announcing the deaths as home runs. A Christian is interrogated by the Roman police in a parody of the prosecution of the contemporary Italian film critic Guido Aristarco, and the Crusades are shown to be a colossal exercise in speculation. Napoleon and Nelson are two little boys squabbling, and the Renaissance originates from a play on words in an argument between two philosophers. The bourgeoisie of the Risorgimento are seen to use the same language and terminology as the postwar Christian Democrats' rhetoric against the Italian Left. In the second part, there are satires of American films, sentimental Italian songs about mothers (parodying the recently established San Remo song festival), postwar building speculation and the legacy of the Krupp family. The Americans attempt unsuccessfully to go to the moon, and an expedition climbing the Himalayas discovers Giulio Andreotti at the top. Finally, the actors take photos of the audience as if they were animals in a zoo.

'The secret to persuasion and entertainment lies in an ability to examine the reality before our eyes by putting a 'finger in the eye', or turning moral interpretations upside down.'
Programme note, 1953, quoted in Claudio Meldolesi, *Su un comico in rivolta*, 1978, p. 38.

'The importance, and the novelty, of *A Finger in the Eye* was the fact that it was the first critical revue in Italy, and that it pursued a satirical line that was rigorous rather than whimsical and frothy, in attacking certain aspects of our mores and particularly our culture. Its importance lay in presenting an anti-academic angle on areas dominated by the historical, cultural and social traditions of academicism.'
Morando Morandini, *Sipario*, June 1954, pp. 9-10.

'We didn't give it a precise label, but naturally it was soon referred to as cabaret. Its synthesis of situations, range of subject matter, fragmentary scenes and musical interludes were like cabaret, but we would prefer to call it revue or *avanspettacolo* [see below] which are the two theatrical genres which have developed in Italy in the absence of a cabaret tradition. Naturally we went beyond the normal notion of revue, which was notable for its lack of political commitment and an artificial linear unity. Our linear unity came from a satirical critique of every conceivable subject.'
Dario Fo, in Roberto Mazzucco, *L'avventura del cabaret*, 1976.

'*Avanspettacolo*: began in about 1930. A very popular performance genre consisting of brief sketches, songs and various acts. These shows, which lasted about an hour, were performed in the interval at film screenings.'
Dario Fo, *Manuale minimo dell'attore*, 1987, p. 327.

'Fo's first "serious" play . . . was immediately referred to as an anti-revue. From the moment the curtain went up it was a shock for the audience. The innovation of its staging was so incredibly different from the sumptuous, overblown costumes and millionaire-type sets of normal revues. The acting was dominated by mime, pratfalls, and acrobatic leaps and bounds. Its content was non-conformist, and political satire that was intelligent rather than clumsy and trivial, made its first appearance on the postwar Italian stage.'

Chiara Valentini, *La storia di Dario Fo*, 1977, p. 39.

Fit to be Tied (*I sani da legare*)

A revue in two acts by Franco Parenti, Dario Fo and Giustino Durano.
First production: Piccolo Teatro, Milan, 19 June 1954 (dir. the authors).

Twenty-four scenes about life in a big city from dawn until dusk, from the point of view of the underdogs: tramps, thieves, the unemployed, prisoners, factory workers and lovers. A sketch satirising newspapers' manipulation of public opinion shows a foreign correspondent working from his armchair at home. Rich society women organise works for charity to alleviate their boredom, but end up eating all the minestrone they have made for the local tramps. In 'The Compromise', a dissident Soviet scientist asks his son to kill him as punishment for his deviation, and the director of the story, which is being filmed, appeals for the approval of the censors. A man applying for a factory job is subjected to a severe psychological test, and workers sing a song parodying the monotony of the production line. A worker on a bus has only a 10,000-lire note, which the conductor refuses to change; other workers on the bus club together to change the note, at which point the conductor offers to change the note and reimburse them. There are satires of film buffs and government initiatives to exploit illiteracy and the mass media.

'. . . A form of popular theatre . . . a collective text . . . almost surreal, recalling the late French decadent poets . . . the language is freed by concrete representations which give a human value to some of the characters in situations which are synthetic (and at times overloaded).'

Salvatore Quasimodo, *Il Tempo*, 1 July 1954.

'The authors have conceived and executed this revue with a new polemical and critical spirit which is aimed in various different directions. As well as specific targets of contemporary mores which the various scenes attack, there is an assault on revue itself, with its ostrich feathers and multi-million-lire budgets . . . the young authors of a play which is brilliantly integrated with Lecoq's mime and Carpi's music have something to say . . .'

Roberto Rebora, *Sipario*, July 1954, p. 24.

'Left-wing cant, already a dubious feature of *A Finger in the Eye*, becomes patent bad faith here, to the point of being cheeky.'

Nicola Chiaromonte, *Il Mondo*, 5 Apr 1955.

'On opening night, the Piccolo Teatro audience was scattered with police armed with scripts and torches, ruining their eyes checking that not a single line or word had escaped from the cuts ordered by the censor.'

Franca Rame, in Valentini, *La storia di Dario Fo*, 1977, p.48.

Thieves, Dummies and Naked Women (*Ladri, manichini e donne nude*)

Four one-act farces.
First production: Piccolo Teatro, Milan, 6 June 1958 (dir. Fo). *Bodies to be Despatched* (truncated title) transmitted on RAI TV, 3 Feb 1959, *One Was Nude and One Wore Tails* on 27 Feb 1962, and *Housepainters Have No Memories* on 20 Mar 1962. *The Virtuous Burglar* revived at Teatro Leopardi, Rome, Oct 1980

(dir. Marco Lucchesi). *One Was Nude and One Wore Tails* and *Housepainters Have No Memories* revived at Teatro Filodrammatici, Milan, Mar 1990 (dir. Arturo Corso).

British production: *The Virtuous Burglar* at Mitchell Theatre, Glasgow, 1989 (trans. Joe Farrell, dir. Morag Fullerton).

American production: *The Virtuous Burglar* at Cubicolo, New York, Aug 1969 (trans. & dir. Maurice Edwards).

Australian productions: *Bodies to be Despatched* at Flinders University, Adelaide, 25 Aug 1972 (dir. Bruno Ferraro). *Every Burglar Has A Silver Lining* (trans. Tim Fitzpatrick) at Seymour Centre, Sydney, 1982.

The Virtuous Burglar is a '*pochade*' about a burglar who is surprised in the act of robbing a house by the owner and his mistress. The burglar's wife rings him 'at work' and becomes jealous of the other woman. Then the owner's wife arrives with her lover, and in the ensuing complications the burglar manages to escape. *One Was Nude and One Wore Tails* is a 'musical farce' about an ambassador who is forced to flee when he is discovered by his mistress' husband, and is found naked in a street sweeper's cart. The street sweeper becomes involved in a complicated ploy to obtain a dinner suit for him, which he obtains from a flower-seller and ends up being treated with great respect. *Housepainters Have No Memories* is a 'clown farce' in which two housepainters arrive to decorate a brothel, where the madam's husband has been embalmed by his jealous wife. One of the housepainters receives the daily injection by mistake, and in the ensuing chaos the madam is also injected, leaving the three men to pair off with girls. In *Women Undressed and Bodies to be Despatched*, a 'thriller farce,' three women kill their husbands, and despatch their bodies through the Italian postal service in parcels. As a result a transvestite detective investigates a woman theatre costumier who is running a divorce agency, which is a cover for a service for women to eliminate their unwanted husbands.

'I realised conclusively that all real theatre is theatre of situation. Every theatrical action arises from a situation on stage which is full of possibilities for developing the action. The dialogue is only one of the tools to express these developments. For example: a naked man hides in an empty street sweeper's cart. This is already a situation; when the street sweeper discovers him, an innumerable series of situations can develop from that first situation. Theatre based on autonomous dialogue developing action which doesn't express potential action isn't theatre, it's literature. Theatrical language is synthetic, and can't accommodate descriptive digressions about states of mind, unless they are part of the momentum one wishes to sustain.'

Fo, in Erminia Artese, *Dario Fo parla di Dario Fo*, 1977, p. 22.

'A taste for paradox, misunderstanding, absurdity and surrealism is expressed by making maximum use of stagecraft. Thus the often-expressed parallel between Fo's "surrealism" and the Theatre of the Absurd (Ionesco and Adamov are most often cited) breaks down. . . . The satirical barbs of the two earlier works have disappeared . . . and the staging has moved from innovation to a naturalism with grotesque ramifications.'
Marina Cappa and Roberto Nepoli, *Dario Fo*, 1982, pp. 39-40.

'Fo and Ionesco both operate in a landscape which is, culturally and spiritually, far removed from the salons of Feydeau's Belle Epoque, but they are equally removed from one another. . . . In his early pre-political farces, Fo ridicules the bourgeois characters because of the way they behave, because of the beliefs they hold, and because of discrepancies between the two. His outlook is limited to the here and now, presenting a world capable of improvement, and therefore one in which optimism and hope have meaning . . . He undermines the "normality" of the bourgeois order but always in the name of an alternative order. In this sense, Fo is the distorted mirror image of Feydeau; where Feydeau asserts that all is well, Fo replies that all could be made well.'

Joseph Farrell, 'Fo and Feydeau: Is Farce a Laughing Matter?', *Italica*, 1995, p. 318.

Comic Finale (*Comica finale*)

Four one-act farces.
First production: Teatro Stabile, Turin, 10 Dec 1958 (dir. Fo
& Gianfranco De Bosio). *Corpse for Sale* transmitted on RAI TV,
20 Feb 1962, and *Marcolfa* on 6 Mar 1962.
British production: *Corpse for Sale*, Derby Playhouse, Apr
1986 (trans. Ed Emery, dir. Claire Grove).
North American productions: *Marcolfa* at Cubicolo Theatre,
New York, Aug 1969. *Corpse for Sale* at New Theatre '83,
University of Windsor, Ontario, Canada, 15 June 1983 (trans.
Walter Temelini).

In *When You're Poor You'll Be King*, based on the carnival 'feast
of fools', a group of strolling players dissuade an old man from
his belief that he will become king if he squanders all his money
and becomes a pauper. *Marcolfa* updates an archetypical
character similar to *commedia dell'arte* figures, who is the mother
of the deceptively wise fool Bertoldo. She becomes a servant
who is courted by everyone in an aristocratic household after
she wins the lottery, but opts for her good-for-nothing fiancé.
In *Corpse for Sale*, some card sharks kill a simpleton after he beats
them at cards, and then discover that he is a dangerous criminal.
The dead man revives and marries the landlord's daughter. *The
Three Suitors* revolves around a misunderstanding between three
daughters of a wealthy landowner and three 'ghostbusters' he
employs to rid his castle of evil spirits, whom the daughters
mistake for suitors.

'Fo has revived a comic vitality which has almost become
extinct and retraced its origins, finding clear historical links with
contemporary society. He has used the scenarios . . . performed
by one of the most outstanding nineteenth-century comic family
troupes, the Rame family of Piedmont . . . He has retained the
essential aspects . . . but embellished them with a completely
new succession of situations, extending and multiplying the
surprises . . . with a completely modern freedom of invention.'
Giorgio Guazzotti, *Il Dramma*, Nov 1958, p. 59.

'Because of this unusual mixture of popular and high cultural elements, and an attempt to combine the refined lessons of mime and the French avant-garde with the gags of the nineteenth-century *guitti*, the *lazzi* [see below] of the *commedia dell'arte*, circus tricks and Brechtian anti-naturalism into a single theatrical form, the critics found themselves in a dilemma: were Dario Fo's plays vaudeville, *pochades*, a new kind of revue, or avant-garde theatre? Probably this confusion was the greatest strength and popularity of a type of theatre which had too much vitality to be easily labelled.'

Valentini, *La storia di Dario Fo*, 1977, p. 60.

'*Guitto*: actor from a travelling theatre company of the lowest order, the so-called 'mountain climbers'. An expression used pejoratively to describe an actor who performs without care or discrimination, without taking any care over makeup or costumes.'

Fo, *Manuale minimo dell'attore*, 1987, p. 337.

'*Lazzi*: the most ancient form of "improvisation". The scenarios of the *commedia dell'arte* are literally crammed with the expression *lazzi* or *lazzo*. It means a comic device, either mimed or verbal, which is almost never described. The way in which the scenarios developed was never written down in order to pass on the various theatrical devices to others who did not belong to the companies. For the actors in the *commedia* companies they served exclusively as memos, and they preferred to keep the development of the comic details and grotesque devices to themselves, virtually secret.'

Ibid., p. 338.

'Political commitment took a back seat for a while. These plays were primarily devices to make people laugh, although a populist subtext was already detectable; a popular nose-thumbing at the rich and powerful.'

Gianfranco De Bosio, in Valentini, *La storia di Dario Fo*, p. 59.

Archangels Don't Play Pinball (*Gli arcangeli non giocano al flipper*)

Three-act play, partly based on a short story by Augusto Frassineti.
First production: Teatro Odeon, Milan, 11 Sept 1959 (dir. Fo).
British productions: BBC Radio 3, May 1986 (adapt. & dir. James Runcie, trans. R.C. McAvoy & A.M. Giugni); Bristol Old Vic, 10 Sept 1986 (trans. McAvoy & Giugni, dir. Glen Walford).
US production: American Repertory Theater, Cambridge, Mass., 5 June 1987 (trans. Ron Jenkins, dir. Fo & Rame); Dad's Garage Theatre, Atlanta, Georgia, 1 May 1998 (dir. Brian Griffin).
Australian production: University of New South Wales, Sydney, 2 Sept 1986 (trans. & dir. Tony Mitchell).

A group of young Milanese petty criminals play a trick on one of their number, Stretch, a modern version of the clever fool Bertoldo, and marry him off to a fake Albanian beauty (who is actually a prostitute) in a mock marriage ceremony. Stretch then tries to get his identity papers in order so that he can draw a disability pension, only to find that he has been registered as a hunting dog, a bureaucratic error he can only rectify by going to a kennel and posing as a dog. The play follows his attempts to extricate himself from the desperate demi-monde of pranks and petty crime, get his papers in order, and find an identity for himself. This includes impersonating a politician whose trousers he steals on a train, and re-encountering the prostitute, who is posing as the politician's wife. At the end, he discovers everything has been a dream, although not manipulated as he thought by the archangels in a game of human pinball.

'If it weren't for the liberal dose of madness he possesses, Fo would be a preacher, a moralist. Luckily for him (and us) he is a preaching clown. Farce represents a tool of moral corrosiveness for him, which by its very nature provides a pretext for escapism and paradoxical exercises ... But here all the congenial acrobatics of farce are rediscovered, along with some pointed references to reality.'

Ghigo De Chiara, *Sipario*, Sept 1959, p. 37.

'The play contains two clearly heterogeneous elements: the nucleus comes from a Frassineti story with its typical fantastical-satirical romantic humour. Bureaucracy becomes a symbol of modern technocracy and its oppressive hierarchy is mocked. The combination of Fo and Frassineti in the second act results in the most evocative and distinctive moments of the play, embodied in exhilaratingly crazy set pieces in which Fo reveals his ability to turn contemporary reality upside down and reveal its underbelly. The rest of the play is made up of witty comic turns which are artfully sustained by his *brio*.'

Vito Pandolfi, *Storia del teatro drammatico*, 1962.

'Genial but toothless ... What Fo is doing is clear: drawing on popular Italian culture, including the Harlequin and Columbine story while at the same time aiming a few swipes at the chicanery, corruption, nepotism and time-wasting form-filling of his native land. But Fo's good nature swamps the social and political protest.'

Michael Billington, *The Guardian*, 17 Sept 1986.

'A collector's item ... though it is not explicitly political ... instead of satirising actual cases of terrorism or police corruption, *Archangels* offers a generalised farcical world of haves and have-nots ... It is a wonderful piece of theatrical legerdemain and also a defiant gesture in which you can read the future author of *Can't Pay? Won't Pay!*'

Irving Wardle, *The Times*, 21 Sept 1986.

'Technically it is a quick-moving farce which draws on some of the classic situations of the French tradition of Labiche and Feydeau, with bedroom confusions and pompous officialdoms.

Its use of the transformation of the hero into an animal looks further back to the literature of the Roman Empire – to the story of Apuleius and his golden ass, who suffered the same fate. The intervention of the archangels at the end is an irresistible reminder of the *deus ex machina* of classical theatre and an interesting parallel to the part played by the gods in Brecht's *Good Person of Szechwan* ... The social provenance of the characters is also unusual. The young men in what one might call their "real life" sequences – for the bulk of the play is a dream – are youths from the sub-proletariat who recall the wide boys Pasolini describes in his novels set in the working-class suburbs of Rome. Their butt is Lofty, a simple young man who describes himself as "the Rigoletto of the poor" – as, in fact, a *giullare* [see below], the innocent who by his literal reading of situations reveals them in all their absurdity.'

Stuart Hood, Introduction to Fo, *Archangels Don't Play Pinball*, Methuen, 1987, pp. xiv–xv.

'*giullare*: medieval actor, acrobat and juggler of distinctly popular origins. The *giullari* performed in taverns, piazzas, courtyards and were often invited into the courts of the gentry and princes. On special occasions they also performed in churches.'

Fo, *Manuale minimo dell'attore*, 1987, p. 336.

'*Archangels* might be called an expressionist farce. . . . This loose framework supports a diverse collection of one-line sallies at political targets; Fo has updated these to include television evangelists, stranded garbage barges, and current politicians, especially during an extended monologue ... played to a cardboard cutout of the President. Fo's style is unabashedly theatrical, full of song, slapstick, and vaudeville turns. But politics always lurks behind the tomfoolery ... a curious blend of sensibilities, somewhere between 1950s Italy and 1980s America. The references are contemporary, and Tiny's plight of getting lost in a world out of control becomes more relevant with each passing year. But the flavor of an older, less jaded European world lingers in the music, in the character of the good-hearted prostitute ... and in Tiny's innocence. These diverse moods unite easily in the play's carnival atmosphere (there is even a live dog on stage). Fo's ability to juggle multifarious elements – farcical and political, Italian and American, new and old – may be his most effective tool for portraying our chaotic world.'

Sam Abel, *Theatre Journal*, Dec 1987, p.504.

He Had Two Pistols with White and Black Eyes (*Aveva due pistole con gli occhi bianchi e neri*)

Three-act play.
First production: Teatro Odeon, Milan, 2 Sept 1960 (dir. Fo).
British production: Sherman Centre, Cardiff, 1985 (as *Two Pistols*, trans. Katy Dimoke).

'An (allegedly false) victim of amnesia is in a psychiatric institution, dressed in a priest's cassock. He meets Luisa, who recognises him as her old lover who has gone to the war, and takes him home with her. The amnesiac does not recognise either the home or the lifestyle the woman explains were his; instead of the harsh and arrogant man she expected, he is docile and full of remorse for the past. Meanwhile the real "gent", the roguish Giovanni Gallina, returns; the other man is merely his double. There is a series of misunderstandings and mistaken identities, until the crook discovers the confusion and decides to hold the amnesiac priest prisoner. Giovanni resumes his life of crime, flees from a police ambush and appears to have caused the death of his double at the hands of the police, who think he is Gallina. He organises a thieves' strike, demanding a percentage of the advantages which upstanding members of the community (insurance companies, dog trainers, crime reporters . . .) gain from their thefts. Luisa discovers that the co-ordinator of the strike is not Giovanni (as the gang of thieves had assumed) but the amnesiac. He is about to be arrested for impersonating a priest when he is recognised by the director of a prison rehabilitation centre as his beloved Don Filippo.'

Cappa and Nepoli, *Dario Fo*, 1982, pp. 49-50.

'Its intentions are very clear but not fully realised, and the play becomes stodgy and monotonous at times where it could have been fast and entertaining . . . The transformation . . . of the priest . . . has not been followed through by Fo with sufficient attention to detail . . . Fo's favourite gags, although amusing, are too dominant, fragment the dialogue and prevent any real development of the characters and events . . . Nonetheless highly enjoyable and at times irresistible.'

Roberto Rebora, *Sipario*, Oct 1960, p. 25.

'. . . Resembles Brecht's *Threepenny Opera* which had just been staged by Strehler at the Piccolo Teatro, and is a kind of gangster story, a black comedy based on an exchange of personalities – a fascist bandit and a Christian Democrat priest . . . The jibes at authority were clear from the moment the curtain went up . . .'

Valentini, *La storia di Dario Fo*, 1977, pp. 70-1.

He Who Steals a Foot is Lucky in Love (*Chi ruba un piede è fortunato in amore*)

Two-act play.
First production: Teatro Odeon, Milan, 8 Sept 1961 (dir. Fo). Revived at Teatro Belli, Rome, 25 Jan 1987 (dir. Antonio Salines).
British production: Channel 5 Theatre, Glasgow, 11 Aug 1983 (trans. Helen Russell).

'A thief (Apollo) and an aspiring taxi driver steals the foot of a statue of Mercury from a museum with an accomplice, and buries it in the ground where a construction company is building, in order to blackmail the owner of the firm. The fraud is successful – the two thieves disguise themselves as archaeologists and turn up at the construction company. They are given three million lire to keep quiet and not obstruct the works. Apollo buys a taxi, and meets the wife of the boss of the

construction company (Daphne) . . . She offers him money to
pretend that he has been involved in a car accident with her, in
order to hide a nose operation from her husband. When he
arrives home, the building contractor does not recognise the
fake archaeologist, but assumes he is having an affair with
Daphne – permissible in their social class. A series of
misunderstandings culminates in the arrival of a doctor, who
pronounces that the woman is suffering from a mortal illness
which is curable by continuous blood transfusions between her
and the taxi driver, who is the only person with the same blood
group. This "medical" union between them . . . continues . . .
because Apollo pretends to be pregnant with Daphne's child.
The husband . . . demands a divorce, and the love story . . . is
interrupted by her escape (since happiness is impossible between
people of such different social classes). She is substituted with
the mythical plant (Daphne, or laurel), which Apollo embraces
affectionately.'

Cappa and Nepoli, Dario Fo, 1982, p. 52.

'. . . A collection of little inventions – stealing the foot and
planting it on the two building speculators is more of an
apology, really. In a sense it is the play that comes closest to our
'revues', because the main thread of the story is very thin – a
pretext for a series of barbs against the authorities of the time.'

Fo, in Artese, Dario Fo parla di Dario Fo, 1977, p. 46.

'Fo returns to one of his starting points, the *fabulatori*.
Consequently the protagonist of this new play is an emigrant
from the south of Italy who represents a different culture from
the sophisticated bourgeois environment of the play. . . . The
plot is a reworking of the classical myth of Daphnis and Chloe.
Formally, it is partly a farce for clowns, and partly a bedroom
farce . . . It is the only play of Fo's not to use songs, and comes
closest to a traditional comic form.'

Bent Holm, The World Turned Upside Down: Dario Fo and
the Popular Imagination, Stockholm, 1980, pp. 71-2.

Isabella, Three Sailing Ships and a Con Man (*Isabella, tre caravelle e un cacciaballe*)

Two-act play.
First production: Teatro Odeon, Milan, 6 Sept 1963 (dir. Fo).
TV version: transmitted on RAI 2 on 11 & 13 May 1977.
Revived at the Centro Dramático Nacional, Valencia, 1992
(dir. Fo).

'An actor [is] condemned to death for acting in a play by Rojas
which has been banned. At the gallows he is allowed to perform
the story of Christopher Columbus, which he drags out as long
as he can in the hope that a pardon will arrive. This does not
materialise, however, and in the end he loses his head. The play
about Columbus presents the Genoese hero as an obsessive, wily
individual, pitting his wits against Isabella, Filippo, Giovanna
the madwoman, the [Spanish] court, sailing ships, enemies, a
trial, and eventual obscurity, a consequence of the fact that
cunning and unscrupulousness (even to honourable ends) is not
enough if the powers that be are not on your side.'

Roberto Rebora, *Sipario*, Oct 1963, p. 28.

'. . . The theatrical language is becoming more developed, the
stagecraft is embellished with complex theatrical machinery, and
the dialogue more streamlined and based on thematic concepts
rather than isolated gags. The results are remarkable, indicating
that Fo is exploring a less gratuitous and more committed use of
theatrical forms. The text of the play is less provisional than
usual, and tends to lose the function of a summarising scenario
which is secondary to the performance, and assume an
autonomy of its own as a piece of writing. The play deserves to
be considered as central to Fo's work, as a "watershed" between
the typically "farcical" output and his later plays.'

Lanfranco Binni, *Dario Fo*, 1977, pp. 31-2.

'Fo's most Brechtian play, in its attempt to reconstruct a character, Columbus, who symbolises a particular epoch and mentality, in its use of songs which do not merely provide support for the action but function as commentary, and for the careful historical research which lay behind the plot.'

Valentini, *La storia di Dario Fo*, 1977, p. 85.

Seventh Commandment: Thou Shalt Steal a Bit Less (*Settimo: ruba un po' meno*)

Two-act play.
First production: Teatro Odeon, Milan, 4 Sept 1964 (dir. Fo).
TV version: RAI 2 on 6 May 1977.
Australian production: University of Queensland, 1973 (trans. T. Schonell).

Enea, a female gravedigger, is persuaded by her colleagues in a practical joke that the cemetery where she works is being demolished by building speculators. She is then convinced she should pursue a vocation as a prostitute, and witnesses a clash between police and striking workers, in which she sympathises with the police. She encounters a victim of 'coffin mania' who wants to rent a coffin, and discovers that the owner of the cemetery is in fact planning to sell it to speculators. Enea disguises herself as a nun, and infiltrates a mental asylum to obtain compromising documents with which to blackmail people in positions of authority. There she again meets the 'coffin maniac', who promises to help her expose corruption in high places. But in the end, in order to prevent a scandal that would be 'worse than an atomic bomb', everyone is subjected to brainwashing with a trephine, except for Enea, who vows to 'go back where she came from'.

'The social satire is more open and direct than in the other plays. Behind the plot and its twists and turns is the most rampant and astonishing building speculation and the impetus of recurrent scandals in Italian politics. . . . the bitterness and cruelty are dispersed rather than submerged by the breadth and complexity of imagination which as always in Fo's plays manifests itself in the action and develops continuously without allowing the audience any respite.'

Franco Vegliani, *Sipario*, Aug–Sept 1964, p. 39.

'A successful synthesis of all the "values" of [Fo's] theatre: an almost perfectly balanced farcical mechanism, comic poise and clever mime, ironic impulse and satirical flights of fancy . . . achieving by its continual and inexorable inventiveness a kind of "chain reaction" which appears to be governed by a rigorous necessity . . . lively, bold and generous . . . the language is both popular, due to the presence of dialect, and highly proficient in its cultured comic effects (puns, assonance, etc.).'

Arturo Lazzari, *L'Unità*, 5 Sept 1964.

'There are two main starting points; a cemetery about to be demolished because a group of speculators have bought up all the buildings around it and want to remove the unpleasant view for their tenants, and a bank vault in a psychiatric institution run by nuns who subject the patients to electroshock therapy twice a day. The nuns also make them vote for the Christian Democrats and teach them "current beliefs" such as telling jokes about unimportant ministers and even priests can calm their nerves, that they may talk about prices and taxes being too high, but that going on strike is wrong because it makes the pope angry, that [the state] sends all its petty cash off to Switzerland, finances foreign companies which don't pay taxes, but is good because it provides work. In the farce that develops around these two basic ideas we put in as many references to corruption as possible. A female character provides the central thread of the story: the play is dedicated to Franca.'

Fo, in Artese, *Dario Fo parla di Dario Fo*, 1977, p. 47.

'. . . The cemetery could be seen . . . from the point of view of popular mythology as the "world of the dead". In realistic terms, the psychiatric hospital alludes to scandals and corruption in the public sector, symbolically it is a political and satirical image of official society, and from the point of view of popular mythology it is the world of the mad, the universe of demons, where constitutional order is turned upside down in an anarchic, carnivalesque universe.'

Bent Holm, *The World Turned Upside Down*, 1980, p. 223.

Always Blame the Devil (*La colpa è sempre del diavolo*)

Two-act play.
First production: Teatro Odeon, Milan, 10 Sept 1965 (dir. Fo).

Set at the end of the thirteenth century, the play is about Amalasunta, a female charlatan who is unjustly accused of being a witch, and decides to become one as a result. She enlists the aid of Brancaleone, a devil-dwarf, and when she is employed for her magical powers in the court of a Duke, he becomes a kind of incubus to her. They both plot to assassinate the Duke, and after they are successful, the Duke's body is made into a marionette by a wizard in order to prevent the people from revolting. But Brancaleone gets inside the body and persuades the members of the Cathar commune to instigate a revolution, so that they will then be killed by the imperial forces, which are about to arrive. As a result Brancaleone becomes the new Duke.

'. . . A farce which brings invisible devils and false witches on to the stage, and manages to attack Catholicism as an instrument of power without resorting to parables. The authorities claim that the Gospels are too abrasive to be put into practice and that they are dangerous, because if they were applied they would abolish all their privileges. Some of the songs in the play are based on heretical songs of the time. Clearly we had to expand the

boundaries of farce to attack the clergy and religion of the 1960s
. . . Unlike *Mistero buffo* it is not a *giullarata*, or a reconstruction
of medieval texts, but a totally invented story in a farcical vein,
which takes advantage of its medieval setting to tell a few truths
about Catholicism.'

> Fo, in Artese, *Dario Fo parla di Dario Fo*, 1977, p. 49.

'Provides particular evidence of a contradiction between
conflicting interests in Fo's "poetics": on the one hand an
unmistakable tendency towards farce, with explicit connections
with the tradition of Italian comedy and *avanspettacolo*, and on
the other a need to develop a complex argument in theatrical
form which gets its motivation from farce and makes it into a
weapon of theatrical discourse. This amounts to a need for a
deeper theoretical base in theatre, and stronger links with
cultural and political reality which the less passive sections of the
audience were experiencing more and more intensely.'

> Binni, *Dario Fo*, 1977, p. 3.

'. . . Almost too rich in inventiveness and somewhat underdeveloped satirical sallies. At the politico-historical kernel of the
play is the struggle between the Holy Roman Emperor and the
Cathars, the communitarian and evangelic sect wiped out for
heresy in the late thirteenth century . . . the allegory is obvious.
The Cathar communards stand for the Italian communists, the
Imperial forces represent the USA which, at the time, was
stepping out of its commitment in Vietnam. An interesting
pointer to the later Fo is his attempt here to disinter
authentically revolutionary episodes from the history of popular
culture, especially those involving pre-Reformation evangelical
religion, which challenges the corrupt and reactionary
orthodoxy for an, as it were, left-wing point of view.'

> Lino Pertile, 'Dario Fo', in Caesar and Hainsworth (eds.),
> *Writers and Society in Contemporary Italy*, 1984, p. 174.

Dump the Lady (*La signora è da buttare*)

Two-act play.
First production: Teatro Manzoni, Milan, 15 Sept 1967 (dir. Fo). TV version: RAI 2 on 9 & 11 Nov 1976.

A clown show satirising America, personified by 'the Lady', and presented as a battle between two rival circuses. A religious ceremony centred on a refrigerator opens the show, which is a series of disconnected sketches which were updated and changed for the 1976 TV version of the play. The Lady is succeeded by the Bride, who is assassinated at Dallas. 'Clown Dario' conducts a tortuous ballistic test tracing the trajectory of the bullet that has killed her, which has hit a stray dog, a chauffeur and an ice-cream van on its way to its target. There is a trial investigating the murder of Lee Harvey Oswald, and an inquest into the murder of a black man, interspersed with circus acts such as peeping-tom clowns and a flea trainer who has to have his fleas removed from his appendix. In another sketch, unborn children are conscripted into the army, and their mothers sent to Vietnam, where orders are transmitted by telephone into the mothers' stomachs. Fo also added a cele-brated sketch in which he plays St George as a dwarf, riding a three-metre-high dragon which symbolised imperialism.

'. . . A highly proficient clown show, in which the circus device assumes a complex technical, aesthetic and narrative function . . . he has avoided giving his clowns poetic, symbolic or meta-theatrical significance, as playwrights and directors who draw on circus devices often do . . . This clown show becomes political theatre, preserving a balance which only rarely topples (at times in the second act it lapses into didacticism) . . . For the freshness of its invention, its sense of pace and timing . . . its use of "distanced" farcical and grotesque devices, and especially for its biting references to social and political issues, it recalls the far-off days of *A Finger in the Eye*, although it is undoubtedly superior, more mature, polished and assured . . .'

Arturo Lazzari, *L'Unità*, 16 Sept 1967.

'. . . There were real clowns in it – the Colombaioni (Alberto, Charlie and Romano, and Alberto's wife, an acrobat) – and I had to employ various effects and breakneck acrobatic tricks, explosions, trapeze acts, walking on springy stilts, and falling vertically into a dustbin. The Colombaioni know how to perform these to perfection, and taught us a lot of other tricks which weren't in the script. I've learned almost everything I know of and about clowns from them, including how to play the trombone. Franca learned how to work on a trapeze and do falls, hanging from her feet with her legs crossed. Because of the vast range and complexity of techniques that a clown has to acquire, it could be said that an actor who picks up this technical know-how is at an enormous advantage . . . not only in comic roles, but – and I can see the "armchair" theatre critics shuddering in horror at this – in tragic roles too . . . The clown goes back a very long way: clowns existed before the origins of the *commedia dell'arte*. It could be said that the Italian *commedia* masks were born from an obscene marriage of female *jongleuses*, *fabulatori* and clowns, and then after incestuous relationships, *commedia* gave birth to scores of other clowns.'

Fo, *Manuale minimo dell'attore*, 1987, p. 256.

Grand Pantomime with Flags and Small and Middle-Sized Puppets (*Grande pantomima con bandiere e pupazzi piccoli e medi*)

Two-act play.
First production: Nuova Scena at Camera di Lavoro, Sala di Vittorio, Milan, autumn 1968 (dir. Fo). Revised version entitled *Death and Resurrection of a Puppet* performed by La Comune, Capannone di via Colletta, 4 Dec 1971 (dir. Fo).

A giant puppet representing fascism gives birth to a King and Queen, Capital, the Bourgeoisie, a General, a Bishop, and the Confederation of Industry. These allegorical figures combat the revolt of the people, represented by an enormous Chinese dragon. A bourgeois Dolly Girl seduces the leader of the Rebels, who succumb to a Wizard who sells them football and advertising as a means of letting off their steam. A Television Director, trying to make a powerful documentary about the Russian invasion of Czechoslovakia, inserts some stock footage from Vietnam. Prospective factory employees are subjected to a psychological and political interrogation, and then trained for an assembly line by a ballet teacher. The Minister of the Interior is wrongly arrested when he becomes entangled in a student demonstration during an amorous rendezvous. The play ends with a song by Mikis Theodorakis celebrating 'the youth of the month of May'. In *Death and Resurrection of a Puppet*, a later version of the same play, Fo, wearing a mask, played Communist Party leader Palmiro Togliatti, whose policies were contrasted with those of Lenin and Mao, represented by puppets. The play attacked the revisionism of the Communist Party, American imperialism, and right-wing terrorism.

'Not his best play, but more than any other play it justifies its existence through its rapport with its audience . . . He is aware of the dangers of didacticism . . . and has attempted, often successfully, to dress his arguments up in theatrical inventiveness.'

Ettore Capriolo, *Sipario*, Jan 1969, pp. 43-4.

' . . . A political satire of the past quarter of a century of Italian history. It dealt with the struggle between the proletariat and the bourgeoisie, which was conveyed primarily through the use of puppets that the actors moved about on the stage or manipulated with strings or sticks in full view of the audience. The manipulation of puppets by warring political factions became a vivid stage metaphor. The continual presence of the monstrous puppet on stage served as a sinister reminder of the omnipresence of political oppression . . . Many of the masks were based on those of the Roman comedy and the *commedia dell'arte*. The puppets resembled Georg Grosz cartoons but lacked their horror.

Despite the seriousness of the theme, Fo's productions retain the surface charm and magic of children's theatre.'

> A. Richard Sogliuzzo, 'Dario Fo: Puppets for a Proletarian Revolution', *Drama Review*, Sept 1972, pp. 75–6.

'When we got involved with ARCI [the cultural and recreational wing of the Communist Party, PCI], it was in the hope that the spirit of 1968 was moving things in a new direction, even though we were well aware of what cooperatives involved, and who was behind the *case del popolo* [Communist Party community centres], and in whose interest they were. We had the illusion that working on a grassroots level, we could change the organisational structures, and that the PCI had adopted a revolutionary line as a result of the pressure of the student and workers' movements. We saw it as the only possible solution, the only representative of the working class.'

> Fo, 'Per una nuova gestione degli spazi e degli spettacoli', in Franco Quadri, *Il teatro del regime*, 1976, p. 143.

'Full, perhaps too full, of things left unsaid for many years, lines cut by the censor or self-censored. The play has a wildly comic structure, using a number of elements from popular theatre (masks and Sicilian puppets adapted to a similar theatrical use to what the Bread and Puppet Theatre were doing at the same time in the USA) in an epic set-up, aspects of which recall Brecht's didactic plays . . . It deals with Italy from the Resistance to the consumer society, the transformation of the ruling class, and the continuation of many elements of fascism into the new society.'

> Valentini, *La storia di Dario Fo*, 1977, p. 12.

'If, in the simplistic dialectical interplay the play uses, Togliatti is the thesis, Mao the antithesis, and the victorious dragon the synthesis . . . polemic against the party has taken Fo to such an extreme that he doesn't realise the shifting sands he is getting into . . . And it is a pity, because his power as a popular author and actor comes through even in this play.'

> Edoardo Fadini, *Rinascita*, 14 Jan 1972.

'*Death and Resurrection of a Puppet* attacked revisionism in an unintelligent way . . . on an ideological level, and . . . stopped at a point of destruction without indicating any constructive way ahead or signs of political reorganisation . . . enabling revisionists to attack us as anti-communist, and this falsehood gained a certain degree of credibility on a mass level. We took this experience into account in *Law and Order for God and Money's Sake*, where the attack on revisionism was much clearer but less frontal and more deep-seated . . .'

Document released by La Comune, Sept 1972, quoted in
Artese, *Dario Fo parla di Dario Fo*, 1977, pp. 131–2.

'*Grand pantomime* was revived in the 1971–72 season with a lot of revisions, since we realised that it couldn't remain unchanged after 1969 and its struggles for workers' contracts, the "hot autumn" with its wave of workers' and students' struggles, and the "state massacres". The script of the second version of the play was discussed in an analytical meeting at which the main workers' nuclei of the vanguard of various factories in Milan were present, and there was a second analysis after the first rehearsal . . . There were also puppets of Marcos and Joe Mo' [Stalin]. They appeared on the stage of a little theatre where their arguments took place. The little theatre was used to distance these leaders of the people, who were symbols of different ways of conceptualising relations with the proletariat. . . . the history of the years 1943 to 1972 was reconstructed from the point of view of proletarian struggles and every part of the play was viewed from this perspective . . . To extend the job of writing a play to a collective means accepting an idea of theatre and its political function which is substantially different from plays by playwrights . . .'

Fo, in Artese, pp. 129–34.

Mistero buffo

A '*giullarata popolare*' in fifteenth-century Padano dialect.
First production: Sestri Levanti, 1 Oct 1969 (dir. Fo). TV

version transmitted on RAI 2 on 22 & 29 Apr, 18 & 25 Nov 1977, and again on RAI 2 in 1991. Revived in Mar 1993 by Coop. Aquarius at Teatro dell'Aquario, Cosenza (dir. Claudio Russo, perf. Antonio Venturino).

British productions: Puppet versions trans. & dir. Malcolm Knight, Maskot Puppet Theatre, Glasgow, 15 Aug 1983; 1982 Theatre Company at the Half Moon Theatre, London, Feb 1984 (trans. Ed Emery); Borderline Theatre, Glasgow and on tour, Jan–Feb 1990 (trans. Ed Emery, dir. Morag Fullerton, perf. Robbie Coltrane). Fo performed *Mistero buffo* at the Riverside Studios, London, 26 Apr 1983, and in the USA in May & June 1986 (first perf. at the American Repertory Theater, Cambridge, Mass., May 1986), and at the National Theatre, London, Jan 1991.

US production: American Repertory Theater Institute, Cambridge, Mass., spring 1998 (dir. François Rochaix).

Australian productions: Adelaide University, 17 Sept 1987 (trans. & dir. Antonio Comin). The Fringe Club, Adelaide, 2 Mar 1988 (trans. Ed Emery, dir. and perf. Leonard Kovner).

A series of one-person performance pieces based on medieval texts originally performed by the *giullari*. *The Hymn of the Flagellants* opens a series of pieces of varying lengths which include *The Drunkard* (later called *The Marriage at Cana*). A drunken guest present at Christ's miracle of the changing of water into wine recounts the story from a highly Dionysian, irreverent point of view, after chasing away an angel who is trying to tell the official version of the story. In *The Slaughter of the Innocents* a mad woman has substituted a sheep for her dead baby. She is accosted by a Roman soldier who takes it for a real baby, and then tells her story to the Madonna, who unsuccessfully attempts to console her. In *The Resurrection of Lazarus*, Christ's miracle is narrated by 15 different characters in the crowd waiting for the miracle. When it finally occurs, people are sprayed with maggots as Lazarus revives, and the final narrator has his pocket picked in mid-sentence. *Boniface VIII* dresses up in all his papal finery, ordering his altar boys around in a display of fascistic arrogance and vanity. He encounters Christ, who refuses to recognise or acknowledge him as a pope, and finally gives him a series of invisible kicks in the backside for his decadence and corruption. The two protagonists of *The Morality Play of the Blind Man and the Cripple* join forces in an attempt at self-sufficiency, the cripple riding on the blind man's back. They attempt unsuccessfully to avoid being 'miracled' by Christ, which will involve having to work and be exploited by a master. *The Birth of the Villeyn* relates the creation of a peasant-serf 'from an ass's fart', so that the master can have someone to do his dirty work. The master then proceeds to give the serf religious instruction, teaching him that he is a vulgar, menial and repellent creature, who nonetheless has an eternal soul which will bring him joy and fulfilment in the hereafter. An Angel calls the master's bluff and sows the seeds of a peasants' revolt. There are also four *Texts from the Passion*, starting with *Death and the Madman*, in which a madman draws the tarot card of death in an inn where Christ and the apostles are staying. A female figure of Death arrives, and the Madman seduces her away from her duty. In *Mary Comes to Know of her Son's Sentence*, the Virgin Mary's friends conceal her son's death from her, but she sees the imprint of his face on Veronica's shroud. In *The Madman beneath the Cross*, the protagonist watches the Roman soldiers betting on how many blows it will take to nail Christ up to the cross. He then offers the 30 pieces of silver Judas has thrown away in return for Christ's body. In *Mary's Passion at the Cross*, Mary tries to bargain with the Roman soldiers for her son's body, and is unconvinced by the Archangel Gabriel's attempts to explain the importance of the Crucifixion. In later performances, Fo added *A Fresh Fragrant Rose*, a discourse on the way popular erotic poetry was censored by clerics and bourgeois scholars and transformed into 'high culture' as courtly love poetry. *Zanni's Grammelot* (see below), is about a starving peasant who is so hungry he imagines eating himself, then dreams of having a Gargantuan meal. He awakes to find himself still hungry, and catches and eats a fly. *The Birth of the Jongleur* is the story of a peasant whose wife is raped by a greedy landowner who also confiscates his land. About to hang himself, the peasant is visited by Christ, who makes him into a *giullare*, giving him 'a new language which will cut like a knife'. Three other *Grammelots* deal with an *English Lawyer* who saves a nobleman's skin in a rape case by proving that the peasant girl he raped exerted her seductive powers on him. *An American Technocrat* presents a potted history of aviation from the Wright brothers to space travel. *Scapino's Grammelot* contains instructions to an actor about how to impersonate French nobility. All the pieces are preceded by explanatory Prologues which are often considerably longer than the pieces themselves.

'*Grammelot*: onomatopoeic patter used to imitate foreign languages and exotic dialects.'

Fo, *Manuale minimo dell'attore*, 1987, p. 337.

'There are no references to Mayakovsky – perhaps Fo is merely being coquettish in giving this title to his latest play, in which he is the sole and absolute protagonist . . . the didactic aspect, which uses slides of old woodcuts and etchings, is unable to get rid of vestiges of paternalism, although Fo communicates with his audience with an enormously congenial charge . . . rather than the lecture on the conditions of the lower classes, using poetry and medieval theatre, that it undoubtedly is, . . . it is a lecture on the theatre: everything that Fo shows and tells us is a representation of the main aspects of a popular theatre which has faded away or been lost in time, and which Fo unearths for us by way of contemporary analogy.'

Arturo Lazzari, *L'Unità*, 4 Oct 1969.

'*Mistero* [Mystery] is the term used since the second and third centuries AD to describe a sacred spectacle or performance. Even today in the Mass we hear the priest announce, "In the first glorious mystery . . . In the second mystery . . ." and so on. So *Mistero* means a sacred performance, and *Mistero buffo* means a grotesque spectacle.'

Fo, *Mistero buffo*, 1977, p. 9.

'The inventors of the *Mistero buffo* were the people. From the first centuries after Christ the people entertained themselves – although it was not merely a form of entertainment – by putting on and performing in spectacles of an ironic and grotesque nature. As far as the people were concerned, the theatre, and particularly the theatre of the grotesque, had always been their chief means of expression and communication, as well as putting across ideas by means of provocation and agitation. The theatre was the people's spoken, dramatised newspaper.'

Fo, *Mistero buffo*, p. 9.

'The kind of relationship with his audience that Fo is attempting to establish in *Mistero buffo* is that between the *giullare* and the peasants. Fo operates continually the double register of medieval satirical, entertaining and abrasive portrayals which are "buffo" in the *jongleuresque* sense of the term, and his analogous references to present-day reality. As a result he never loses sight of the ultimate aim of the performance . . . to raise his audience's consciousness of the repressiveness of the capitalist system . . . His shifts from one register to the other are by no means mechanical, but have a remarkable comic and political alienation effect, which is perhaps the best way of interpreting the success and incisiveness of *Mistero buffo*.'

Mauro Ponzi, *Rinascita*, 28 May 1976, p. 43.

'. . . Unilaterally violates fundamental religious values shared by many citizens . . . a clear violation of reforms which provided for pluralism, but also mutual respect . . . This programme reminds one of the book-burning of the Nazis, or the fascist attacks on the Vatican newspaper offices and the members of "Catholic Action".'

Mauro Bubbico, MP and head of Government Media Watch Committee, 1977, quoted in Fabrizio Carbone, *Proibito in tv*, 1985.

'His one-man show is the opposite of a personal exhibition. Certainly Fo is here, in his everyday clothes, apparently without any accessories (nothing in his hands, nothing in his pockets, and only a microphone around his neck is visible) on a bare stage, where spectators even sit on the floor. But he is not revealing himself. He is there to perform and show us other people. . . . In renouncing any concern with revealing himself and in seeking refuge in characters, Fo is able to compensate for a refusal to be histrionic with another form of histrionics: his virtuosity and his ubiquity. . . . Fo is able to play on the timing and the astonishment of metamorphoses. And that is where his commentaries come in . . . In relation to Brechtian epic theatre, Walter Benjamin talks about the "interrupted act" and the "*gestus* of quotation". This can be applied here to the letter. Fo engages in continual interruptions. His gestures are abruptly suspended. He observes them, comments on them, laughs at them, repeats them or extends them . . . Through his uncompleted gestures, suspended as it were between past and present, and his words which call up these gestures but are never completely resolved in them, Fo not only appeals to the spectators' imaginations; he activates the spectators. He obliges them to "accommodate" him continually, to multiply their perspectives and points of view. He engages them in debate.'

Bernard Dort, *Théâtre en jeu 1970–1976*, 1977, pp. 207, 208, 210–11.

'All the greater pity, then, that on this occasion Dario Fo has kept to the relatively safe ground of religious satire. In Italy, naturally this reaches into everyone's life. But when we in England (or most of us at least) laugh at the Pope, our fun comes easily – we have nothing to lose . . . Italian society has for a sort of shadow, or unconscious structure, all the ceremony, hierarchy and mysticism of the Church. Without this all-pervading ritual it may be that the English will never produce clowns like Fo.'

Michael Stewart, 'A unique clown', *Tribune*, 6 May 1983.

'Where English Fo-actors are crude and hysterically over-keen on making you laugh, the original is subtle, at ease with his audience and confident of the intrinsic interest of his material

. . . It is great to see someone reviving the traditional enmity between the actor and the church.'

James Fenton, 'The subtle satire of Dario Fo', *Sunday Times*, 8 May 1983.

'. . . A revelation comparable to London's first sight of the Berliner Ensemble . . .'

Irving Wardle, *The Times*, 5 Jan 1984.

'Like all great comics, his humour disgorges itself from dark wellsprings of pity and terror. . . . Letting his plays leap out of headlines, he never releases them from history. . . . As a writer, he stands unsquarely in a mixed tradition of overflowing Elizabethans such as Ben Jonson and the more furious conceits of Molière. Eclectic, at war with God and at peace with himself, he is, in a word, Italian. . . . The laughter, especially, is about . . . victims who still know how to outsmart the victimisers.'

Gordon Rogoff, 'Mistero buffo', *Village Voice*, 10 June 1986.

'If there is a single work that embodies the essence of Fo's epic clown it is *Mistero buffo*. . . . Fo's masterpiece. It provides a key to understanding the extraordinary performance techniques required to animate the texts of his large-cast plays. . . . Fo infuses every story with the rhythmic drive of a jazz improvisation, the immediacy of a newspaper headline and the social scope of a historical novel. There is a Marxist slant . . . but it is far subtler than the cartoon politics that are often found in commercialised adaptations of Fo's plays in the US. Fo's politics are skilfully embedded into the comic structure of his material. Instead of blatantly proclaiming his opposition to economic injustices, Fo creates stories that centre on the tension between freedom and oppression. He then orchestrates his comic climaxes so that they coincide with the victim's liberation from servitude, so that laughter and the defeat of tyranny are simultaneously linked in the audience's mind.'

Ron Jenkins, 'Clowns, Politics and Miracles', *American Theatre*, June 1986, pp. 13-4.

'I have studied the camera movements of the cinema, but what I am really trying to recreate is the effects that were employed by medieval painters of the mystery processions. When painters tell a story they are outside language. They don't show the perspective of only one person. They show diverse points of view. In the sacred presentations of the Mystery plays in the Middle Ages, people would play a variety of scenes from the life of Christ, showing the actions of Jesus, the Madonna, the devils, etc. And when the painters designed their religious frescoes, they recreated mechanically the things that they had seen from different points of view: the same scene from behind, from the front, from a distance. The techniques of cinema were not born with the invention of the camera. They have been used by painters and storytellers for hundreds of years.'

Fo, 1986, in Jenkins, p. 15.

The Worker Knows 300 Words, The Boss Knows 1,000 – That's Why He's the Boss (L'operaio conosce 300 parole, il padrone 1,000 – per questo lui è il padrone)

Two-act play.
First production: Teatro della Gioventù, Genoa, 3 Nov 1969 (dir. Fo).
British production: Yorick Theatre Co., Latchmere Theatre, Apr 1985 (trans. David Hirst, dir. Michael Batz).

A group of workers are clearing out a library in a Communist Party community centre to make way for billiard tables. Some of the books they look through come to life in a series of flashbacks. The first scene deals with the Stalinist trials of the Czechoslovakian activists Kvcanic and Slansky. The second shows Gramsci as a young student, talking to workers about socialism and persuading them that they must become the intellectuals of the Communist Party. In the second act Franca

Rame performed the first of her one-woman shows, about the mother of the Sicilian trade unionist Michele Lu Lanzone, who was murdered by the Mafia after discovering a spring in an area of drought. The mother recalls the events from a mental institution. The final episode deals with Soviet censorship of the poet Mayakovsky's work, his suicide and his mythologisation into a hero. At the end of the play, the workers replace the books and the library, realising that it is still needed.

'What does the 300 words mean? It's not our title; it comes from Barbiana, where a group of farm workers wrote a book in which they used this expression . . . It means that the boss has built up his own culture, and imposes it on the worker from above, imposing his laws and his vocabulary and way of writing. At home you have a dialect and a culture . . . but the boss cuts you off from it. You have 1,000 words of your own culture, but the boss . . . insists that you use his, so the 1,000 words refers to the boss's culture . . .'

Fo, debate with an audience, *Compagni senza censura*, 1970, p. 221.

'The epic theatre, or the didactic theatre, if you prefer, opens out its backcloth to expose all the tricks of the trade, and involve the audience in the "technical aspects" of the performance. In *The Worker Knows 300 Words* . . . the Worker shows that an awareness of theatrical representation is essential for learning and the cultural activity he recognises the need for . . . the play assumes a reality which is the aim of didactic theatre: the critical involvement of the audience. And since our audiences are proletarian audiences, workers are the protagonists of this reality which we imagine has come about; they are the authors and actors of a theatre which expresses their own culture. And what culture is it that these workers present on stage? A political culture . . . They have learned Gramsci's lesson that "if we don't know where we come from, it's hard to understand where we're going." In other words, for someone who is exploited, knowing their own history, how they came to be exploited and for what reasons, and the methods the boss has used to exploit them, is important.'

Fo, in Artese, *Dario Fo parla di Dario Fo*, 1977, pp. 114–15.

'Fo . . . had an expression of Brecht's in mind: "The people know how to say profound and complex things with great simplicity; populists who swoop down from above to write for the people say things that are empty and banal, with great simplicity." His ambition was . . . to "make the people speak" and represent on stage problems he had become aware of in his first year, and issues he had heard raised during debates with audiences. His encounter with the world of militants, workers and trade unionists had had a profound effect on him, and stimulated him to express himself in a new way.'

Valentini, *La storia di Dario Fo*, 1977, p. 111.

'Although the underlying themes of Dario Fo's plays are always serious, his attempts to articulate them in sustained, serious language are frequently unsuccessful. His theatrical text tends to become sententious when he incorporates into it lines taken from political writers such as Gramsci, Lenin, Rosa Luxemburg and so forth. In these cases he breaks the continuity of his direct, "popular" discourse and mounts, as it were, on to a platform. *L'Operaio* . . . is one of the few plays he has written in a predominantly serious vein, and for the most part it is a moving, thought-provoking work, with some scenes of extraordinary dramatic intensity. However, its chief weakness lies in the . . . rhetorical tone of its language. Perhaps the real problem . . . concerns the subject: unlike most of Fo's plays, which revolve around a concrete and specific political issue, this work is based on an essentially theoretical question; namely, the role and function of culture as an element of political consciousness (and here, also of political praxis) in the working class. An ambitious theme, but one which is undoubtedly better suited to a Brechtian *Lehrstück* or to Peter Weiss than to a writer like Dario Fo, rooted as he is in the tradition of popular comic theatre and in the bedrock substance of practical political activity. One gets the impression . . . that Fo's rather abstract theme needed a correspondingly abstract language which lies outside his normal mode of discourse.'

Suzanne Cowan, 'The Militant Theatre of Dario Fo',
PhD thesis, 1977, p. 208.

'Dario Fo is not only a brilliant satirist: he is also a thinker. He thinks that "the people" have a vast culture which has almost been obliterated by their oppressors – the church, the state and capitalism. It's the work of his popular theatre to rediscover it. But is there anything to rediscover? *The Worker Knows 300 Words* ... is more about telling the workers what's good for them than about rediscovering.'

Desmond Christy, *The Guardian*, 4 Apr 1985.

Chain Me Up and I'll Still Smash Everything (*Legami pure che tanto io spacco tutto lo stesso*)

Two one-act plays.
First production: Teatro della Gioventù, Genoa, 5 Nov 1969 (dir. Fo). *Law and Order for God and Money's Sake!!!*, Capannone di via Colletta, Milan, autumn 1972 (dir. Fo).
British production: *The Boss's Funeral*, Essex University Theatre, 27 Mar 1987 (trans. David Hirst, dir. Chris Adamson).
Australian production: *The Boss's Funeral,* University of New South Wales, Sydney, 9 Oct 1984 (trans. & dir. Tony Mitchell).

In *The Loom* (a shorter, earlier version of *Law and Order,*) a communist family who do piecework at home on weaving looms discover that they have to work 16 hours a day to meet their overheads. The Mother is staunch in her belief that it is important to follow the precepts of the PCI expressed in their newspaper *L'Unità* although she never has time to read it. But she becomes aware that the party, in the person of an official who is distributing the piecework they do, is exploiting them. The Father, exhausted by the work and shocked by the fact that his daughter is sleeping with her boyfriend, goes berserk, smashes the looms, and hits his wife on the head. The Mother, unconscious, dreams about a new, reformed Communist Party in which revisionists and deviationists have been kicked out. This play was extended into the two-act farce, *Law and Order for God and Money's Sake!!!* adding two characters: a prostitute and an extraparliamentary, revolutionary son. In *The Boss's Funeral* a group of workers occupying a factory are evicted by the police and decide to stage a play to draw the attention of other workers on their way to work to their predicament. They 'borrow' some costumes and improvise a carnivalesque play about the death of their boss, an unsuccessful attempt at a heart transplant, and the effects of pollution. This develops into a satire about industrial accidents, in which a butcher is brought onstage to slaughter a goat in a bizarre ritual illustrating the need to maintain the daily average of industrial fatalities. This final theatrical device extends into the play's 'third act': a debate with the audience.

'The characters in the farce . . . which the workers perform are the bosses: the boss's widow, the priest, and so on . . . As in Carnival or on New Year's Eve, when you bury the old year. But the worker characters complicate the farce with a device which is intended to give it more impact . . . But the "sacrifice" would have meant primarily an emotional involvement, which the actors and workers reject. The theatre still serves the function of debating *in front of* an audience and *with* an audience with the tools of farce and satire, and theatrical dialectic, the themes of class struggle, so that everyone . . . is a protagonist . . .'

Fo, in Artese, *Dario Fo parla di Dario Fo*, 1977, pp. 115, 117.

'There is nothing more removed from "agit-prop" in the banal sense of the word, or, on the other hand, from a Pirandellian game in which theatre and reality exhaust each other by reflecting each other. Or rather, it is precisely because Fo's farces use both openly, that they become something else. . . . in *The Boss's Funeral* there are three levels interacting: an almost naturalistic account of a factory occupied by its workers surrounded by the police; then the ludic level of the death and burial of the boss enacted by his workers; and the fairy tale intervention of the Great Vulture "who transports heavenly souls", also played by a worker. In this detour into fairy tale and cheap romance we recognise the reality of the factory: its smells, pollution, work accidents and exploitation. In the end, the theatre is turned upside down, and reveals its innards. It appears as what it is: the space where a fiction destroys itself in the course of being acted out and extends into the area of class struggle.'

Bernard Dort, *Théâtre en jeu 1970–1976*, 1977, pp. 204-5.

'The anti-technological and anti-exploitation topography expressed in these two short plays draw their inspiration from the necessity of the moment, that is, by adapting previous works to new situations. . . . Studying the differences between the two versions, one can easily explain Fo's militant approach to theatre and particularly the emphasis he places on its didactic and polemical value, over and above its purely aesthetic qualities. In the later version, stress is laid on the message that the only way to bring about any radical social, political and economic change is by building a genuinely revolutionary party. The play is thus not a static presentation of one fixed, immutable message, but a flexible and dynamic instrument of analysis.'

Mario B. Mignone, 'Dario Fo: Jester of the Italian Stage', *Italian Quarterly*, no. 85, 1981, p. 56.

'. . . These one-acts are interesting for their criticism, from a left-wing point of view, of the PCI, which is accused of collusion with the bourgeoisie and reminded of its radical revolutionary duties at exactly the moment when it was widening its power-base towards the centre and evolving the concept of the national path to socialism. What . . . emerge . . . are Fo's increasingly Maoist views – views not easily tolerated by the PCI.'

Lino Pertile, 'Dario Fo', in Caesar and Hainsworth (eds.), *Writers and Society in Contemporary Italy*, 1984, pp. 179-80.

I'd Rather Die Tonight If I Had To Think It Had All Been In Vain (*Vorrei morire anche stasera se dovessi pensare che non è servito a niente*)

Two-act play subtitled: 'Resistance: The Italian and Palestinian People Speak' (*Resistenza: parla il popolo italiano e palestinese*)
First production: Capannone di via Colletta, Milan, 27 Oct 1970 (dir. Fo).

The title comes from a poem of the Italian Resistance by Renata Viganò, and the play combines readings, songs, mimes and monologues based on accounts of experiences of Italian partisans (in the first act). These are compared and contrasted with personal testaments by participants in the Palestinian Liberation Movement (in the second act). Put together after only one day's rehearsal, the play was a response to the events of the Black September of terrorist events in the Middle East. It includes an account by Franca Rame of Luisa, a woman from Bologna who was tortured and raped by fascists, but who still holds out hopes that Communism will come. There is also an account by Fo of the partisan Angiolino Bertoli who goes on an expedition to blow up an army barracks, and has to hide in a septic tank. In 'The Bestiary', the Russian bear pretends to help the weaker animals of the Middle East against the American tiger, but ends up making an agreement with the tiger and tramples on the rights of the other animals. Another animal fable pits the roosters of Amman against the pigs of King Hussein's police force.

'What emerges is a cry of disappointment and revolt rather than a re-evocation; it is an attempt to convey to a present-day audience the revolutionary impulse which inspired the Resistance . . . Fo and Rame reproduce only the more advanced aspects of the Fedayin resistance, those which inspired the overthrow of the old feudal regime before the war against Israel . . . in the second act Fo and his company seek a positive outlet for the disappointments exposed in the first part, talking about a "people's" war ... The discussion after the play included among other things not only a violent attack against the USSR, but also an attack against the PCI, which had been presented in the first part as the sole motivating force of the Resistance. ... This really raises the question of who Fo is addressing himself to ... Who does he expect to listen to him?'

Edoardo Fadini, Rinascita, 13 Nov 1970.

'... An extremely effective play; its scrupulous montage was "scientific", to use Fo's expression ... in the careful precision of the timing, rhythm and tension between performed texts and songs ... and its effectiveness and ability to "keep the audience nailed to their seats" and lead them into a situation of dialectical conflict and compel them to take up a position ... '

Lanfranco Binni, Attento te!, 1975, p. 320.

Accidental Death of an Anarchist (*Morte accidentale di un anarchico*)

Two-act play.
First production: Capannone di via Colletta, 10 Dec 1970 (dir. Fo).
British and Irish productions: Belt and Braces, Dartington College, Jan 1979; Half Moon Theatre, London, Oct 1979; Wyndham's Theatre, London, 5 Mar 1980; Oscar Theatre, Dublin, 10 Feb 1981 (dir. Jim Sheridan); Contact Theatre, Manchester, 3 Mar 1982; Druid Theatre Co., Galway, 13 Apr 1982; Hawks Well Theatre, Sligo, 10 May 1982; Belltable Theatre, Limerick, 17 May 1982; Lyric Players Theatre, Belfast, 18 May 1982; New Vic Studio, Bristol, 18 May 1982; Central Studios, Hampshire, June 1982; Wolsey Theatre, Ipswich, 24 Nov 1982; Liverpool Playhouse, 25 Nov 1982; Cork Theatre, 26 Jan 1983; Chester Gateway Theatre, 26 Jan 1983; Newcastle Playhouse, 10 Feb 1983; Theatre Workshop, Edinburgh, 1 Mar 1983. TV version, Channel 4, 14 Sept 1983 (trans. Gillian

Hanna, adapt. & dir. Gavin Richards); Bloomsbury Theatre, 1
Nov 1988 (dir. Andy Arnold); Towngate Theatre, Pagel Mead,
Basildon, Essex, 2 Oct 1990; Cottesloe Theatre, Royal National
Theatre, London, 4 Jan 1991 (trans. Alan Cumming & Tim
Supple, dir. Tim Supple); Contact Theatre, Manchester, 1997
(trans. Ed Emery).
North American productions: Open Circle Theater,
Toronto, 13 Mar 1980 (trans. Suzanne Cowan, adapt. & dir. R.
G. Davis); Mark Taper Forum, Los Angeles, Jan 1983 (adapt.
John Lahr, dir. Mel Shapiro); Arena Theater, Washington, 9
Feb 1984 and Belasco Theater, Broadway, 15 Nov 1984 (adapt.
Richard Nelson, dir. Douglas C. Wager); Eureka Theater, San
Francisco, Nov 1984 (adapt. Joan Holden, dir. Anthony
Taccone).
Australian productions: Nimrod Theatre, Sydney, 15 Jan
1981; Fortune Theatre, Canberra, 12 Sept 1981 and Melbourne
Theatre Company, 2 Feb 1983 (trans. Tony Mitchell, adapt. &
dir. Brent McGregor); T.N! Theatre, Brisbane, 29 Feb 1984
(dir. Rod Wissler); State Theatre of South Australia, the
Playhouse, Adelaide, 16 Apr 1994; Footbridge Theatre, Sydney,
20 May 1994 (trans. Alan Cumming & Tim Supple, adapt. &
dir. Robyn Archer).

A 'Maniac' infiltrates the Milan Police Station, where an
anarchist suspect has 'fallen' to his death from a fourth-floor
window during interrogation about a series of bomb explosions
in Milan. The Maniac poses as an examining magistrate
conducting an inquiry into the anarchist's death, interrogating
the police officers who were present at the time of the 'leap'.
After demolishing any semblance of credibility in the conflicting
and implausible police accounts of events, he convinces them
the only solution is to follow the anarchist's example and leap
out the window. He then persuades them to construct a new
version of events which will win them public sympathy, and
which involves singing an anarchist song to prove how well
disposed they were to the suspect. In the second act, a woman
Journalist arrives to interview the police about the case for a

magazine. The Maniac 'disguises' himself first as a forensic expert, then a bishop, to conceal his 'identity' from her, while managing to convince her the police are responsible for the anarchist's death. Unmasked, the Maniac handcuffs the police, and produces a detonator for a bomb which has been shown as evidence. He then reveals that he has taped the entire proceedings and will give the tape to the media.

'I realised we needed a decoy character, a surety, so to speak. And then I got the idea that this surety could be a madman who holds the key . . . to all the madness, and he becomes normal, while everything else is abnormal. A total reversal. Another important thing we noticed in explanations of the story was indignation . . . we realised that indignation is really a means of catharsis, liberation and letting off steam. This . . . became central . . . The play was conceived in a grotesque style to avoid any dramatic catharsis. If we had created a dramatic play instead of a comic, grotesque and satirical play, we would have created another liberating catharsis. But this play doesn't allow you this outlet, because when you laugh, the sediment of anger stays inside you, and can't get out. It's no wonder dictatorial governments always forbid laughter and satire first, rather than drama.'

Fo, 1970, in Meldolesi, *Su un comico in rivolta*, 1978, pp. 178-9.

'. . . A grotesque farce about a tragic farce . . . popular theatre has always used the grotesque and farce – which was invented by the people – to develop dramatic arguments . . . Anger and hatred must become conscious action in collaboration with others, and not just the individual letting off steam in an impotent way . . . This play about the assassination of Pinelli has two main features, which are also pointers towards work and hence confrontation for anyone who is active on the cultural front. First and foremost the "documentary theatre" aspect; a theatre which sets out to interpret the current movement of class struggle, which participates in it as a form of critical consciousness, which is against any position of flat, naturalistic description of "phenomena", but has instead a conscious desire for historical and political "synthesis". The second feature is that of language which has its roots in the rich cultural heritage of popular culture, satire and grotesque farce.'

Fo, Introduction to *Pum, pum! Chi è? La polizia!*, 1974, pp. 11-3.

'But what has been the real reason for the show's success? It is not so much the way it mocks the hypocrisies, the lies that are organised so grossly and blatantly (which is putting it mildly) by the constituted organs of the State and by the functionaries who serve them (judges, police chiefs, prefects, under-secretaries and ministers); it has been above all the way it deals with social democracy and its crocodile tears, the indignation which can be relieved by a little burp in the form of scandal; scandal as a liberating catharsis of the system . . . But unluckily for them, they will have to realise that there are a lot of us . . . and this time their burp is going to stick in their throats.'

Fo, Postscript to *Accidental Death of an Anarchist*, trans. Ed Emery, *Dario Fo Plays: One*, 1992, 1997, pp. 77-8.

'. . . An exemplary farce which, using the paradoxical techniques of his "mid period" plays, dismantles and continually reassembles, with rapidly mounting pace and entertainment, the false and conflicting versions of the outrageous judicial case presented by the police. This is an example of great theatre, in which the wild inventiveness of the writing blends harmoniously with the aims of counter-information, and succeeds in having a concrete effect on consolidating public opinion in a way one rarely sees happen.'

Franco Quadri, Introduction to *Le commedie di Dario Fo*, vol. 3, 1989, pp. xiii-xiv.

'Obviously, the shows *have* to be altered when they're transported into a British context. They take on other values, other modes of expression, other cultural styles, etc. But at the same time, some of the shows – I am thinking of the production of *Accidental Death* . . . which I saw here in London – seem to me very overloaded, verging terribly on the grotesque. Many people, though, have said that they liked that production . . . even with the excessive buffoonery that they introduced into it. . . . In my opinion these productions lack subtlety. They lack detachment, which must be the first main quality of an "epic" actor.'

Fo, in *Theatre Workshops at Riverside Studios*, 1983, pp. 67–8.

'Despite the moralising tone of the last half-hour, *Morte accidentale* is certainly Fo's best achievement in the vein of dramatic topicality. Differing from the more broadly didactic *Mistero buffo*, it captures the moment of direct intervention, when popular awareness, restored to the people by the jester, is enlisted into the daily praxis of class struggle. And it captures, more vividly than any literary work of the time, the enthusiasm, the agitation, the anxiety and fear which swept Italy.'

Lino Pertile, 'Dario Fo', in Caesar and Hainsworth (eds.), *Writers and Society in Contemporary Italy*, 1984, p. 183.

'The capacity of Fo's buffoon to impersonate policemen, anarchists, judge, and bishop fosters a comic, carnivalesque vision of society where, as Bakhtin said of the carnival in Rabelais's world, people become interchangeable in their mass body. Fo becomes a one-man carnival, and amply represents the collectivity . . .'

Joel Schechter, *The Un-American Satire of Dario Fo*, 1984, pp. 116–17.

'Don't call my play a comedy. There is a misunderstanding of the word. I call it farce. In current language, farce is understood as vulgar, trivial, facile, very simple. In truth, this is a cliché of official culture. What they call comedy today has lost the rebellious strain of ancient times. What is provocative and rebellious is farce. The establishment goes for comedy, the people for farce.'

Fo, Programme note for Washington Arena production of *Accidental Death*, 1984.

'Can the killing of *Accidental Death of an Anarchist*, at the Arena
Stage in Washington, be an accident? The answer to that
question could go to the bone of American politics if such a
sweeping view wouldn't seem to exonerate adaptor Richard
Nelson, director Douglas Wager, and producer Zelda
Fichlander from responsibility for the loss of nerve, intelligence,
and focus that has occurred in their adaptation of Dario Fo's
"tragic farce". . . . Nelson has ruthlessly Simonized it,
substituting random gags for forceful satire. Fo never writes
gags, hit-and-run jokes grabbing laughs. Nelson's utterly deflect
the play's political urgency.'

Elinor Fuchs, 'Their Fo is Folly', *Village Voice*, 20 Mar 1984.

'It didn't work at the Mark Taper Forum . . . and . . . it doesn't
really work on Broadway. But finally an American company has
got Dario Fo's *Accidental Death of an Anarchist* right. . . . the
Eureka Theatre of San Francisco . . . had the sense to go to Joan
Holden for an adaptation . . . Holden has been writing scripts
for the San Francisco Mime Troupe for 15 years – the closest
thing we have to Fo's radical theatre troupe in Italy. Like Fo,
Holden knows that the first thing that people's theatre has to do
is be entertaining. . . . Holden's *Accidental Death* does so, the
message snaking in underneath.'

Dan Sullivan, 'Bicoastal *Accidental Death*', *Los Angeles Times*,
25 Nov 1984

'All the North American productions of *Anarchist*, including
my own, have failed to match the author's intentions, have
misunderstood the structure of the work, and have not given
enough importance to the casting of a recognisably political
actor in the lead. . . . So far, most US productions of
Anarchist have tried to downplay or ignore the politics.
Producers, directors and players have aimed for a slapstick
hit. Their thinking seems to be that the more the play is de-
politicised, the better will be its reception from the public
and the critics. The rub is that when you ignore the political
content of *Anarchist* you swamp both the politics *and* the
comedy. It will not serve to cast a clown in the main role. A

way must be found to politicise the comedy and fill the politics with humour.'

R. G. Davis, 'Seven Anarchists I Have Known', *New Theatre Quarterly*, Nov 1986, pp. 313, 318.

'My chief memory of the original Belt and Braces production back in 1979 is of a breakneck farce with Alfred Molina as the protagonist looking like Tommy Cooper on speed; this new version by Alan Cumming and Tim Supple is far less funny but politically more potent.

'It treats the play as moral satire rather than grotesque farce. . . . the quality that makes Fo uniquely powerful, the ability to wring wild laughter out of insidious corruption, is here deliberately muted: instead of guilty ecstasy we get careful point-scoring. . . . This is Fo shrewdly updated but without his carnivalesque danger.'

Michael Billington, *The Guardian*, 9 Jan 1991.

'Dario Fo's play is a farce; but it is written by a man who combines the hilarious impertinence of a music hall comic with the moral fervour of a Savonarola. Supple directs it as simply a batty farce; he forgets that farce can be dangerous, and that Fo exploits this brilliantly, with a sense of menace which is both hilarious and shocking.

'This is essentially a harmless, jolly English production, constantly tipping a wink to the audience, and having fun with a Prince Charles take-off and references to Chief Constable Anderton. Fo has written a lethal parody of a very real and very nasty political crime story; Supple has turned it into a flaccid sitcom.'

John Peter, *Sunday Times*, 13 Jan 1991.

'Dario Fo has not always been pleased with British performances of his moral farces. The production of *Accidental Death of an Anarchist* that introduced West End audiences to his work in 1980 struck him as lacking in satiric bile and bite, too often "exclusively comic". Yet the National Theatre's revival of the same play last year he thought too solemn and didactic. The balance, as he is the first to agree, is diabolically hard to catch and, as he is too polite to add, does not come easily to Anglo-Saxons.'

Benedict Nightingale, *The Times*, 15 Apr 1992.

United We Stand! All Together Now! Oops, Isn't That the Boss? (*Tutti uniti! Tutti insieme! Ma scusa, quello non è il padrone?*)

Two-act play, subtitled: 'Workers' Struggles 1911–1922' (*Lotte operaie 1911-1922*).
First production: Casa del Popolo, Varese, 27 Mar. 1971 (dir. Fo).

The play follows the political education of Antonia Berazzi, a dressmaker, who develops from an apolitical, naive representative of the world of high fashion into a revolutionary activist. Her husband, Norberto, a militant in the revolutionary wing of the Italian Socialist Party, is killed by a fascist squad. Antonia, pretending to be a police informer, infiltrates police headquarters, where a secret deal is taking place involving a trade unionist, an industrialist's wife, a police superintendent, a colonel and a fascist. Antonia avenges her husband by shooting the fascist, and the body is dumped in the same rubbish tip where Norberto was shot along with 20 other comrades. Antonio regrets her action, however, since she has 'killed the dog instead of the masters'. The story proceeds through a series of flashbacks. In 1911, Antonia is caught in a police raid of a subversive meeting at which she is an unwitting participant, and Norberto is arrested after she criticises Mussolini. Her wedding coincides with Italy's entry into the First World War and clashes between patriots and socialists opposed to the war. In 1917 Antonia visits Norberto in prison, and tells him the Socialist Party leaders have refused to support the insurrectionary struggles in Turin. In 1920 the factory occupations by workers in Turin, led by Gramsci, are shown to be betrayed by the socialist leaders and trade unionists who make a deal with the government.

'Even though the play's predominant form is certainly not grotesque, much of the action which the dressmaker is the protagonist of is made up of farcical gags. Antonia's language is full of proverbs and jargon which have their roots in popular culture. Her character is built around one of the *commedia* masks: the *étourdie*. She is a kind of vamp who gradually acquires political awareness and becomes *étourdie* (scatterbrained) in a cunning and calculating way.'

Fo, in *Sipario*, Mar 1971.

'While we were touring around the employment centres and cooperative headquarters where the working class invited us for discussions, this historical period kept on coming up – 1911 and the arrival of fascism. A lot of old people who had lived through this period demonstrated in what they said that even they had not become aware of the historical significance of those years. So there was a need for, first, a clear understanding of them, and then sustained research into them. Since we'd left the bourgeois theatre to put ourselves at the service of the "working class", we had an obligation to develop this subject, and untangle the confusion, since it involved the origins of the whole workers' movement in Italy. And now that there is a resurgence of fascism it's even more important to understand the origins and reason for today's fascism, even if the situations are different from an objective viewpoint.'

Fo, 'Teatro di situazione uguale teatro popolare',
Sipario, May 1971, p. 43.

'Fo's play has a curious and quite innovative structure . . . It is built on a farcical form based on striking gags, historical and documentary events inserted in flashbacks (relating the dressmaker's life story) . . . and violent, political songs which deliberately provoke the audience and break up the dramatic narrative, giving the play a street-theatre quality which Dario Fo has perhaps incorporated for the first time. He does so prudently, like the old hand he is at theatrical experimentation . . . a noteworthy advance on *Accidental Death of an Anarchist.*'

Edoardo Fadini, Rinascita, no. 18, 1971.

'. . . The internal structure is marked by a violent play of emotional chiaroscuro which is sustained by a desire to involve the audience, totally manipulating and controlling them through the mechanism of identification and projection. This is evidenced by the rigid alternation between serious, emotional sequences (which are not tragic, however . . .) and comic sequences . . . an often congenial and wildly scatological thread places certain aspects of the play in the equivocal area of provincial vaudeville and popular *avanspettacolo*. Hence it would almost seem that the Gramscian lesson, cited openly here as elsewhere by Fo, of the need for a class culture . . . is interpreted in reverse, by retaining from this lesson its ambiguously populist aspects, whereby melodrama and vaudeville are seen as real models for an audience that is more petit bourgeois than working class. For Gramsci, these models were intended to be used in an . . . introductory fashion, to initiate a certain type of lively, authentic dialogue with the target audience.'

Paolo Puppa, L'erba voglia, Apr 1972.

'Undoubtedly in terms of playwriting, the form of *United We Stand!* . . . is different from the other plays of that period, like *Anarchist* . . . and there is a lack of pace and spontaneity which appears to be due to the didactic structure within which the play develops. There are a number of static parts, and signs that a story is being told rather than represented on stage.'

Lanfranco Binni, Attento te! . . . , 1975, p. 319.

'. . . In the story of the sub-proletarian woman in *United We Stand! All Together Now!* which is about her gaining political awareness, there is a clear historical situation: the disunity of the workers' movement, for which the leaders of the Communist Party are largely responsible on both an ideological and an organisational level. This, together with the split and the lack of faith in the power of the proletariat, are the basis of a real political situation.

'The play is about the consciousness of a woman in conflict with her situation of being a woman and being exploited. It even involves a love story, which is not presented in metaphorical terms, but as the living relationship between a woman and a man which is the consequence of this consciousness, and the cultural, political and moral transformation, the ideological and moral change, which is fundamental for this woman.'

Fo, 'Aspects of Popular Theatre', *New Theatre Quarterly*, May 1985.

Fedayin (Fedayn)

Two-act play subtitled: 'The Palestinian Revolution through its Culture and Songs' (*La rivoluzione palestinese attraverso la sua cultura e i suoi canti*).
First production: Capannone di via Colletta, Milan, Jan 1972 (dir. Fo).

A documentary play about the Palestinian struggles, performed by Franca Rame and eight members of the Popular Front for the Liberation of Palestine, with simultaneous translation from Arabic to Italian, slides, masks and songs. A 13-year-old girl narrates how she joined the Fedayin at the age of nine, and had to kill another nine-year-old who was wounded, so that she wouldn't be captured and interrogated by King Hussein's Jordanian bedouins. In a modern version of the story of Judith and Holofernes, a Palestinian woman sleeps with and then kills a captain from Hussein's police force, a well-known torturer of the Fedayin. A thief gives up his life of crime to join the guerillas, and a man fighting on the Al Fatah side sees the error of his ways and joins the Popular Front. Women try to prevent ancient traditional customs like their exclusion from funeral services and the whipping of brides on their wedding night. A woman whose Fedayin son has been killed pleads for him not to be made a hero, because 'our stories should be true stories about men who trip up, who have constant doubts, who are afraid, but who don't run away.'

'You are trying to distinguish between honest and dishonest Fedayins. This argument is not political, nor is it acceptable; you can't split a resistance movement, which should be united, into honest and dishonest factions, into right and left, as you are doing.'

Union of Palestinian Students representative, in Valentini, *La storia di Dario Fo*, 1977, p. 143.

'. . . This is not a play conceived along classical lines, nor does it follow any rigidly expository or narrative thread. It is a montage of testimonies, songs, slides, readings from documents, théâtre-vérité sketches, explanatory speeches and asides, reflections and comments on particular events, more or less along the lines pursued by Piscator in 1925 when he produced *Trotz alleden!* . . . through these means the play achieves more than any work of the imagination could in managing to convey a sense of the upheaval that the Palestinian people have gone through, and gives a desperately epic quality to their struggle for survival . . . the question as to whether or not this is theatre seems an idle one.'

Aldo Paladino, 'Dario Fo nipotino politico di Piscator', *Il Dramma*, Sept–Oct 1972, pp. 28, 30.

'Apart from the riots and the often pretentious polemics, and despite the later, partly self-critical statement by La Comune and the PFLP that they had dealt too directly with the internal problems of the Palestinian resistance movement in a situation of general lack of information (which may have led to sectarian interpretations of the play, particularly its criticisms of the Al Fatah position), *Fedayin* remains a coherently internationalist play, in its production aspects as well as its content . . . a militant play in the fullest sense of the word, arising from specific political needs of the [revolutionary] movement in Italy and a concrete response to the need for "support" on every level, requested by a liberation movement.'

Lanfranco Binni, *Attento te! . . .*, 1975, p. 338.

'They were theatrical statements which theatre people made in order not to feel paralysed by the struggles of particular people. They are useful because they can help others to break out of the same sort of feeling, which is natural because of the alarm which events caused . . . *Fedayin* dealt with the significance of the split between the right and the left of the Palestinian resistance movement, and the crisis in the movement after the massacre in July at Gerashea Ajlun. The limitations of these plays and the information they provide, seen in retrospect, are due to the need for a quick statement, which can sometimes lead to presenting arguments which are provisional and hasty.'

Fo, in Artese, *Dario Fo parla de Dario Fo*, pp. 127-8.

Knock Knock! Who's There? Police! (*Pum, pum! Chi è? La polizia!*)

Two-act play.
First production: Circolo Quarticciolo La Comune, Rome, 7 Dec 1972 (dir. Fo).

A sequel to *Accidental Death of an Anarchist*, performed as a rehearsed reading, and written for the third anniversary of the bomb explosions in Milan's Piazza Fontana, after which the anarchist Pinelli was interrogated. It is set in the Italian Ministry of the Interior, with a chorus of civil servants who sing songs commenting on the action. The play begins with investigations into the bomb explosion at the Banca dell'Agricoltura and the police manhunt for the anarchists Valpreda and Pinelli. A taxi driver's evidence suggests that fascists are implicated in the bombing. But the Chief of Secret Police (played by Fo) instructs that fascist leads should not be followed up, despite the known involvement of one Valerio Borghese in an attempted right-wing coup d'état. In the second act, Andreotti gives orders to direct the police inquiry into right-wing terrorist groups. Specific people and events of the 'strategy of tension' are mentioned by name, and continual news updates on events are telephoned in to the Chief. He repeatedly asks what the man in the street thinks about the situation, and attempts to quell the mass movement of mobilisation against the 'state massacres' by offering the people sex and mass executions. The Chief also performs *Scapin's Grammelot*, a lesson in theatrical hypocrisy taken from Molière, which is presented as a demonstration of 'the real art of a Christian Democrat minister'. The play ends with a song inviting people not to 'hang their head, or the boss will break their neck.'

'. . . Extends the argument begun in my play about the death of comrade Pinelli. It is a didactic play, and an attempt to synthesise the historical process which is underway: three years of history of the "state massacres" and their class enemy, the working class and its supporters, who have caused the angry and defensive reaction of the Italian bourgeoisie to action which has been largely spontaneous. In this case the weapon of demystification is again the grotesque . . . the "state massacres" and their criminal developments have been reconstructed in grotesque form from the point of view of the authorities, in an office which played a fundamental role in the Piazza Fontana operation.'

Fo, Introduction to *Pum, pum!*, 1974, pp. 13-4.

'. . . Written in seven or eight days, and rehearsed in eight days . . . a long gag lasting a good two and a half hours; convulsive and frenetic with telephone calls, functionaries coming and going, orders from the ministry, and the arrival and departure of documents, information, instructions to the police, news, etc. . . . In the first act the attacks against the PCI are cautious. In the second act a squalid biliousness emerges, culminating in the final debate, which instead of being a discussion embellishing and correcting the play ... is a tirade indicting our party as the real enemy of the working class.'

Edoardo Fadini, *Rinascita*, 22 Dec 1972.

'As usual, truncheons speedily interpret the need for law and order ... The play was not in fact designed to please the police force ... But Fo and Rame have been making a nuisance of themselves for quite a number of reasons ... Guaranteeing Fo the freedom to perform does not mean talking about the freedom of art and culture, nor is it the same thing as fighting for Marlon Brando's right to use butter ... In our permissive society comics have not been a cause for alarm for some time now. But this comic is a cause for alarm, to the extent that there are attempts to get rid of him with police warrants as well as by other means, and to give him a brutal warning: "If you carry on the way you're going, you're a dead man." ... Is there any real difference between a country where an MP is beaten up for speaking in parliament and a country where a woman is tortured because she talks about political problems on a stage?'

Umberto Eco, 'Pum, pum! Chi è? Fascisti!', *L'Espresso*, 18 Mar 1973.

The People's War in Chile (*Guerra di popolo in Cile*)

Two-act play.
First production: Palazzo dello Sport, Bolzano, 20 Oct 1973 (dir. Fo).

A montage of monologues, songs and sketches written and performed by Fo, Rame and the Sicilian *cantastorie* Cicciu Busacca, in response to the coup in Chile. A duet on the last transmission of the Chilean radio station MIR is followed by a digression on international politics and in particular the Middle East, comparing Golda Meir with a parrot. A song about

Murieta, a Chilean activist in the miners' struggle who becomes an outlaw and is killed in a battle is followed by the Chilean Christian Democratic party, personified as the madam of a brothel, who backs the coup and appeals to the Pope for support. An 'incident' occurs in which police messages received in the theatre indicate that there has been a *coup d'état* in Italy. In the second act, a monologue and songs celebrate the songs and revolutionary example of Victor Jara. *Cicciu Corno*, a piece by Busacca, tells how the donkey used to have a horn with which it defended weaker animals. It was tricked by the powerful animals into cutting it off so they could kill the other animals, proving that 'only the revolution can save the proletariat.' The last piece is *Mamma Togni*, a monologue about a woman who drives away fascist speakers from a platform with a stick. She is arrested, but released to general public acclaim. The play ends with a discussion with the audience.

'. . . We tried out improvisation techniques; it was a play in which all the actors came on stage one at a time and played characters who were apparently unrelated to one another – it was basically a series of interlinked monologues. But the main element was provocation, which is why we were attacked by some left-wing magazines, and by comrades from some groups, for the play's violence and realism in terms of provocation. They said we'd played a "dirty trick" on them and treated serious matters too lightly, namely the possibility of a coup d'état. . . . [in] popular theatre you find the same techniques, namely "incidents", ruthless violent provocation which makes you sit up straight . . . You find the same sort of provocation in El Teatro Campesino, and again in the stories which comrades tell us now about Porto Margera, where there were demonstrations with Christs on crosses in the streets . . . We realised that our recent experiences had given us the courage to overturn the rules of a theatre which has always been looked upon like the Parthenon.'

Fo, 'Popular Culture', *Theater*, Summer/Fall 1983, p. 53.

'It is probably the first time in the history of the theatre that an

actor was taken directly from the stage to prison, before he had
even begun his performance, with an armed escort usually
reserved for important criminals.'

Chiara Valentini, Panorama, 22 Nov 1973.

'My opinion of Dario Fo and his work is so negative that I refuse
to talk about him. Fo is a kind of plague on the Italian theatre.
I should say the worst possible things about him, but this doesn't
seem an appropriate time.'

Pier Paolo Pasolini, Panorama, 22 Nov 1973.

'[Pasolini] is undoubtedly one of the greatest cultural figures of
our time. He had an extraordinarily coherent relationship with
his own life. He was a literary figure of great strength and
geniality. But he wasn't a playwright. I understand why he
disapproved of me, since I had previously indicated that he was
unable to "create theatre", in connection with a play he was
attempting to stage. His work just didn't stand up; it was merely
literature, and didn't have the necessary basic grounding in
theatre, or the dialogue necessary for theatre, or the timing or
the structure. He was greatly offended by this; he was furious.
That's my explanation for his negative statement about me.'

Fo, Moda Italia, Sept 1985, p. 340.

Can't Pay? Won't Pay! (Non si paga! Non si paga!)

A Farce in Two Acts.
First production: Palazzina Liberty, Milan, 3 Oct 1974 (dir.
Fo). New, revised version, Palazzina Liberty, 16 Sept 1980
(dir. Fo).
British and Irish productions: (as *We Can't Pay? We Won't
Pay!*, trans. Lino Pertile, adapt. Bill Colville and Robert
Walker:) Half Moon Theatre, London, 22 May 1978 (dir.
Robert Walker); Oxford Theatre Group, Edinburgh Festival,
Aug 1980 (dir. Tim Sebel); Overground Theatre Company,
Kingston-upon-Thames, Oct 1980 (dir. Philip Partridge);

Phoenix Arts Theatre, Leicester, Jan 1981; Leeds Playhouse, Apr 1981. (As *Can't Pay? Won't Pay!*:) Criterion Theatre, London, 15 July 1981 (dir. Robert Walker); Victoria Theatre, Stoke-on-Trent, 6 Oct 1982; Drumbeat Company, Plymouth, 7 Feb 1983; Project Arts Centre, Dublin, May 1983; Cambridge Theatre Company, May 1983; Legit Theatre Company, Dublin, June 1983; Crucible Theatre, Sheffield, July 1983; Spectacle Theatre Company, Glamorgan, Wales, 13 Feb 1984; Civic Theatre, Chelmsford, 13 Feb 1984; Dukes Playhouse, Lancaster, 4 Apr 1984; Torch Theatre, Milford Haven, Oct 1985 (dir. Les Miller); Royal Lyceum, Edinburgh (with additional Scottish material by Alex Norton), 1988; Lyric, Hammersmith, 19 Mar 1990 (dir. Alexander Bridge).

North American productions: (as *We Won't Pay! We Won't Pay!*:) Tamahous Theater, Vancouver, Sept 1980 (adapt. & dir. R. G. Davis); Chelsea Theater Center, New York, 16 Dec 1980 (adapt. & dir. R. G. Davis); Empty Space Theater, Seattle, 12 May 1981 (dir. Richard Edwards); San Francisco Mime Troupe, 1981 (dir. Joan Holden); (as *We Can't Pay? We Won't Pay!*:) Open Circle, Toronto, Sept 1981 (dir. Sylvia Tucker); Los Angeles Actors' Theater, Sept 1981; Wisdom Bridge Theater, Chicago, 1985.

Australian productions: (as *We Can't Pay? We Won't Pay!*:) Wood Street Theatre, Newcastle, May 1980 (trans. Margaret Kunzle, dir. Brent McGregor); New Theatre, Sydney, July 1980; New Theatre, Melbourne, Apr 1981; Q Theatre, Penrith, June 1981; Troupe Theatre, South Australia, 8 Oct 1981; Theatre South, Wollongong, Mar 1982; TN! Theatre, Brisbane, 24 Mar 1982; Murray River Performing Group, Dec 1982 (trans. Lino Pertile, adapt. Bill Colville & Robert Walker); Universal Theatre, Melbourne, June 1983 (dir. Lois Ellis); (as *Don't Pay! Don't Pay!*:) Theatre ACT, Canberra, 7 Sept 1985 (trans. Tony Mitchell, dir. John Derum).

Antonia, a working-class Milanese woman, has pilfered some goods from her local supermarket after a protest against rising prices has developed into a riot of looting. She and her neighbour Margherita set about trying to hide the stolen goods from their line-toeing PCI husbands, and Margherita stuffs a bag of groceries down her coat. Giovanni, Antonia's husband, catches sight of Margherita on his arrival home, and Antonia tells him Margherita is pregnant but has been hiding the fact. Antonia goes to Margherita's place to borrow something for dinner. Giovanni is visited by a Maoist police constable who is searching their apartment block for stolen goods, but is in favour of civil disobedience. Antonia returns with Margherita, and they are searched again by more police, who end up taking both women to a maternity hospital for a 'baby transplant'. Luigi, Margherita's husband, arrives with news that he, Giovanni and their workmates have been retrenched. Giovanni tells him of his wife's 'pregnancy', and they set off for the maternity hospital. In Act Two, Antonia and Margherita, after giving police and hospital the slip, return home and start transporting their 'shopping' to a garden shed. Luigi and Giovanni meet the Maoist constable again at a road accident involving a truckload of stolen sacks of sugar, rice and flour. Encouraged by the constable, they steal some sacks and transport them home in a coffin. A police sergeant apprehends the two women with their 'pregnant' bellies, but they convince him he has gone blind when the electricity is cut off. They then blow up his stomach with oxygen in an attempt to revive him after he knocks himself unconscious. Finally, the thefts by both the husbands and the wives are revealed to one another. Giovanni is convinced that civil disobedience is the only effective way of fighting oppression and exploitation, and the police sergeant revives, convinced he is pregnant. Finally, in a riot in the street hundreds of women drive away a battalion of police.

'We've tried to avoid the pitfalls of ideological didacticism by means of a "theatre of situation". This is a means similar to that of "epic theatre", where it's not the characters who advance the action, but the situation, the theatrical mechanism. The development is determined and sustained by events, and the characters involved in the situation are the gears which move or manoeuvre this mechanism. This flick of a switch can release a mechanism of paradox, then blow it up like a photo, intensify it, stand it on its head, speed it up, or explode it.

'This isn't a "career" choice, even if the career aspect of this type of theatre is important. It's a cultural choice, because being involved in a theatre of situation means representing a story rather than acting it. It means not being involved in the "drama" arising from the individual character and his or her private and individual problems and relationships with others, but rather dealing with everybody's problems in the context of a collective drama. These problems emerge in an explosive way in a dialectical conflict of relationships within a "situation". The actual drafting of the play is my sole responsibility, but from the first improvised reading to the final *mise en scène* the text has been discussed repeatedly, not only among our collective, but above all with workers' groups and committees from various different factories in Milan. . . . This is, in our opinion, the correct way to run a "collective" theatre.'

Fo, 1974, Editorial note to *Non si paga! Non si paga!*

'Deals with the very vital current issue of civil disobedience, in the form of battles against increases in market and service prices, new instances of which are continually being reported in the newspapers. But what is outstanding about it is that Fo, with the sensibility and awareness that make him one of the most extraordinary figures in Italian theatre, has imagined these episodes before they actually happened. Then reality began to imitate art.'

Alberto Blandi, *La Stampa*, 3 Oct 1974.

'A real farce in the 1958–59 mould: all the comic ingredients are there, from coffins in the cupboard to cross-dressing, from *coups de théâtre* to grotesque miracles; here and there didactic declarations about current events are badly integrated into the play's fabric (a typical example being the final "epic" song).'

Lanfranco Binni, *Dario Fo*, 1977, p. 78.

'. . . Amidst the laughter at the implausible twists and turns of this extremely threadbare story, or one of Fo's gags, which are getting more and more recycled and almost as if quoted from his arsenal in a process of self-codification like Eduardo [de Filippo], amidst the *lazzi* and the games, embarrassment and annoyance crept in . . . [and] a discomfort not at the politics, but at the rhetoric of the politics.'

Ugo Volli, *La Repubblica*, 19 Sept 1980.

'It is rare to find a farce original enough to forget bedroom antics and find jokes in rising prices and quips in unpaid bills and redundancy notices. This Dario Fo does with ease, thanks to an ever-bubbling onrush of comic ideas and a natural liking for anyone in a desperate fix. He makes you glad to be alive.'

John Barber, *Daily Telegraph*, 17 July 1981.

'As the ascent of Vaclav Havel has shown, there must always be hope that art will prevail over tyranny. Mediocrity, though, is a more pernicious enemy, and it is by numbing mediocrity that Dario Fo's comic satire is grievously shafted in Alexander Bridge's flaccid revival. . . . there is nothing political or Italian or satirical or even funny about this wheezing production, played by the cast as if it were *Move Over, Mrs Markham* at Leatherhead. It makes for one of those limbo evenings in the stalls which chillingly remind us that the price of freedom in theatre is that directors like Bridge may take their pick of plays from the shelf at French's. Appallingly, most of his audience will now, presumably, think of Fo as kith and kin to Ray Cooney.'

Michael Wright, *Time Out*, 7 Mar 1990.

Fanfani Kidnapped (*Il Fanfani rapito*)

A play in three acts and two interludes.
First production: Palazzina Liberty, Milan, 5 June 1975 (dir. Fo).

'A bitterly hilarious indictment of the Christian Democratic Party (DC), personified by one of its most important leaders: former Italian Prime Minister and one-time DC Secretary, Amintore Fanfani. The action begins with a political kidnapping: Fanfani is abducted on the orders of none other than the Christian Democratic Prime Minister Giulio Andreotti, for the purpose of arousing a wave of public outrage and sympathy calculated to win votes for the DC in the forthcoming elections. (The first performance of the play was held on 5th June 1975, just ten days before nationwide regional elections.) Believing he is in the hands of an authentic terrorist group, Fanfani blurts out a hysterical "confession" in which he admits to all the corruption, clericalism, repression and unscrupulous opportunism which have marked the party's 30-year-old administration. At a certain point, faced with the impending discovery of their hideout, the kidnappers are obliged to move Fanfani to a new location: a private, very exclusive abortion clinic directed by nuns. They disguise him as a woman and, terrified by the prospect of mutilation or death, he is assailed by a violent attack of intestinal gas, which swells his stomach to pre-delivery proportions. In order to avoid a veritable explosion, he must undergo a Caesarean section. When his stomach is cut open, releasing a violent stream of gas and smoke, Fanfani gives birth to a remarkable infant: a fascist puppet decked out in fez and black shirt. During the grotesque delivery, Fanfani dies and is immediately transported to heaven. Jesus, Mary and St Michael – represented as militant leaders and defenders of the poor – are waiting to sit in judgment on him. During the trial, the most scathing indictment of Fanfani's crimes comes from the Virgin, who condemns him and his party to perdition. Before being banished from heaven, however, he is forced to listen to Mary's prediction of the future. In a madly surrealistic climax, a sort of witches' Sabbath in heaven, she foretells the eventual disaster which awaits the Christian Democrats and the ultimate triumph of the revolutionary working class. At this point Fanfani wakes up in his office to discover that the entire episode has been a dream. However, in one of Fo's most clamorous surprise endings, the dream proves to be real after all. No sooner does he come to his senses than a group of kidnappers – flesh-and-blood ones this time – breaks into his office. They inform him that the abduction has been arranged by Andreotti, and drag him away, screaming.'

Suzanne Cowan, *Dario Fo: Bibliography, Biography, Playography*, 1978, p. 20.

'A more coherent farce [than *Can't Pay!*] . . . it uses a trick from medieval theatre already used in *Always Blame the Devil*: Fo reduced to the grotesque dimensions of Fanfani *au naturel* (one and a half hand-spans tall, an idiot and a troublemaker) . . . The theatrical effectiveness of the play once again consists mainly of Fo's great comic abilities as an actor, freely entertaining the audience in a wildly satirical game.'

Binni, *Dario Fo*, 1977, p. 78.

'A complicated . . . fable which is unchecked by any artistic restraint, freewheeling in a ramshackle and haphazard way with a crudeness that lashes out at any target; sometimes the Communist Party, sometimes, obviously, the Christian Democrats – frontally and indiscriminately. . . . Once again the extremist parameters of Fo's vision, combined with his demagogy, take him a long way outside the concrete reality of political struggles in Italy. When all is said and done, his *Fanfani Kidnapped* is an innocuous squib.'

Arturo Lazzari, *L'Unità*, 7 June 1975.

Mother's Marijuana is the Best (*La marijuana della mamma è la più bella*)

Two-act play.
First production: Palazzina Liberty, Milan, 2 Mar 1976 (dir. Fo).

'In a working-class family, mother (Rosetta, Franca Rame) and grandfather (Fo) use various types of drugs, from "grass" to scorpion punctures [sic], also growing their own and dealing on a small scale among their neighbours. After a series of arguments with their son/grandson Luigi and his friend, who is on "hard" drugs, the by-now experienced drug-takers unmask a priest, who is an informer and member of the Mafia, and throw him out of the window together with a policeman from the narcotics squad . . . The defenestration is the culmination of a series of ritual punishments to these symbols of authority, carried out in order to damage their dignity and physical wellbeing: their trousers are pulled down and their bottoms branded, and there is an account of the injuries Rosetta inflicts on the *carabiniere* Antonio. The couple finally reveal to the youngsters that their addiction has been faked, as a strategy to teach both of them a lesson. Ordinary cigarette smoke and plastic scorpions have been used to demonstrate the class and ideological function of drugs, which divert, mystify and dissipate authentic class struggle.'

Cappa and Nepoli, *Dario Fo*, 1982, pp. 116–17.

'We do not tell stories from the past . . . we are exclusively interested in what is happening now. We deal with drugs that are still distributed under the name of psycho-pharmaceuticals to make workers work harder, and we attempt to make young people understand, and to understand better ourselves, all the pitfalls which the authorities, and not only the authorities, have surrounded this problem with.

'We have attempted to be as informative as possible . . . without providing any definitive solutions. And above all we have tried to involve people by entertaining them, making them laugh themselves rigid, if possible. We think that the intelligence that operates through satire and mockery, along with the rationality of irony, is, when all's said and done, the best and healthiest of drugs, particularly when obtuse authorities are trying to repress every citizen who has any ideas about freedom.'

Fo, 'The Invention of Drugs', *La marijuana della mamma è la piu bella*, 1976, p. 23.

'Not one of his most accomplished plays. Perhaps more similar than others to the early farces, but substituting moralism for irrational mechanisms, on the pretext of providing a lesson rather than a crazy outburst. There is probably a lack of any precise and easily recognisable target, necessary for Fo's comic powers, against which to strike. Its inventions are stagnant. The problem it deals with, however, is a very real one, and the discussions it provoked were effective, and no one felt inclined to attack the basis of the play, even if there were a number of negative reviews . . . there were also criticisms of Fo for having produced a play which ignored the new developments of the youth movement . . .'

Valentini, *La storia di Dario Fo*, 1977, pp. 167–8.

'The initial impetus is excellent, and some of the gags (like the grandfather's surreal monologue and LSD trip) . . . are of a high standard. Less plausible from a theatrical point of view is the series of strictly didactic speeches, where the counter-information aspects break the farcical structure . . . But when the antidote of satire restores the balance of this thesis play and reaches the extremes of lunacy that are a trademark of Fo's plays, the play displays an inventiveness and comic force.'

Cappa and Nepoli, p. 117.

Female Parts (aka It's *All House, Bed and Church*) (*Tutta casa, letto e chiesa*)

Monologues by Franca Rame and Dario Fo.
First production: Palazzina Liberty, Milan, 6 Dec 1977 (dir. Fo).
Second version, Teatro Cristallo, Milan, 27 Feb 1981 (dir. Fo). Performed by Rame (as *It's All Bed, Board and Church*) at Riverside Studios, London, 11 May 1982, and in Apr 1983, also at the Edinburgh Festival in Aug 1983, and on tour in the USA in 1986, beginning at the American Repertory Theater, Cambridge, Mass. in May 1986.
British and Irish productions: (as *Female Parts*, trans. Margaret Kunzle, adapt. Olwen Wymark, dir. Michael Bogdanov, with Yvonne Bryceland:) National Theatre, London, 26 June 1981; Glasgow Theatre, Scotland, Aug 1982; Borderline Theatre Company, Irvine, Scotland, Jan 1983; Project Arts Centre, Dublin, 17 Feb 1983; Northern Lights Theatre, Yorkshire, June 1983; Worcester Repertory Company, 13 Feb 1984; Contact Theatre, Manchester, June 1987 (dir. Sheryl Crown). (Second version, as *The Fourth Wall*, trans. Gillian Hanna, dir. Penny Cherns, with Paola Dionisotti:) Monstrous Regiment, the Drill Hall, London, March 1983.
North American productions: Pepsco Summer Fair, Novoton, USA, 21 July 1982; The New Stagecraft Company, New York, 4 Nov 1982; The New Rose Theater, Portland, Oregon, 3 Mar 1983; H.T. Studios, Toronto, Mar 1983; Empty Space Theater, Seattle, spring 1984; Los Angeles Actors' Theater, 1984. (First and second versions, as *Orgasmo Adulto Escaped from the Zoo*, adapt., dir. and performed by Estelle Parsons:) Public Theater, New York, 27 July 1983. *Orgasmo Adulto Escaped from the Zoo* performed and directed by Shelley Mitchell, No Exit Theater, San Francisco, 6 Nov 1998.
Australian productions: Nimrod Theatre, Sydney, 10 Feb 1982 (dir. Fay Mokotow); T.N! Theatre, Brisbane, 24 Mar 1982; Winter Theatre, Fremantle, 4 June 1982; Theatre ACT, Canberra, 8 Oct 1983 (dir. Anne Harvey); Universal Theatre, Melbourne, Feb 1984 (dir. Lois Ellis, with Evelyn Krape).

Second version (as *Whore in a Madhouse*, trans. Gillian Hanna:)
Belvoir St Theatre, 11 Apr 1985.

A series of monologues dealing with female oppression. In
Waking Up, a working-class woman goes through her morning
chores preparing for work and to take her baby to the nursery,
but cannot find her key. In order to work out where she has left
it, she retraces everything she has done since arriving home the
night before, including a prolonged argument with her husband
– who sleeps throughout the play – about the injustice of her
situation. Having found the key, she realises that it is Sunday. In
A Woman Alone, an attractive housewife is locked in the house
by her suspicious husband, whose brother, confined to a
wheelchair, gropes at her periodically, while a peeping-tom
spies on her from the building opposite. She recounts her life
story to a neighbour, telling her of a sexual escapade with her
English teacher, who appears and harasses her, followed by one
of her husband's creditors. At the end of the play, she takes a gun
and shoots all the men who are oppressing her. In *The Same Old
Story*, a woman falls pregnant to her left-wing, intellectual lover,
whom she cannot persuade to be considerate of her. In a
prolonged, scatological children's story, she tells about a little
girl with a dolly who uses swearwords, and influences her to
marry a engineer who exploits her as a sex object. After the
engineer tries to kill the doll, she blows him up until he
explodes, and ends up under a tree with a group of other girls
who all have 'the same old story'. In *Freak Mother*, a woman
becomes a hippy in order to pursue her son, who has joined a
commune of 'Metropolitan Indians'. After experimenting with
promiscuity, becoming a witch, and resorting to crime, she
hides in a church, where she recounts her story to a priest in
confession. Then there is a *Medea* based on the popular shows of
the magicians of Umbria and Tuscany, a Medea who does not
kill her own children out of anger and jealousy, but out of her
awareness that the children are the links of a chain society hangs
around the neck of women 'like a heavy wooden saddle that

makes us easier to milk and easier to mount' (from the Riverside Studios programme).

The second version of the show added a *Prologue* developing an extended word-play on the names of male and female sex organs. Other pieces added later were *Contrast for a Single Voice*, in which a woman gains the upper hand in seducing her silent suitor by tricking him into believing her parents are sleeping in the next room and he must be extremely furtive. A *Roman Lysistrata* recounts a brief version of Aristophanes' play in Roman dialect. Other monologues Rame performed were *Monologue of a Whore in a Madhouse*, in which a prostitute tells her life story to a psychiatrist interviewing her in a mental institution. In *Alice in Wonderlessland* Carroll's Alice is cast adrift in a porno-world of sexual harassment run by a porno film director, a monkey who is a friend of the white rabbit, and ends up being produced on a conveyor belt as a compendium woman. *Michele Lu Lanzone* is a monologue taken from *The Worker Knows 300 Words*. Rame also performed two monologues about the Baader-Meinhof group. In *Ulrike Meinhof*, the German terrorist-activist recounts her experiences of 'sensory deprivation' in Stammheim, and condemns the complicity of the European bourgeoisie and intelligentsia with the oppressive legislature of the German state. In *Tomorrow's News* Irmgard Moeller tells the story of her 'suicide' in Stammheim, presenting a scenario in which she is stabbed by a number of guards.

In 1983 three further monologues were added (and sometimes performed with the two-hander *The Open Couple*). In *The Rape* (also known as *I Don't Move, I Don't Scream, My Voice is Gone*) a woman is abducted, tortured and raped by three men in a van, who finally dump her in a park. She finds herself unable to go through the ordeal of reporting the rape to the police. In *The Mother* a woman discovers from the TV that her son has been arrested as a terrorist. She is strip-searched when she visits him, and has a nightmare in which she strangles him during his trial. In *Coming Home* a woman leaves her husband in disgust at his using her as a sexual convenience, and sleeps with a colleague in a sordid hotel room. In the evening, drunk, bewildered and exhausted, she returns home in a heavy fog, and is reconciled with her husband in a darkened bedroom. In the morning she discovers she is in the wrong apartment, with the wrong family and the wrong husband.

'I would never have been able to write female characters that were substantial enough, and – without being modest about it – which have a certain weight, if it hadn't been for Franca. She is a formidable critic and has an extremely good theatrical ear. This is not by chance, but because of the fact that she was literally born on the stage, and as a result breathed the air of performance before she was even aware of it. Franca's input, not only in drafting characters that involved her directly, but in the overall construction of the comic–grotesque–satirical situation of the plays, has always been a theatrical resource for me.'

> Fo, in *Il teatro politico di Dario Fo*, 1977, pp. 149–50.

'. . . Not a play, or a drama, or even a farce. They are bits and pieces of reality that fly through the air and land on us, eliciting wry smiles and uncomfortable admissions.'

> S. Borelli, *L'Unità*, 11 Dec 1977.

'. . . High-grade feminist farce . . . This, of course, is against the English tradition. We tend to put serious business into straight plays and reserve popular forms, like panto, farce and sitcom, for trivia.'

> Michael Billington, *The Guardian*, 28 June 1981.

'The pieces are comic, grotesque, on purpose. First of all because we women have been crying for two thousand years. So let's laugh now, even at ourselves. And also because a certain gentleman of the theatre, who knew a lot, a certain Molière, used to say: When you go to the theatre and see a tragedy, you identify, empathise, cry, cry, cry, then go home and say, 'What a good cry I had tonight,' and you have a good night's sleep. The social significance went by like water over glass. But for us to provoke you to laughter – and it's always Molière who speaks – you have to have a brain, you have to be alert . . . to laugh you throw open your mouth and also your brain and into your brain are hammered the nails of reason. We hope tonight that someone will go home with his or her head nailed down.'

Rame, 'Prologue', 1981, adapt. Estelle Parsons, *Orgasmo Adulto*, p. 4.

'Why does this show, which is so anachronistically ideological, so irritatingly didactic, so intolerant of mediations, and so explicit in its propaganda, work? In a word – bravura. The bravura of a text full of traps, deviations, games and well-chosen exaggerations; the bravura of a performer who uses a style developed in common with Dario Fo, but which she takes off in her own direction, with a flair for paradox, verbal compression and non-acting, and a refusal of illusion which is not ideological but practical, and completely personal and admirable.'

Ugo Volli, *La Repubblica*, 27 Sept 1981.

'In Italy she is a star, and she acts like a star. While her text, delivered rather casually, relies on music-hall broadness and speaks of women in chains, everything about her being triumphantly attests to the power of female sexuality. In Italy this may sugar the pill; in Britain . . . it looks like a case of wading in into one of feminism's embarrassing grey areas.'

Victoria Radin, 'Good Shape', *The Observer*, 16 May 1982.

'What most immediately strikes one about Franca Rame is that she is sexy. But rather than serving to undermine the message of her plays, as her detractors allege, it is this very sexiness which gains her access to the women that adamantly feminist theatre will never reach. . . . Rame's alternately coy, bawdy and careless sensuality invites women who still aspire to Physical Glamour and the Institution of the Family to relate to and sympathise with characters very much like themselves, while the poignant ironies of the situations enacted gently prod them to broach the issue of their own exploitation. . . . Hers is a "popular" approach to feminism, a blend of mime, story-telling, burlesque and stand-up comedy – all traditions rooted in popular theatre – which can be appreciated by the masses, not just the converted.'

Barbara Schulman, 'It's All Bed, Board and Church',
Plays and Players, July 1982, p. 33.

'There is a quarter of an hour of great theatre in . . . Franca Rame's new show . . . the monologue of *The Rape*. Few know it, only her close friends, but the actress is playing herself: she transposes an appalling experience which actually happened a few years ago (a kidnapping and rape by a group of fascists in the darkness of a van) into pure theatrical expressiveness. Beyond the moral and political impetus which has propelled this fiercely committed performer for years on the civil rights front, the gamble of "replaying oneself" on stage is an enormous challenge. Rame meets it completely, insofar as she manages to overcome any naturalistic identification, while still conveying all the horror of the degradation she underwent.'

Guido Davico Bonino, *La Stampa*, 18 Feb 1984.

Tale of a Tiger and Other Stories (*La storia della tigre e altre storie*)

A '*Giullarata*'.
First production: Palazzina Liberty, 2 Feb 1978 (dir. Fo). Annotated version included in TV programme *Tricks of the Trade*, RAI 3, Mar 1985. Updated version (with Prologue about Tiananmen Square) performed at a solidarity rally for Chinese students, Milan, spring 1989.
First British performance of *Tale of a Tiger* by Chris Adamson, Essex University, 25 Mar 1987 (trans. Ed Emery, dir. Chris Adamson).
First US performance of *The Story of the Tiger,* Charlestown Working Theater, Boston, Oct 1989 (trans. and dir. Ron Jenkins, perf. Tommy Derrah).
Australian performances of *Tale of a Tiger,* Zootango

Theatre, Tasmania, Oct 1987 (trans. Ed Emery, perf. Ian Laing);
Seymour Centre, Sydney, 12 Feb 1992 (dir. Anni Finsterer,
perf. David Wenham).

'His *Tale of a Tiger* comes from a Chinese piece which Fo says
he saw delivered by a peasant storyteller to an audience of
20,000 when he visited the Chinese People's Republic in 1975.
. . . The "tiger story" is a fable about a Chinese soldier of Mao's
army who returns from the war of liberation. He is wounded
and takes refuge in a cave where he is taken care of by a tigress.
He gets better and becomes a friend of the tiger family which he
takes with him back to his village. The tigers become
inseparable friends of the people and help them to rout the last
members of Chiang-Kai-shek's army. The "People's
Government" then takes over and doesn't approve of the tigers.
An official wants them to be sent to the zoo. The "people" now
have a democratic government so shouldn't need "tigers" to
protect them. In the end, however, the villagers set the tigers
against their new leaders.'
John Francis Lane, International Daily News, 1 Apr 1980.

In *The First Miracle of the Boy Jesus*, an 'apocryphal' gospel story,
Christ and the Virgin Mary are Palestinian migrants in Egypt.
Jesus is ostracised by the other children because he is Palestinian,
until he starts creating real birds out of paper ones. The jealous
son of the city's biggest landowners destroys the children's
games, so Jesus, with permission from his father in heaven,
performs a miracle on him. His eyes emit lightning bolts and the
boy turns into terracotta. Mary persuades Jesus to change him
back, as she and Joseph have managed to find work and do not
want to have to be on the run again. Jesus does so, but gives the
boy a kick in the bum in the process. *Abraham and Isaac* deals
with the result of a bet between God and the Devil about the
extent of Abraham's love for God. This is revealed to Isaac only
after the Angel has appeared to stop Abraham from carrying out
the sacrifice of his son. Isaac throws a stone which hits Abraham
on the head, and tells his father the stone has fallen from heaven.

Daedalus and Icarus begins with the father and son getting lost in the labyrinth they have constructed for Knossos, and ends with the fall of Icarus after their attempts to fly. Fo uses the story to attack patriarchal power and stress the importance of the imagination, as opposed to surrogates for the imagination like drugs, horoscopes and UFOs.

'Dario Fo does all this (performing? speaking? miming?) without using words. He moves a few centimetres and becomes the teacher, then becomes the pupil, strains his vocal chords to an almost frightening extent, saws the air with his long paws, does both the real roars and the apprentice ones, and multiplies his hands, legs and utterances to let us "see" rather than just hear the roaring class. And he succeeds. He succeeds because he has adopted everything that's been going around the theatre theory scene about gesture, mime, the *giullare*, body language, metaphor and audience involvement, and he incorporates it all into the sole ingredients of dust and sweat, without mediators, without indirect asides, and without playing his cards close to his chest.'

Renzo Tian, *Il Messaggero*, 30 Mar 1980.

'. . . I performed [*Tale of a Tiger*] in public for a good two years using only improvisation, and I only decided to write it down fairly recently . . . The first performance of this *giullarata* took place in Florence several years ago . . . I decided to try a new piece. I had made a rough draft of the story, but it wasn't written down, the sequence of various passages was in my head . . . and then I took off! . . . No one, not even Franca, knew I was going to try it out. It was a surprise for the whole company. The performance lasted exactly 25 minutes. It was an immediate success . . . But I'd made mental notes that a lot of the elaborations didn't quite work yet, and there were useless repetitions . . . passages that were underdeveloped, or too descriptive . . . and a lot of approximation. The next day I listened to the tape [of my performance] . . . Ten days later, after more cutting, editing and compressing, finally *The Tiger* lasted

55 minutes. It might seem paradoxical, but it's true. In the theatre, often when you cut words the playing time expands because pauses, laughter, and the enjoyment of the actor and the audience come into play.'

Fo, *Manuale minimo dell'attore*, 1987, pp. 215–16.

Trumpets and Raspberries (*Clacson, trombette e pernacchi*) (aka *About Face*)

Two-act play.

First production: Cinema-Teatro Cristallo, Milan, 14 Jan 1981 (dir. Fo).

British productions: (as *Hooters, Trumpets and Raspberries*, trans. R.C. McAvoy and Anna-Maria Giugni:) Riverside Studios, 3 Jan 1984 (reading, dir. George Byatt); (as *Trumpets and Raspberries*, trans. McAvoy & Giugni:) Palace Theatre, Watford, 4 Oct 1984, and Phoenix Theatre, London, 15 Nov 1984 (dir. Roger Smith); Borderline Theatre, Murray House Theatre, Edinburgh, Aug 1985 (dir. Morag Fullerton).

American productions: (as *About Face*, trans. Dale McAdoo & Charles Mann, dir. Andrei Belgrader:) Yale Repertory Theatre, New Haven, 8 Apr 1983; Eureka Theater, San Francisco, Aug 1986; Tomi Park Royale Theater, New York, 1 Nov 1987 (dir. Richard Seyd).

Australian productions: (trans. McAvoy-Giugni:) Melbourne Theatre Company (dir. John Sumner), 8 Nov 1985; T.N! Theatre, Brisbane, June 1986; Theatre South, Wollongong, June 1986 and Seymour Centre, Sydney, Jan 1987 (dir. Des Davis); West Australian Theatre Company, Perth, Sept 1986 (dir. Simon Phillips); (trans. Tony Mitchell, adapt. Greg McCart:) New Moon Theatre, Queensland, 18 Sept 1985 (dir. Helmut Bakaitis); TAU Theatre, Canberra, 16 June 1987 (dir. Tina Van Raay); State Theatre Company, Darwin, June 1987 (dir. Aubrey Mellor).

Antonio Berardi, a Fiat worker, unwittingly rescues Fiat boss Gianni Agnelli from a car accident following a botched attempt by terrorists to kidnap him. Agnelli's face is disfigured in the crash. After Antonio flees, leaving his jacket over Agnelli, the latter is mistaken for Antonio and undergoes plastic surgery, giving him Antonio's face. Antonio's wife Rosa takes Agnelli home from hospital, believing him to be her husband (the real Antonio has been living with his mistress, Lucia). Antonio goes into hiding for fear he will be implicated in the terrorist kidnapping, but police suspicions are instead directed at Agnelli. In the ensuing confusion of identities, Rosa believes Antonio and Agnelli are one and the same person, and Agnelli persuades her to hide him. The house is invaded by rival factions of the Italian secret police in a series of disguises. Agnelli reveals he has plagiarised Aldo Moro's letters to the government, requesting an exchange of political prisoners for his safety. The request is successful, proving that wealthy industrialists have more political weight than prominent politicians.

'At the end of one of the first performances . . . three women, relatives of prisoners from Trani, got up on stage and asked if they could read a document. The document . . . was simply a complaint which they . . . had sent to the magistrate in that city. . . . in the eyes of the three journalists who reported on the evening, ten people out of the seven hundred plus who packed the theatre were transformed into a tidal wave, a chorus of indignant revolt. The document, which was published in [a number of left-wing Italian newspapers] was transformed into a bulletin for the Red Brigades, even a proclamation calling for a general revolt.'

Fo, 'Newspaper Terrorism', in *Clacson, trombette e pernacchi*, 1981, p. 101.

'The years go by, and along with them new political developments, but Dario Fo remains the most abrasive figure in Italian theatre, and goes on putting a finger in the eye of his audience, while his polemical objectives are never small or insignificant . . . the important thing missing from this play is terrorism, the real variety, that kidnaps and kills. It is not merely a question of secret services and the interests of "the authorities" in having victims! Fo refuses to deal with it, certainly not out of any complicity, because he is totally removed from guerilla logic . . . a restricted argument which loses its bite and lapses from satire into preaching, a political lapse that is also theatrical.'

Ugo Volli, *La Repubblica*, 17 Jan 1981.

'It's true, Fo is repeating himself but then so do most great artists. Someone will say that great artists don't waste their energies on propaganda but express their views in metaphors. This is true, too, but Dario Fo has created a genre of political farce that nobody else can do as well as he. His plays are very much about Italian politics but they translate surprisingly well . . . Though there is as always a certain amount of ideological confusion in Fo's new play . . . the satire is on target . . . absurd situations in the great traditions of theatrical farce on the case of mistaken identity of twins, such as dramatists from Plautus to Goldoni have exploited to the full.'

John Francis Lane, *International Daily News*, 21 Feb 1981.

'Targets include not only Italian plutocrats and the red-faced Red Brigade, but also everyone from Yuri V. Andropov to James G. Watt and everything from microsurgery to macrobiotics. Nothing is sacrosanct, least of all the theatrical form. Actors step out of character and address the audience, the walls have eyes and the windows have feet . . . In a time of media-minded revolutionaries and laboured industrial relations – and in a theatre in which political satire is otherwise close to a secret – Dario Fo is a maestro and *About Face* is a bracing antidote to the news.'

Mel Gussow, *New York Times*, 17 Apr 1983.

'Even with Agnelli's final paean to economic power, in New Haven the play hardly offers the universal affront that it poses in Milan. . . . Moreover, Fo's political critique is more complex and sophisticated than an American audience may be used to, especially in the theatre, for Fo not only jabs the bourgeoisie and the powerful, or simply pits left against right. He also criticises the left from the left and presents various viewpoints within a broad political spectrum, none of which fare too well under his scrutiny. This complexity is difficult to transfer to America where the left is often perceived and referred to as a single, unified, Soviet-inspired position. But instead of undertaking the difficult task of finding a way to translate the play into a version that could explore these issues for an American audience, the Yale Rep production remains in safely distant Italy.'

Alisa Solomon, *Performing Arts Journal*, no. 20, 1983, p. 65.

'Fo remains consistent in a theatrical form which speaks the language of politics and ideology to the point of verbose preaching and to the limits of a public debate, and defends his exclusive speciality, the ever-more indiscriminate and mechanical entertainment of an audience which has reached very high figures at his plays. The theatrical quality has declined, and instead of a unified inventiveness and a consistently sustained central idea there is a rigid, schematic application of infantile or simplistic pedagogical and political conceptions.'

Sergio Colomba, *La scena del dispiacere*, Ravenna, Longo, 1984, p. 189.

Obscene Fables (*Il fabulazzo osceno*)

Four monologues.
First performance: Cinema Smeraldo, Milan, 11 Mar 1982 (dir. Fo).
British production: Young Vic, London, 31 Mar 1987 (trans. Justin Gregson, dir. Michael Batz).
Australian production: Adelaide Festival, March 1988 (trans. Ed Emery, perf. Lenny Kovner).

'His first tale concerns the revolt of a large band of Bolognese citizens in 1324. The revolt is not prominently featured in history books, for reasons that become apparent as the story unfolds. After they suffered huge losses in misguided religious wars, angry Bolognese citizens rebelled against papal legates and the Provençal troops protecting the Vatican's emissaries. The papal delegation, well supplied with food and whores inside a fortress, found itself besieged by a people's army that used the only weapon available to it at the time: its own excrement. After eleven days, during which excrement was constantly thrown over the fortress walls, the refined papal sensibilities could take no more. The Provençal troupes and legates left the region under a shower of human ordure.'

Joel Schechter, 'Dario Fo's Obscene Fables', *Theater*, Winter 1982, p. 88.

The Bologna Riot is followed by *The Butterfly-Mouse*, a twelfth-century sexual fable about a wealthy but simple-minded goatherd who is tricked on his wedding night by his wife. She has been married off to him to avoid the scandal arising from her affair with the local parish priest. When her new husband finally returns from a wild goose chase, she, tired from frolicking with the priest, tells him she has left her sex (the 'butterfly-mouse') at her mother's house. The goatherd goes there and is given a cardboard box with a cloth and a mouse in it, and told not to open it until he gets back to his wife. But he opens it and the 'sex' escapes. When he returns empty-handed and exhausted to his wife, she takes pity on him and shows him where the 'butterfly-mouse' really is. *Lucio and the Donkey* is loosely based on Apuleius' *The Golden Ass*. A poet suffering from 'phallocratophantasmagoria' tries to transform himself into an eagle, but ends up as a donkey, who is then forced to carry the beautiful daughter of a wealthy family. He is constantly kicked in the testicles by all and sundry, but manages to rescue the girl from brigands and return her to her parents. They try to gratify his insatiable sexual appetite with horses. They then discover he can write, and sell him to a circus, where he is rented out to an aristocratic lady for sexual purposes, and he takes part in a live sex act with a slave girl. He discovers the antidote to his transformation potion and changes back into a man. He then seeks out the aristocratic lady, who rejects him since he is now only a man. The fourth monologue is *Ulrike Meinhof*, performed by Franca Rame as an 'obscene tragedy' of modern times, and used to focus attention on the Italian 'supergrass' laws for 'repentant' terrorists.

'*Obscene Fable*s is a text which originated directly on the stage, quite unexpectedly. Dario had adapted an improvised scenario from a picaresque French *fabliau* . . . and called it *The Butterfly-Mouse*. He revised and changed it for me . . . I was supposed to perform it . . . The general structure of the piece was certainly profoundly poetic, on the same level as the best *giullarate* in *Mistero buffo*, but certain passages . . . were so crude in their erotic satire, and so ruthless in their paradoxicality, that they made me feel uneasy. I would have had to do violence to myself to manage to play it: the perennial condition of sexual inhibition of a woman faced with the blackmailing myth of modesty and shame.'

Franca Rame, Introduction to *Il fabulazzo osceno*, 1982, p. 1.

'The subjects dealt with in these fables are obscene in their character and flavour. I repeat, obscene – not vulgar or scurrilous. The main aim of the storytellers was to overturn the idea of scandal imposed in a terroristic way by the authorities, through a play of eroticism. Erotic obscenity is used as a weapon of liberation. These days we could synthesise it into an exclamation: "Obscene is beautiful!" '

Fo, *Il fabulazzo osceno*, p. 5.

'Few of the tales that Fo recites can readily be found in books. He discovers them in obscure sources, invents details, and turns them into performance scenarios. In doing this he brings to the public some chapters of Italian history and folklore that went unrecorded because the scholars who preserved past culture favoured the ruling class; it was not in their interest for stories of political and sexual unrest to survive . . . Fo notes that Popes and noblemen in the Middle Ages were free to write obscene literature, and circulate it among their friends, while stories for the general public survived – if they survived at all – through the oral tradition of minstrelsy in which Fo places himself. His narratives of repression and resistance to it are "obscene" insofar as they would have been declared blasphemous or treasonous by medieval church authorities, nobility and scholars.'

Schechter, *Dario Fo's* Obscene Fables, p. 87.

'This effect of collectivity and communality is fundamental to Dario Fo's theatre which due to force of circumstances is less militant, less ideological and less instrumental than it has been in the past, but it still does not shirk from being partisan . . . Fo's improvisation, which has some definite fixed points and gags which are repeated in many performances, runs a riotous, abundant course, with deviations and self-quotations which are hardly signposted . . . but also with a kind of torrential taste for exaggeration, precise but imaginary detail, hyperbole and list-making: in short a Rabelaisian transfiguration of reality into a showcase of extremely comic and monstrous animals, who move around in a dislocated and unchecked way in a world full of pitfalls and weird happenings.'

Ugo Volli, *La Repubblica*, 26 Jan 1983.

The Open Couple (*Coppia aperta – quasi spalancata*)

One-act comedy by Franca Rame and Dario Fo.
First production: Teatro Comunale di Monfalcone, 30 Nov 1983 (dir. Fo, with Franca Rame); also in the USA, May–June 1986; at the Assembly Rooms, Edinburgh Festival, Aug 1986, and Covent Garden, Sept 1986 (with *The Mother* and *The Rape*); and in a double bill with *A Day Like Any Other*, as *Parti femminili*, Teatro Nuovo, Milan, 9 Oct 1986.
British productions: Sir Richard Steele Pub Theatre, London, 23 Jan 1985 (trans. Ed Emery, dir. Simon Usher); The Last Theatre Co. at Camden Studio Theatre, 17 Aug 1993 (trans. Stuart Hood, dir. Paul Plater).

First American production: Eureka Theatre Company, San Francisco, 15 Jan 1987 (dir. Susan Marsden).
Australian productions: Universal Theatre, Melbourne, 7 Jan 1986 (dir. Lois Ellis); Zootango Theatre, Hobart, Tasmania, 2 Apr 1987 (dir. Richard Davey).

In a series of extended flashbacks, events after a couple's decision to have an 'open relationship' are presented by the wife. She has undergone a crisis since her husband has started having affairs, and even tries to commit suicide with a pistol. Her husband then accidentally shoots her in the foot with it. It becomes clear that the arrangement works from the husband's point of view as long as he has other relationships, but when his wife does likewise, he breaks down and wants to go back to the conventional couple situation. When he discovers that his wife has an (invented) lover, a Nobel Prize-winning nuclear physicist and rock musician, he commits suicide with a hairdrier in the bath.

'*Open Couple* is about a couple in crisis, in which the man tries to overcome their problems with false solutions, based on a presumed notion of individual freedom, with great declarations of tolerance and rationality, as long as he is the one running the game. But it is all destined to collapse in the most dramatic way, which is grotesque at the same time, as soon as the situation is reversed and the woman communicates to her companion her own experiences, following the dictates of the mythical freedom of the open couple. The man goes off his head when the woman tells him she has decided to go off with another man.'
    Dario Fo and Franca Rame, Introduction to *Parti femminili*, 1987, p. 6.

'The contribution of Franca Rame to Fo's plays has been undervalued for a long time. Even confined to the dramaturgical aspect, leaving aside her organisation of a company which has always explored new avenues, and their work on stage in which her presence has always been most notable, a lot of things which have been traditionally attributed to her husband also, or even predominantly, come from her. The political animus, or the more simply realistic aspect of Fo's company, the punctilious attention to phenomena of the real world and its stories great and small (if we can contrast this for convenience's sake with the imaginative, grotesque, storytelling and clownish attributes of Fo), is largely hers . . . This is very apparent in this piece.'

Ugo Volli, *La Repubblica*, 12 Oct 1986.

'Fo and Rame, themselves a couple, finger the hypocrisy of the so-called trendy, modern liberal man who espouses equality but doesn't want it on his own doorstep, and concurrently bewail the political backlash against the ideals of 1968. It's a cleverly constructed play, stacked against the "caring, sharing" (in this case '70s) man who wants a mother-figure for a wife plus sexual freedom with others – while always being engagingly sweet about it all. Women, the play suggests, are more loyal, less predatory and very imaginative. But no advocacy emerges either for old-style marriage or new-wave companionship.'

Caroline Rees, *What's On*, 25 Aug 1993.

Elizabeth (*Quasi per caso una donna: Elisabetta*)

Two-act play.
First production: Riccione, 7 Dec 1984 (dir. Fo).
British productions: Half Moon Theatre, 31 Oct 1986 (dir. Michael Batz & Chris Bond, trans. & perf. Gillian Hanna); Battersea Arts Centre, 31 Oct 1991 (dir. Anna Farthing).
First American production: Yale Repertory Theatre, New Haven, 1 May 1987 (trans. Ron Jenkins, dir. Anthony Taccone).

'The action is set over the two days of a coup d'état which the young Robert Essex, ex-lover of the queen, who is still very much in love with him, has organised to dethrone her. It is 1601 and the play is set in Elizabeth's bed chamber, dominated by a huge wooden horse, which the sovereign's father used to construct an equestrian statue. From the bedroom window everything that happens in the Earl of Essex's palace can be monitored. With him is Southampton, Shakespeare's patron and theatrical impresario. Elizabeth suspects that Shakespeare is not a poet who is above partisan struggles, and out of curiosity, starts reading all his plays. The queen is quickly convinced that Shakespeare's characters are talking about her and her court. Though this applies to all the characters (she sees herself mirrored in both Richard II and Cleopatra and sees the Earl of Essex in Antony), it is with Hamlet that she finds the most profound identification, not just through precise allusions, but also in turns of phrase and mannerisms . . . Fo plays a female part, Donnazza, a type of witch whose job is to restore a youthful appearance to the queen, a highly solitary woman who is prepared to make any sacrifice to get her lover back and persuade him he is on the wrong track. Real events unfold as Shakespeare predicted: the cultivated queen is capable of great cruelty and vulgarity, as well as false madness like Hamlet. Behind the arras there is always a spy or an assassin lying in ambush, and after victory over the enemy at home the more serious and definitive battle with the enemy abroad appears on the horizon. Fortinbras arrives from Norway when Hamlet dies, and James of Scotland will arrive in England when Elizabeth dies.'

Anon., in La Nazione, 28 Nov 1984.

'The action takes place in 1601, but its theme is very topical. It's about the commitment of the intellectual, and the need to participate in world events and take a position. It's worth emphasising that it's a political play, but it's also moral, and makes a statement about the function of theatre. . . . [Elizabeth's] is the first modern state. She invented the secret service and modern politics. There's even a sort of Moro affair, when three lords are kidnapped and held to ransom by rebels. She, naturally, doesn't give into this, and maintains a hard line. . . . The theatre shouldn't be regarded in an idealistic way, as if it dealt with stories that have no relation to reality. The intellectual should be committed, and so much the better if he can intervene in the world around him. Authority often has very similar forms, which can be laughed at.'

Fo, in La Repubblica, 6 Dec 1984.

'It's a huge mosaic of ideas and language. Fo's Elizabeth has many obsessions: She's obsessed by Mary Stuart; she's obsessed by "thespian guttersnipe" Shakespeare who she's convinced is subversive and revolutionary and that all his plays are allegories of her life. A joke which runs throughout the play is that Elizabeth believes he steals all his best lines from her. The play is really a farce about a woman's relationship to power and about a woman growing old. Elizabeth is so obsessed with trying to regain her youth and beauty that she goes through literal torture. Here Fo's making a point about the crap that some women put themselves through: the plastic surgery, the tummy tucks, the face lifts.'

Gillian Hanna, Women's Review, Dec 1986/Jan 1987, p. 44.

'*Elizabeth* is an excessively bawdy, vulgar comedy too fatuous to have been a revolutionary text in the early 17th century, too unfocussed for the political satire we might expect for today. . . . If we accept the premise of a deep reactionary fear of gynaeocracy, the fear that has made a harpy out of Thatcher, this is a deeply comforting piece. . . . Elizabeth, to our relief, is not much more than a woman. The kindest one can say of the play is that it cuts both ways: both confirming and mocking a misogyny deeper rooted, I suspect, in Fo's native culture than our own.'

Alex Renton, 'Gloriana goes for a bust job', The Times,
8 Nov 1986.

'Problems like excessive literary references and a careless structure mar this theatrical practical joke, but Hanna's triumph is her recreation of Grossmith (superbly played by Bob Mason) speaking "Stepney-Italian", a doggerel which sounds like a ludicrous mix of an Elizabethan Stanley Unwin and Cockney Mrs Malaprop.'

Anne McFerran, Time Out, 12–19 Nov 1986.

'... What is so remarkable about Fo's satire is its humanity. It may cut to the bone and draw blood, but it's remarkably unmalicious. ... The play isn't one long laugh fest, simply because even Fo finds it difficult to keep satire afloat for two acts, especially when he has to unravel such a convoluted plot ... the play is rich with raunch and scatology – it may be offensive to the unwary.'

Markland Taylor, *New Haven Register*, 3 May 1987.

'Fo's play highlights the parallels between Elizabethan imperialism and modern world politics. Some of the Queen's dialogue was taken almost verbatim from newspaper accounts of Italian political scandals. Italian audiences acknowledged the accuracy of Fo's satiric aim by punctuating their laughter with applause every time he scored a bull's eye that reminded them of current events. The parallels played themselves out so smoothly that audiences often lost track of where Elizabethan history ended and contemporary fact began. These blurred boundaries only served to reinforce Fo's contention that political injustices repeat themselves.'

Ron Jenkins, Translator's Preface to *Elizabeth*, in *Theater*, Summer/Fall 1987, p. 64.

'I know you are a sophisticated man of theatre who understands the use of allegory and anecdotes to make a point, so I don't want you to leap to any false conclusions about possible parallels between the story of Elizabeth in my play, and your own Presidency. Just because my play is about an aging leader whose advisers don't tell her what they're doing behind her back, a leader who tends to get confused and forgetful about certain details, don't think for a moment that it has anything at all to do with you. Everything in this play happened a long time ago to a queen who was at the end of her reign, and there is absolutely no parallel to the current situation in America. ... Also be assured that the minor urinary problems Elizabeth suffers in the play have nothing to do with your well-publicised prostate operations, and that her obsessive concern with her image and with cosmetic beauty treatments has no relation whatsoever to the dyeing of your hair, your face-lifting, or the polyps that disappeared mysteriously from your nose. And don't let anyone try to convince you that Elizabeth's love for horses has anything to do with your image as a galloping cowboy. . . . '

Fo, Letter to President Reagan, Prologue to *Elizabeth*, in *Theater*, p. 66.

'Anna Farthing has wisely avoided the pitfall of so many English productions of Fo – turning it into witless, artless slapstick – but imposes almost too much restraint on her players. . . . The box of tricks is offered almost mechanically – a little bit of *commedia* here, a little bit of Gerry Cottle there, a Laurel and Hardy chase there – but just as the words of a joke without timing aren't funny, so clowning without conviction is not amusing to watch.'

Clare Bayley, *What's On*, 6 Nov 1991.

Harlequin (*Hellequin, Harlekin, Arlecchino*)

Two-act play based on *lazzi* compiled by Ferruccio Marotti & Delia Gambelli.
First production: Palazzo del Cinema, Venice, 19 Oct 1985.

'Four extended monologues written for the Venice Biennale on the 400th anniversary of the birth of Harlequin. In a lengthy *Prologue*, Marcolfa tells a story based on Giordano Bruno's play *The Candlestickmaker*, about a woman who discovers her husband is having an affair with a prostitute. She confronts her, and the prostitute teaches her her skills so she can win back her husband's sexual attention. This is repeatedly interrupted by Harlequin, who constructs a ship on stage and makes extended jokes about contemporary Italian politicians. In *The Gravediggers*, Harlequin and Razzullo are digging a grave for a suicide. They both piss in the grave, and are rebuked by a skeleton. Another skeleton appears, and the gravediggers hit and kick them. The funeral procession arrives, and a brawl breaks out, in which the dead man's brother kills the priest, and is in turn killed by the widow's lover, who dies in the process. The widow invites the gravediggers to the wake, and there is a final dance by all the dead in the graveyard.

'Act Two opens with *The Lock*: on one side Colombina is lovingly polishing an enormous lock. Harlequin enters on the other side with an equally enormous key, which he polishes and cuddles. He asks Colombina to let him try turning his key in her lock. She gets angry at the idea of her sensitive plaything suffering such a vulgar and bulky object. They both sing the praises of their possessions; the lock belongs in heaven, and the key belongs to the emperor. But nothing can break the impasse until Colombina is hungry, and Harlequin reveals that he has a piece of bread. Colombina gives in out of hunger. The scene is played naturally, without vulgarity, and without immediately revealing the game as a sexual encounter.'

Fo, in *Europeo*, 19 Oct 1985, p. 63.

In *The Donkey* Harlequin is terrorised by two dogs who turn out to be Razzullo and Scaracco in masks. His girlfriend Franceschina sneers at his cowardice. He then has a long conversation with a donkey, only to discover it is again his two friends in disguise. A lion escapes from a Sultan's serraglio, and Harlequin, thinking it is his two friends playing another trick, tames it by force and impresses Franceschina. There is a final dance of animals. Two other pieces, *Harlequin and the Flying Cat* and *The Shepherds' Song: A Journey with the Madonna*, were later discarded.

'In the beginning, Harlequin was on stage for no more than a fleeting appearance. Two or three brief "comic entrances" and that was it. If they were cut, nobody would even notice. The primordial Harlequin was a superfluous character, and the action he took part in was quite gratuitous, even senseless. What's more, his actions were horribly obscene and bloodthirsty, gratuitously violent and irrational. . . . He'd come on like a mindless moron, but then he'd suddenly start philosophising in the language of a Rabelaisian scholar. . . . He was incongruous, unpredictable and absurd. . . . There is no other mask in the history of the theatre in every country and epoch that can boast so many centuries of life and such success wherever he appeared. . . . He was born from the commodious belly of *commedia dell'arte*, who was a real slut – one can only imagine how many lovers she had. So Harlequin has hundreds of fathers . . . We're not interested in discovering the most likely father, but in discovering his gestures, his imagination, his tricks, the games he improvised, his accidents, and to learn the hops, skips and jumps, the *lazzi*, lampoons, rambling misunderstandings, complicated deceptions, quick changes, long-winded tirades and boasts. . . . if we want to be able to perform *commedia dell'arte* today, we need to improvise . . . We tried to be scientific without being stuffy. Our ambition was to concoct a show made up of fragments which are as entertaining as possible.'

Fo, 'A Mask Four Centuries Old', in *XXXIII° Festival Internazionale del Teatro*, 1985, Venice Biennale, pp. 46–8.

'Professionally I am still a product of those [post 1968] years, even though I can no longer do plays of direct intervention like *Fanfani Kidnapped* or *Can't Pay? Won't Pay!*. In the past few years I have dealt with apparently less political subjects, from *Obscene Fables* to *Harlequin*. But I believe there is still a very important difference between my work and the bourgeois theatre. Naturally, there is a technical difference, because my work continually breaks with naturalism, but there is also a difference in content and meaning in my work. My theatre is a moral theatre . . . but also a comic theatre.'

Fo, interviewed by Ugo Volli, *Europeo*, 19 Oct 1985, pp. 65, 67.

'In reality Fo has always been Harlequin in a sense, just as Eduardo de Filippo was always Pulcinella, in a personalised and somewhat secret way, but within a tradition. Outside Italy he is considered to be an authentic continuation of the *commedia dell'arte*, and even *Mistero buffo* is read in this way, which is incorrect historically, but visibly real. The fact remains that Fo has always preferred to leap from the medieval *giullari* to contemporary politics, keeping his distance from the sixteenth and seventeenth centuries, the centuries of the *commedia* masks.'

Volli, *Europeo*, p. 63.

'"Faithful" without being philological, above all to Fo, who even recycles some of his old gags (while Rame redoes her Marcolfa), and to a certain type of theatre based on improvisation and nose-thumbing at the taboos of sex and death imposed by the powers-that-be, which after the *commedia dell'arte* became farce and variety and ended up in the cinema. When he takes off his demonic mask, Harlequin does not lose his colourfulness, and Fo's face achieves a surreal minstrelsy in a collection of pieces which is enjoyable without being earth-shattering.'

Oliviero Ponte di Pino, *Panorama*, 3 Nov 1985.

'... Costume, spirit, the paradox and the imagination, the authentic sources of *lazzi*, are all part of the *Commedia dell'arte*, but mingle irresistibly with other undeniable strengths of Fo's comic stage personality, which no amount of justification and research in the world will turn into a Harlequin of history. The very twentieth-century targets, from the anachronisms of satires of cabinet ministers to Fo's propensity for "gags off the wall" are, in the end, the result of Fo's stage personality, as robustly satisfying as it ever was, which tends to spill out in performance and break free from the "academic" framework of the *Commedia dell'arte*, in an instinctive rapport (itself authentic) with audiences in the here and now, which will not be boxed and pigeonholed. And in the end, this is itself what the *Commedia dell'arte* means today: the *freedom* to adapt to "modern" purposes a pan-European theatrical tradition ... With the innate subversive charge of the radical, Fo is today's Harlequin (at least since the death of Chaplin), and the encounter (confrontation?) in 1985–6 with academic pretensions was a liberating of his stage personality, not a caging of it.'

Christopher Cairns, *Dario Fo and the* Commedia dell'arte, 1993, p. 261.

A Day Like Any Other (Una giornata qualunque)

One-act play by Dario Fo and Franca Rame.
First production: Teatro Nuovo, Milan, 9 Oct 1986 (as *Parti femminili*, with *The Open Couple*, dir. Fo).
First British production: (as *An Ordinary Day,* trans. Joe Farrell, dir. Morag Fullerton), Mitchell Theatre, Glasgow, 1989.
First American production: Eureka Theatre Company, San Francisco, 7 Jan 1988 (dir. Richard Seyd).

'*A Day Like Any Other* is, predictably, the story of an incredibly unusual day: every moment situations that are both tragic and grotesque break out. It begins with a woman in her own apartment-office making a video tape to send as a letter to her husband, from whom she has lived apart for some time. The woman warns her ex-husband that she has decided to commit suicide. Her taping of her farewell speech is interrupted by a number of telephone calls. They are the voices of women who have contacted her in the belief that they are talking to a psychoanalyst. Her phone number has been printed by mistake in a medical magazine, with the name of a famous psychiatrist who has experimented in Japan with effective methods of curing neurosis. They all ask her for advice and refuse to acknowledge the woman's protesting attempts to explain their misunderstanding. Finally our protagonist is forced, unwillingly, to accept the role of an analyst and listen to the patients' stories, which are by turns pathetic, comic and tragic. The last voice on the telephone, which to begin with sounds like the calmest, is revealed to be that of a female doctor. Our false analyst is immediately forced by the situation to assume the classic role of a "Samaritan" and try to make the "patient" see reason and convince her not to go ahead with the insane and desperate action she is about to commit.'

Fo and Rame, Introduction to *Parti femminili*, 1987, pp. 5-6.

'Backed up by an original technological device, a video camera which blows up the performer's image on a large screen set up on the back wall, showing Fo's intention to find new solutions for stage settings, the play combines measured doses of comedy and melancholy, wild gags and pointed social observation. Fully appropriating the language of advertising from women's magazines and daily bla bla [sic], the text contains an exhaustive manual of current affectations, fashions, mannerisms and banalities, which accumulate obsessively to produce the paradoxical, surreal outbursts which are typical of Fo. The subject is brought to life and made concrete in human terms, and at times exhilarating, by the decisive contribution of the performer's intense stage presence. With her penitent gestures, her idiosyncratic timing and her dismay and stupefaction Rame builds up a multi-faceted portrait which expands from one invention to another into a fractured mirror-image – at times affectionate, at times cruel – of "days like any other" in which we find ourselves involved for better or for worse.'

Renato Palazzi, *Corriere della Sera*, 17 Oct 1986.

Kidnapping Francesca (*Il ratto della Francesca*)

Two-act play.
First Production: Teatro Sloveno, Trieste, 3 Dec 1986 (dir. Fo).
British production: (as *Abducting Diana*): Pleasance Theatre, Edinburgh Festival, 10 Aug 1994 (trans. Rupert Lowe, adapt. Stephen Stenning, dir. Jonathan Banatvala).

Francesca Bollini de Rill, a wealthy banker, is doing an AIDS test on a prospective young lover when kidnappers burst into her apartment disguised as firemen. She has just told her young man that she is in fact Francesca's lookalike secretary, but manages to convince the kidnappers, and the audience, that she is Francesca. They take her to a farmhouse in the country, wearing masks of prominent Italian politicians to disguise their identity. It transpires that they have done her a favour, since she was just about to be arrested for bankruptcy. The kidnapping appears to have been organised by Francesca's lawyer and lover, whom she has instructed to give the kidnappers two billion lire in ransom money. While three of the gang are collecting the money, she manages to free herself and terrorise the fourth member. In Act Two, she rings her mother, instructing her to bring two shotguns to the farmhouse. A priest arrives, supposedly to bless the house, and ends up performing an exorcism on the kidnapper, who has become delirious due to his torture, and has been put in the refrigerator. The mother, who is a medium, arrives and joins in until the walls of the house start moving in. The kidnappers return with the money in a suitcase, which has a bomb inside. Only Francesca knows the combination number to open it, and she refuses to do so until the kidnappers bring her their leader. This turns out to be her mother, in cahoots with Francesca's husband, who has disguised himself as the priest, and who takes over the ransom money at gunpoint. Then the real Francesca enters, revealing that the other woman is in fact her secretary, and that she has been monitoring proceedings throughout, partly through the young man. She attaches the suitcase-bomb to the ceiling, sets the timer, and exits with the young man, only to return to assure the audience that the play will not end with an explosion. She then distributes the ransom money to the kidnappers, and promises them a job in her bank.

'This is a play in defence of rich people . . . Of course Dario and I haven't got a very good public profile or reputation in this respect. On a number of occasions, we must admit, we've gone a bit overboard with our satire against the wealthy and powerful. But allow us to redeem ourselves. Nowadays we feel it is our duty to rush to the defence of the rich against the insane campaign which is being organised against them . . . some people really hate and abhor the rich: magistrates, for example

. . . terrible examining magistrates who rise from the lower classes, and in the guise of avenging angels, beat the drum for justice being equal for all, and throw industrialists, bankers and farm owners into prison . . . make no mistake, these days the workers have given up the class struggle, and the only ones who still carry it on, fearlessly but alone, and with great difficulty, are the employers. They never give up!'

Rame, *Il ratto della Francesca*, 1986, pp. 18, 20.

The Pope and the Witch (*Il Papa e la strega*)

Two-act play.
First production: Teatro Faraggiana, Novara, 31 Oct 1989 (dir. Fo; ass. dir. Arturo Corso).
'Updated' production: Teatro Pergola, Florence, 25 Mar 1990.
First British production: West Yorkshire Playhouse, Leeds, 1 July 1991 (trans. Ed Emery, adapt. Andy de la Tour, dir. Jude Kelly); transferred to Comedy Theatre, London, 13 Apr 1992.
US productions: American Repertory Theater, San Francisco, 1992 (trans. Joan Holden, dir. Richard Seyd); Yale School of Drama, New Haven, 1996 (dir. Stephan Genn).

'The Pope (a nameless Pope, but not exactly difficult to recognise, played in grand style by Fo) is suffering from a strange syndrome: he is afraid of children, even though he has always loved them. To cure him a famous specialist . . . is sent for, and arrives accompanied by a would-be missionary nun (Franca Rame in excellent form). She is, of course, not a nun, but a healer, hypnotist and "witch". She succeeds in solving the Pope's problem by involving him in an imaginary (and highly diverting) "child hunt" which sublimates and overcomes his phobia. But the Pope's troubles are far from over. He is immobilised by a sudden mysterious attack of arthritis, which Fo delights in giving bizarre scientific names to, with his arms raised and locked in a blessing. The Witch releases him from this new affliction, thanks to a ridiculous aerial massage for which the unfortunate Pope has to be harnessed and suspended from the ceiling on a chandelier. But the cure only lasts a few minutes. Informed by two very alarmed cardinals . . . of the real identity of the fake nun, as well as her activities in support of legalising drugs and birth control, the Pope throws her out, only to be immediately paralysed once again. . . .

'Unable to shake off his paralysis, the Pope visits the healer incognito in her clinic, where she dispenses low-priced drugs under her own organised medical supervision. Here, after a series of tumultuous events (a gang of drug dealers obviously hostile to her enterprise break in, the Pope is forced to inject heroin, an executioner-cum-drunk intervenes, etc.) the illustrious patient undergoes a "conversion" to the anti-prohibitionist cause. This conversion eventually leads him to issue a papal encyclical which is revolutionary, to say the least. An unprecedentedly vast schism ensues, and a number of governments fall in a chain reaction, leading to the (perhaps only temporary) elimination of the Pope, after a series of comic failed assassination attempts.'

Giovanni Raboni, *Corriere della Sera*, 2 Nov 1989.

'Using the Pope was a surreal idea which enabled us to talk about the ongoing carnage that goes on right under our eyes: eight or nine deaths a day from overdoses, AIDS, hepatitis, and all the other catastrophes caused by drugs.

'The Pope provided us with a device to present arguments which people perhaps no longer wish to hear, or which they listen to only with a sense of moral piety. We needed something out of the ordinary and paradoxical which enabled us to destroy the logic behind the criminalisation of drugs, since we are convinced (perhaps we are the only ones, given all the doubts that have been raised about the subject) that prison is not the way to save drug addicts. This is not a play about religion. Nor is it a satire on the Pope and the Vatican, which are not central to the play. Our concerns lie elsewhere.

'Our Pope becomes involved in the situation and the problem as a victim. He is above all a man who becomes conscious, who sees reality for the first time and realises that legalisation, while it may not be the solution, is at least a recourse worth trying, and perhaps the only one that can prevent young addicts from dying on the streets. We have used his authority as a symbol to explore this paradox in a light-hearted and sympathetic way. It is a serious and involving subject, but it's too easy to dismiss it as no laughing matter. All we can do is try to deal with it in an ironic way, without demonising it. We don't laugh it off, but we don't cry over it either.'

Fo and Rame, Note to *Il papa e la strega*, 1990, p. 43.

'A Herodian spirit burns in this Pope's heart, and he proclaims the need for population control because "the condom is not the devil's raincoat". A grotesque situation typical of Fo: right from the beginning his Pope is placed in a gallery of crazed, surreal characters straight out of this actor-playwright's best plays, which stop at nothing, whether it be staging anarchists "falling" out of windows, or the kidnapping of Agnelli or Fanfani. He takes a highly personalised view – which sometimes I agree with and sometimes not – of the more violent aspects of our society: discrimination, drugs, terrorism. His plays are sometimes written "to the beat of a drum", following the dreams and utopias of a political theatre. But *The Pope and the Witch* . . . is, like Fo's best plays, a text which has been "thought out": it is not a political pamphlet, rather a grotesque fresco whose protagonist is an absolutely astonishing Pope.'

Maria Grazia Gregori, *L'Unità*, 9 Nov 1989.

'The most successful aspect of Fo's latest play is the fusion of entertaining comedy and a theatre of ideas. Once again a mixture of irony and sharp perception result in a successful theatrical representation of a vital and painful reality, or in this case, a most terrible and devastating social problem: drug abuse. But the particular quality of the writing in *The Pope and the Witch* is also notable: the play has a considerable sense of rhythm, levity and modernity of language. . . . There are some quite

Molière-like touches at the beginning, and a sense of fully-fledged imagination, as well as some intuitions worthy of Genet. In the second act the play bends slightly towards didacticism, but soon explodes into great comic anarchy when the Pope is subjected to an overdose by the drug dealers. This is Fo at his best, most strategic and well thought-out, a metaphysical farce which is able to deal with tragedy with the knowledgeable and measured detachment of a liberating sense of laughter.'

Sergio Colomba, *Il Resto del Carlino*, 7 Dec 1989.

'It's the kind of show you'll see, if you're lucky, half a dozen times in a lifetime of theatregoing. Outrageous ideas pour out in an uninhibited stream. Comic invention is piled on comic invention until you're left physically exhausted from laughter. As you wipe away the tears, you become aware that in the process of reducing you to convulsions, Fo and Rame have also confronted you with a world upside down. They have invented a Pope who puts out an Encyclical urging "the distribution of drugs at reasonable prices by all national governments." . . . Fo's triumph is to make the Pope's behaviour seem entirely reasonable.'

Albert Hunt, 'Papal Bull', *Plays and Players*, June 1991, p. 7.

'Dario Fo's *The Pope and the Witch* would seem to have lost something in the translation . . . it appears to have been designed as a holdall for a vast range of anti-Vatican jokes only some of which retain their ability to shock or satirise in Andy de la Tour's frenetic local translation . . . the scattershot principle allows too many blanks . . . we get a collection of cartoons and caricatures and one-line Catholic gags but no real sense that anyone has worked out what to do with them or why. The result is a lot of sound and fury signifying little more than increasing desperation on the part of adaptor and director.'

Sheridan Morley, *Herald-Tribune*, 22 Apr 1992.

'I can only concur with the chorus of disapproval that this sting-less swipe at Vatican corruption has elicited. It's too unstruc-tured to work as farce – Berwick Kaler . . . and Frances de la Tour . . . go directly for postcard-humour romp . . . the whole idea seems to be that religious leaders with portable phones, saying "fuck", nudge-nudging with talk of shares, is enough. . . . Something has gone badly amiss in Andy de la Tour's version: having worked "from a literal translation" his "adaptor's note" in the programme reads like veiled apology.'

Keith Stanfield, *City Limits*, 30 Apr 1992.

Hush! We're Falling! (*Zitti! Stiamo precipitando!*)

Two-act play.
First performance: Teatro Asta, La Spezia, 21 Nov 1990.

'Cruel clandestine experiments have been carried out on the inmates of an asylum, and have produced an antibody against AIDS, which can only be transmitted sexually. A prominent industrialist (Dario Fo) who is obsessed with diseases arrives here by mistake, and decides to seduce a patient to obtain immunity against the virus. She is a poetic, mad scientist with a sexual phobia (Franca Rame), who handles toads and snakes, carries out mysterious research and believes she is being persecuted by extraterrestrial beings. To get her into bed, the industrialist funds her research and then pretends to be bankrupt and abandoned. Love ignites but before the necessary number of embraces for immunity, the word is spread about the madwoman's powers, and everyone tries to jump on her. Nonetheless she succeeds in inventing a simple, free and revolutionary solar engine which terrorises the industrialist because it is a threat to his business. Finally the madwoman lets herself be captured (or rather assumed into heaven) by her extraterrestrial friends.'

Ugo Volli, 'Indomitable Fo in the Madhouse with AIDS',
La Repubblica, 4 Dec 1990.

'There is a certain dose of vulgarity and lines that are not exactly in a lofty spirit, but which contribute to the construction of a vortex of nonsense; there is also a certain amount of the ideological pronouncements which are never absent from Fo's work.

'Franca Rame's tender, crazed character is a great creation, and there is an overwhelmingly demented plot mechanism, a good company of actors, and Dario Fo is in great form. The result is an improbable, enjoyable, offensive and rather entertaining play, which is also . . . very neo-baroque. And it flies in the face of the deadly theatre of Aristotelian unities and their passionate advocates.'

Volli, *ibid.*

'Ironically, the heavily fur-coated first-night audience almost certainly contained some of the play's chief targets . . . If there is any moral to this sadly disjointed tale, it is that most of us are pretty incorrigible, and any saints around would be well advised to depart forthwith to a better world.

'The staging and production were of a standard any provincial rep company would have been ashamed of. The large cast were used mainly for clowning and general rushing about, between large chunks of Fo and Rame on stage, hugging most of the dialogue. Fo . . . seems . . . a long way removed from the people he used to reach by performing in factories and other venues more accessible to the great masses he claims to champion. At 64, the court jester has become emperor, and this particular emperor hasn't many clothes on anymore.'

Della Couling, 'A cautionary tale with no moral',
The Independent, 7 Jan 1991.

Johan Padan Discovers the Americas (*Johan Padan a la descoverta de le Americhe*)

Monologue in two parts (with a Prologue).
First production: Teatro Romana, Trento, 5 Dec 1991 (dir. Fo).

Johan Padan escapes from the Inquisition in Venice on a fishing boat bound for Spain. He reaches Seville, where he gets a job making and setting off fireworks, and then as a banker's scribe writing fraudulent letters of credit. When he is discovered by the Spanish Inquisition, he escapes on Columbus' fourth voyage to the Americas, where he is forced to look after the animals. After Indians are taken on board, Johan begins to learn their language, and becomes an interpreter for the Spaniards. After a storm, Johan and four other animal attendants are left behind with the Indians when the rest of the Spanish crew take off in lifeboats. They attach themselves to the pigs, who tow them through the sea to the coast. They are then sold as slaves and carried off by another group of Indians in canoes to Florida. Johan survives an attempt at cannibalism, and after saving the life of the village shaman and predicting a storm, he is proclaimed a saint and leads the villagers south. After two months, they meet a group of Incas, who refuse to acknowledge Johan's saintly authority because he is too similar in appearance to the Spaniards. Johan performs two miracles – a 'fishleap' in a lake at full moon which provides fish to eat, and a comic rain dance which turns a drought into a flood. After he and his Indian followers successfully ambush a group of Spaniards with Indian prisoners, Johan realises that Christianity is the only cause for the Spaniards' persecution of the Indians. He decides to teach the natives – with great difficulty – the basic precepts of Christianity, with a few tropical adaptations. Seven years after his escape from the shipwreck with the pigs, Johan and 8,000 Indians arrive at the Spanish headquarters at Catchoches in Florida. The Spanish governor sets the Indians to work, but after they disappear he threatens to hang Johan. As he is about to be hanged, thousands of Indians appear carrying torches, and threaten to burn down the city. The Spaniards are forced to surrender, and are later shipwrecked in a storm after Johan uses his magical powers and consults the moon. Johan remains in Florida for another 40 years, until King Carlos declares it a no man's land.

'Fo–Johan creates and populates the stage with phantasms, situations, sounds, phonemes, guffaws and improvised laughter, then in a calm, pleasant voice, proceeds to narrate another episode of his story. Then there are more improvised excursions, choruses of voices, concise rhythms, characters entering and exiting. Fo–Johan pursues the visions in his mind, seizes them, elaborates on them, embellishes and transports them into the realm of comedy with his counter-attacks and unsynchronised gestures. The audience's imagination is stimulated. It sets off in pursuit of the narrator-character's visions, participating in and inhabiting with him this fantastic theatre. Fo–Johan oscillates from one side of the stage to the other, becoming agitated, constructing characters and objects with his own idiosyncratic, caricatured, allusive gestures, and integrating them into his own pataphysical world, without leaving any loose ends. He is as adventurous as an acrobat, moving from one invention to the next. Situations are built up and developed to their maximum degree of theatricality. Fo–Padan, the juggler of languages, takes you by the hand, captures your imagination and sense of abandon and takes you with him on this journey into the imagination. Then he leads you back into the narrative, changes gear, and lets you go, only to lead you off again into a vortex of situations, as if in an embrace, right up to the "discovery of the Americas". Through this game of intelligence, this jongleur's journey, Fo also demonstrates his own sympathies, his attitude towards this historical event which is celebrated by everyone, but which in Johan Padan's view we should be ashamed of because of its abuse of unprotected natives. Fo works inside your head while he tickles your stomach. Fo the actor describes, comments on and constructs grotesque situations, orchestrating voices, stories and objects. His imagination elaborates on characters, animals and other elements, at times debasing and degrading images to an almost obscene level, only to immediately raise the tone. His comic tone becomes confused with a poetic tone, his vocal and gestural mannerisms multiply into a unique chorus, a unique concert.'

Mario Mattia Giorgetti, *Sipario*, Mar 1992, p. 2.

'Considering Fo's age . . . and the energy it takes to perform a one-man show for over two hours, this may very well be one of his last major solo pieces. *Johan Padan* is an appropriate crowning for the *giullaresque* phase of his long career – a mature, well-balanced, multidimensional work, a masterpiece that rates with *Mistero buffo*.'

Antonio Scuderi, 'Framing and Improvisation in Dario Fo's *Johan Padan*', *Theatre Annual* 49, 1996, p. 85.

Seventh Commandment: Steal a Bit Less No. 2 (*Settimo: ruba un po' meno no. 2*)

A monologue in two acts by Dario Fo and Franca Rame.
First production: Teatro Animosi, Carrara, 20 Nov 1992 (dir. Fo).

A long, topical monologue about Italy's corruption scandals of the early 1990s, performed by Rame in front of a triptych of 108 photographs of politicians, businessmen and state officials implicated in the Milan 'Tangentopoli' scandals. Sketches deal with corrupt officials' secretaries committing suicide, the activities of Mario Chiesa of the Socialist Party, who tries to flush 37 million lire down the toilet, and 'Clean Hands' magistrate Antonio di Pietro. The trivia of Italian TV chat shows is parodied, and the nihilism of the 1990s contrasted with the naive political activism of the 1960s. Andreotti and other corrupt government politicians are satirised, as well as the new mood of festivity and excess which the scandals have generated. 'A Tragedy of Jealousy' recounts a news story of a family where the son is having an affair with his mother-in-law, and the couple are discovered and killed by the father and daughter. Rame then relates stories from her adolescence and about her marriage and her son's adolescent sexual activities. After satirising the Northern League, she constructs a hell full of corrupt politicians, where the Pope pays a visit. There is a

Utopian 'happy end' where scandals such as the Piazza Fontana bombings, the plane shot down at Ustica, the bribery scandals, the squalid conditions in hospitals, the dominance of the country by industrialists and the Mafia, and the political partitioning of RAI TV and other mass media are all resolved.

'About 25 years ago Franca and I staged a play called *Seventh Commandment: Steal a Bit Less*. It was an absurd, paradoxical story about building speculation in a cemetery. A bunch of rogues were running a black market in corpses, and taking bribes for graves and even council coffins. It reached the point of evacuating the whole cemetery to turn it into land for building on. Recently we discovered we had been robbed. You can read about it in the newspapers: a whole army of building inspectors and contractors have stolen our idea, our plot and even the paradoxical technique we invented to rob and swindle public institutions, and naturally without paying us a single lira in royalties. What thieves!

'So Franca and I decided to get our revenge. For the 1992/93 season we would put on a play where, without too much fantasy or absurdity, as there's no need, we would narrate this dance of thieves that is coming to light every day like an enormous, impossible fireworks display. . . . Every time we narrated one of these impossible events we would project on to a screen upstage the newspaper article which proved that it was true. But make no mistake, as we are honest people, we will pay royalties to these geniuses of fraud and theft who have invented the greatest masterpieces of administration in the world'.

Fo, 'The thieves' ball', *Sipario*, Nov 1992.

'A *tourbillon* of cops and robbers taken word for word from current affairs to prove that at the moment reality has surpassed satire. Dario Fo and Franca Rame have written it in a hurry but the text is like Penelope's loom: something is always added every morning, because every morning *Tangentopoli* offers something new. And they observe the effect on the audience: Fo as director and Rame alone on stage with a lectern and a pile of newspapers in a monologue lasting more than two hours which nails the audience to their seats.'

Manuela Zadro, 'Dances with Thieves', *La Repubblica*, 22–23 Nov 1992.

Dario Fo Meets Ruzzante (Dario Fo incontra Ruzzante)

Two-act play, based on texts by Angelo Beolco (Ruzzante).
First production: Teatro Nuovo, Spoleto, 8 July 1993.

Dario Fo Performs Ruzzante (Dario Fo recita Ruzzante)
First production: Florence, 1995.

A series of monologues and short plays adapted from Ruzzante. 'The Oration' is an address given by Ruzzante to Cardinal Marco Cornaro in 1521, in which he asks the church to change its laws so that peasants no longer have to fast, wear clothes, or make love in moderation. He also asks them to legislate against poets and writers using refined language, for priests taking wives, and against the discrimination against peasants by the citizens of Padua, and to allow peasants to have four spouses. In 'Galileo Galilei' a doctor and the peasant Nelo discuss the cosmos and the universe in terms of cheese, omelettes, polenta, chickpeas, etc. In 'Betìa' Nale is married to Tamìa (Franca Rame) but in love with Betìa, who is married to Zìlio, Nale's best friend, and Tamìa is in love with Meneghèllo. Zìlio discovers Betìa's relationship with Nale and stabs him. They all believe Nale is dead, but he is not, and he appears to a distraught Tamìa to tell her about life in hell, which is as bad as their lives as peasants. Nale then makes peace with Zìlio, and the two women, Nale and Zìlio decide to live together as a foursome, leaving Meneghèllo, who resolves to join them.

The second part begins with 'Life', a short philosophical treatise. This is followed by 'Bertevèlo the Fisherman's Dream', in which a fisherman finds a woman's handbag full of gold, silver and precious stones after a storm at sea, and dreams of all the food and sexual activity he will indulge in now that he is rich. His dream ends with him drowning in a sea of love and luxury. In the final piece, 'Ruzzante Returns from Battle', a soldier ravaged by the experiences of fighting for the Venetian republic returns to Venice in a miserable state, looking for his wife Gnua, only to discover that she has found another man. She explains that she needs a man to provide for her so she can eat. Her man arrives and beats Ruzzante with a stick, leaving him lying on the ground. He tries to convince his friend Menato that he has been attacked by 100 men, and then tries to laugh about his situation. Menato suggests it has been 'like a comedy', which makes Ruzzante laugh even more.

'. . . Ruzzante, thanks to his eccentricity, and the protection of his patron, Cardinal Cornaro, was able to say things with a ferocity and violence which have never been equalled, even by Shakespeare. And who knows how many of his jokes were not transcribed because they were censored. . . . Angelo Beolco is a great intellectual, cultivated, curious and wise. He was Galileo Galilei's favourite author. He is a poet who took the side of the peasants, but not in any populist sense. His approach is far from populist, in fact he is very hard on the figure of the peasant. On the one hand he attacks the authorities and crushes them, and on the other he shows the peasant's arrogance and cowardliness. He shows the peasant who steals from another peasant, who is contemptuous of others simply because they have become victims, and hence objects of contempt. He also shows the peasant's racism against those who are not like him and don't speak the same language. Although he is partisan, Ruzzante portrays a peasant who is enclosed in his shell and never comes out. . . . Often Ruzzante talks about being and not being. Not being present in flesh and blood but a fiction, outside of time. Being a ghost, being already dead, going to hell, which is a medieval idea of journeying to another world, before the Greeks. This is also in Shakespeare and Dante. . . . It is a mechanism which he often uses to describe directly and violently what he wished was a reality but is not. This is undoubtedly a subversive element, a grotesque and satirical device which functions to expand his perspective on the world through comedy. '

Fo, in Walter Valeri, 'Dario Fo: tra Goldoni e Ruzzante',
Sipario, Sept 1993, pp. 96-7.

Mummy! The Sans-culottes! (Mamma! I sanculotti!)

Two-act play.
First production: Teatro Animosi, Carrara, 6 Nov 1993 (dir. Fo, ass. dir. Arturo Corso).

'For the title of what he defines as "a mechanical farce in the manner of Feydeau", Fo chooses the French Revolution, where the parallel between the eighteenth and the twentieth centuries is drawn through the sanguine revolutionaries the *sans-culottes* ... The play proceeds according to a classic scenario of role reversals and a proliferation of gags. In the guises of a magistrate and vet, Fo creates a Buñuel-like scenario with an operating table which is set up like a banquet table, on which there is a man instead of a calf. Going back to the roots of a popular theatre where death and food provoke the same kind of laughter, the actor laughs scornfully at a society which is devouring itself. But he also takes the opportunity to move away from archetypes and reprise his satire of contemporary life. The victim of the operation is a corrupt medical supervisor (we are in the times of De Lorenzo) who is well aware of the dangers facing the doctors he has authorised to operate on him, but refuses any kind of medication. Fo, after his Dame Grosslady in *Elizabeth*, is again in drag, complete with high heels, while Rame plays the part of a seemingly schizophrenic policewoman.'

Cappa and Nepoli, *Dario Fo*, 1997 edition, p. 150.

'You might expect *Mummy! The Sans-culottes!* to be a natural, inevitable development of the play we staged last year (*Seventh Commandment: Steal a Bit Less No. 2*): a satirical ballad for a single voice, on a 'Thieves' Ball' theme, with bribes, corrupt politicians and a chorus of infinite public and private scams. But it isn't. The structure of this play is quite different. It is a *pochade* for several actors, with a grotesque detective thriller plot, theatrical effects and reversals. Besides the game of deceit which transparently alludes to our current situation of a tissue of lies – about the real perpetrators of state massacres, and the obsessive collusion of the Mafia, terrorists and the more or less 'deviant' secret services – there is a series of over-the-top clown effects, which we have included not as light relief or digressions from the play's indictments, but as another way of demonstrating the horrendous political events we are living through.

'At the play's centre is an event which seems to be endless: the judiciary in conflict with the perennial mendacity of those in power. A carousel of investigations conducted by some judges who are clearly respectable and by others who are clearly corrupt. A kind of grotesque dance performed, mimed and sung, inside the red-hot mechanism of which we are more or less conscious spectators or performers – a spectacle where everything is mixed up and ground down into fairground balls which are thrown at targets which are often authentic, but more often fake, and simply diversionary. . . .

'In this play, with its liars, thieves, demagogues, bribe-obsessed maniacs and murderers, we have not been able to privilege anybody. We have brought everyone out on to the stage, including those who prefer to remain backstage. You will find it easy to recognise them if you have been following the events and revelations that have by now surpassed our imagination. Every day we are forced to invent situations and facts that are more and more absurd and improbable, in order to escape the intrepid snares of current events. But we are aware that this kind of escape derives from the oldest mechanisms of satirical theatre from the time of Aristophanes. And the character played by Dario could be from that era, a judge who by chance finds himself conducting an inquiry which leads him straight to the truth about who organised all the state massacres (from Piazza Fontana onwards), the collusions with obscure organisations linked to military apparatuses and the police . . . It's all too much for our protagonist to be able to bear, but he is engulfed by the situation.

'It is a farce based on misunderstandings in which there is transvestism and absurd 'surgical operations' involving transplants of animal organs, backed up by songs and dances. I play the classical antagonist, the character who conducts and directs the game: a volatile woman police officer, appointed to head the bodyguards who protect the poor judge, who risks being eliminated at any moment. This policewoman appears to be a judicious woman, full of common sense, but we soon realise she is the craziest character in the whole team.'

Franca Rame, 'Do We Remind You of Something?',
programme note to *Mamma! I sanculotti!*, Milan,
26 Oct 1993.

Sex? Thanks, Don't Mind If I Do! (*Sesso? Grazie, tanto per gradire!*)

Monologue by Franca Rame, Dario and Jacopo Fo, performed by Franca Rame.
Based on *Zen and the Art of Fucking* by Jacopo Fo.
First production: Teatro Comunale, Cervia, 18 Nov 1994 (dir. Fo).

A long, rambling, comic monologue-lecture, performed by Rame in front of a backdrop representing the garden of Eden. 'The Old People' is a grotesque sketch enacting an imagined proposal by the Berlusconi government to get rid of old people by throwing them off balconies to save on pensions. A comic sketch about Loreena Bobbit's castration of her husband leads into a chronicle of some of the follies of the Berlusconi government. In 'Adam and Eve's First Sexual Encounter,' based on a Boccaccio story, the couple discover sexual pleasure simultaneously with guilt and the devil. 'Mazzapegol' presents a little sex-maniac demon kept in a sack. 'The Abortion' recounts Rame's first sexual experiences and her abortion, leading into an extended comic sketch about American gymnastic lessons in faking orgasms. It is followed by sketches about promiscuity, frigidity, post–coital sadness, impotence, pornographic films, Jacopo's adolescent sexual insecurities, ways of avoiding premature ejaculation, and the importance of Zen in the sexual act. 'Where We Came From' traces the transition from ancient matriarchal societies to patriarchal societies. 'Virginity' exposes the myth of the intact hymen. 'The Clitoris' uses paintings by Fo of flowers to demonstrate the topology of the female sexual organs and the 'G spot'. 'The Male Sex Organ' explores the myths of the penis and penetration. Rame relates her own first sexual encounters, and demonstrates the need for pelvic gymnastics. The final piece is 'The Story of the Three Desires', a sexual fable translated into the Padano dialect of *Mistero buffo*. A couple are granted three wishes by a goldfish, and discover that finding new forms of love is not the same as exploring new forms of sexual adventure.

'As a mother and a respectable person I am upset about being censored and restricted to people over 18. A play is not a novel, and needs to be seen before it is judged. We turned Jacopo's book into a play in which basic aspects of sexual relationships are explained, and love is celebrated as the expression of pure, uninhibited feeling based on affection. Our aim was also to inform young people and adults about the danger of AIDS. We thought that in a politically squalid, dark and confused period like this it was indispensable to go back to the personal, and start off with the essential things of life: love, feelings and pleasure.'

Rame, *Il Giorno*, 28 Dec 1994.

'A fast, felicitous monologue full of imagination, combining ingenuity, enchanting mischief, poetic observations and objections solidly based on common sense, exposing the absurd cruelty of those who confuse the word love with the devil. This piece by France Rame presents at last an Eve who is modern, lucid and amiable. . . . In her hands, representing hell becomes a portrayal of malice, cynicism, ignorance, pornography, pernicious politicians, abstract theology, the natural inexperience of any adolescent transformed into illness and guilt by a society regulated only by haste, the invasion of social norms and the degradation of our personal lives, which have become a repository and an incinerator for the daily violence from which sexuality and its fantasies suffer.'

Walter Valeri, *Sipario*, Dec 1994, pp. 83–4.

'. . . Members of the audience preferred to respond to the humorous side of this semi-serious chat about a subject which is still shrouded in reticence or embarrassment or worse. They seemed to exorcise their own phobias to a certain degree, since many of the more adult members of the audience would have been victims of the same ignorance or sexual mis-education (from their family, school or a repressive society) which Franca Rame . . . sympathetically confesses to on her own behalf. Not only those of Rame's generation, but also today's young people can relate to Jacopo's personal experiences, which are recounted in various ways.

'The intention to contribute to the dissipation of fears and the breaking down of taboos which have always ensnared the pleasures of love is laudable. As is the call to combine sex and love (along with an implicit appeal for behaviour which will prevent the spread of AIDS). The "no frills" argument, which is backed up with some scientific information, risks turning into an anatomy lesson. But there are at least three moments in which the actress produces pieces of real theatre, moving away from the lectern which she is stuck behind for a large part of the performance (an hour and forty minutes without an interval). The first and the third of these elaborate, in a language à la *Mistero buffo*, where Dario Fo's hand is especially evident, a Boccaccioesque sketch (taken from the delightful tenth novella of the third day of the *Decameron*), which is softened somewhat in the adaptation, and a Provençal medieval fable which also provide the edifying "moral" of the whole show. . . . The re-enactment of a (perhaps) imaginary American "course" for women in learning how to have an orgasm is a pure parody . . .

'As for Zen, . . . it is mentioned only in passing. But the most notable omission, considering the open-mindedness and courage which Dario and Franca have displayed . . . during their long period of artistic activity, is elsewhere. The sex which is talked about here is exclusively that between men and women, with or without love. Homosexuality remains a mere word, almost hidden, in one hurriedly pronounced and hardly convincing sentence.'

Aggeo Savioli, *L'Unità*, 31 Dec 1994.

The Emperor's Bible and the Peasants' Bible (*La bibbia dell'imperatore, la bibbia dei villani*)

Monologues.
First production: Palasannio, Benevento, 6 Sept 1996 (dir. Fo).

A 'supplement' to *Mistero buffo*, consisting of monologues performed by Fo and Rame, including *The First Miracle of the Boy Jesus* and *The Massacre of the Innocents* and some new material. 'Adam and Eve's First Sexual Encounter' and other material from *Sex? Thanks, Don't Mind If I Do!* is also included. There is a lengthy prologue by Fo comparing the official ('Emperor's) version of the bible with various plebeian apocryphal versions which he has unearthed from research throughout different regions of Italy. These express a far more direct relationship between God and humanity, and he also refers to current political events. In 'Pigs without Wings' a pig asks God for wings, and then uses them to enjoy himself. He goes to heaven, where he romps about with a sow, and even God is amused by the spectacle. But the pig is eventually punished, and falls into a sewer, making such a big splash that it reaches heaven. 'Two Lovers Entwined like Beans in a Pod', a piece in Southern Italian dialect, is performed by Rame, as are the apocryphal biblical pieces *Mary at the Cross* and *The Madonna Meets the Marias*. In *Abraham and Isaac* God forces Abraham to sacrifice his son after making a bet with the devil. 'The Dung-Fest' is a scatological piece in *grammelot* based on one of Aesop's fables, with the addition of a medieval Christ figure. 'The Shepherd's Cantata' is a piece in Neapolitan dialect about a miracle performed by the Madonna, originally included in the 1985 play *Harlequin*:

> 'Two *zanni* spy a blackbird, then a cat, then a dog, waiting for each animal to eat up the former in order to catch them all at once. Predictably, the animals escape and the *zanni* have to be content with the crumbs the blackbird was pecking. This is followed by the arrival of the virgin Mary *en route* for Jerusalem and needing porters. Understanding *Pellestrina* (on the coast not far from Venice) for *Palestina*, the *zanni* attempt to take her there by a boat which is almost wrecked in a storm and only saved by invocations to the virgin who of course is present). Thus the mistaken identity gag is sustained to the end, supported by songs sung in chorus.'
>
> Christopher Cairns, 'Dario Fo and the *Commedia dell'Arte*', 1993, p. 257.

The Devil in Drag (*Il diavolo con le zinne*)

Two-act play.
First production: Teatro Vittorio Emmanuele, Messina, 7 Aug 1997 (dir. Fo).
British production: National Theatre Youth project, summer 1999.

'Alfonso Ferdinando de Tristano, an incorruptible, progressive magistrate (who disapproves of torture as an instrument of persuasion) investigates an arson in the cathedral. Unhappy about being subjected to his investigation, the prominent citizens of the town launch a campaign to discredit him, employing a couple of devils. One of them is instructed to enter the magistrate's body "through the most suitable orifice, the anus", transforming him into a rogue, a debauchee, a hypocrite and a black marketeer. Due to a misunderstanding, the devil Barlocca enters the body of Pizzocca Gannàssa, Alfonso's elderly and ungainly housekeeper, who is transformed into a delectable, busty lady (the 'tits' of the title). Led astray by this beauty, the magistrate is dragged into court, but the she-devil allows him to be acquitted. Nonetheless he is condemned to become a galley slave in a subsequent trial.'

Cappa and Nepoli, *Dario Fo*, 1997 edition, pp. 153–4.

'In about two hours plus an interval, adapting situations from the comic theatre of the Renaissance, Fo tells the story of a sprightly and open-minded lay magistrate, operating in a sixteenth-century city in the Po valley. In the course of his investigations into a sacrilegious theft, the magistrate unwittingly treads on the toes of the church authorities, who place him under surveillance. At the same time a group of devils, who are also hostile to him, cause his old housekeeper to sprout enormous breasts and buttocks. Coming home drunk – something which one would never expect of him – the magistrate goes to bed with the housekeeper turned whore, is caught *in flagrante delicto* and put on trial for immorality. But before they can testify, the key witnesses in the case are all eliminated . . . Finally the judge is absolved of the main charges but sentenced to five years's imprisonment for heresy, and rows away into the sunset with other galley slaves. These are the bare bones, but as in *commedia dell'arte*, the story is embellished with various digressions and bits of comic business, some of which are organised with Fo's usual expertise as a director (for example, the shrunken devil substituted with a marionette), others based on situations that have become rather hackneyed over the centuries (the greedy cardinal who eats horse manure, mistaking it for a sumptuous feast). The overriding impression is that in writing the piece Fo had no real desire either to organise a solid or particularly politically committed plot which goes beyond the usual equation of corruption with power, or to foreground any opportunities for added pleasure. This time his creative faculties have been absorbed in inventing a semi-imaginary language, or rather languages, which all the characters express themselves in, whether it be the Lombardian of most of the citizens or the ersatz Neapolitan of the horned devils.'

Masolino D'Amico, *La Stampa*, 9 Aug 1997.

Marino at Large (*Marino libero! Marino è innocente!*)

Monologue in two acts.
First production: Teatro Nazionale, Milan, 16 Mar 1998 (dir. Fo). Televised on RAI 2 on 18 Mar 1998.

On the last night of December 1999, the three former left-wing activists imprisoned for the murder of Milan police inspector Luigi Calabresi in 1972, Adriano Sofri, Ovidio Bompressi and Giorgio Pietrostefani, assemble in prison. They are joined by the magistrates who carried out investigations and sentenced them, all represented by life-sized cardboard cut-outs, and the informer who gave evidence against them, Leonardo Marino, represented by a ventriloquist's dummy manipulated by Fo, who is the judge. The play begins with an analysis of the crime scene after Calabresi's murder and follows the long series of contradictions and untruths involved in the "120 lies" of Marino's evidence. Illustrated by over 100 comic-strip-like paintings and drawings by Fo, which are projected as slides, it goes on to give his interpretation of 30 years of Italian political history, from the bombs in Piazza Fontana to the present, and the involvement in them of the secret services, neo-fascists, corrupt magistrates, the ultra-left newspaper *Lotta Continua*, the *carabinieri* and journalists.

'Marino is present in the form of a loutish puppet, along with cut-outs of the suspects, maps and television-style blackboards, in a family-like atmosphere which suggests a community meeting, with Franca (whose tragic abduction is alluded to delicately in the story) acting as prompt and manipulator of the images, operating the comic strips projected on the centre-stage screen and already in the hands of some of the audience in the form of the instant book published by Einaudi. But the investigation-like set up and the community atmosphere detract in no way whatsoever from the performance aspect of the show, since here once again every issue becomes a spectacle, a pantomime, developed to an absurd and imaginary extreme, provoking laughter, as in the enchanting story of Johan Padan, another "con man" from Dario's great repertoire, where the fulcrum was also in the magical illustrations in a huge book which were transformed into visual and sonic action. The one difference being, as is well known, that this is a real and painful story, even though it is full of the improbabilities and the mysteries of Italian public life and fits ideally into the repertoire of the imagination.'

Franco Quadri, 'Fo, il giullare militante ritorna',
La Repubblica, 19 Mar 1998, p. 49.

CHAPTER 11

MINOR PLAYS

The 999th of the Thousand (Il 999° del mille)

One-act farce, written 1959, published 1976.
First production: Teatro Mobile Globo, Milan, Sept 1959
(dir. Fo). Also broadcast on Italian radio.

'A "miles gloriosus" boasts that he has taken part in the
expedition of the Thousand, which he describes to his fellow
townspeople in the rhetoric of military publicity. Caught out by
one of Garibaldi's real soldiers, the young man is saved from
disgrace by the unexpected arrival of the "general" who
pretends to recognise him, and drags him off with him for his
next action.'

Cappa and Nepoli, Dario Fo, 1982, p. 44.

The True Story of Piero Anghera, Who Wasn't at the Crusades (La vera storia di Piero Anghera, che alla crociata non c'era)

Three-act play, written 1960, published 1981.
First production: Gruppo della Tosse, Teatro Stabile, Genoa,
21 May 1984 (dir. Tonino Conte, des. Emanuele Luzzati).

A large-cast play with songs, about the medieval communes and
the political opportunism of the crusades. Piero Anghera is a
scribe who finds he is able to fly. Due to the purity of his

thoughts, he loses this ability when he falls in love with his stepmother, the Duchess Federica. He organises the subjects of the realm into opposition against her husband, the Duke Oddo, on his return from the crusades.

'. . . This is the play that prompted me more than any other to invent new solutions and rhythms, pantomime tricks and scores of other frenetic situations.'

Fo, Introduction to *La storia vera di Piero Anghera*, 1981, p. 7.

'The pleasure in its stylistic and formal derivations, its irreverence towards high cultural concerns, its explosion of gestural devices and popular entertainment are leavened by what seems at times an excessively undisciplined and incomprehensibly rich concept. Fo borrows unlimitedly from any theatrical forms (including Brecht) which stimulate the imagination.'

Mauro Mandotti, *Secolo X*, 23 May 1984.

The End of the World, or God Makes Them and then Matches Them (*La fine del mondo, o Dio li fa, poi li accoppia*)

Two-act play, written 1963. Unpublished.
First production: Teatro Belli, Rome, Feb 1979 (dir. Jose Quaglio).

Abelard and Heloise survive a world cataclysm by hiding in a sewer, and believe they are the sole remaining people in the world until they encounter a corrupt General of Intelligence and an Angel. The world is in the process of being taken over by cats in the absence of human power figures. The play deals with sexual relationships, and satirises the 'historic compromise', in which the PCI negotiated entering the government.

The Pinball-Dummy Boss (*Il pupazzo giapponese*)

One-act play, written 1967, published 1976.
First performed as 'The Japanese Puppet' in the TV show
Let's Talk about Women, RAI TV, May 1977 (dir. Fo).

A short play in which the manager of a factory is paralysed by
an electric shock during repairs to the production line because
he refuses to turn off the power. A naive female worker,
Armida, has lost two fingers in an accident and spent time in a
mental hospital due to taking too many tranquillisers. Two
workers persuade her that a new Japanese experiment, in which
workers can vent their frustrations against an effigy of their boss,
has been initiated in the factory. Armida discovers the paralysed
manager in an office, and believes he is a 'pinball jukebox
dummy'. She 'plugs him in' to a heating device, inserts a 100-
lire coin in his mouth, squashes his nose and twists his ear. She
then proceeds to insult him, draw on his face, and then smear
him with disinfectant, creosote and other cleaning fluids. The
factory boss and a doctor, who have been summoned by other
workers, arrive and discover the anguished, smouldering
manager.

On the Seventh Day God Created Prisons (*Il settimo giorno Dio creò le carceri*)

Two-act play, written 1972. Unpublished. Unperformed.

'... A direct contribution to the militant prison campaign ...
The plot is based on one of Fo's most familiar comic schemes,
the inadvertent confusion of one person for another. A judge is
called in to quell a prison revolt; in the course of turmoil, he
himself is mistaken for a convict, beaten, and locked up. In jail,
he is forced to experience personally all the horrors which make

up the daily lives of the inmates. When an official finally discovers the mistake and procures his release, the judge initiates such a violent, rabid campaign in denunciation of existing prison conditions that he is assumed to be insane and is locked up in another kind of prison – a state mental institution – for the rest of his life.'

Mario B. Mignone, Dario Fo: Jester of the Italian Stage,

p. 58.

Stop the Fascists! (*Basta con i fascisti!*)

An audiovisual show, written in 1973.
First performance: Toured in factories, workers' halls, etc., in northern Italy in summer 1973, by Franca Rame and members of La Comune. *Mammi Togni* first performed in a piazza in Pavia 25 April 1971, published 1989.

A documentary about fascism past and present, based on personal accounts by Second World War partisans and contemporary political militants. Includes the monologue *Mamma Togni*, later included in *The People's War in Chile*, and urges the outlawing of fascism and the spread of 'militant anti-fascism'.

The Plates (*I piatti*)

One-act sketch, written 1976, published 1978, 1991.
First performance: In the TV show *Let's Talk about Women*, May 1977.

An anarchic comedy in which a family, fed up with consumerism, game shows and advertising, start throwing hundreds of plates and smashing up their living room.

The Giullarata (*La giullarata*)

Two-act play, published 1976.
First production: Palazzina Liberty, Milan, 11 Nov 1975 (dir. Fo, with Cicciu, Concetta & Pina Busacca).

A series of songs and sketches demonstrating the art of the *cantastorie* (singer-storyteller), beginning with *The Birth of the Jongleur* from *Mistero buffo*, and including *The Ballad of Cicciu Corno* from *The People's War in Chile*, as well as a number of songs and sketches from Busacca's Sicilian repertoire, and songs by Fo.

'. . . I am a *giullare cantastorie* . . . the *giullare* strips the king, the bishops and government ministers down to their underpants with his satire. The people's laughter and sneers have always been the most dangerous threat to the authorities.'

Cicciu Busacca, in *La Giullarata*, 1976, pp. 19-20.

'The acting is done by Cicciu, who makes observations on the status and role of popular culture, quoting Brecht and stressing the connection between his ballads and the recent history of oppression. There are numerous motifs and narrative sections from Fo's repertoire in the collection. Music is the most prevalent part of the play . . .'

Cappa and Nepoli, p. 115.

Eve's Diary (*Il diario d'Eva*)

Monologue, written 1978, published 1989.
First performance: Milan, Dec 1984.
First US production: Artists' Foundation, Massachusetts, Oct 1985 (trans. Cristina Nutrizio & Ron Jenkins, dir. Anna-Maria Lisi & Ron Jenkins).

'I read Mark Twain's "Eve's Diary" and was inspired to rewrite the entire story as a madrigal. . . . As it progressed it confirmed an intuition I have always had about the superiority of women right from the origins of the human race, an intuition confirmed by anthropology. This woman is an intellectual in the way she organises her life: she creates artefacts such as vases and utensils, and decorates and paints them. And even in pre-matriarchal society she introduces a different and richer form of nutrition: agricultural food. She cultivates a garden, and picks and crushes seeds, as well as domesticating animals. In my story she also invents language. When she is nearly 50 years old, Eve finds her diary and re-reads it, interpreting and explaining her life and her relationship with the idiotic Adam, whom she has given the benefit of her knowledge and her wisdom, as well as loving him to the point that he was led to believe that he was the real genius. . . . My "Eve's Diary" stops at the death of Abel. The structure of the story is simple, and like some of my other plays, based around choruses. Its language was greatly influenced by Boccaccio.'

Fo, Prologue to *Eve's Diary*, *Le commedie di Dario Fo,* vol. 8, 1989, p. 125.

The Tragedy of Aldo Moro (*La tragedia di Aldo Moro*)

Play in one act, written and published in 1979.
First performance (as a reading by Fo): Palazzetto dello Sport, Padua, 21 June 1979.

Written in the style of a Greek tragedy, with a central situation based on Philoctetes, a dramatisation of some of the letters Moro wrote to his Christian Democrat colleagues in the government while he was being held by the Red Brigades in a 'people's prison' between March and May in 1978. The play is set up as a forum in which Moro debates with his colleagues, and denounces the refusal of the government to negotiate with the Red Brigades as a desire to make him a scapegoat. The play is presented by a Jester and there are dances by Satyrs and Bacchanals. Fo discarded the play after only one reading.

'I have been working on the Moro play for a long time now, but I have had great difficulty finding a direction and a style for the second act, because current events keep on overtaking the development of the play. The powers-that-be are continually attempting to mystify the issues involved, and sweep them under the carpet. They are cleverer than I am, and always one step ahead of me. However, the political situation since the death of Moro has developed exactly as I predicted in the play. But I am left with a format – that of Greek tragedy – 15 characters, but no performance date.'

Fo, interview on RAI Radio 3, 17 Oct 1979.

Patapumfete

A Clown Show in two parts, written in 1982. Unpublished.
First production: Cinema Teatro Cristallo, Milan, Mar 1983 (dir. Fo, with Alfredo and Ronald Colombaioni).

'Seven clown routines (including *The Morality Play of the Blind Man and the Cripple* from *Mistero buffo*) written for the Colombaioni brothers. As well as a sketch satirising TV quiz shows, and a short trick sequence with metal rings, there is a story about the violence of the city, which ends up in a series of clowns' slaps and somersaults; a worker is turned into a robot by a new automatic production system, where he believes he can relax and drink coffee and smoke cigarettes, but is soon afflicted by an alienation not very dissimilar from that of his old workmate on the production line. There are video games in which "one becomes a little robot in the service of a big robot, who leads you through a process which even involves punishment, exploitation, and the addiction principle." There is a relatively moral confrontation between an old and cheerful drunk and his friend who rebukes him for this disgusting vice, but pops tranquillisers, sniffs cocaine, injects heroin, and finally turns a backward somersault and dies.'

Ugo Volli, *La Repubblica*, 6 Mar 1983.

'This text originated from a collective workshop begun in Perugia in the summer of 1982 with Alfredo and Ronald Colombaioni ... and their already rich and full repertoire of acrobatics, techniques and comic tricks of a wide range of clown routines, and the desire to do a show together. We began to work on their repertoire and build it up into scenes based on current issues ... I would like to develop this research into clowns further, placing it in a closer relation to *commedia dell'arte*, the origins of comedy, buffo and so on. Naturally translating it into the reality of today, as I think we have done in this work ...'

Fo, programme note to *Patapumfete*, 1983.

'Although the sketches are entertaining and worthwhile, as a product they are much less convincing. To the observer it is the defects rather than the merits of its clown aspect and Fo's writing which are apparent. There is a certain uneasiness in the performers when it comes to straight acting, outside of the gags, and in the somewhat verbose ideological content which Fo often produces at the beginning of his plays and then modifies and prunes once he makes contact with his audience and finds the right balance.'

Ugo Volli, *La Repubblica*, 6 Mar 1983.

The Candlestickmaker (*Il candelaio*)

Monologue, written 1983. Unpublished. Unperformed.

A sketch loosely based on the general situation of Giordano Bruno's sixteenth-century comedy of the same name, and used in a modified form in *Elizabeth* and *Harlequin*. A dresser informs the audience that the play they are about to see has been called off due to the illness of the lead actress, and begins telling them the story. A candlemaker has grown tired of his wife and begun to frequent a prostitute. The wife approaches the prostitute, who trains her in her art, enabling the husband to rediscover his wife as prostitute.

God Makes Them and Then Wipes Them Out (*Dio li fa poi li accoppa*)

Two-act play, written 1984. Unpublished. Unperformed.

'. . . Written . . . in the light of the new wave of revelations about the Mafia and its activities at the centre of power politics . . . a wide-ranging satirical farce in the style of . . . Fo's plays of the 1960s. All the characters reveal an identity different from the person they claim to be, and are involved in criminal gangs connected with top-level politicians (there is a "quasi" Andreotti in the play). The comic climax is reached by way of a grotesque device (involving a fake castration), a *tour de force* which takes place in the lounge of a famous criminal surgeon. It is a play of masks, involving a comic situation based on misunderstanding. Towards the end the rival criminal organisations form a consortium . . . and set the surgeon up as a scapegoat. He objects, and the farce ends in a general massacre. But first the action is interrupted to accommodate a brief discussion among the actors as to whether it is legitimate to present all the characters as either negative or corrupt.'

Bent Holm, *The World Turned Upside Down*, chapter 4, p. 32.

Letter from China (*Lettera dalla Cina*)

Monologue, written 1989 and performed by Franca Rame. Subtitled: 'Sent to Paris by a Girl from Beijing' (*Mandata a Parigi da una ragazza di Pekino*).

A young Chinese student militant reflects on the aftermath of the Tiananmen Square massacre: the disappearance of all the foreigners in fear 'like the audience at a circus when a lion escapes from its cage', and the violence of the massacre, 'like a film full of special effects'. She recounts a visit to one of her professors, who is hiding out in the country. He explains why the authorities' backlash was so violent: because the students had dared to discuss their rights and desire for freedom directly with the emperor without intermediaries, and caused a public spectacle which had never been seen in China since the days of the Long March. As she watches her comrades being arrested, the girl decides not to try to escape, and is reminded of the photos she has seen of the Communists arrested in 1927 by Chiang-kai Chek. The radio broadcasts warnings to the students to give themselves up and to others to denounce them, and the anonymous letter-writer concludes with a plea to foreign observers not to 'turn off your memories of us with your TV sets', and to sing the 'Internationale' as a way of remembering them.

Let's Talk about Women (*Parliamo di donne*)

Two one-act plays, *Heroine* (*L'eroina*) and *The Fat Woman* (*La donna grassa*) by Franca Rame.
First production: Ravenna, 4 Dec 1991 (dir. Fo).

In *Heroine*, Rame is Carla, a 'Mater Tossicorum', and ex-Latin mistress who has become a travelling saleswoman, dealing in pornographic videos, fake mobile phones, contraceptives and other gadgets. She waits on the fringes of a public park in the outer suburbs of Milan for a drug dealer to sell her heroin to administer to her daughter, who is an addict and whom she keeps at home tied to the bed. She has already lost two sons to heroin, and dreams of taking her daughter to Liverpool, which she thinks is a good environment to get her daughter off drugs. To raise the money for the trip she also works as a prostitute. After an unexpected windfall of two bags full of money turns out to have been part of a dream, she is accidentally killed in the crossfire between two armed robbers, one of whom snatches a bag of money from under her vendor's stall. In *The Fat Woman*, Rame plays Mattea, a 50-year-old woman separated from her husband, who has gone off with another woman, and suffering from obesity. She has a hidden conversation with a man who visits her under the mistaken impression she is his estranged wife, and then an argument with her daughter, who is having problems with her husband and her lover. Finally she orders her daughter out of her house and seeks refuge in the solitary world of her successful invention, an electronically simulated lover.

'. . . These two one-act plays talk about women, about their suffering and their solitude. An abandoned woman seeks refuge in eating and a mother becomes a criminal from watching her daughter taking drugs.

'I don't know if passing a law to legalise drugs is good. I do know that *the present* law is not a good law. I know that it causes three deaths a day and that every day there are 300,000 addicts who have to get through the day, snatching handbags, breaking into houses and risking AIDS. My play is about this as well. It's a show I'm very involved with because I have managed to say everything I've had bottled up inside for many years. The audience understands that, because when I perform it they pay incredible attention. They know I'm talking about issues that are a daily drama for many families. They know that what we say at the end, that after all the great battles and mobilisation for divorce, abortion and rape laws, in everyday life women are women's own worst enemy.'

Rame, in *L'Unità*, 14 Dec 1991.

CHAPTER 12

ADAPTATIONS

I Think Things Out and Sing Them (*Ci ragiono e canto*)

A 'Popular Representation' in two acts (*Rappresentazione popolare in due atti*) based on original material edited by Cesare Bermani and Franco Coggiola.

First production: Il Gruppo Nuovo Canzoniere Italiano, Teatro Carignano, Turin, 16 Apr 1966 (dir Fo). Second version by Nuova Scena, Camera di Lavoro, Sala di Vittorio, Milan, 8 Apr 1969. Third version by La Comune, Teatro della Gioventù, Genoa, 27 Feb 1973.

Australian production (as *Dear Boss, I Want to make You Rich*):, 26 May 1979, Flinders University, Adelaide (dir. Antonio Comin).

'A musical show based on about a hundred traditional Italian workers' and peasant songs from various different regions which were researched by Il Nuovo Canzoniere, and choreographed by Fo.

'In the first part, popular traditions, festivals and the war seen from the point of view of the lower classes were brought to life with very precise rhythms. The second part was glossier, and included a series of beautiful paintings which showed the intuitions of Fo the painter, with the work of washerwomen, a wedding, the passion of Christ according to apocryphal gospels, ending in a great crescendo with the popular anarchist song "Our Home is the Whole Wide World", sung by everyone at the top of their voices, often with . . . the audience joining in.'

Valentini, *La storia di Dario Fo*, 1977, pp. 98–9.

The second version of the show, performed without Il Nuovo Canzoniere, included about a dozen songs written by Fo, such as 'I Saw a King' (later recorded by Enzo Jannacci) and 'Don't Wait for St George'. The third version included the Sicilian *cantastorie* Cicciu Busacca, and some Sicilian material which was later used in *The Giullarata*. This third version was released on LP and cassette by La Comune.

'We were constantly concerned with philological precision, out of respect for the material, which we wanted to use as it was. We were worried that altering the songs would mean that their class point of view would not be so predominant. Dario's concern was with trying to pull the songs apart and make them more theatrical. We were constantly running into obstacles; we refused to do things which seemed absurd to us at the time, like putting on makeup and moving to a theatrical rhythm.'

Ivan della Mea, in Valentini, p. 97.

' "If we don't know where we come from it's impossible for us to know where we're going" said Gramsci; but every time there is any serious proposal to do research into the people and history which really overturns the "false culture" that bourgeois education has perpetrated for centuries, then you see a lot of "revolutionaries" turning up their noses ... the bosses aren't producers, they don't cut cane, they don't make ladders or build walls and so when they have to fight on territory and with rules set up by the people, they always lose ...'

Fo, 'Towards an Introduction to an essay on Popular Culture', *Ci ragiono e canto 3*, 1973, pp. 89, 98.

The Sunday Walk (*La passeggiata della domenica*)

Two-act play by Georges Michel, translated from the French and adapted by Dario Fo.
First production: Teatro Durini, Milan, 18 Jan 1967 (dir. Fo).

'*The Sunday Walk* was a fable about petit bourgeois apathy represented by the Sunday walk of a family in pursuit of its little myths and wellbeing, oblivious to the violence and massacres in the world around it, which in the original play were the Algerian war and the OAS. In Fo's rewritten version, these become clashes between police and demonstrators, and the Americans in Vietnam. The modifications which Fo made to the text were not restricted to political allusions. Michel's play was adapted, its provocative elements accentuated, and any residue of pathos was eliminated.'

Valentini, p. 101.

'Dario Fo . . . has saved all the play's intelligence, and substituted its delicacy with a bitter polemic taste, backed up by a beat group, "Oscar and the Bit-Niks" . . . who become the fundamental aspect of the play, rather than the secondary element they should be . . . Fo is only to blame for having adopted and stressed all the familiar arguments of political propaganda in his enthusiasm for protest . . . These are wall posters which need to be filtered through other means in the theatre.'

C.M.P., *Il Dramma*, Feb–Mar 1967.

The Soldier's Tale (*La storia del soldato*)
'Stage Action by Dario Fo with music by Stravinsky (*Histoire du Soldat*, Octet).'
First production: Teatro alla Scala, Teatro Ponchielli, Cremona, 18 Nov 1978. (dir. Fo).

A free adaptation of Ramuz' libretto for Stravinsky's chamber opera, turning it into a 'choral' political satire about migration from the south of Italy, with *grammelot* and a cast of 32 students from La Scala instead of the four in the original version. The soldier-protagonist is played as a kind of Zanni, by a number of different actors, and there is a series of large-scale stage 'pictures' of the city, the stock exchange, war, a market, and a 'ship of fools', as well as a gigantic cane puppet.

'*The Soldier's Tale* can be read as a kind of accusation against capitalism, which speculates on the concept of patriotism and uses the peasant, the poor devil who is eradicated from his land, and entices him with traffic, business and bogus dreams, taking away his fields and his culture.'

Fo, *Panorama*, 7 Mar 1978, p. 113.

'Fo tries to turn the sanctimoniousness of the story upside down, maintaining a dialectical position towards its development. He keeps some of its essential aspects, like the exchange of the violin for the book of riches, and the story of the princess. But the devil is "for the safeguarding of institutions, for order against disorder, for a balance of payments in the black", and the soldier "could be an emigrant". The original action is substituted with not so much an alternative course of events, as a series of images, which do not proceed one after the other, but are ideally alongside one another. A kind of world theatre in which different incarnations of the soldier are explored.'

Ugo Volli, 'Leggere il teatro come un rebus', in Dario Fo, *La storia di un soldato*, 1979, p. 16.

The Opera of Guffaws (*L'opera dello sghignazzo*)

Adapted from John Gay's *The Beggar's Opera* and some ideas by Jacopo Fo.
First production: Teatro Il Fabbricone, Prato, 1 Dec 1981 (dir. Fo). Revised version, Teatro Nazionale, Milan, Apr 1982 (with Fo as Peachum).

Originally an adaptation of Brecht's *Threepenny Opera* commissioned but rejected by the Berliner Ensemble. Fo later based the play more on Gay's original play. This is a rock opera version, with songs based on motifs from Jimi Hendrix, Janis Joplin, Bob Dylan, etc., in which Macheath becomes a Mafioso-type financial criminal, Peachum runs a fraud agency for drug addicts, drop-outs and social security dodgers, and there is satire on mechanisation, electrical appliances, drugs, sex and violence. Lockit becomes associated with Lockheed, and Macheath's escape from prison takes place during the Notting Hill Carnival.

'Right from the first time the Berliner Ensemble proposed I do a production of *The Threepenny Opera*, I immediately felt it was necessary to apply the same wilful irreverence to Brecht's play that Brecht himself advised: "When you are faced with staging a play by an illustrious author, escape from the terrorism of the classics," he insisted; "treat them without any respect if you want to show the slightest consideration for the ideas that these classics express." Personally, since Brecht himself has now been reduced to a classic, I took his advice at his word, and jumped straight into it (the play, that is), boots and all . . . certainly Brecht, if he were still alive today, would have to redraft the play, and introduce current problems like drugs, kidnappings, the international and industrialised organisation of terrorism, crime, the robot-ised sex market, low-grade mass psycho-analysis, mass media, etc., not to mention the pretty vulgar level that politics has descended to all over the world . . . I must admit that nothing is left of Brecht's play, not even a single line . . . there are references, but only in the form of comments, which are often in an intentional play of antithesis.'

Fo, Introduction to *L'opera dello sghignazzo*, 1982, pp. 5, 7, 8.

'Dario Fo brushed off the nostalgic wickedness of *The Threepenny Opera* and made the shark, who had lost his teeth, bite again. His up-to-date Mack the Knife acts in a world of mass media and business crime; he is no longer the noble villain in his best suit, but a young, dynamic criminal, sitting behind a desk, whose face looks just like the faces of all these multinational salespersons. The Mack, who in the grand-style production of the Turin "Teatro Stabile" was finally allowed to present himself, is a big business gigolo made in Italy, a cynic, but somehow likeable. He is the hero of a spectacle which has not much to do with the Puritan theatre of Brecht, but a lot with a parody of a Broadway supershow: see-saws, sex machines, revolving and suspended stages, acrobats as in a circus. Sure, the beggars are still begging, thieves are stealing, whores whoring, but their faces already show the death of irony and the boredom of an advanced industrial society: instead of a pub-like atmosphere there is a bright neon light, instead of Weill-sound, there is a mixture of rock and cocktail bar music.'

Der Spiegel, 7 Dec 1981, quoted in Vittorio Felaco, 'New Teeth for an Old Shark', in Fuegi *et al.*, *Beyond Brecht*, 1983, p. 67.

'Without politics there wouldn't be Fo – it is his mark of Zorro. But this time his aim doesn't go as deep as usual, and nudges often become merely slaps on the cheeks of politicians and bankrupt businessmen, high-finance entrepreneurs and the financial police. Rinsed in the ascetic water provided by the Teatro Stabile of Turin, who produced the play, the usual red flags Fo waves with justified violence seem faded here . . . Fo is sure that Brecht would have liked his irreverence, but it certainly did not delight his daughter Barbara . . .'

Rita Cirio, *L'Espresso*, 10 Jan 1982, pp. 68, 69.

The Barber of Seville (*La barbiera di Seviglia*)

An Adaptation of the Opera by Rossini.
First production: Amsterdam Musiktheater, 24 Mar 1987 (dir. Fo, music dir. Richard Buckley, televised in 1992). Revived at the Teatro Petruzzelli, Bari, 1988, and at the Opéra Garnier, Paris, 1992.

A version of Rossini's opera directed and designed by Fo, with a *commedia dell'arte* troupe added to the singers and the use of banners and placards with political slogans.

'. . . This particular opera – or the Beaumarchais play on which it is based – does have a kind of relationship with the *commedia dell'arte*, and so has Dario Fo . . . The trouble is that like most producers coming fresh to opera, particularly comic opera, Dario Fo has no faith in the music as being worthy of attention in itself . . . Fo will do anything – fly a kite, paddle a gondola, sit on a swing, toss a doll in a blanket – anything to distract his audience from Rossini.'

Gerald Larner, *The Guardian*, 26 Mar 1987.

The Doctor in Spite of Himself and *The Flying Doctor* (*Il medico malgrado lui* e *Il medico volante*)

Two one-act plays by Molière, adapted by Fo.
First production: Comédie Française, Paris, 18 June 1990 (dir. Fo). Revived 1991.

A highly physical, acrobatic production of two Molière farces based on the repertoire of the sixteenth-century *comici italiani* in Paris, featuring Sganarelle, and incorporating *lazzi* from the *commedia dell'arte*, a chorus and a good deal of extraneous stage business.

'Predictably, Fo retrieved from the "historic memory" of the *comici dell'arte* verbal and gestural elements and improvised *lazzi* which were surprising and sometimes downright obscene, but always highly entertaining, and which had been "behind" these farces by Molière. He then made a skilful attempt to incorporate these into the high-quality acting practice of the "sociétaires"

452

and "pensionnaires" of the Comédie, which, as is well known, is noted for an acting style which has its strong points in the effective interpretation of a great poetic repertoire. For Fo it was ultimately important to succeed in getting a cultivated, international audience to appreciate a type of theatre which is fundamentally farcical, based more on uninhibited gesture than on logical, consistent discourse.'

Federico Doglio, Sipario, Sept 1990, p. 30.

'Viewed through distinctly Fo-vian bifocals, Molière's world became a split-level society that was to include not just the speaking characters provided for in the text, but a second social strata, an active chorus of townspeople, not-so-silent conspirators in the antics of Sganarelle. Not for Fo the individualistic, virtuoso servant, the superhero who miraculously rights all wrongs, but rather a community working together against the old order. . . .

'What Fo had accomplished was not simply to make Molière funnier than ever. True, he had concocted marvels, and inspired the cast to carry it off with remarkable flair. Yes, he had seduced the Comédie Française's refined audiences into the warm enjoyment of so-called low comedy. But above all, he had used the power of raw farce to bring to theatrical life Molière's world of disguise, deception and social upheaval.'

John Towsen, 'Molière "à l'Italienne": Dario Fo at the
Comédie Française', Theater, Summer/Fall 1992, pp. 55, 61.

CHAPTER 13

FILMS

The Screwball (*Lo svitato*)

Dir. Carlo Lizzani, screenplay by Fo, Lizzani, Massimo Mida & Augusto Frassineti, starring Fo & Rame. 1956.

'Fo plays Achilles, a Hulot-like factotum for an evening newspaper, who travels around looking for a scoop in the Milan of the "economic miracle".'

Cappa and Nepoli, *Dario Fo*, 1982, p. 22.

'In reality *The Screwball* was misunderstood because it was different to what people were used to seeing in the cinema at the time. There was an element of fantasy separate from any commitment to content, and a very effective use of pantomime by Fo. Its main defect was in the co-ordination of words and speeches with the language of images. This made it prolix, full of gaps, and using a mode of expression which had little to do with the cinema.'

Carlo Lizzani, in Valentini, p.53.

'The only film I made of any value . . . [it] had its defects, but its comedy was too unusual in comparison with the low-level sort that predominated at the time. It was a precursor of Woody Allen and surreal comedy. It had the lowest box-office takings of that year, and despite being a fiasco, it had pieces of good cinema in it, as is proved by the fact that it is now in the cinemathèques.'

Franca Rame, *Domenica del Corriere*, 3 Oct 1981, p. 44.

'The Screwball is the first character worthy of this term created by Dario Fo. Like the other figures who populate the gallery of the Milanese writer, the Screwball is a pure, candid, naive character who lacks the malice and cynicism of future Fo characters. ... *The Screwball* was a peculiar film, perhaps too surreal and paradoxical for its time, and it was not appreciated. Basing it on a reinvention of silent comedy, its creators wanted it to forge a new direction in Italian film comedy, which had been weighed down and vulgarised by a trivial and joky type of comedy in the films of that time. With obvious reference to Tati, Keaton, Chaplin and Ridolini, *The Screwball* contains a poetic germ which Fo would begin to develop systematically at the end of the 1950s when he returned to the theatre.'

Chiara Casarico, *La vera storia di Dario Fo*, Gremese, Rome, 1998, pp. 19–20.

Souvenir d'Italie (It Happened in Rome)

Dir. Antonio Pietrangeli and Fo, screenplay by Fo, Age & Scarpelli, with Fo in the role of Carlino. 1957.

'An example of "pink neorealism", similar to the summer-holiday film genre. In the role of Carlino, Fo offers a small taste of his storytelling capabilities in a brief, hyperbolic and paradoxical "tirade".'

Casarico, *op. cit.*, p. 17.

Rascel Fifi
Dir. Guido Leoni, screenplay by Fo & Dino Verde, with Fo & Franca Rame. 1957.

'A parody of gangster films in which Dario Fo develops another character which will become typical in his plays, the "dumb Lothario".'

Casarico, *op. cit.*, p. 17.

Fo also collaborated on the screenplays of *Nata a marzo* (*Born in March*, dir. Pietrangeli, 1958) and *Follie d'estate* (*Summer Madness*, 1964).

CHAPTER 14

RADIO PLAYS

Poor Dwarf (Poer nano)

18 monologues written and performed by Fo on RAI Radio weekly from December 1951.

A series of well-known biblical and classical stories performed in popular, 'illegitimate' versions, some based on the stories of the *fabulatori* of Lake Maggiore. The usual endings and morals of the stories are turned upside down and satirised. The stories included 'Cain and Abel', 'Abraham and Isaac', 'Samson and Delilah', 'Romulus and Remus', 'David and Goliath,' 'Nero', 'Daedalus and Icarus', and short, burlesque versions of *Hamlet, Othello, Julius Caesar, Romeo and Juliet*, etc.

'The key point of these stories was always paradox, reversals and opposites . . . Cain was the victim and not the executioner, God knew everything but was absent-minded and caused confusion which his son had to remedy – hence the story of original sin . . these reversals were not done for their own sake, but were a stubborn refusal to accept the logic of convention, and a rebellion against the moral contingent which always sees good on one side and evil on the other . . . The comedy and the liberating entertainment lies in the discovery that the opposite stands up better than the commonplace . . . There is also the fun of desecrating and demolishing the sacred and untouchable monuments of religious tradition.'

Fo, Preface to Poer nano, 1976, p. 5.

Fo also participated in the scripting and performance of two other radio comedy series: *Chichirichì* (1952–53, with Giustino Durano, in which Fo created the character of the civil servant Gorgogliati); and an 11-part series called *You Don't Live on Bread Alone* (*Non si vive di solo pane*, 1955, with Franco Parenti).

'At that time I wasn't used to performing a written text. At the most I jotted down a scenario or a few notes. I wasn't used to the literary dimension. And in fact it was absent from these texts. They were full of inserts, expressions in Lombardy dialect, backtracking, and comments on situations. It was an expression of a tradition which had never been written down, and for which it was necessary to reinvent a form of writing.'

Fo, interview with Enzo Magri, in Valentini, p. 36.

In 1982 Stuart Hood wrote and presented *Throwaway Theatre,* a 30-minute assessment of Fo's work and the problems involved in presenting it in the UK, for BBC Radio 4, which concluded that 'part of the success of Fo's work in the West End must be attributed to the fact that it can be enjoyed on a non-political level.'

In November 1985 a 90-minute radio programme, *Dario Fo and Franca Rame: Comics of the People,* compiled by Tony Mitchell, and produced by Jane and Phillip Ulman and Tony Mitchell, was broadcast on 2FC by the Australian Broadcasting Corporation.

CHAPTER 15

TELEVISION PLAYS

Who's Seen Them? (*Chi l'ha visto?*) *Canzonissima*
Who's seen Them? transmitted by RAI 2, 1962.
Canzonissima transmitted by RAI 1, 1962.

A series of sketches and songs transmitted in one programme on
RAI 2 and in eight parts on RAI 1. The theme song to
Canzonissima was 'Children of the Economic Miracle', and
other songs included 'That Ugly City of Mine', about Milan.
The sketches satirised the entertainment industry, industrial
accidents, the Mafia, conditions in prisons and mental
institutions, scandals and corruption, industrial relations and
building speculation. In one sketch, Fo was 'arrested' by two
'policemen' for breaches of censorship. The programme was
taken off after the eighth episode, when Fo and Rame refused
to drop a sketch referring to a current strike, and they were
effectively banned from Italian TV for 14 years.

'My main idea was to look beyond the surface of the economic
miracle and the conciliatory attitude of the bosses. The gist of
what they were saying was "Times have changed, we're all one
big family now." I wanted to show how exploitation was even
worse than before, and how scandals were proliferating. And
how the authorities tried to deceive people by tranquillising
them with the entertainment industry, pop songs, song festivals,
and programmes like *Canzonissima*. In fact, right from the first
episode I tried to turn it upside down from the inside, and use
its structures to send it up.'

Fo, in Valentini, pp. 83-4.

'Before *Canzonissima* we did a show for the second channel called *Who's Seen Them?* which very few people saw, but in which we were allowed to say virtually whatever we liked. Then to show that TV was open to the Left, since there was a centre-left government, they asked us to do *Canzonissima* . . . We got to the eighth episode. We had already done programmes on the Mafia, and the toll collectors, which had caused a lot of fuss, because the Mafia was, and still is, very powerful, and the toll-collectors were on strike. In the eighth episode there was to be a sketch about the building trade, about deaths and the indifference of bosses to the excessive number of work accidents. The TV channel said no to that piece, and to two others in the same episode. They even said they couldn't understand why we were so stubborn about defending them: they weren't even funny.'

Rame, *Domenica del Corriere*, 3 Oct 1981, p. 45.

The Level-Crossing Woman (*La casellante*)

One-act sketch, written 1962, published 1991.
First performed in *Canzonissima*, RAI 1, 1962.

A journalist interviews a woman working for the railways, who lives with her family in an isolated, smoke-filled shack by the railway line without electricity, gas or heating. She cheerfully recounts all her hardships in this 'vale of tears', where her chickens are often run over by trains, her garden polluted by smoke and her children have to travel ten kilometres to school and are kept awake by the trains. She reveals that her husband is in prison awaiting trial for damage caused by a railway colleague, and they have no fixed contract or pension. Nonetheless she is full of sympathy for her employer.

'When . . . *The Level-Crossing Woman* was performed on RAI 1 . . . a fracas of hitherto unknown dimensions broke out. The

460

television management had blithely rubber-stamped the piece for transmission. The censorship inspectors had completely missed the satirical game hidden in the piece; restricting their inspection to the dialogue and reading the text with the bureaucratic logic of the obvious, they found the subject and the staging of it quite acceptable, even though it was a bit paradoxical. The censors were caught on the wrong foot by the fact that they were dealing for the first time with a text which took its subject from current events, and actual facts connected with the exploitation of workers, and which illustrated, with data from union cases, the inhuman conditions which casual railway workers were forced to undergo. All this was put across casually and amicably . . . As we know, censors' reflexes are a bit slow, and the public realised what was going on much quicker than they did. Reactionary viewers howled with indignation, while democratic progressives applauded enthusiastically. Avalanches of letters and telegrams arrived at the RAI full of insults and charges (the letters of support, which were in the majority, don't count), the absent-minded censors were suspended, and one particular "doormat" bureaucrat was made a scapegoat and fired.'

Fo, Introduction to *Le commedie di Dario Fo IX,* 1991, p. v.

'A very biting satire of the awful conditions of life experienced by women and their families when the women are compelled to accept health-threatening jobs in order to survive. By alternating short descriptions of the disastrous effects of such a job on a woman worker's family life with comments voicing the authority's point of view, the woman's discourse ironically reveals the unfairness of her situation. . . . Rame's parody is apparent when the worker tries to minimalise the responsibilities of the authorities . . . raised an enormous controversy. Although this was the first time that Rame's transgressive voice shook the Italian political system, it was not the last one.'

Marga Cottino-Jones, 'Franca Rame on Stage',
Italica, vol. 72, no. 3, 1995, p. 327.

Let's Talk about Women (*Parliamo di donne*)

Transmitted: RAI 2 in two parts, 18 and 20 May 1977, as part of two retrospective 'cycles' of Fo's plays in the spring and autumn of 1977, recorded live with audiences in the Palazzina Liberty. (Other plays televised were *Mistero buffo, Throw the Lady Out, Isabella, Three Sailing Ships and a Con Man, Seventh Commandment, Steal a Bit Less* and *I Think Things Out and Sing Them*.)

A series of songs, sketches and pieces from other Fo plays, like the monologues *Michele Lu Lanzone* and *Mamma Togni*. The programme also included the short farce *The Plates* and *Waking Up*. In 'The Creation', the first woman immediately kneels in submission to the first man; in 'The Holy Family' the roles of Mary and Joseph are reversed, with Joseph riding the donkey; St Augustine expresses his bewilderment about the existence of a female soul; the use of boys for female roles in the Elizabethan theatre is satirised; Fo boycotts Rame when she attempts to sing the feminist song 'Io sono mia' (I Am Mine); Rame sings a blues song which is completely upstaged by Fo's accompaniment. In 'The Pregnant Man' a wealthy industrialist who is president of the anti-abortion league becomes pregnant through a process of parthenogenesis. His wife and daughter are also pregnant, and he decides to have an abortion.

'Subjects dealt with more fully by the women's movement remained in the shadows (as various feminist groups noted). The "talking about women" consisted mainly of putting female characters on stage, without dealing with specific aspects of women's problems. When it did, it was in fairly traditional ways, like the scene in which a woman and a man become "pregnant". Perhaps the sole exception was the wonderful sketch *Waking Up* . . .'

Valentini, p. 174.

Buona sera con Franca Rame

20 half-hour programmes written and directed by Fo, transmitted on RAI 2 from Dec 1979 to Jan 1980.

In between the opening song, a satirical reversal of 'Little Red Riding Hood' in which the wolf is kidnapped and held to ransom, and the closing song by Fo satirising UFOs and superheros as devices to distract people's attention from social and political problems, are a series of satirical songs and sketches. These include a piece about the charges against Social Democrat Defence Minister Tanassi for fraud and corruption in the Lockheed affair, and his 're-education' by Rame. In 'The Old Age Problem' old people are thrown out of windows in order to save on pensions and old people's homes. In 'The Black Out' a woman makes elaborate preparations, including blindfolding herself, for a possible power cut, watched by her bemused husband. It is their daughter's twentieth birthday, and three of her boyfriends, and her grandparents, are due to arrive for a party. There is a blackout as the first boyfriend arrives, and the grandparents are stuck in the lift. The fire brigade arrive, and everyone helps the woman to cook the 20 kilos of food in the fridge. As the daughter blows out the candles on her birthday cake, the lights come back on, and the woman tells all the guests to leave so she can save the food for another energy crisis.

The Tricks of the Trade (*I trucchi del mestiere*)

Six one-hour programmes, transmitted on RAI 3, Feb–Mar. 1985.

A live recording of the performance-seminars Fo gave at the Teatro Argentina in Rome in October 1984, which were later included in the book of the same title.

Forced Transmission (*Trasmissione forzata*)

Eight 90-minute programmes, transmitted on RAI 3, 12 Apr –
31 May 1988 (dir. Alida Fanoli).

A variety series incorporating new satirical sketches about RAI
television, Italian politicians and topical events like the
celebration of Liberation Day on 25 April. There are also items
from Fo's and Rame's repertoire such as *Can't Pay? Won't Pay!*
and *The Bologna Riot* from *Obscene Fables*. Also included are
excerpts from *Canzonissima* and Rame's *Buona sera con Franca
Rame*, a number of Fo's *grammelots*, and songs by Enzo Jannacci.
Pieces subsequently published include 'Italian Rape Weather
Forecast', a satirical 'weather report' about rape statistics in Italy
and a fashion parade of rape safety clothing. In 'A Friendly
Voice' a woman recounts to a Samaritan-style help phone
service her pregnancy and her complicated sexual relations with
all the male members of a family. In 'I Had Plastic Surgery' a
grandmother records a secret video for a close friend about her
humiliating experiences after undergoing rejuvenating surgery.
'The Pregnant Grandmother', based on a case in South Africa,
is the story of a middle-aged woman who becomes a 'rent a
womb', first for her daughter whose husband doesn't want her
to undergo the physical deformations of pregnancy, then for a
wealthy industrialist's wife. In 'Test-tube Baby', a couple discuss
whether to attempt in-vitro fertilisation, with the husband
eventually refusing to be a 'Frankenstein'. 'Paris–Dakar' is a
satire of the motor race in which a couple terrorise the desert
with a series of roadkills and their vehicle finally explodes.

In Britain, the Belt and Braces version of *Accidental Death of an
Anarchist* was broadcast on Channel 4 on 14 Sept 1983, while a
one-hour programme, *Dario Fo*, directed by Dennis Marks, was
shown in the BBC 2 *Arena* series on 26 Feb 1984. This included
parts of *The Resurrection of Lazarus* and *Boniface VIII*. Channel 4
also broadcast a programme, directed by Stuart Hood, entitled

Dario Fo: Modern Jester, in December 1985, in which John McGrath and Griff Rhys Jones discussed sections of *Mistero buffo* from the RAI TV cycle.

Robbie Coltrane's performance of *Mistero buffo*, directed by Morag Fullerton, was broadcast on BBC TV Scotland in 1990.

CHAPTER 16

SONGS

Ballate e canzoni

Dario Fo, *Ballate e canzoni*, Bertani, Verona, 1974. Second edition, Newton Compton, Rome, 1976.

An anthology of the texts of more than 100 songs from Fo's plays from 1953 to 1973. Includes songs from *Canzonissima* and *Who's Seen Them?* and 10 other one-off songs, many written for Enzo Jannacci, with music for 16 of the songs.

'The songs clearly follow Dario Fo's general development, from songs of purely imaginative play . . . to songs of sympathy for the "louts" of the underworld of the city's outskirts . . . to a mockery of the pop songs of the culture industry . . . to songs of political satire . . . to choral songs propagating the principles of socialism and a proletarian conception of the world.'
        Lanfranco Binni, Introduction, *Ballate e canzoni*, p. 24.

Recordings of songs by Fo include Dario Fo, *Ma che aspettate a batterci le mani,* (Ricordi, Serie Orizzonte, 1977), and *Le canzoni,* vol. 1, vol. 2 and vol. 3 (Edizioni F.R. La Comune), which contain songs from his plays.

Songs by Fo have been recorded by Enzo Jannacci in *Nuove registrazioni 1980.* (Ricordi, Serie Orizzonte, 1980), *I successi di Enzo Jannacci* (International Joker production CD, 1990), and *Il musicista che ride* (1998), which contains a 1998 duet with Fo, 'C'è la luna in mezzo al mare' (The Moon in the middle of the Sea).

There is an extensive discography of songs recorded by Fo up to 1976 in Binni's Introduction to *Ballate e canzoni*, but almost all of these have been deleted.

CHAPTER 17

BOOKS AND ESSAYS

Don't Tell Me About Arches, Tell Me About Your Prisons
(Non parliamo degli archi, parliamo delle carceri)

Edited by Franca Rame. Edizioni F.R. La Comune, 1984.

A book based on the diaries kept by the mother of Alberto Buonoconto, a member of NAP (Armed Proletarian Nucleus). He went insane and committed suicide at the age of 27, after being subjected to years of imprisonment in various jails all over Italy on the basis of scant evidence and charges of possession of arms and false documents.

'The book . . . gives evidence of an inhumanely repressive system. Franca thinks that the middle classes washed their hands of terrorism, although often it was happening next door. A reading of this book, which compares to that of seeing movies such as *El Norte* or *The Killing Fields*, reveals worlds of cruelty beyond imagination. Besides being a historical document, the book also speaks about Franca: she emerges as a writer close to the simple, painful facts . . .'
                    Serena Anderlini, 'Franca Rame: Her Life and Works',
                                        Theater, Winter 1985, p. 36.

A Short Manual for the Actor (*The Tricks of the Trade*) (*Manuale minimo dell'attore*)

With a section by Franca Rame. Einaudi, Turin, 1987.

An edited transcript of various seminar-workshops which Fo gave in the 1980s, particularly *The Tricks of the Trade*, *The History of Masks* and the Riverside Workshops, and workshops held at the 'Free University of Alcatraz' in Santa Cristina, in Gubbio, near Perugia. Divided into six Days, it covers *commedia dell'arte*, the Rame family, the theatrical text, Diderot, masks, gestures, laughter, songs, dance, movement, mime and 'breaking the fourth wall'. There are also sections on *grammelot,* the *giullari,* theatre of situation, the role of the spectator, theatre of commitment, and filmic aspects of theatre perspective (with illustrations from *Tale of a Tiger*). Other topics include makeup, ancient Greek theatre, the voice, improvisation, clowns, theatre and literature, epic theatre, female clowns, and women in theatre. There is also a glossary of theatrical terms.

A Provocative Dialogue about Comedy, Tragedy and Reason (*Dialogo provocatorio sul comico, il tragico, la follia e la ragione*)

By Dario Fo & Luigi Allegri. Laterza, Rome, 1990.

A book-length interview with Fo which proceeds in rough chronology from Fo's early works through to more recent plays.

Fabulazzo

'Theatre, Culture, Politics, Society, Sentiments: Articles, Interviews, Playtexts, Documents, 1960–1991'. Edited by Lorenzo Ruggiero, revised by Walter Valeri, with a Preface by Franca Rame. Kaos Edizioni, Milan, 1992.

An anthology of Fo's occasional writings about politics and theatre, and interviews from Italian newspapers and magazines. There are also sketches and extracts from some of his plays, and translations of a number of foreign-language reviews and interviews.

Totò: A Manual for the Comic Actor (Totò: Manuale dell'attore comico)

Vallecchi, Florence, 1995.

A series of short, illustrated essays on the 'poetics' of the Neapolitan film actor, with a dictionary of quotations and a filmography.

Molière's *Don Giovanni*

Translated by Delia Gambelli and Dario Fo. Marsilio, Milan, 1997.

A translation of Molière's playtext into a sixteenth-century Neapolitan dialect partly invented by Fo, based on a literal Italian translation by Gambelli.

NOTES

All translations of quotations are by the author, unless otherwise indicated.

Introduction

1. Dario Fo, *Fabulazzo*, Milan, Kaos Edizioni, 1992, p. 273.
2. The Swedish Academy, Press Release, 9 October 1997, 'The Nobel Prize for Literature 1997: Dario Fo'.
3. Antonio Scuderi, *Dario Fo and Popular Performance*, New York, Legas, 1998, p. 106.
4. *Dario Fo and Franca Rame Theatre Workshops at Riverside Studios, London, 28 April, 5, 12, 13 and 19 May 1983,* London, Red Notes, 1983, pp. 40–1.
5. *Corriere della Sera,* 11 October 1998.
6. Steve Grant and Tony Mitchell, 'An Interview with Dario Fo and Franca Rame', *Theater*, vol. 14, no. 3, Summer/Fall 1983, p. 46.
7. Dario Fo, 'Dialogue with an Audience', *Theatre Quarterly*, vol. IX, no. 35, Autumn 1979, p. 15.
8. Joseph Farrell, 'The Actor Who Writes: Dario Fo and the Nobel Prize', forthcoming in Joseph Farrell and Antonio Scuderi, *Dario Fo: Stage, Text and Tradition*, Carbondale, Southern Illinois University Press, 1999.
9. Paolo Puppa, 'Tradition, Traditions and Dario Fo' (translated by Joseph Farrell), in Farrell and Scuderi, *op. cit.*
10. Dario Fo, *Manuale minimo dell'attore,* Turin, Einaudi, 1987, p. 4.

Chapter 1

1. Dario Fo, *Mistero buffo*, Verona, Bertani, 1977, p. xix.

2. *Ibid.*, p. 9.
3. *Ibid.*, p. 9.
4. Antonio Scuderi, 'Updating Antiquity', forthcoming in Joseph Farrell and Antonio Scuderi, *Dario Fo: Stage, Text and Tradition, op. cit.*
5. Lanfranco Binni, *Dario Fo*, Florence, Il Castoro, 1977, p. 52.
6. *Mistero buffo, op. cit.*, pp. 4–5.
7. Walter Valeri has argued that the term 'grommelot' was coined in 1918, when it appears in the writings of a French critic, Leon Chancerel, who was a collaborator of the director Jacques Copeau. Copeau's daughter has claimed that the term derived from 'gremeau', meaning in French argot to improvise on sounds and rhythms. Fo's use of the term 'grammelot' may be an Italian corruption of this word. Another possible origin is 'grelot', a rattle or bell, or 'avoir les grelots' (to be scared stiff), a term used by *commedia dell'arte* players in Paris in the sixteenth century. This 'denotes the nervous and garbled speech of someone who is too frightened or upset to articulate clearly'. (Walter Valeri, 'Dario Fo: Actor-playwright', in Farrell and Scuderi, *op. cit.*)
8. Dario Fo, *Pum, pum! Chi è? La polizia!*, Verona, Bertani, 1974, pp. 234–5.
9. Various authors, *teatro politico di Dario Fo*, Milan, Mazzotta, 1977, p. 6.
10. In Chiara Valentini, *La storia di Dario Fo*, Milan, Feltrinelli, 1977, p. 125.
11. *Il teatro politico di Dario Fo, op. cit.*, p. 60.
12. In Valentini, *op. cit.*, p. 128.
13. Ugo Volli, in *La Repubblica*, 3 March 1979.
14. In Erminia Artese, *Dario Fo parla di Dario Fo*, Cosenza, Lerici, 1977, pp. 53–5.
15. Michele Straniero, *Giullari e Fo*, Milan, Lato Side, 1978.
16. In *Panorama*, 21 November 1978.
17. In Artese, *op. cit.*, pp. 84–5.
18. *Mistero buffo*, p. vii.
19. In Artese, p. 19.
20. *Mistero buffo*, p. xx.
21. *Il teatro politico di Dario Fo, op. cit.*, p. 72.

22. In Artese, pp. 51, 68.
23. *Ibid.*, p. 140.
24. *Mistero buffo*, p.100.
25. In Artese, pp. 139-40.
26. Paolo Puppa, *Il teatro di Dario Fo*, Venice, Marsilio, 1978, pp. 113-14.
27. In *Mistero buffo*, p. 215.
28. *Ibid.*, p. 213.
29. *Ibid.*, p. 217.
30. *Ibid.*, p. 184
31. In *Il Messaggero*, 30 March 1980.
32. Dario Fo, *La storia della tigre*, Milan, La Comune, 1980, p. 3.
33. In *Il Messaggero*, 30 March 1980.
34. In the *International Daily News*, 1 April 1980.
35. In *Il Messaggero*, 30 March 1980.
36. *Theater*, vol. 13, no. 4, Winter 1982, p. 88.
37. Dario Fo, *Il fabulazzo osceno*, Milan, La Comune, 1982, p. 1.
38. *La Repubblica*, 30 May 1981.
39. Mikhail Bakhtin, *Rabelais and his World*, translated by Helene Iswolsky, Bloomington, Indiana University Press, 1984, pp. 92-3.
40. Dario Fo and Luigi Allegri, *Dialogo provocatorio sul comico, il tragico, la follia e la ragione*, Rome, Laterza, 1990, p. 112.
41. Antonio Scuderi, *Dario Fo and Popular Performance*, *op. cit.*, p. 107, note 12.
42. Antonio Scuderi, 'Updating Antiquity', *op. cit.*
43. Ron Jenkins, *Subversive Laughter: The Liberating Power of Comedy*, New York, The Free Press, 1994, pp. 123-4.
44. *Sipario*, April 1993.
45. In Marisa Pizza, *Il gesto, la parola, l'azione: Poetica, drammaturgia e storia dei monologhi di Dario Fo*, Rome, Bulzoni, 1996, p. 367.
46. *Ibid.*, p. 364.

Chapter 2

1. Bianca Fo Garambois, *Io, da grande mi sposo un partigiano*, Turin, Einaudi, 1976, pp. 10-1.

2. Artese, *op. cit.*, pp. 8-9.

3. Valentini, *op. cit.*, p. 21.

4. *Ibid.*, p. 25.

5. In Claudio Meldolesi, *Su un comico in rivolta: Dario Fo il bufalo il bambino*, Rome, Bulzoni, 1978, pp. 25-6.

6. Dario Fo and Jacopo Fo, *Poer nano*, Milan, Ottaviano, 1976, p. 5.

7. In Luigi Ballerini and Giuseppe Risso, 'Dario Fo Explains', (translated by Lauren Haliquist and Fiorenza Weinpple), *The Drama Review* 77, vol. 22, no. 1, March 1978, p. 36.

8. In Valentini, *op. cit.*, pp. 39-40.

9. *Ibid.*, p. 35.

10. Lanfranco Binni (ed.), in Dario Fo, *Ballate e canzoni*, Rome, Newton Compton, 1976, p. 26.

11. In Meldolesi, *op. cit.*, p. 42.

12. In Valentini, *op. cit.*, p. 53.

13. In Chiara Casarico, *La vera storia di Dario Fo*, Rome, Gremese, 1998, pp. 36-7.

14. In Valentini, *op. cit.*, p. 55.

15. *La Repubblica*, 25 October 1980.

16. Joe Farrell, 'Fo and Feydeau: Is Farce a Laughing Matter?' *Italica*, vol. 72, no. 3, 1995, pp. 314-16.

17. *Ibid.*, p. 320.

18. Dario Fo, *Fabulazzo*, *op. cit.*, p. 36.

19. In Valentini, *op. cit.*, p. 58.

20. *Ibid.*, p. 64.

21. *Le commedie di Dario Fo*, vol. 1, Turin, Einaudi, 1966, p. 26.

22. Puppa, *op. cit.*, p. 37.

23. In Lanfranco Binni (ed.,) Dario Fo, *Ballate e canzoni*, *op. cit.*, p.50.

24. Joseph Farrell, 'The Actor Who Writes: Dario Fo and the Nobel Prize', forthcoming in Joseph Farrell and Antonio Scuderi, *Dario Fo: Stage, Text and Tradition*, *op. cit.*

25. Ballerini and Risso, *op. cit.*, p. 46.

26. In Binni, 1976, *op.cit.*, p. 42.

27. Puppa, *op.cit.*, pp. 47-8.

28. *The Scotsman*, 29 August 1983.

29. *La Repubblica*, 24-5 April 1977.

30. In Binni, 1976, *op.cit.*, p. 51.
31. Franca Rame, in *Domenica del Corriere*, 3 October 1981, p. 45.
32. In Valentini, *op. cit.*, p. 85.
33. *Le commedie di Dario Fo*, vol. 2, Turin, Einaudi, 1966, p. 44.
34. *Ibid.*, p. 86.
35. Puppa, *op.cit.*, p. 61.
36. Joseph Farrell, 'The Actor Who Writes: Dario Fo and the Nobel Prize', *op. cit.*
37. *La Repubblica,* February 1979.
38. *Le commedie di Dario Fo,* vol. 2, *op. cit.*, p. 172.
39. In Valentini, p. 91.
40. Puppa, *op.cit.*, p. 91, note 19.
41. *Ibid.*, p. 62.
42. In Artese, *op. cit.*, p. 49.
43. Puppa, *op.cit.*, p. 77.
44. Marina Cappa and Roberto Nepoli, *Dario Fo*, Rome, Gremese, 1982, p. 66.
45. In Meldolesi, *op. cit.*, p. 104.
46. In Valentini, *op. cit.*, p. 99.
47. *Ibid.*, p. 101.
48. A. Richard Sogliuzzo, 'Dario Fo: Puppets for a Proletarian Revolution', *The Drama Review*, 55, vol. 16, no. 3, September 1972, p. 73.
49. In Ballerini and Risso, *op. cit.*, p. 43.
50. *L'Espresso*, 23 November 1969.

Chapter 3
1. *Libération*, 9 January 1974.
2. Dario Fo, 'Per una nuova gestione degli spazi e degli spettacoli', in Franco Quadri, *Il teatro del regime*, Milan, Mazzotta, 1976, p. 143.
3. Sogliuzzo, *op. cit.*, p. 72.
4. *Le commedie di Dario Fo, vol. 3*, Turin, Einaudi, 1975, pp. 21-2.
5. *Ibid.*, p. 107.
6. *Ibid.*, p. 128.
7. In Valentini, *op. cit.*, p. 112.
8. *Ibid.*, p. 113.

9. In *Playboy* (Italian issue), December 1974, quoted in Lanfranco Binni, *Attento te!* . . . , Verona, Bertani, 1975, p. 385.

10. David L. Hirst, *Dario Fo and Franca Rame*, London, Macmillan, 1989, p. 174.

11. *Le commedie di Dario Fo, vol.3, op. cit.*, p. 164.

12. Bernard Dort, *Théâtre en jeu*, Paris, 1977, p. 205.

13. In Quadri, *Il teatro del regime, op. cit.*, p. 137.

14. Valentini, *op. cit.*, p. 112.

15. In Binni, *Attento te!* . . ., *op. cit.*, p. 263.

16. Cappa and Nepoli, *op. cit.*, p. 90.

17. *Rinascita*, 13 November 1970.

18. Valentini, *op. cit.*, p.132.

19. In *Playboy* (Italian issue), December 1974, quoted in Binni, *Attento te!* . . ., *op.cit.* p. 385.

20. Piero Sciotto (ed.), *Il teatro di Dario Fo e Franca Rame: rappresentazioni al estero dal 1960 al 1989*, Milan, 1990, quoted in Christopher Cairns, 'Italy', in Ralph Yarrow (ed.), *European Theatre 1960–1990: Cross-cultural perspectives*, London, Routledge, 1992, p. 136.

21. In *Sipario*, May 1971.

22. Dario Fo, *Morte accidentale di un Anarchico*, second edition, Turin, Einaudi, 1975, p. 115.

23. *Ibid.*, p. 112.

24. Valentini, *op. cit.*, p.135.

25. Pina Piccolo, 'Farce as the Mirror of Bourgeois Politics: *Morte accidentale di un anarchico*', *Forum Italicum*, vol. 20, no. 2, Fall 1986, p. 573.

26. Dario Fo and Luigi Allegri, *Dialogo provocatorio sul comico, il tragico, la follia e la ragione*, *op.cit*, pp. 14-5.

27. *Morte accidentale di un anarchico, op. cit.*, p. 106.

28. *Ibid.*, p. 6.

29. *Ibid.*, p. 31.

30. *Ibid.*, p. 39.

31. *Ibid.*, p. 43.

32. *Ibid.*, pp. 65-7.

33. Paul Taylor, 'Window of opportunity', *The Independent*, 9 January 1991.

34. *Dialogo provocatorio, op. cit.*, p. 41.
35. Joylynn Wing, 'The Performance of Power and the Power of Performance: Rewriting the Police State in Dario Fo's *Accidental Death of an Anarchist'*, *Modern Drama*, vol. 33, no. 1, March 1990, p. 140.
36. Piccolo, *op. cit.*, p. 173.
37. *Morte accidentale di un anarchico, op. cit.*, pp. 88–9.
38. Wing, *op. cit.*, pp. 145–6.
39. *Morte accidentale di un anarchico, op. cit.*, p. 102.
40. Dario Fo, 'Andiamo a ridere', *A.R.T. News.*, vol. 7, no. 4, May 1987, p. 1.
41. *Morte accidentale di un anarchico, op. cit.*, p. 106.
42. *Ibid.*, p. 107.
43. *Ibid.*, p. 108.
44. Valentini, *op. cit.*, p. 138.
45. Dario Fo, *Pum, pum! Chi è? La polizia!*, Verona, Bertani, 1974, pp. 11–2.
46. Valentini, *op. cit.*, p. 137.
47. Binni, *Attento te!, op. cit.*, p. 338.
48. Puppa, *op. cit.*, p. 173–4.
49. Valentini, *op. cit.*, p. 141.
50. Binni (ed.), *Ballate e canzoni, op. cit.*, p. 27.
51. In Valentini, *op. cit.*, p. 143.
52. *Ibid.*, p. 145.
53. Dacia Maraini, *Fare teatro*, Milan, Bompiani, 1974, p. 73.
54. *Pum, pum!, op. cit.*, p. 134.
55. Umberto Eco, 'Pum, pum! Chi è? Fascisti!', *L'Espresso*, 18 March 1973.
56. Suzanne Cowan, 'The Throwaway Theatre of Dario Fo', *The Drama Review*, vol. 19, no. 2, June 1975, pp. 112–13.
57. Chiara Valentini, 'Pum, pum! Il questore', *Panorama*, 22 November 1973, p. 57.
58. In Valentini, *op. cit.*, p. 57.
59. In Valentini, *op. cit.*, p. 56.

Chapter 4
1. Dario Fo and Luigi Allegri, *Dialogo provocatorio sul comico, il tragico, la follia e la ragione, op. cit.*, p.89.

2. Dario Fo, *Non si paga! Non si paga!*, Milan, La Comune, 1974, p. 4.

3. Piero Sciotto (ed.), *Il teatro di Dario Fo e Franca Rame: rappresentazioni al estero dal 1960 al 1989*, Milan, 1990, quoted in Christopher Cairns, 'Italy', *op. cit.*, p. 131.

4. *Non si paga! Non si paga!*, *op. cit.*, p. 1.

5. *Ibid.*, p. 18.

6. *Ibid.*, p. 25.

7. Binni, *Attento te! . . .*, *op. cit.*, p. 389.

8. Dario Fo and Luigi Allegri, *Dialogo provocatorio sul comico, il tragico, la follia e la ragione*, *op. cit.*, p. 108.

9. Ugo Volli, *La Repubblica*, 19 September 1980.

10. Joel Schechter, 'The Un-American Satire of Dario Fo', *Partisan Review*, vol. 51, no. 1, 1984, pp. 117-18.

11. Martin W. Walsh, 'The Proletarian Carnival of Fo's *Non si paga!*', *Modern Drama*, vol. 28, no. 2, June 1985, pp. 213, 214, 219.

12. Lino Pertile, 'Dario Fo', in Michael Caesar and Peter Hainsworth (eds.), *Writers and Society in Contemporary Italy*, New York, St Martins Press, 1984, pp. 186-7.

13. *Ibid.*, p. 188.

14. Domenico Rigotti, *Vent'anni di teatro milanese (1960-1980)*, Milan, Pan, 1981, p. 28.

15. Fo and Allegri, *Dialogo provocatorio*, *op. cit.*, p. 64.

16. Fo, *Fabulazzo*, *op. cit.*, p. 273-4.

17. *Panorama*, 12 June 1975.

18. Binni, *Attento te! . . .*, *op. cit.*, pp. 389, 395.

19. In Valentini, *op. cit.*, p. 163.

20. In Valentini, *op. cit.*, p. 162.

21. *La Repubblica*, 19 September 1980.

22. Valentini, *op.cit.*, p. 163.

23. Dario Fo, *La marijuana della mamma è la più bella*, Verona, Bertani, 1976, p. 24.

24. *Ibid.*, p. 67.

25. *Ibid.*, p. 93.

26. *Ibid.*, p. 135.

27. *Ibid.*, pp. 61-2.

28. In *Le commedie di Dario Fo*, vol. 8, *Venticinque monologhi per una donna*, Turin, Einaudi, 1989, pp. 31-2.

29. *Panorama*, 20 December 1977.
30. In *Le commedie di Dario Fo*, vol. 8, *op. cit.*, p. 16.
31. *Ibid.*, p. 49.
32. Maggie Günsberg, *Gender and the Italian Stage: From the Renaissance to the Present Day*, Cambridge University Press, 1997, p. 227.
33. Dario Fo and Franca Rame, *Venticinque monologhi per una donna*, *op. cit.*, pp. 67–70.
34. Sharon Wood, 'Parliamo di donne: Feminism and Politics in the Theatre of Franca Rame', forthcoming in Farrell and Scuderi, *op. cit.*
35. Sciotto in Cairns, 'Italy', *op. cit.*, p. 131.
36. Serena Anderlini, 'Franca Rame: Her Life and Works', *Theater*, vol. xvii, no. 1, Winter 1985, p. 39.
37. Sue-Ellen Case, *Feminism and Theatre*, London, Macmillan, 1988, p. 92.
38. Marga Cottino-Jones, 'Franca Rame on Stage: The Militant Voice of a *Resisting* Woman', *Italica*, vol. 72, no. 3, 1995, p. 334.
39. Günsberg, *op. cit.*, p. 220.
40. *Ibid.*, p. 232.
41. *Ibid.*, p. 231.
42. In *Il teatro politico di Dario Fo*, 1977, *op. cit.*, pp. 144–5.
43. *The Mother*, in *Dario Fo and Franca Rame Theatre Workshops at Riverside Studios, London*, 1983, *op. cit.*, p. xiv.
44. *Domenica del Corriere*, 26 December 1981, p. 60.
45. *Panorama*, 7 March and 14 March 1978.
46. *Ibid.*
47. Anna Bandettini, 'La satira a scatafascio', *La Repubblica*, 12 January 1998.
48. Dario Fo, *Il caso Moro*, in *Fabulazzo*, *op. cit.*, p. 182.
49. *Panorama*, 5 June 1979.
50. *La Repubblica*, 1 September 1983.
51. *Ibid.*
52. *Il papa e la strega e altre commedie*, Turin, Einaudi, 1994, p. 71.
53. *Ibid.*, p. 141.
54. Chiara Valentini, in *Scena*, vol. VI, no. 1, February 1981, p. 31.

55. Ed Emery, 'Dario Fo's *Trumpets and Raspberries* and the Tradition of Commedia', in Christopher Cairns (ed.) *The Commedia dell'Arte from the Renaissance to Dario Fo*, Lewiston, The Edwin Mellen Press, 1988, pp. 332-4.
56. Stuart Hood, Introduction to Dario Fo, *Can't Pay? Won't Pay!*, London, Methuen, 1987.
57. Franco Quadri, *Panorama*, 3 February 1981.
58. Irving Wardle, *The Times*, 17 November 1984.
59. Cappa and Nepoli, *op. cit.*, p. 133.
60. *La Repubblica*, 12 November 1981.
61. Dario Fo, *L'opera dello sghignazzo*, Milan, La Comune, 1981, p. 25.
62. *Plays and Players*, January 1983, p. 41.
63. In Tony Mitchell, 'Theater in Milan: Open House with Dario Fo and Franca Rame', *Theater*, vol. 15, no. 3, Summer/Fall 1984, p. 65.
64. *Ibid.*, p. 66.
65. *Ibid.*, p. 66.
66. *Ibid.*, p. 67.
67. *Ibid.*, p. 67.
68. *Ibid.*, p. 68.
69. Giorgio Strehler, programme note to *Minna von Barnhelm*, Piccolo Teatro, Milan, 1983.
70. Fo and Allegri, *Dialogo provocatorio*, *op. cit.*, p.59.
71. Stuart Hood, 'Open Texts: Some problems in the editing and translating of Dario Fo', in Cairns (ed.), *The Commedia dell'Arte from the Renaissance to Dario Fo*, 1988, *op. cit.*, p. 348.
72. *Corriere della Sera*, 16 February 1984.
73. Dario Fo, *Il candelaio*, unpublished manuscript, p. 12.
74. In anon., 'Le peripezie ed i successi all'estero', *Nuovo paese*, November 1997, p. 17.

Chapter 5
1. *La Repubblica*, 18 October 1984.
2. Chiara Casarico, *La vera storia di Dario Fo*, Rome, Gremese, 1998, pp. 84-5.
3. In Nicola Javarese (ed.), *Anatomia del teatro*, Rome, Casa Usher, 1983, pp. 36, 142.

4. *La Repubblica*, 24 October 84.

5. *Il Globo* (Melbourne), 12 November 1984.

6. Fo, *Fabulazzo, op. cit.*, p. 325.

7. *La Repubblica*, 6 December 1984.

8. *Ibid.*

9. *Ibid.*

10. *Oggi*, 9 January 1985.

11. *La Repubblica*, 20 January 1983.

12. *Ridotto*, no. 8-9-10, August–October 1984, p. 73.

13. *Ibid.*, p. 83.

14. *Ibid.*, pp. 94-5.

15. Hirst, *Dario Fo and Franca Rame*, 1989, *op. cit.*, p. 35.

16. *Ibid.*, p. 158.

17. David L. Hirst, *Giorgio Strehler*, Cambridge University Press, 1993.

18. John Rutlin, *Commedia dell'Arte: An Actor's Handbook*, London, Routledge, 1994, p. 228.

19. Christopher Cairns, 'Dario Fo and the Commedia dell'Arte', in David J. George and Christopher J. Gossip (eds.), *Studies in the* Commedia dell'Arte, Cardiff, University of Wales Press, 1993, p. 233.

20. Fo, *Il fabulazzo, op. cit.*, p. 117.

21. Cairns, 1993, *op. cit.*, p. 238.

22. Rutlin, *op. cit.*, p. 38.

23. Fo, *Il fabulazzo, op. cit.*, p. 108.

24. Cairns, 1993, *op. cit.*, p. 261.

25. Rutlin, *op. cit.*, p. 229.

26. Dario Fo, *Il Papa e la strega e altre commedie*, Turin, Einaudi, 1994, p. 160.

27. Marcantonio Lucidi, 'Che bella predica', *Il Messaggero*, 20 December 1987, p. 16.

28. Dario Fo, 'Lettera dalla Cina', in Dario Fo and Franca Rame, *Coppia aperta, quasi spalancata* in *Le commedie, vol. 9*, Turin, Einaudi, 1991, pp. 197-202.

29. Antonio Scuderi, 'Subverting Religious Authority: Dario Fo and Folk Laughter', *Text and Performance Quarterly*, vol. 16, no. 3, July 1996, p. 226.

30. Fo, *Il Papa e la strega e altre commedie, op. cit.*, p. 286.

31. *Ibid.*, p. 277-8.
32. Giovanni Raboni, *Corriere della Sera*, 2 November 1989.
33. In Albert Hunt, 'Papal Bull', *Plays and Players*, June 1991, p. 8.
34. *La Repubblica*, 2 November 1989.
35. *L'Unità*, 9 November 1989.

Chapter 6

1. John Towsen, 'Molière "à l'Italienne": Dario Fo at the Comédie Française', *Theater*, vol. 23, no. 3, Summer/Fall 1992, p. 54.
2. *Ibid.*, p. 56.
3. *Ibid.*, p. 61.
4. Dario Fo, *Zitti! Stiamo precipitando!*, Copione di scena a cura di Franca Rame e Nora Guazzotti, Milan, 1990, p. 35.
5. *Ibid.*, p. 36.
6. *The Independent*, 7 January 1991.
7. *La Repubblica*, 4 December 1990.
8. *La Repubblica*, 10 October 1997.
9. Franca Rame, *Parliamo di donne*, Milan, Kaos Edizioni, 1991, p. 79.
10. Maggie Günsberg, *Gender and the Italian Stage: From the Renaissance to the Present Day*, op. cit., p. 229.
11. Cappa and Nepoli, *Dario Fo*, Rome, Gremese, 1997 edition, p. 145.
12. Dario Fo, *Johan Padan a la descoverta delle Americhe*, Prato, Giunti, 1992, p. 10.
13. Antonio Scuderi, *Dario Fo and Popular Performance*, New York, Legas, 1998, pp. 100-5 and p. 107, note 12.
14. Ron Jenkins, *Subversive Laughter: The Liberating Power of Comedy*, op.cit., p. 135.
15. Antonio Scuderi, *Dario Fo and Popular Performance*, op. cit., p. 103.
16. *Ibid.*, p. 104.
17. Marisa Pizza, *Il gesto, la parola, l'azione: Poetica, drammaturgia e storia dei monologhi di Dario Fo*, op. cit., p. 295.
18. Sergei Prokofiev, *Pierino e il lupo*, (ri)scritta e narrata da Dario Fo, Orchestra Sinfonica di Milano Giuseppe Verdi, dir. Alun Francis, Amadeus, 1996. This CD became

available as a special offer, together with a videotape of the 1977 television production of *Isabella, tre caravelle e uno cacciaballe*, with the Italian newspaper *L'Unità* in 1998.

19. Dario Fo and Franca Rame, *Settimo: ruba un po' meno no. 2*, in *Sipario*, no. 528, November 1992, p. 19.

20. Joseph Farrell, 'Fo and Ruzzante: Debts and Obligations', forthcoming in Farrell and Scuderi, *op. cit.*

21. Dario Fo, *Dialoghi su il Ruzzante*, Copione di scena, 1993, pp. 4, 7.

22. In Walter Valeri, 'Dario Fo: tra Goldoni e Ruzzante', *Sipario*, September 1993, p. 97.

23. *Ibid.*, p. 97.

24. Cappa and Nepoli, *Dario Fo*, 1997 edition, p. 150.

25. Antonio Scuderi, *Dario Fo and Popular Performance*, *op. cit.*, p. 65.

26. *Il Giorno*, 28 December 1994.

27. Cappa and Nepoli, *op. cit.*, 1997 edition, p. 152.

28. Franca Rame, Dario & Jacopo Fo, *Sesso? Grazie, tanto per gradire!*, in *Sipario*, no. 552, September 1994, pp. 67–79.

29. *Ibid.*, p. 3.

30. Cappa and Nepoli, *op. cit.*, 1997 edition, p. 152.

31. *L'Unità*, 31 December 1994.

32. Dario Fo, *The Devil in Drag*, translated and adapted by Ed Emery, unpublished manuscript, 1998. This version was produced as part of the London National Theatre's national youth theatre project in summer 1999.

33. In Cappa and Nepoli, *op. cit.*, 1997 edition, p. 153.

34. *La Stampa*, 9 August 1997.

35. *La Repubblica*, 9 August 1997.

36. The Swedish Academy Press Release, 'The Nobel Prize for Literature', The Permanent Secretary, 9 October 1997.

37. Quoted in Tony Kushner, 'Fo's last laugh – I', *The Nation*, 3 November 1997, p. 4.

38. *La Repubblica*, 10 October 1997, p. 16.

39. *Ibid.*, p. 15.

40. *La Stampa*, 9 October 1997.

41. *La Repubblica*, 8 October 1998.

42. *Famiglia Cristiana*, November 1997.

43. *La Repubblica*, 11 December 1997.
44. *La Repubblica*, 16 October 1997.
45. Kushner, *op. cit.*, pp. 4-5.
46. *The Times*, 10 October 1997.
47. *La Repubblica*, 8 December 1997, p. 4.
48. Jim Heitz, 'Dario Fo gives manic, unorthodox Nobel Prize lecture', Associated Press, 7 December 1997.
49. *Corriere della Sera*, 13 January 1998.
50. *Corriere della Sera*, 5 January 1998.
51. Desmond O'Grady, 'Nobel Fo of the Establishment', *Sydney Morning Herald*, 10 January 1998, p. 10s.
52. *La Stampa*, 27 July 1998.
53. *Corriere della Sera*, 11 October 1998.
54. Dario Fo, *Marino libero! Marino è innocente!*, Turin, Einaudi, 1998, and *Il diavolo con le zinne*, Turin, Einaudi, 1998.
55. Dario Fo, 'L'orrendo papocchio del caso Sofri', *La Repubblica*, 6 April 1998.
56. *La Stampa*, 9 October 1998.

Chapter 7
1. Jørgen Stender Clausen, 'Il teatro di Dario Fo in Danimarca', *Il Veltro*, no. 25, 1981, p. 393.
2. *Tribune,* 14 March 1980.
3. Fo and Allegri, *Dialogo provocatorio, op. cit.*, p. 152.
4. *Ibid.*, p. 63.
5. David Groves, in *Act* (NZ), March 1985, p. 8.
6. Stuart Hood, 'Open Texts: Some problems in the editing and translating of Dario Fo', in Cairns, 1988, *op. cit.*, p. 345.
7. R.G. Davis, 'Seven Anarchists I Have Known: American Approaches to Dario Fo', *New Theatre Quarterly*, vol. 2, no. 8, November 1986, p. 315.
8. Tim Fitzpatrick and Kzenia Sawczak, 'Accidental Death of a Translator: the Difficult Case of Dario Fo', in *About Performance: Working Papers 1*, 1995: Translation and Performance, Sydney University, p. 15.
9. Hood, 1988, *op. cit.*, p. 345.
10. *Ibid.*, p. 344.

11. Valeria Tasca, 'Dario Fo from One Language to Another', in Patrice Pavis (ed.), *The Intercultural Performance Reader*, London, Routledge, 1996, p. 117.

12. *Ibid.*, p. 120.

13. Hood, 1988, *op. cit.*, p. 349.

14. Dario Fo, *Accidental Death of an Anarchist*, adapted by Gavin Richards from a translation by Gillian Hanna, London, Methuen, 1987, p. 73.

15. David L. Hirst, *Dario Fo and Franca Rame*, 1989, *op. cit.*, p.92.

16. Ed Emery, 'Did Dario Fo Write *Accidental Death of an Anarchist?*, Working Notes towards a Small Contribution on Theatre Translation', unpublished paper presented at the Conference on Dario Fo and Franca Rame, Essex University, March 1987, p. 5.

17. *Ibid.*, p. 9.

18. Ron Jenkins, Translator's Preface to *Almost by Chance a Woman: Elizabeth*, translated with Introduction by Ron Jenkins, *Theater*, Summer/Fall 1987, p. 65.

19. Ron Jenkins, 'The Rhythms of Resurrection', forthcoming in Farrell and Scuderi, *op. cit.*

20. Emery, 1987, *op. cit.*, p. 9.

21. *Plays and Players*, August 1983, p. 18.

22. Dario Fo, *We Can't Pay? We Won't Pay!*, translated by Walker and Colvill, London, Pluto Press, 1978, p. 29.

23. *Non si paga! Non si paga!*, Milan, La Comune, 1974, p. 98.

24. Hirst, 1989, *op. cit.*, p.98.

25. *Ibid.*, pp. 83-4.

26. *Ibid.*, p. 105.

27. *Canberra Times*, 9 September 1985.

28. *Sipario*, September 1983, p. 38.

29. *Ibid.*, p. 37.

30. Lloyd Trott, 'So You Think That's Funny, Making Revolution into Money?' *The Leveller*, 21 August–3 September 1981, p. 18.

31. *Daily Telegraph*, 17 July 1981.

32. *Time Out*, 7 March 1990.

33. *The Times*, 21 March 1990.

34. *Financial Times*, 20 March 1990.
35. *Time Out*, 28 March 1990.
36. *Tribune*, 15 March 1990.
37. Fo, *Accidental Death of an Anarchist*, adapted by Gavin Richards from a translation by Gillian Hanna, London, Pluto Press, 1980, p.vi.
38. *Punch*, 24 October 1979, p. 731.
39. *Time Out*, 16 March 1979, p. 17.
40. Fitzpatrick and Sawczak, *op. cit.*, p. 29.
41. *Accidental Death of an Anarchist*, 1980, *op. cit.*, p. 43.
42. Fitzpatrick and Sawczak, *op. cit.*, p. 15.
43. *Theater*, Summer/Fall 1983, p. 49.
44. Jennifer Lorch, '*Morte accidentale* in English', forthcoming in Farrell and Scuderi, *op. cit.*
45. *Accidental Death of an Anarchist*, 1980, *op. cit.*, p. iv.
46. *Ibid.*, p. 41.
47. *Ibid.*, p. 41.
48. Hirst, 1989, *op. cit.*, p. 77.
49. *Ibid.*, pp. 84, 89.
50. *Ibid.*, p. 81.
51. *Tribune*, 13 April 1979.
52. *The Leveller*, April 1980, p. 27.
53. *The Socialist Challenge*, 12 April 1979.
54. *The Observer*, 2 March 1980.
55. *The Leveller*, April 1980, p. 26.
56. *The Observer*, 9 March 1980.
57. *Dario Fo and Franca Rame Theatre Workshops at Riverside Studios, London*, 1983, *op.cit.*, p. 43.
58. Emery, 1987, *op.cit.*, p.3.
59. *Theatre Workshops at Riverside Studios*, *op.cit.*, p. 43.
60. Lorch, *op. cit.*
61. Fo, *Accidental Death of an Anarchist*, adapted by Alan Cumming and Tim Supple, London, Methuen, 1991, p. xxiii.
62. *Ibid*, p. xxiv.
63. *Evening Standard*, 8 January 1991.
64. *The Times*, 15 April 1992.
65. *The Times*, 9 January 1991.
66. *The Guardian*, 9 January 1991.

67. *Sunday Times*, 13 January 1991.
68. *Tribune*, 11 January 1991.
69. *The Times*, 9 January 1991.
70. In Christopher Cairns, Introduction to Dario Fo, *Accidental Death of an Anarchist*, 1991, *op. cit.*, p. xx.
71. Lorch, *op. cit.*
72. *The Sun-Herald* (Sydney), 29 May 1994.
73. Mary Karen Dahl, 'State Terror and Dramatic Countermeasures', in John Orr and Dragan Klaic, *Terrorism and Modern Drama*, Edinburgh University Press, 1990, p. 116.
74. *The Times*, 27 June 1981.
75. Dario Fo and Franca Rame, *Female Parts*, adapted by Olwen Wymark, London, Pluto Press, 1981, p. 6.
76. Franca Rame in conversation with Tony Mitchell, May 1982.
77. Sharon Wood, 'Parliamo di donne: Feminism and Politics in the Theatre of Franca Rame', *op. cit.*
78. *The Guardian*, March 1983.
79. *Sipario*, September 1983, p. 37.
80. Gillian Hanna, Introduction to Franca Rame and Dario Fo, *A Woman Alone and Other Plays*, London, Methuen, 1991, p. xvi.
81. Steve Grant, 'Laughter on the Ramparts', *Time Out*, 7 May 1982, p. 7.
82. Jim Hiley, 'Singing of Dark Times', *The Observer* Supplement, 24 April 1983.
83. *The Guardian*, 29 April 1983.
84. *Financial Times*, 30 April 1983.
85. *Sunday Times*, 1 May 1983.
86. *Daily Telegraph*, 30 April 1983.
87. *The Spectator*, 6 May 1983.
88. *The Times*, 5 January 1984.
89. *Evening Standard*, 29 February 1984; *The Observer*, 26 February 1984.
90. *The Times*, 28 February 1984.
91. *The Times*, 12 August 1984.
92. *The Scotsman*, 28 August 1984.
93. Hirst, 1989, *op.cit.*, p. 115.

94. *Time Out*, 25 August 1993.
95. *The Independent*, 25 August 1993.
96. *What's On*, 25 August 1993.
97. Hirst, 1989, *op. cit.*, p. 77.
98. *The Guardian Weekly*, 25 November 1984, p. 20.
99. Dario Fo, *Trumpets and Raspberries*, translated and adapted by R. C. McAvoy and A.-M. Giugni, London, Pluto Press, 1984, p. 3.
100. Hirst, 1989, *op.cit.*, p. 77.
101. *The Guardian Weekly*, 25 November 1984, p. 20.
102. *The Times*, 17 November 1984.
103. *The Age*, 7 November 1985.
104. 'Popular Theatre and the Changing Perspective of the Eighties: John McGrath interviewed by Tony Mitchell', *New Theatre Quarterly*, vol. 1, no. 4, November 1985, p. 394.
105. *Dario Fo, Plays: Two*, London, Methuen, 1997, p. 128.
106. Emery, 1987, *op.cit.*, p. 10.
107. *Ibid.*, p. 6.
108. *Sunday Times*, 9 November 1986.
109. *The Independent*, 8 November 1986.
110. *Financial Times*, 9 November 1986.
111. *The Times*, 8 November 1986.
112. *The Independent*, 5 November 1991.
113. *What's On*, 6 November 1991.
114. *Time Out*, 6 November 1991.
115. *The Times*, 21 September 1986.
116. *The Guardian*, 17 September 1986.
117. Dario Fo, *The Pope and the Witch*, adapted by Andy de la Tour, London, Methuen, 1992, p. xv.
118. *Ibid.*, p. 5.
119. *The Observer*, 19 April 1992.
120. *Herald-Tribune*, 22 April 1992.
121. *Tribune*, 1 May 1992.
122. *Evening Standard*, 14 April 1992.
123. *The Times*, 15 April 1992.
124. *Sunday Telegraph*, 19 April 1992.
125. *Daily Telegraph*, 15 April 1992.

126. *City Limits*, 22 April 1992.
127. *The Observer*, 19 April 1992.
128. Dario Fo, *Abducting Diana*, adapted by Stephen Stenning, London, Oberon Books, 1994, p. 5.
129. *Ibid.*, p. 37.
130. *The Times*, 15 April 1992.
131. Fo and Allegri, *Dialogo provocatorio*, *op.cit.*, pp. 149-50.
132. *Financial Times*, 15 April 1992.
133. Nicholas de Jongh, 'The century's top twenty plays', *Evening Standard*, 16 September 1998, pp. 28-9.

Chapter 8
1. Walsh, 'The Proletarian Carnival of Fo's *Non si paga!*', *Modern Drama*, June 1985, *op. cit.*
2. R.G. Davis, 'Dario Fo Off-Broadway: The Making of Left Culture under Adverse Conditions', *Theatre Quarterly*, no. 40, 1981, pp. 130-9, and 'Seven Anarchists I Have Known', *New Theatre Quarterly*, vol. 2, no. 8, November 1986, pp. 313-19.
3. Ron Jenkins, 'The Roar of the Clown', *The Drama Review*, vol. 30., no. 1, Spring 1986, p. 172.
4. Walsh, *op. cit.*, p. 221.
5. Dario Fo, *We Won't Pay! We Won't Pay!*, North American version by R.G. Davis, New York, Samuel French Inc., 1984.
6. *New York Times*, 18 December 1980.
7. *Variety*, 24 December 1984.
8. Alisa Solomon, Reviews of *About Face* and *No Se Paga!*, *Performing Arts Journal*, vol. VII no. 2, 1983, p. 66.
9. Dario Fo, *Accidental Death of an Anarchist*, adapted by Richard Nelson, New York, Samuel French Inc., 1987, p. 6.
10. Programme of Washington Arena Stage production of *Accidental Death of an Anarchist*, 1984.
11. Fo, *Accidental Death of an Anarchist*, adapted by Richard Nelson, *op. cit.*, p. 18.
12. *New York Times*, 15 February 1984.
13. Elinor Fuchs, 'Their Fo was Folly', *Village Voice*, 20 March 1984.

14. Robert Brustein, 'Exploding an Anarchist Play', *New Republic*, 17 December 1984, p. 26.

15. Dario Fo, 'Cercavo King Kong: Era a farsi una dose', *Oggi*, 5 December 1984, p. 47.

16. *Ibid.*, p. 47.

17. Eric Bentley, 'Was This Death Accidental?', *Theater*, vol. xvi, no. 2, Spring 1985, p. 66.

18. *Accidental Death*, adapted Nelson, *op. cit.*, p. 9.

19. *Ibid.*, p. 84.

20. *Ibid.*, p. 86.

21. Davis, 'Seven Anarchists I Have Known', *op.cit.*, p. 316.

22. *Ibid.*, p. 316.

23. *Ibid.*, p. 316.

24. *Ibid.*, p. 316.

25. *Los Angeles Times*, 25 November 1984.

26. Franca Rame and Dario Fo, *Orgasmo Adulto Escapes from the Zoo*, adapted by Estelle Parsons, New York, Broadway Play Publishing Inc., 1985, p. xi.

27. Dario Fo, *About Face*, translated by Dale McAdoo and Charles Mann, in *Theater*, vol. 14, no. 3, Summer/Fall 1983, p. 92.

28. Fo, *Clacson, trombette e pernacchi*, Milan, Edizioni F.R. La Comune, 1981, p. 140.

29. Fo, *About Face*, *op. cit.*, pp. 41-2.

30. Solomon, *op. cit.*, p. 65.

31. *New York Times*, 17 April 1983.

32. Mimi D'Aponte, 'From Italian Roots to American Relevance: The Remarkable Theatre of Dario Fo', *Modern Drama*, vol. xxxii, no. 4, December 1989, p. 539.

33. Ron Jenkins, 'Clowns, Politics and Miracles: The Epic Satire of Dario Fo', *American Theatre*, vol. 3, no. 3, June 1986, p. 12.

34. *New York Times*, 29 May 1986.

35. *Village Voice*, 10 June 1986.

36. *Boston Globe Magazine*, 27 April 1986, p. 64.

37. *Theatre Journal*, September 1987, p. 80.

38. Dario Fo, *Archangels Don't Play Pinball*, translated by Ron Jenkins, New York, Samuel French Inc., 1987.

39. Ron Jenkins, *Subversive Laughter: The Liberating Power of Comedy*, *op.cit.*, p. 133.

40. Dario Fo, *Almost by Chance a Woman: Elizabeth*, translated by Ron Jenkins, in *Theater*, Summer/Fall 1987, p. 80.
41. *The New Haven Register*, 3 May 1987.
42. Dario Fo, *The Story of the Tiger*, translated by Ron Jenkins, in *Theater*, vol. 21, nos 1/2, Winter/Spring 1990, p. 3.
43. D'Aponte, *op. cit.*, p. 541.

BIBLIOGRAPHY

Primary Sources in English

Plays

Can't Pay? Won't Pay!, trans. Lino Pertile, adapt. Bill Colvill and Robert Walker, Pluto Press, 1978 and 1982; revised edition, with Introduction by Stuart Hood, London, Methuen, 1988.

Accidental Death of an Anarchist, trans. with Introduction by Suzanne Cowan, in *Theater*, vol. 10, no. 2, Spring 1979.

Accidental Death of an Anarchist, trans. Gillian Hanna, adapt. Gavin Richards, Pluto Press, 1980; revised edition, with Introduction by Stuart Hood, London, Methuen, 1987.

Ulrike Meinhof and *Tomorrow's News*, trans. with Introduction by Tony Mitchell, in *Gambit*, vol. 9, no. 36, 1980.

Female Parts (One Woman Plays), trans. Margaret Kunzle, adapt. Olwen Wymark, with Introduction by Stuart Hood, London, Pluto Press, 1981.

About Face, trans. with Introduction by Dale McAdoo and Charles Mann, in *Theater*, vol. 14, no. 3, Summer/Fall 1983.

Trumpets and Raspberries, trans. and adapt. R.C. McAvoy and Anna-Maria Giugni, with Introduction by Stuart Hood, London, Pluto Press, 1984.

Orgasmo Adulto Escapes from the Zoo, trans. and adapt. Estelle Parsons, New York, Broadway Play Publications, 1984, 1998.

The Open Couple – Very Open, trans. Stuart Hood, in *Theater*, vol. 17, no. 1, Winter 1985.

Accidental Death of an Anarchist, trans. Suzanne Cowan, adapt. Richard Nelson, Samuel French Inc., 1987.

Archangels Don't Play Pinball, trans. R.C. McAvoy and Anna-Maria Giugni, with Introduction by Stuart Hood, London, Methuen, 1987.

Elizabeth: Almost by Chance a Woman, trans. and adapt. Gillian Hanna, with Introduction by Stuart Hood, London, Methuen, 1987.

Almost by Chance a Woman: Elizabeth, trans. with Introduction by Ron Jenkins, *Theater*, Summer/Fall 1987, and Samuel French Inc., 1989.

Mistero buffo, trans. Ed Emery, edited with Introduction by Stuart Hood, London, Methuen, 1988.

Archangels Don't Play Pinball, trans. Ron Jenkins, Samuel French Inc., 1989.

About Face, American version by Ron Jenkins, Samuel French Inc., 1989.

The Story of the Tiger, trans. Ron Jenkins, *Theater*, vol. 21, nos 1–2, Winter/Spring 1990.

A Woman Alone and Other Plays, trans. Gillian Hanna, Ed Emery and Christopher Cairns, with Introductions by Stuart Hood and Gillian Hanna, London, Methuen, 1991.

Accidental Death of an Anarchist, trans. and adapt. Alan Cumming and Tim Supple, with Introduction by Christopher Cairns, London, Methuen, 1991.

The Pope and the Witch, trans. Ed Emery, adapt. Andy de la Tour, with Introduction by Stuart Hood, London, Methuen, 1992.

Dario Fo Plays: One (Mistero Buffo, trans. Ed Emery, *Accidental Death of an Anarchist*, trans. Ed Emery, *Trumpets and Raspberries*, trans. and adapt. R.C. McAvoy and Anna-Maria Giugni, *The Virtuous Burglar*, trans. Joe Farrell, *One Was Nude and the Other Wore Tails*, trans. Ed Emery), with Introduction by Stuart Hood, London, Methuen 1992, 1997.

Dario Fo Plays: Two (Can't Pay? Won't Pay!, trans. Lino Pertile, adapt. Bill Colvill and Robert Walker, *Elizabeth*, trans. and adapt. Gillian Hanna, *The Open Couple,* trans. Stuart Hood,

An Ordinary Day, trans. Joe Farrell), London, Methuen, 1994, 1997.

Abducting Diana, trans. Rupert Lowe, adapt: Stephen Stenning, London, Oberon Books, 1994.

The Pope and the Witch and *The First Miracle of the Boy Jesus*, trans. Ed Emery, London, Oberon Books, 1996, and New York, Theatre Communications Group, 1998.

The Pope and the Witch, trans. Joan Holden, Samuel French Inc., 1997.

The following plays, all translated by Ed Emery, can be obtained in English versions by writing to The Fo-Rame Forum, 111 Albion Road, London N16 9PL: *One Was Nude and One Wore Tails, The Good that a Burglar can Bring, Corpse for Sale, Housepainters Have No Memories, Women Undressed and Bodies to be Despatched, Marcolfa, Three Bold Lads, He Who Steals a Foot is Lucky in Love, Dump the Lady, I'd Rather Die Tonight If I Had To Think It Had All Been in Vain, The Tale of a Tiger, The Opera of Guffaws, Coming Home, The Mother, The Rape, The Open Couple, The Butterfly-Mouse, Mister Christopher Columbus, Johan Padan, Sex: Don't Mind If I Do!, The Devil in Drag, Marino at Large.*

Prose writings

The Tricks of the Trade, trans. Joe Farrell, edited with notes by Stuart Hood, London, Methuen, 1991.

Articles and documents

'Dialogue with an Audience' (trans. Tony Mitchell), *Theatre Quarterly*, vol. 9, no. 35, Autumn 1979, pp. 11-6.

'The Sandstorm Method' (trans. by Peter Caravetta, James Cascaito and Lawrence Venuti), *Semiotext(e)*, vol. 3, no. 3, 1980, pp. 214-16. (On terrorism.)

Dario Fo and Franca Rame Theatre Workshops at Riverside Studios, London, 28 April, 5, 12, 13 & 19, May 1983. (Includes texts of *Waking Up, I Don't Move, I Don't Scream, My Voice is Gone*, trans. Jytte Lollesgard, and *The Mother*, trans. Ed

Emery, and an interview with Fo and Rame by Ed Emery.) London, Red Notes, 1983.

'Popular Culture' (trans. Tony Mitchell), *Theater*, vol. 14, no. 3, Summer/Fall 1983, pp. 50-4 (also in an abbreviated version in *Trumpets and Rasberries*, London, Pluto Press, 1984.)

'When they beat us, we suffer', *Index on Censorship*, vol. 14, no. 1, 1985, p. 59. (On censorship in Italy and the USA.)

'Aspects of Popular Theatre' (trans. Tony Mitchell), *New Theatre Quarterly*, vol. 1, no. 2, May 1985, pp. 214-16. (Contains 'Theatre of Situation' and 'Retrieving the Past, Exposing the Present'.)

'Totò: The Violence of the Marionette and the Mask' (trans. Stuart Hood), *Theater*, Summer/Fall 1987, pp. 6-12. (On the famous Italian comic.)

'Hands off the Mask!' (trans. Gail Macdonald), *New Theatre Quarterly,* vol. 5, no. 19, August 1989, pp. 207-9. (On masks from ancient Greece to *commedia* and beyond, and their function as a ritual of disguise.)

'What Passion! What Generosity! What Corruption!' (trans. Ron Jenkins), *New York Times Magazine*, 5 December 1993, pp. 64-5. (On 'Tangentopoli' and the corruption scandals in Italy.)

Johan Padan (extract) in Lawrence Ferlinghetti (ed.), *Ends & Beginnings: City Lights Review #6*, San Francisco, City Lights, 1996.

Interviews

Luigi Ballerini and Giuseppe Risso, 'Dario Fo Explain' (trans. Lauren Hallquist and Fiorenza Weinpple). *The Drama Review*, vol. 22, no. 1, March 1978, pp. 34-48. (An overview of Fo's work to 1978 and the return to TV, and *Throw the Lady Out*.)

Catherine Itzin, 'The "How-to" of Political Theatre'. *Tribune*, 14 March 1980, p. 9. (On *Accidental Death of an Anarchist* and *Mother's Marijuana*.)

David Groves, 'Fo Interviewed'. *Act* (NZ), vol. 3, no. 2, April 1982, pp. 18-20. (On *The Opera of Guffaws*.)

Michael Billington, 'Everybody's Favourite Fo'. *The Guardian*, 26 April 1983.

Steve Grant and Tony Mitchell, 'An Interview with Dario Fo and Franca Rame'. *Theater*, vol. 14, no. 3, Summer/Fall 1983, pp. 43-9. (On *Female Parts*, *The Opera of Guffaws* and politics in Italy and the USA.)

Derek Boothman, 'Popular and Political Theatre'. *Marxism Today*, August 1983, pp. 37-9. (On La Comune.)

Tony Mitchell, 'Open House with Dario Fo and Franca Rame'. *Theater*, vol. 15, no. 3, Summer/Fall 1984, pp. 65-8. (On *The Open Couple*.)

Scott Rosenberg, 'Dario Fo, Italy's Political Clown, Pays a Visit'. *New York Times*, 25 May 1986.

Joseph Farrell, 'Fo and Rame'. *Plays and Players*, June 1987, pp. 9-10. (On *Kidnapping Francesca* and *A Short Manual for the Actor*.)

Albert Hunt, 'Papal Bull'. *Plays and Players*, June 1991, pp. 6-8. (On *The Pope and the Witch*.)

Secondary Sources in English

Monographs

Tony Mitchell, *Dario Fo: People's Court Jester*, London, Methuen, 1984; revised and expanded version, Methuen, 1986.

Tony Mitchell, *File on Dario Fo*, London, Methuen, 1989.

David L. Hirst, *Dario Fo and Franca Rame*, London, Macmillan, 1989.

Antonio Scuderi, *Dario Fo and Popular Performance*, New York, Legas, 1998.

Joseph Farrell and Antonio Scuderi (eds.), *Dario Fo: Stage, Text and Tradition*, Carbondale, Southern Illinois University Press, 1999, forthcoming. (Includes Jennifer Lorch, '*Morte accidentale* in English; Bent Holm, 'Dario Fo's "Bourgeois Period": Carnival and Criticism; Joe Farrell, 'Fo and Ruzzante: Debts and Obligations; Paolo Puppa, 'Tradition,

Traditions and Dario Fo; Costantino Maeder, '*Mistero buffo*: Dario Fo Fatalist?; Ron Jenkins, 'The Rhythms of Resurrection: On Stage with Fo; Antonio Scuderi, 'Updating Antiquity; Walter Valeri, 'Dario Fo: Actor Playwright; Tony Mitchell, '*The Moon is a Lightbulb* and Other Stories: Dario Fo the Songwriter; Sharon Wood, '*Parliamo di donne*: Feminism and Politics in the Theatre of Franca Rame; and Joseph Farrell, 'The Actor Who Writes: Dario Fo and the Nobel Prize'.)

Articles and chapters in books

A. Richard Sogliuzzo, 'Dario Fo: Puppets for a Proletarian Revolution'. *The Drama Review*, vol. 16, no. 3, September 1972, pp. 72-7. (On Nuova Scena.)

Suzanne Cowan, 'The Throw-away Theatre of Dario Fo'. *The Drama Review*, vol. 19, no. 2, June 1975, pp. 103-13. (On Nuova Scena and the early years of La Comune.)

Suzanne Cowan, 'Theatre, Politics, and Social Change in Italy since the Second World War'. *Theatre Quarterly*, vol. 7, no. 27, Autumn 1977, pp. 25-38. (The social, political and theatrical background to Fo's work.)

Tony Mitchell, 'Dario Fo's *Mistero buffo*: Popular theatre, the *Giullari*, and the Grotesque'. *Theatre Quarterly*, vol. 9, no. 35, Autumn 1979, pp. 1-10.

Tony Mitchell, 'Dario Fo: The Histrionics of Class Struggle'. *Gambit*, vol. 9, no. 36, 1980, pp. 55-60. (On *Ulrike Meinhof*, *Accidental Death*, *Mistero buffo* and *Archangels Don't Play Pinball*.)

Charles Mann, 'Fo No-Show Doesn't Mean No Fo Show'. *Village Voice*, 17-23 December 1980. (Overview, Fo's refused visa to the USA, *Can't Pay? Won't Pay!*.)

Mario B. Mignone, 'Dario Fo: Jester of the Italian Stage'. *Italian Quarterly*, no. 85, 1981, pp. 47-62. (Overview to 1980.)

Lloyd Trott, 'So you think that's funny, turning rebellion into money'. *The Leveller*, 21 August–3 September 1981, pp. 18-9. (On London productions of *Anarchist*, *Can't Pay? Won't Pay!* and *Female Parts*.)

Bibliography

R.G. Davis, 'Dario Fo Off-Broadway: The Making of Left Culture under Adverse Conditions'. *Theatre Quarterly*, vol. 10, no. 40, Autumn–Winter 1981, pp. 30-6. (On Davis' attempts to stage *Can't Pay? Won't Pay!* in the USA.)

David Groves, 'Laughter has become a *Sghignazzo*', *Act* (NZ), vol. 7, no. 2, April 1982, pp. 16-8. (On *The Opera of Guffaws*.)

Vittorio Felaco, 'Notes on Text and Performance in the Theatre of Dario Fo'. In Michael Herzfeld and Margot D. Lenhart (eds.), *Semiotics 1980*, New York, Plenum Press, 1982, pp. 57-71. (Notes towards a semiotic analysis of *Mistero buffo*.)

Joel Schechter, 'Dario Fo's Obscene Fables'. *Theater*, vol. 14, no. 1, Winter 1982, pp. 87-90.

Jim Hiley, 'Singing of Dark Times'. *Observer Magazine*, 24 April 1983, pp. 28-31. (Also in *Riverside Workshops* – overview, interview, *The Obscene Fable*.)

Brian Glanville, 'Master Class from a Master Clown'. *Sunday Times*, 1 May 1983 (Also in *Riverside Workshops*.)

Sally Banes, 'Dario Fo's Theater of Blasphemy'. *Village Voice*, 2 August 1983, pp. 1, 33-5. (Overview and *Mistero buffo*.)

Joel Schechter, 'The Un-American Satire of Dario Fo'. *Partisan Review*, vol. 51, no. 1, 1984, pp. 112-19. (*Anarchist, Can't Pay? Won't Pay!* and *About Face* considered in the light of the USA visa refusal.)

Lino Pertile, 'Dario Fo'. In Michael Caesar and Peter Hainsworth (eds.), *Writers and Society in Contemporary Italy*, New York, St Martins Press, 1984, pp. 167-90. (Overview to 1984.)

Vittorio Felaco, 'New Teeth for an Old Shark'. In John Fuegi et al. (eds.), *Beyond Brecht: Brecht Yearbook,* vol. 11, 1982, Detroit, Wayne State University Press, 1983, pp. 57-71. (Fo and Rame as inheritors of Brechtian theatre concepts; *The Opera of Guffaws*.)

Joel Schechter, 'Beyond Brecht: New Authors, New Spectators'. In Fuegi *et al.*, *Beyond Brecht*, op.cit., pp. 43-53. (Fo as one of a number of modern playwrights who have extended Brecht's precepts.)

Eric Bentley, 'Was This Death Accidental?'. *Theater*, vol. 16, no. 2, Spring 1985, p. 66. (On the Broadway *Anarchist*.)

Martin W. Walsh, 'The Proletarian Carnival of Fo's *Non si paga!*'. *Modern Drama*, vol. 28, no. 2, June 1985, pp. 211-22.

Joel Schechter, 'Dario Fo: The Clown as Counter-Informer'. In *Durov's Pig: Clowns, Politics and Theater*, New York, Theatre Communications Group, 1985, pp. 142-57. (On *Can't Pay? Won't Pay!*, *Accidental Death*, *About Face* and *Throw the Lady Out*.)

Serena Anderlini, 'Franca Rame: Her Life and Works'. *Theater*, vol. 17, no. 1, Winter 1985, pp. 32-9. (Detailed assessment of Rame's career from childhood to *Elizabeth*.)

Ron Jenkins, 'Dario Fo: The Roar of the Clown'. *The Drama Review*, Spring 1986, pp. 172-9. (On *Mistero buffo* and *Tale of a Tiger*.)

Ron Jenkins, 'Clowns, Politics and Miracles: The Epic Satire of Dario Fo'. *American Theater*, vol. 3, no. 3, June 1986. (Similar to the above.)

Pina Piccolo, 'Farce as the Mirror of Bourgeois Politics: *Morte accidentale di un anarchico*'. *Forum Italicum*, vol. 20, no. 2, Fall 1986, pp. 170-81.

R.G. Davis, 'Seven Anarchists I Have Known: American Approaches to Dario Fo'. *New Theatre Quarterly*, vol. 2, no. 8, November 1986, pp. 313-19.

Jerry Palmer, *On Film and Television Comedy*, London, BFI Publications, 1989, pp. 194-9. (On *Accidental Death* as an example of the 'logic of the absurd'.)

Pina Piccolo, 'Dario Fo's *giullarate*: Dialogic Parables in the Service of the Oppressed'. *Italica*, vol. 65, 1988, pp. 131-43. (*Mistero buffo* and *Tale of a Tiger* considered in the light of Bakhtin's theories of carnival, grotesque realism and the dialogic.)

Joseph Farrell, 'Dario Fo – *Zanni* and *Giullare*'. In Christopher Cairns (ed.), *The Commedia dell'Arte from the Renaissance to Dario Fo*, Lewiston, The Edwin Mellen Press, 1988, pp. 315-28. (The combined influences of the *giullari* and *commedia dell'arte* in Fo's work.)

Ed Emery, 'Dario Fo's *Trumpets and Raspberries* and the Tradition of *Commedia*'. In Cairns, *ibid.*, pp. 330-4.

Stuart Hood, 'Open Texts: Some problems in the editing and translating of Dario Fo'. In Cairns, *ibid.*, pp. 336-52. (Fo's use of dialect in *Mistero buffo* and *Elizabeth* and his debate with Pasolini; Fo and Rame's extensive textual emendations.)

Mimi D'Aponte, 'From Italian Roots to American Relevance: The Remarkable Theatre of Dario Fo'. *Modern Drama,* vol. 32, no. 4, December 1989, pp. 532-44. (Positive responses to Fo in the USA, analyses of *Can't Pay?, Anarchist* and *About Face.*)

Joylynn Wing, 'The Performance of Power and the Power of Performance: Rewriting the Police State in Dario Fo's *Accidental Death of an Anarchist*'. *Modern Drama,* vol. 23, no. 1, March 1990, pp. 141-9. (Political cover-up as a form of theatrical representation.)

Mary Karen Dahl, 'State Terror and Dramatic Counter-measures'. In John Orr and Dragan Klaic (eds.), *Terrorism and Modern Drama,* Edinburgh University Press, 1990, pp. 109-21. (*Accidental Death of an Anarchist* as a countermeasure to state terror.)

John Towsen, 'Molière "à l'Italienne": Dario Fo at the Comédie Française'. *Theater,* vol. 23, no. 3, Summer/Fall 1992, pp. 52-61.

Christopher Cairns, 'Dario Fo'. In Ralph Yarrow (ed.), *European Theatre* 1960–1990, London, Routledge, 1992, pp. 130-7. (Overview of Fo's work in the context of Italian theatre to 1991.)

Christopher Cairns, 'Dario Fo and the *Commedia dell'arte*'. In David J. George and Christopher J. Gossip (eds.), *Studies in the* Commedia dell'arte, Cardiff, University of Wales Press, 1993, pp. 247-65. (Detailed analysis of Fo's *Harlequin.*)

J.L. Wing, 'The Iconicity of Absence: Dario Fo and the Radical Invisible'. In *Theatre Journal* 45, 1993, pp. 303-15. (Fo's imaginative and carnivalesque use of space and perspective in *Mistero buffo.*)

Ron Jenkins, 'Clowns and Popes in Italy'. In *Subversive Laughter: The Liberating Power of Comedy,* New York, The Free Press,

1994, pp. 107-40. (Analysis of *Mistero buffo, Female Parts, Accidental Death, Elizabeth* and *Johan Padan* in terms of subversion and the *giullari*.)

Angela Montgomery, 'The Theatre of Dario Fo and Franca Rame: Laughing all the Way to the Revolution'. In Brian Docherty (ed.), *Twentieth-century European Drama*, London, Macmillan, 1994, pp. 203-20. (Partial overview of Fo and Rame's work, focusing on *Archangels, Mistero buffo, Anarchist*, and *All House, Bed and Church*.)

John Rutlin, 'Dario Fo'. In *Commedia dell'Arte: An Actor's Handbook*, London, Routledge, 1994, pp. 226-31. (Brief, critical overview of Fo as a performer in the *commedia* tradition.)

Joe Farrell, 'Fo and Feydeau: Is Farce a Laughing Matter?'. *Italica*, vol. 72, no. 3, 1995, pp. 307-21. (Analysis of Fo's early farces.)

Marga Cottino-Jones, 'Franca Rame on Stage: The Militant Voice of a *Resisting* Woman'. *Italica*, vol. 72, no. 3, 1995, pp. 321-38. (Feminist analysis of Rame's work, concentrating on *Waking Up* and *Medea*.)

Tim Fitzpatrick and Kzenia Sawczak, 'Accidental Death of a Translator: The Difficult Case of Dario Fo'. In *About Performance: Working Papers 1, 1995: Translation and Performance*, Sydney University, 1995. (Compares four different English versions of a scene from *Anarchist*; argues that translating Fo involves varying degrees of adaptation.)

Valeria Tasca, 'Dario Fo from One Language to Another'. In Patrice Pavis (ed.), *The Intercultural Performance Reader*, London, Routledge, 1996, pp. 114-20. (Fo's French translator on some of the difficulties of rendering his work into French.)

Antonio Scuderi, 'Framing and Improvisation in Dario Fo's *Johan Padan*'. *Theatre Annual*, no. 49, 1996, pp. 76-91. (Fo's use of *giullaresque* techniques of breaking the fourth wall.)

Antonio Scuderi, 'Subverting Religious Authority: Dario Fo and Folk Laughter'. In *Text and Performance Quarterly*, vol. 16, no. 3, July 1996, pp. 216-22. (Fo's use of carnivalesque clownery in *Mistero buffo, The Pope and the Witch* and *Johan Padan*.)

Maggie Günsberg, 'Centrestage: Franca Rame's Female Parts'. In *Gender and the Italian Stage: From the Renaissance to the Present Day*, Cambridge University Press, 1997, pp. 203-42. (Analysis of Rame's monologues in the context of the representation of women in Italian theatre since the Renaissance.)

Tony Kushner, 'Fo's Last Laugh – 1'. *The Nation*, 3 November 1997, pp. 4-5.

Margaret Spillane, 'Fo's Last Laugh – 2', *The Nation*, 3 November 1997, pp. 5-6.

Christopher Hitchens, 'Lotta Continua'. *The Nation*, 10 November 1997, p. 8.

Ron Jenkins, 'The Nobel Jester'. *American Theatre*, February 1998, pp. 22-4. (Includes short extract in English from *Johan Padan*.)

Other reference sources

Anon., 'Dario Fo' in Michael Anderson *et al* (eds.), *A Handbook of Contemporary Drama*, London, Pitman, 1974, pp. 152-3.

Suzanne Cowan, 'The Militant Theatre of Dario Fo', PhD Thesis, University of Minnesota, 1977.

Suzanne Cowan, 'Dario Fo: Bibliography, Biography, Playography', *Theatre Quarterly Checklist,* no. 17, 1978.

Web sites

There is a Dario Fo web site in Italian (with some pages in English) at http://www.wema.com/dariofo.html

The San Francisco Fofest web site is at http://www.infinex.com/~berny/fofest.html

Ed Emery's web site, which contains translations of a number of Fo's plays, is http://www.emery.archive.mcmail.com

INDEX

Index